An Outline of the Philosophical Anthropology

Stanisław Kowalczyk

An Outline of the Philosophical Anthropology

PETER LANG
Frankfurt am Main · Bern · New York · Paris

Die Deutsche Bibliothek - CIP-Einheitsaufnahme

Kowalczyk, Stanisław:

An outline of the philosophical anthropology / Stanisław Kowalczyk. - Frankfurt am Main ; Bern ; New York ; Paris : Lang, 1991
ISBN 3-631-44156-8

NE: GT

ISBN 3-631-44156-8

Printed in Germany 1 2 3 5 6 7

CONTENTS

PREFACE

In spite of all the centuries of efforts, the Socratic command "know thyself" has not been fully accomplished and man still remains a creature incompletely recognised and understood. It seems most likely that the mystery of man will never be completely explained. However, the important thing is the fact that man - and man alone in the visible universe - has posed such questions as: What am I? Where do I come from? Why do I exist? How should I live? Man's uniqueness concerns the fact of his coming into being, the connection of nature with person, and the specificity of action. The questions posed above go beyond the scope of exact sciences, natural and sociological, so any attempt to answer them must refer to philosophy.

The term "anthropology" has appeared relatively late (previously the term "anthropological psychology" was used) but interest in man accompanied philosophical thought already in antiquity and early Christian times; perhaps the best evidence can be found in the writings of St. Augustine. Anthropology is connected with many currents in philosophy and, in consequence, one may speak of a variety of its models. Thus, there is Platonic anthropology, Aristotelian anthropology, Stoic anthropology, Augustinian anthropology, Thomistic anthropology, Cartesian anthropology, phenomenological anthropology, existentialist anthropology and so on. Taking into account the methodological aspect, one may distinguish such variants of anthropology as rational and irrational, metaphysical and scientistic, systemic and phenomenological-existentialist, objective and subjective. The ontological criterion makes it possible to distinguish naturalistic - materialistic and personalistic-spiritualistic anthropology. They also speak of such kinds of anthropology as individualistic and collectivistic, realistic and idealistic, ontological, axiological and pragmatic. Various models of anthropology are most often connected with their corresponding conceptions of man and the latter, in turn, manifest various degrees of systemic determination.

The bibliography of studies in philosophical anthropology is quite abundant. The multiplicity of philosophical systems and the variety of the applied methods, though in themselves they are positive factors, often make the fundamental paradigms of man's personal being problematic. Many matters still require further considerations and that is why it is necessary to undertake further analyses in the domain of philosophical anthropology. The present study pertains to the personalistic current in the philosophy of man, so that non-personal (assumed or factual) conceptions of the human being are omitted. The accomplishments of "perennial philosophy", especially those inspired by St. Augustine and St. Thomas Aquinas, may be enriched by contemporary philosophical reflections. Naturally, this enrichment cannot assume the form of indiscriminate incorporation but it must be a selective use and inclusion of some threads of modern and contemporary philosophy in the classical philosophy of man. Thomism implies a global-systemic presentation of the conception of human person, while Augustinianism allows one to apprehend man in his dynamic aspect and existential anxiety, while contemporary philosophy introduces the subjectivistic and axiological views. As some attempts recently undertaken indicate, the philosophy of being and the philosophy of subject may mutually complement each other.

The present study consists of three parts, namely, introductory - methodological considerations, the phenomenology of man, and the metaphysics of man. The first and shortest part touches, among others, problems of a semantic and methodological character. The arrangement of the material in subsequent parts should be viewed flexibly because the borderline between the phenomenology and metaphysics of man is not always clear and unequivocal. Even in the domain of the phenomenology of man there occur problems whose final analysis is possible only within the metaphysics of the human being. However, difficulties of this kind do not seem to negate the validity of the distinction introduced in the study.

Stanisław Kowalczyk

PART I

INTRODUCTION: METHODOLOGICAL REMARKS

Chapter 1

The Philosophy of Man and the Empirical - Descriptive Anthropologies

Man is an object of study in many branches of science which, in consequence, has given rise to a variety of anthropologies. The major variants of the kind in question in the present chapter include: natural anthropology, social anthropology, philosophical anthropology and theological anthropology[1]. The first two have a primarily descriptive character, while the latter two contain evaluative - normative elements.

Natural anthropology examines man as a specimen of the homo sapiens species, i.e. it studies his phylogenesis and ontogenesis, the structure and functions of his organism, evolution in the past and its future possibilities, features distinguishing the human kind and its relations to the biocosmos, the origin of human races etc.[2]. The problems studied in natural anthropology are very rich and one may distinguish there aspects general and particular, as well as systemic and social. Such anthropology covers, among others, the questions of the multiplicity of human races, their origins, transformations, differentiation and so on[3]. Similarly to all natural sciences, natural anthropology describes man in such his dimensions as external-quantitative, somatic, biological, ecological, morphological etc.

Social anthropology, also known as cultural anthropology[4], has a similarly non-philosophical character. It characterizes individual man and society in their relation to culture and civilisation, social organisation etc. Social - cultural anthropology is understood in various ways; some connect it with sociology and psychology, while others - with history, ethnology and ethnography. The latter direction is represented by the founder of structuralism, Claude Lévi-Strauss. The ethnologist Bronisław Malinowski († 1942) explained the phenomenon of culture functionally, opposing the nineteenth-century classical evolutionism. In the United States particularly influential is ethno-psychological anthropology which emphasizes the role of cultural patterns typical of particular nations

---

[1]Cf. O. Marquard: "Anthropologie" [in:] *Historisches Wörterbuch der Philosophie*, Basel 1971, vol. 1, pp. 362-374.

[2]M. Bates: *Man in Nature*, Englewood Cliffs 1964; J.B. Janusch: *Origins of Man. Physical Anthropology*, New York 1966.

[3]J. Czekanowski: *Człowiek w czasie i przestrzeni* [Man in Time and Space], Warszawa 1967.

[4]B. Malinowski: *Man and Culture*, London 1957; A. Waligórski: *Antropologiczna koncepcja człowieka* [The Anthropological Conception of Man], Warszawa 1973.

and of psychic features connected with them. Natural and cultural anthropology does not always occur in a strictly descriptive form; in the writings of many authors one may also find philosophical - universal elements. Yet, in such cases reductionistic approaches to man are usually the result.

Anthropological reductionism occurs in many forms but three of them are most often distinguished, namely, biologism, psychologism and sociologism[5]. The first two often occur jointly, e.g. in S. Freud's († 1939) psychoanalysis. However, these are not the only variants of reductionistic anthropology since one can also speak of such forms as physicism, biologism, psychologism, sociologism and the logicalist - pragmatic models.

Physicism is typical of the representatives of mechanistic materialism whose chief advocates include C. Lévi-Strauss and Tadeusz Kotarbiński († 1981). The founder of structuralism discounted historical thinking and overemphasized the synchronic-structural method, in consequence reducing man's culture to the physico-chemical nature[6]. Thus, the author questioned man's ontical "uniqueness", i.e. the personal "I", society, history, and spiritual culture. He reduced man's psyche to physiology and the latter - to physics and chemistry. In this way anthropology has been degraded to enthropy determined by pure chance and inevitably leading to the disintegration of the human being.

The above conception of anthropology, though starting with ethnological and historical data, contains evidently philosophical elements. In fact, structuralism can be regarded as vulgar materialism which attempts to explain man's personhood by means of data derived from physics, chemistry, physiology, mathematics and logic. This non-personal model of man undermines any psychic-spiritual dimensions, such as reflective thought, conscience, sensitivity to higher values, humanism, sense of life, community. Actually, it constitutes the "death" of man as a person and the offered explanation is in fact a degradation of man-subject to the role of a thing-model.

Biologism is another form of reductionistic anthropology. By the term we do not mean here the methodological biologism which was characteristic of P. Teilhard de Chardin († 1955), who accepted man's ontic specificity while employing a methodology derived from the domain of biological sciences. It is ontological biologism that is in question, as represented by Friedrich Nietzsche († 1900). His materialism has a biological-vitalistic character because it stresses the role of animal life. Man is described as a "tamed animal" whose principal axiological command is "the law of life"[7]. Man's psychic life is to be "an addition" of the nervous system which, through the phenomena of conscience and morality, ultimately becomes a source of vital weakening. The naturalistic-biological perspective was a cause of the depreciation of such phenomena as ethics, religion, love, charity, while simultaneously overemphasizing elements of fight and hatred in man's life. Biologism provides no basis for humanism.

---

[5]V. Frankl: *Homo patiens*, Vienna 1950.

[6]C. Lévi-Strauss: *Anthropologie structurale*, Paris 1958; also his: *La pensée sauvage*, Paris 1964.

[7]F. Nietzsche: *Thus Spoke Zarathustra*, Baltimore 1961, p.279.

A combination of biologism and psychologism appears in the founder of psychoanalysis, S. Freud. This scholar reduced man's conscious ego to the domain of drives and instincts, i.e. to the non-personal id[8]. Consciousness was reduced to subconsciousness, and man's whole psychic life was interpreted as a manifestation of biological drives, especially of the sexual drive. Man's principal pursuit was to be a search for pleasure. Religion, explained as an effect of frustration, was to be regarded as a sublimation of this drive. The naturalistic explication of man also refers to social life whose mechanisms are to be governed exclusively by: the drive to pleasure, a desire to avoid dangers, and the will of talented leaders. The above interpretation of man is obviously one-sided because it cancels out the autonomy of spiritual life, including the domains of morality and religion. Man is explained away as a knot of biological and instinctual energies, so that higher values (justice, love) are deprived of any sense. Hence, biologism and psychologism lead to man's dehumanization because they depersonalize and reify him[9]. Such an interpretation of the human person questions its very core: consciousness, conscience, ethos, love, subjectiveness. Freud perceived only the animalistic-instinctual "archaeology" of man, questioning his ontological teleology and personal sense.

Another form of anthropological reductionism is encountered in sociologism which recognizes the absolute primacy of society over the individual. Such a conception of social life is also called an organicistic theory because the role of human individuals is reduced to that of "social organism": the collective, class, state. Modern trends of sociologism include Marxism[10] whose founder described man as "a totality of social relations"[11]. According to this conception, man has no stable, universal, ontical datum, and that is why the collective is the agent creating the person. Man comes into being only within a community to which he owes all his human features, such as self-consciousness, language, tools, mode of physical and mental labour. "Society produces man as man"[12], i.e. a physical individual is transformed into a conscious, free, active self. Ontological socio-priorism and sociocentrism unavoidably lead to relativisation in the domain of axiology, so that in Marxism they speak of the class character (previously even of the party character) of science, philosophy, ethics etc. The criteria of all values, including the ethical ones, have a social character. Good is that which serves society and its progress.

Sociologism is most often connected with some totalitarian form of governing which has historically been confirmed by Italian Fascism, Hitler's National Socialism or

---

[8]S. Freud: *A General Introduction to Psychoanalysis*, New York 1958; also his: *Moses and Monotheism*, New York 1955.

[9]A sharp critique of Freud has been carried out by V.Frankl; cf. *Homo patiens*, op.cit.

[10]S. Kowalczyk: "*Jednostka a społeczeństwo w interpretacji marksistowskiej*" [The Individual and Society in the Marxist Interpretation], *Studia Płockie* 10 (1982), pp. 159-168.

[11]K. Marks: *Thesen über Feuerbach. K.Marks - F.Engels, Werke*, vol.3, Berlin 1962, p.6.

[12]K. Marks: *Ökonomisch-philosophische Manuskripte*, Leipzig 1974, p.190.

Stalinism[13]. In sociocentric interpretation man - subject is depersonalized because in human nature the autonomy of the person is questioned - its Logos, conscience, freedom, immortality, stable ethos. The individual-personal dimension of man is here explained as an epiphenomenon of social life and, hence, man is regarded as man only in the context of the community and due to his active participation in it. Humanization is to be a result of man's undertaking social life and labour. Human dignity is to constitute a consequence of social relations and therefore man's rights, too, are to be a result of socio-economic systems. Such a relativisation of human rights is extremely dangerous in social life, because it sanctions the claims of a totalitarian authority. It is, in fact, a reification of man, since he is then treated as an element of the play of socio-economic forces. Totalitarian sociologism cannot be reconciled with the personalistic understanding of man. A particularly emphatic expression of it can be found in National Socialism which arbitrarily glorified some races while degrading others. It also treated man in instrumental-pragmatic terms and that is why, among others, it established an organized way of destroying personality in concentration camps. The error of every sociologism consists in the relativisation of cognitive, moral and religious values. This trend subjects to relativization everything, with a single exception, namely, it accepts its own interpretation of man and social life as an absolute truth. The objective values of truth and good are questioned for the sake of the collective subject - race, class, state etc.

The next variant of a reductionistic interpretation of the human person is the analytical-scientistic explication of man. Its typical representative is Bertrand Russell († 1970), an advocate of extreme empiricism[14]. He was under a strong influence of the picture of the world typical of mathematical physics and non-substantial behavioural psychology, so he questioned man's stable personality. Man's subjectiveness is "a logical fiction", accepted exclusively for grammatical-linguistic reasons. The difference between man's material body and mind is to be merely a cognitive-semantic problem, not an ontological issue. Russell's theory of "natural monism" questions the significant difference between subject and object, which is connected with mechanistic materialism. Such ontology provides no foundation for objective axiology, so in consequence Russell questions the category of sin and the existence of universal ethical norms[15].

The theses of the English empiricist, so radical and shocking in their formulations, do not constitute the only expression of anthropological reductionism. The cult of logic, mathematics, empirical sciences and technology is typical of technocratic mentality. In this trend man is apprehended as *homo faber* and *homo inventor*, whose highest vocation in life is technological and scientific activity. Creativity is the source of human dignity[16].

---

[13]L. Janssens: *Personne et société. Théories actuelles et essai doctrinal*, Louvain 1939, pp. 5-120.

[14]B. Russell: *The Analysis of Mind*, London 1961, pp. 141 ff, 308.

[15]B. Russell: *The Conquest of Happinesss*, New York 1955.

[16]Cf. G. Kraus: *Blickpunkt Mensch. Menschenbilder der Gegenwart aus christlicher Sicht*, München 1983, pp.78-102.

The logicalist-technocratic vision of man raises serious objections. The subjection of the human person to strict logic and empiricism gives no chance of a full explanation of its ontical richness. It is a purely quantitative explication of man, ignoring his qualitative "being". Mathematics and empirical methods are incapable of grasping such significant dimensions of humanity as: consciousness, self-consciousness, freedom, conscience, and religious faith. Technocraticism, aiming at technological-scientific progress and exploitation of the cosmos, neglects the domain of higher values, so significant for man. The proposed "rationalism" leads therefore to the depersonalization of man. Russell's conception of man is a repetition of the stipulations of materialism as a postulate of science, which is a reflection of nineteenth-century scientism. Reductionism is never able to disclose an adequate truth about man as a person.

The variants of anthropological reductionism, briefly sketched out above, though differing in details, share common methodological assumptions, namely, they are attempts of constructing anthropology on the basis of pure sciences. Physicism, biologism, psychologism and neo-positivism all fall back on natural sciences, whereas sociologism more strongly emphasizes economic-sociological sciences. A common feature of these trends can also be found in epistemological monism, narrowing down the domain of scientific cognition to the limits of matter apprehensible in sensible cognition. Such methodological exclusiveness is unjustified, because it is not limited to the sphere of facts but it surreptitiously introduces philosophical assumptions derived from materialism[17]. The atmosphere of extreme scientism favours the birth of philosophical materialism which attempts to explain the whole reality - including the psychic-physical personality of man - in terms of categories appropriate to matter. One-sided epistemology unavoidably leads to anthropological reductionism, obliterating or totally negating the spiritual dimension of man. Rationality is often identified with extreme empiricism or even materialism. That is why an attempt to construct a universal theory of man on such a basis constitutes an act of faith rather than knowledge.

The restricted epistemological - methodological perspective, shared by various forms of ontological reductionism, is a cause of a deformed conception of man. Man is no longer a person, i.e. a conscious and free subject, but a physical-chemical "mechanism" in the structuralist approach, a tamed animal in the conviction of Nietzsche, or a knot of drives and vital forces directed by the vital "it" (id) in Freud's interpretation. Sociologism perceives in man the effect of the automatisms of social life, while neo-positivism and technocraticism - an efficient automaton. These are depersonalized conceptions of man, questioning his subjectiveness, freedom, moral sensitivity, self-consciousness, ontical finalism and a being directed towards Transcendence. In such context it is hard to speak about man's inner-spiritual life, universal truth, stable moral norms, absolute beauty, or transcendent Sacrum. The scientistic model of man (physical, biological, sociological etc.) omits in the person precisely what constitutes its *differentia specifica* in respect to the rest

---

[17] S. Kowalczyk: "Nauka a wiara: opozycja czy zgodność?" [Science and Faith: Opposition or Agreement?], *Roczniki Filozoficzne* 31 (1983) nr. 3, pp.93-120.

of the world. Concentrating on the quantitative aspect, natural and economic-social sciences are incapable of explicating the spiritual-personal being. For these reasons the forms of anthropological reductionism mentioned above constitute a blind alley in the search for a solution of the mystery of man.

All these observations make it possible to draw some conclusions about philosophy as a science which should provide an adequate theory of the human person. Pure sciences seem unable to offer a methodological foundation for anthropology since their methods and hypotheses concern only some aspects and dimensions of human existence. Obviously, natural and social anthropology is needed but it is still incapable of taking the place of the philosophical conception of man. Philosophy, understood as a discipline objectively and methodologically autonomous in respect to pure sciences, is necessary. This is how the role of philosophy is understood in Christian thought, although not all of its representatives identically understand the relation between philosophy and pure sciences. Some scholars interpret philosophy as a discipline which is principally incontiguous to scientific-natural cognition, while others perceive a possibility and even a necessity of complementarity of both types of human cognition. The first attitude is typical of the representatives of existentialistic Thomism[18], while the second one - of the contemporary trend of the philosophy of science. It seems that the autonomy of philosophy does not require its separation from the domain of empirical sciences, although their epistemological and methodological distinctness should undoubtedly be recognized. The autonomy of philosophy is doubtful when it is understood as a kind of a meta-science, a logical-linguistic analysis, or a kind of synthesis crowning all the pure sciences. In this interpretation, philosophy loses its reason of being. Only philosophy truly autonomous in relation to other sciences is necessary in the reflection about man[19]. It is this kind of philosophy that examines man's universal - ontic structures: substantive properties, faculties, relation between corporality and psychicism etc. Such a philosophy is not restricted to the aspect of contents but it also analyses the existential level of human existence. Finally, only philosophy is capable of grasping and explaining the mental-spiritual values of man: truth, good, beauty, love, religiousness. Such values escape empirical methods but when those values are ignored, ludicrous images of man are the result.

However, the methodological distinctness of philosophy does not necessitate its separation from sociological and natural sciences. The proponents of existentialist Thomism indicate a lack of substantial connections between philosophical anthropology and modern knowledge. They also claim that truth, in its proper sense, is apprehensible

---

[18] S. Kamiński: "Antropologia filozoficzna a inne działy poznania" [Philosophical Anthropology and other Domains of Cognition] [in:] *O Bogu i o człowieku* [On God and on Man], Warszawa 1968, vol.1, pp. 153-154.

[19] Cf. S. Matczak: *Philosophy. Its Nature, Methods and Basic Sources*, New York 1975.

only in the domain of philosophy[20]. For philosophy exploits the so-called existential judgments, directly grasping the act of existence and thus ensuring a cognitive junction with real being. In empirical sciences truth is apprehensible only indirectly, in so far as the notions and models of these sciences correspond to the reality. Yet, scientific theories and models are not principally connected with truth propositions because their character is mainly instrumental in conquering and controlling the cosmos. The current of Thomism mentioned above describes the role of science in utilitarian-pragmatic terms, questioning its cognitive-theoretical character.

The problem of the mutual relation between philosophy and pure sciences is really complex, nevertheless it does not seem justified to remove the category of truth from the domain of empirical sciences in such a wholesale and aprioristic manner. Eric Lionel Mascall, who is also a representative of existentialistic Thomism, perceives the noetic value of the propositions of natural sciences[21]. They do not constitute a literal description of the world but still they speak about its structure and properties. Scientific theories, which offer models of the world, are to be regarded as tools (*obiectum quo*) which make possible the cognition of the real world. Such models uncover only some aspects of the reality but, within this scope, one may speak about their truth or falsehood. Jean Ladriére also claims that science is not merely a sum total of the observed facts but also a theory, i.e. a certain truth about the world. The language of science is not an arbitrary projection of man or only a symbol, but it is a key to the understanding of the reality and its ontological foundations[22]. The goal of science is the search for truth which is not made invalid by the probabilist language sporadically typical of natural sciences. C.A. Peursen claims that the philosophy of man should be a synthesis of "objective" natural sciences and of "subjective" philosophical sciences[23].

Among modern naturalists and methodologists there often appear subjectivistic tendencies. The advocates of such a position include T.S.Kuhn and P.K.Feyerbend[24]. This kind of a subjectivist - relativistic interpretation of the cognitive value of natural sciences is most often a consequence of certain philosophical assumptions, mainly of idealism (in its varied amplitude) and relativism. Such a lineage causes that the category of truth is eliminated from the area of science. Idealism is a trend inimical to classical Christian thought (including Thomism) and that is why the subjectivistic-idealistic interpretation of the results of pure sciences is invalid. It would be hard to evaluate the theories of natural and sociological sciences, in spite of the subjective elements they

---

[20]M.Krąpiec: "Konfesyjność uczelni i wolność nauki" [The Confessional Character of University and the Freedom of Science], *Zeszyty Naukowe KUL* 1 (1958) nr. 1, pp. 75-81.

[21]Christian *Theology and Natural Science*, London 1957.

[22]*La science, le monde et la foi*, Tournai 1972, pp. 133-142.

[23]*Le corps - l'âme - l'esprit. Introduction à une anthropologie phénoménologique*, The Hague 1979, p.169.

[24]R. Kuhn: *The Structure of Scientific Revolution*, Chicago 1962; Feyerbend: "Consolation for the Specialist" [in:] *Criticism and the Growth of Knowledge*, Cambridge 1970, pp.227 ff.

contain, while excluding the category of truth. Any methodological "imperialism", claimed either by naturalists and by philosophers, is unjustified. Truth is not an exclusive privilege of either the former or the latter, although obviously philosophy and sciences uncover its different elements.

Philosophical anthropology, though it implies a variety of subjects and methods derived from pure sciences and metaphysics, does not exclude their mutual complementarity. This theory, without obliterating the differences between the attitudes of a scientist and a philosopher, implies the need of their cooperation. It is particularly necessary in respect to borderline problems, e.g. the origin of man, determinism and freedom, suffering and death, labour, culture, position in society. Man is an immanent entity in respect to the cosmos and that is why natural sciences are necessary in a description of his ontical status. An analogical role is played by sociological sciences in so far as the relation between man and community is concerned. In both cases the knowledge of science is necessary for a philosopher, at least on an elementary level. The attitude of isolationism from pure sciences exposes the philosopher to the dangers of abstractness and verbalism, so that it is then difficult to speak about the existential description of the human person. Obviously, there are limits to empirical-sociological cognition to which, in principle, the world of the person, with its values and categories, is not apprehensible. It is already a domain of philosophical reflection, making use of its own proper methods. Physico-chemical, biological-physiological, psychological, sociological, ethnic-cultural aspects and others do not exhaust the richness of the human person and therefore a restriction to any of them leads to reductionistic attitudes in anthropology. Natural cognition and philosophical cognition differ in their methods and scopes, therefore they should not be mixed or, even more so, identified. Still, they are complementary in the ultimate explication of human existence. The heuristic value of both types of cognition requires the acceptance and observance of their distinctness, which does not mean their mutual hostility - especially in the mental attitudes of the philosopher and the scientist. In the past, philosophy often inspired pure sciences, while the latter frequently forced philosophy to revise its argumentation or even theses. Philosophy without science is lame, while science without philosophy is blind to values. For this reason a departure from methodological anarchism does not necessitate a separation of philosophical anthropology and pure sciences. Inter-disciplinary openness is the most appropriate attitude in the examination of the phenomenon of man.

LITERATURE

BOCHEŃSKI, I.: *The Methods of Contemporary Thought*, Dordrecht 1965.

BÖHME, G.: *Anthropologie in pragmatischer Hinsicht*, Frankfurt a. M. 1985.

CHAUCHARD, P.: *Des animaux à l'homme. Psychisme et cervaux*, Paris 1961.

EMMET, D.M.: *The Nature of Metaphysical Thinking*, London 1945.

GEHLEN, A.: *Studien zur Anthropologie und Soziologie*, Berlin 1971.

GEHLEN, A.: *Der Mensch. Seine Natur und seine Stellung in der Welt*, Bonn 1965.

GEHLEN, A.: *Anthropologische Forschung*, Hamburg 1971.

HARTSHORNE, Ch.: *Creative Synthesis and Philosophical Method*, La Salle 1970.

HEITLER, W.: *Der Mensch und die naturwissenschaftliche Erkenntnis*, Braunschweig 1961.

KOREN, H.: *An Introduction to the Science of Metaphysics*, St. Louis 1956.

LANDMANN, M.: *Philosophische Anthropologie*, Berlin 1976.

MASCALL, E.L.: *Christian Theology and Natural Science*, London 1957.

WOJCIECHOWSKI, T.: *Wybrane zagadnienia z filozoficznej antropologii* [Selected Problems of Philosophical Anthropology], Kraków 1985.

ŻYCIŃSKI, J.: *Język i metoda* [Language and Method], Kraków 1983.

Chapter 2

Currents in Personalistic Anthropology

In this chapter we shall discuss those philosophical trends which recognize a possibility of personalistic anthropology, either already in their systemic assumptions and the starting point of analysis or at least in their ultimate goals. The latter case occurs in the theories of those modern thinkers (P. Teilhard de Chardin, A.N.Whitehead) who yield to the influence of the trend of methodological empiricism. In the philosophy of man two currents are most often distinguished, namely, the philosophy of being and the philosophy of the subject (resp. consciousness)[1]. The classical philosophy of being was represented by Aristotle and St. Thomas Aquinas, while the philosophy of the subject was accepted, among others, by St. Augustine, Descartes, Hegel, phenomenology and existentialism. The latter two trends are sometimes separated, although methodologically they are undoubtedly connected with the philosophy of consciousness. One may also find another classification of currents in anthropology, distinguishing among them existentialistic and compilatory approaches[2]. The latter classification is based on the ontological criterion, connected with the distinction between existence and essence as constitutive elements of being.

To some extent any classification is bound to be a matter of convention and cannot reflect the richness of currents of philosophical anthropology. The term "classical philosophy", though in itself well justified, is repeatedly and arbitrarily narrowed down only to some thinkers. And yet, classical philosophy is by no means a uniform current, since it can equally well be represented by Aristotle and Thomas Aquinas, on the one hand, and, on the other, by Augustine and Descartes. The distinction between the philosophy of being and the philosophy of the subject is methodologically valid, yet it cannot be employed for the purpose of an uncritical apology of one of these trends and a simultaneous a priori disavowal of the other.

---

[1]K.Wojtyła: *Osoba i czyn* [The Person and the Act], Kraków 1969, pp. 22-23; M.A. Krąpiec: "Idee przewodnie we współczesnej filozofii człowieka" [The Leading Ideas in Modern Philosophy of Man], *Zeszyty Naukowe KUL* 13 (1970) nr. 4, pp.21-34.

[2]M.Gogacz: *Wokół problemu osoby* [On the Problem of the Person], Warszawa 1974, pp. 143-146; also his: "Wielość koncepcji człowieka dominujących we współczesnej antropologii filozoficznej" [The Multiplicity of the Conceptions of Man Predominant in Contemporary Philosophical Anthropology] [in:] *W kierunku chrześcijańskiej kultury* [Towards a Christian Culture], Warszawa 1968, pp.121-148.

In subsequent considerations three leading trends in anthropology will be distinguished, namely, ontological-systemic, existentialistic-subjectivist, and a current tending towards empiricism. The first one is represented by the philosophy of being, the second - by the philosophy of the subject, and the third one, among others, - by A.Gehlen, Teilhard de Chardin and the so-called process theology.

The ontological-systemic trend, usually described as the classical philosophy of man, is primarily represented by St. Thomas Aquinas († 1274). This medieval philosopher devoted to the anthropological problems no fewer than fifteen questions in his *Summa Theologiae* (I. qq. 75-89)[3]. His arrangement of the material is particularly characteristic. He begins with an analysis of the category of the soul as a substantive form of the body, then discusses the problem of the faculties of the soul, cognitive and appetitive, and only then does he undertake the subjects of emotional life, the problems of will and free choice[4]. Subsequent topics concern broadly understood epistemological questions, such as the perception of the object and the subject - the human soul. Final considerations deal with the manner and scope of the cognition of the soul separated from the body. The order of the problems taken up by the author is not accidental since it reflects his systemic and generally ontological understanding of anthropology. At the point of departure no reference is made to the subject's experience, while assumptions are made about the categories of general metaphysics, namely, being, substance, the soul as a form, faculties etc. Due to this procedure, emotional life and the domain of freedom are already being analysed in the light of the above philosophical conceptions rather than constituting the starting point of anthropological considerations.

Obviously, the questions of *Summa Theologiae* devoted to the problem of man should be interpreted in the context of the whole philosophy of St. Thomas, including his epistemology. This is exactly what Jacques Maritain († 1973) did[5]. He devoted much attention to the problems of human cognition, critically evaluating both idealism and sensualism. He especially emphasized the pluralism of the forms of human cognition. The controlling function was ascribed by him to intellect, to thought, but he also brought out the important role of experience. He accepted the value of various kinds of experience, ethical, aesthetic, religious and interpersonal[6] Speaking about man Maritain took into account various kinds of cognition, sensible and intellectual, discursive and intuitive, theoretical and practical, pre-philosophical and philosophical. He duly appreciated advances in natural sciences but he also emphasized the methodological specificity of

---

[3]Cf. St. Thomas Aquinas: *Traktat of człowieku* [The Treatise on Man], prepared and ed. by Stefan Świeżawski.

[4]It is particularly characteristic that Thomas Aquinas first wrote about the faculty of will and only then provided a phenomenological description of man's freedom.

[5]J. Maritain: *The Education of Man*, New York 1962, pp. 45-50.

[6]J. Maritain: *Distinguer pour unir ou les degrés du savoir*, Paris 1948, pp. 265-273, 489 ff; also his: *Creative Intuition in Art and Poetry*, Princeton 1977.

philosophical wisdom[7]. Only philosophy makes it possible to create a global vision of human nature and to discover the existential sense of his life, which naturally goes beyond the scientific cognition of particular causes. Maritain also paid much attention to the problem of freedom, entering into a polemic with the advocates of biological and sociological determinism (Freud and Marxism)[8] The French Thomist was also well inclined to Thomas Aquinas's philosophy of man, but enriched it at the starting point - by making use of broadly understood experience.

In Poland Thomistic anthropology is represented by Father Mieczysław Krąpiec, the author of *I - Man*. Constructing his philosophy of man he employs two methods: he analyses the data of experience and refers to the systemic principles of Thomism. Talking about experience, he states:

> "*Hence, at the very starting point of philosophy, we can accept, in principle, a pre-scientific description of the human 'fact'*"[9].

He describes here the truths apprehensible by means of the so-called common sense, independent of "scientific facts" and, thanks to that, ensuring the absence of any doctrinal assumptions. The accepted conception of experience, typical of existentialist Thomism, is restricted to two types of experience, sensible perception and the recognition of our inner "I"[10]. Such a conception of experience is a derivative of the system, excluding anthropological and axiological experience as a basis of the philosophy of man. This impoverishment of the category of experience exerts a negative influence on the conception of man and his existential experience. Explaining the ontological structure of man Krąpiec analyses in detail the human "fact"[11].Referring to experience, he indicates the opposition between "I" and its proper acts, the latter inhering in the "I" as a subject.

Although the author theoretically acknowledges the important role of experience, yet as a rule he observes the requirements of "systemic thinking". It is evident when he passes from the "I" to metaphysical categories - the soul as a substantive form, act, cause etc. That is why he claims that "*We arrive at the notion of soul solely as a result of systemic philosophical analysis and philosophical explanation of our I. [...] The philosophical interpretation relies above all on the manifestation of those ontical functions that do not contradict the ontical fact originally given to us for explanation*"[12]. Justifying the existence of the soul, Thomism relies on the principle *agere sequitur esse*. This is also the way followed by the Polish Thomist: he begins with the analysis of mental-cognitive and volitional acts, looking for their reason of being. The immateriality of acts implies the

---

[7]*The Education of Man ...*, p.54.

[8]J. Maritain: *True Humanism*, New York 1938, pp. 20-22, 27-32; also his: *Freedom in the Modern World*, London 1935.

[9]*I-Man. An Outline of Philosophical Anthropology*, New Britain 1983, p.30.

[10]M.A.Krąpiec: "Doświadczenie a metafizyka" [Experience and Metaphysics], *Roczniki Filozoficzne* 24 (1976) nr.1, pp.5-16.

[11]*I - Man ...*, pp.94-98.

[12]Ibid., p.100.

immateriality of their subject which can only be an independent (in being but not in operating) soul[13].

The study *I - Man* pays little attention to Augustinian and post-Cartesian philosophy which emphasizes the subjectivist character of man. One is struck by the fact of an almost exclusive use of terminology taken over from the general philosophy of being when explaining the structure of man. This is a terminology ("act", "form", "substance") borrowed from the world of things and for that reason it is hardly satisfactory in explaining and interpreting the world of the human person[14]. The systemic method, preferred by existentialist Thomism, should be more solidly founded on experience and on phenomenological description.

The second trend in anthropology, which is predominant today, has an existentialistic-phenomenological character, usually described as the philosophy of the subject. Its philosophical lineage is quite ancient, since it goes back to the thought of St. Augustine († 430). That thinker focused his attention on man and God[15], discovering the presence of the Absolute in the heart of the human person. Sometimes St. Augustine's epistemological realism is questioned because of the emphasis laid on the *cogito* in his philosophy. Yet, the objection does not seem valid because his epistemology significantly differs from Descartes's idealism. The latter philosopher started from the fact of thought in which he found a justification of man's reality, whereas St. Augustine accepted the simultaneity of the cognition of the three ontical levels of man: existence, life and thinking[16]. He did not infer the reality of man's existence from the fact of thought but perceived the fact of existence in the thinking subject. Therefore, Augustine was undoubtedly a realist; he acknowledged the reality of man and of the cosmos, although he was more interested in the world of spirit than in matter. The realism of St. Augustine is sometimes called "radical psychological empiricism"[17] or "spiritualism" or "noologism"[18]. Perhaps it would be best to use the term "existential realism" because this thinker set his mind on the concrete in human existence. His philosophy of man was discovered in the existential reflection on everyday life, in man's changeable fortunes, in the drama and beauty of life. It was an "ontology of encounter" since it grasped man in relation to other people and community[19].If Thomas Aquinas was interested in existential structures and patterns, then Augustine was interested in the action of the

---

[13]Ibid., pp.108-118.

[14]Cf. J.Tischner: *Myślenie według wartości* [Thinking according to Values], Krak6w 1982, pp.312-338.

[15]St. Augustine: *Soliloquia* 1,2,7 PL 32, 872.

[16]St. Augustine: *De Trinitate* 10,10,13-14 PL 42, 980; 15,12,21 PL 42, 1073-1074.

[17]M.Gilson: "L'avenir de la m6taphysique augustinienne", *Revue de Philosophie* (1930) pp.360-384.

[18]F. Thonnard: "Charact6res platoniciens de l'ontologie augustinienne" [in:] *Augustinus Magister*, Paris 1954, vol.1, p.319.

[19]F. K0rner: *Das Sein und der Mensch. Die existenzielle Seinsentdeckung des jungen Augustin*, Freiburg 1959, pp.30-31.

human person and its values. He perceived the realization and fullness of human existence precisely in action. His existentialism has a dynamic-spiritualistic character; it is an apprehension of the human being - its sense and vocation - in the experiencing of fortunes and in shaping values. He focused his attention on life, action, and the concrete - omitting speculative-abstract problems. Characterizing man, this thinker did not employ a reifying terminology, borrowed from the analysis of non-human beings. Augustine considered man through the prism of his existence - psychic experiences, freedom, action, and in the context of the fundamental values of the human person - thought, truth, good, happiness, faith, love. It was an axiological perspective of anthropology - man is a person living in the world of values, shaped by those values and realizing them. That thinker of early Christianity showed man in his manual activity - labour, in psychic-spiritual acts of cognition, in love, in search for happiness. At the basis of Augustine's anthropology there is not so much the experiencing of being but rather personal experience and the experiencing of values[20].

Augustinian anthropology has found continuation in phenomenology and existentialism. A leading representative of the anthropology of the former trend was Max Scheler (†1928). His philosophy of man was based on specific apriorism, intuitionism, emotionalism and the priority of love over cognition[21]. Apriorism and intuitionism were combined with the method of phenomenological description and phenomenological reduction, omitting the problem of the reality of a cognized object but grasping its essence. The eidetic perception of Edmund Husserl († 1938) was combined with idealism which Scheler tried to overcome. He accepted the "material a priori" which he understood not so much as a subjective form of human mind but rather as a perception of the essence of the object cognized. Such a perception has a pre-reflective character since it is realized through emotional experience. The German thinker accepted emotional intuitionism, ascribing the cognitive function also to the domain of feelings. Among those feelings the one of love predominates and its object is the world of persons[22].

Although Scheler detached himself from Husserl's subjectivism and idealism, still the phenomenological method accepted by him exerted some influence on his conception of man. His anthropology has a programmatically philosophical character and is opposed to naturalistic evolutionism. Man is in possession of "the dignity of spirit"[23], which cannot be established by means of empirical methods. Stressing the dynamic character of the human being, Scheler actually relinquished the category of substance. The human person is not a substantive being but a conjunction of acts and actions - cognitive, appetitive, emotional, manual etc. It was an actualistic conception of person, without becoming an

---

[20]S. Kowalczyk: *Człowiek i Bóg w nauce św. Augustyna* [Man and God in the Teaching of St. Augustine], Warszawa 1987, pp.51-164.

[21]M. Scheler: *Vom Ewigen im Menschen*, Bern 1954, pp.17, 196-197, 207-209.

[22]M. Scheler: *Vom Umsturz der Werte*, Bern 1955, pp.96 ff; H.Leonardy: *Liebe und Person*, Den Haag 1976.

[23]M.Scheler: *Wesen und Formen der Sympathie*, München 1973, pp. 85-87, 168 ff.

extreme psychological actualism[24]. Similarly to St. Augustine, the German phenomenologist emphasized the role of love, moral and religious values, activity and constant self-development in human life. Thus it was an anthropology of a dynamic, axiological and spiritualistic character. At its basis there was a theory of emotional intuitionism and voluntarism.

A particularly creative representative of phenomenological - existentialistic anthropology was Gabriel Marcel († 1973). He accepted the primacy of existence over essence in the sense that existence is never ultimately cognizable. As a consequence, he was averse to the philosophical systems and formulas identified with static philosophy[25]. He himself was an advocate of a dynamic philosophy, which he called a "thinking thought" or a "philosophy of the concrete". Such a philosophy refers to man's concrete experiences, among others, to those in "extreme situations", such as, for instance, the experience of anxiety. Marcel charged idealistic philosophy with the degradation of existence, and scholastic philosophy - with arguing about abstract existence. As a point of departure of realistic philosophy he accepted the experience of existence, ***existo***, and not doubting or thinking[26]. True philosophy is the philosophy of human existence. Obviously, it does not mean the mechanical existence of things, but the conscious and committed existence of the human person.

As the French existentialist repeatedly asserted, anthropology should be based on experience. His understanding of experience departs from the solutions of both extreme empiricism and rationalism. He postulated the use of all forms of experience of the human person, both external and internal[27]. As a constant "pilgrim" in time and space, man is involved in certain situations in respect to the world of nature and that of human communities. He experiences love and rivalry, hope and despair, solidarity and desertion, he is seeking truth and good. Marcel's existentialism is often charged with the label of idealism, yet the objection does not seem to apply because Marcel clearly distinguished subjectivity from subjectivism.

It is often thought that the method of existentialism is primarily connected with introspection. Marcel corrected that view asserting that it is not so much introspection that is the point but rather experiencing oneself in the context of the world and of other people[28]. His philosophical method is connected with the distinction of the so-called primary reflection and secondary reflection. The primary reflection is typical of natural sciences; it is connected with sensible perception and leads to a quantitative apprehension of the reality. The secondary reflection already has of a philosophical character, since it

---

[24]M.Scheler: *Der Formalismus in der Ethik und die materiale Wertethik*, Halle 1921, pp.383-393; also his: *Wesen und Formen der Sympathie*, pp.255-256.

[25]G.Marcel: *De refus à l'invocation*, Paris 1940, pp.21-25, 192 ff, 214 ff.

[26]G. Marcel: *Etre at avoir*, Paris 1935, pp.151-152.

[27]G.Marcel: *Homo Viator. Introduction to a Metaphysics of Hope*, New York 1962, pp.23-26, 166 ff.

[28]G.Marcel: *Présence et immortalit é*, Paris 1959, pp.25-26.

is a consequence of man's freedom and it demands our "participation" in the universe[29]. This is a "recovering reflection" since it makes possible the overcoming of the strangeness of the human subject in respect to the world. Hence, philosophy requires an active participation in the world.

Characterizing the human being Marcel consciously renounced the category of substance, which he regarded as too static. He described man as the subject of experiencing[30]. Immediate experience allows us to grasp the human "I", its self-identity, permanence and subjectivity. Man is a subject, a person and a spirit, while simultaneously he is "a being incorporated" in material reality[31]. Man's vocation is to act and to develop; not ***sum*** but ***sursum***[32]. The phenomenological analysis of the act makes it possible to reveal the very essence of the human person. Action is both man's act and at the same time his self-realization. To a large extent, Marcel's philosophy of man is undoubtedly literary, often resorting to metaphors as a means of presentation. In spite of that, at its basis there is a specific epistemological realism, distancing itself from subjectivism and relativism. In principle, Marcel's aim was not a rational-discursive justification of certain anthropological theses, but a clarification of the authentic truth about the human person[33].

The phenomenological-existential current in anthropology also constitutes a reference point, among others, for Józef Tischner. He constructs his conception (though not a system) of man in opposition to Thomism, turning instead to phenomenologists and existentialists. The point of departure of his anthropology is the "experience of the ego", namely, the fact of man's possessing immanent self-consciousness[34]. This is a Cartesian trend, though enriched with Scheler's axiology. In this context the essence of man is perceived by the author in the fact of experiencing the value. Man is "an axiological I", intuitively reading the rich scale of values[35]. Tischner is less interested in the ontology of values than in their existential experiencing. He even goes as far as to acknowledge the primacy of values over being and he therefore speaks about "thinking according to values". Another characteristic feature of the proposed anthropology is the category of interpersonal communication which is introduced in order to explain the origin of society as a community[36].

---

[29]*De refus* ..., op.cit., pp.30-35; I. Dec: *Tomaszowa a Marcelowa teoria człowieka [St.Thomas's and Marcel's Theories of Man]*, Wrocław 1984.

[30]*Présence et immortalit é*, p.103.

[31]*De refus* ..., pp.29-33.

[32]*Homo Viator*, p.26; cf. *De refus* ..., pp.142 ff.

[33]I. Dec, op.cit., p.258.

[34]J.Tischner: *Świat ludzkiej nadziei* [The World of Human Hope], Kraków 1975, p.119.

[35]Ibid., pp.120-121, 183-200.

[36]*Myślenie według wartości*, pp.78-86.

In this survey of modern variants of personalistic anthropology it would be difficult to exclude the current tending towards empiricism. Its representatives accept the data of natural sciences as their point of departure but they are convinced that in the final effect of their analyses they reach universal-philosophical conclusions. The results of pure sciences are taken into consideration, among others, by H. Plessner and A. Gehlen who strongly rely on biology and psychology, though at the same time they try to preserve the opinion that natural sciences provide important knowledge specificity of philosophical cognition[37]. They are of the about man and that this knowledge should be included in the anthropological-philosophical analysis.

The leading and most influential representative of the empirical trend in anthropology is Pierre Teilhard de Chardin. To the problem of man he has devoted many of his writings, of which perhaps the best known is the study *The Human Phenomenon*. The author programmatically omitted the former metaphysics of man, accusing it of apriorism and staticality. In its place he proposed a new phenomenology of man which he understood as "an external description of man as a phenomenon - to the extent to which, on the basis of earthly observation, we are justified in considering scientifically the human being in relation to the development of other living beings and as the highest - at least so far - phase of their evolution"[38]. Naturally, Teilhard's phenomenology differs from Husserl's, since it incorporates scientific-naturalistic experience. In fact, in his phenomenology Teilhard saw a new "philosophy of existence", that is, a totally homogeneous explanation of the world and man[39]. In his writings he discussed problems proper for philosophical anthropology, such as the nature of man, the relation of the psychical-spiritual and bodily-material factors, its genesis, moral and religious values, the sense of life, the problems of humanism and so on. The phenomenology of the French scholar is neither exclusively descriptive nor extremely scientistic, since it also contains philosophical and theological elements. His philosophy of man has an inductive-synthetic character[40]. Its point of departure is the scientific experience, especially in physico-biological sciences. A particularly fundamental role is played by the idea of evolution, from the perspective of which he explains the appearance and the nature of man[41]. The idea of evolution has been interpreted as a pan-ontological principle, since it allows an adequate explanation of the totality of cosmic transformations, from the process of the corpuscularization of inorganic matter to the fact of hominization. The human phenomenon was explained by Teilhard in the context of the totality of the pre-human and extra-human world. In consequence of such methodological assumptions

---

[37]H.Plessner: *Condition humana*, Pfullingen 1964; also his: *Die Stufen des Organischen und der Mensch*, Berlin 1928; A. Gehlen: *Der Mensch. Seine Natur und seine Stellung in der Welt*, Bonn 1965.

[38]P.Teilhard de Chardin: *La place de l'homme* [in:] *Oeuvres*, Paris 1964, vol.8, p.165.

[39]*Esquisse d'un univers personnel* [in:] *Oeuvres*, Paris 1962, vol.6, p.88.

[40]M.Wrede: *Die Einheit von Materie und Geist bei Teilhard de Chardin*, Limburg 1964, pp.61-62.

[41]*Comment je crois?* [in:] *Oeuvres*, Paris 1969, vol.10, p.115; *La mystique de la science* [in:] *Oeuvres*, vol.6, pp.212-214.

he was critical of the "pernicious dualism" in the existing Christian anthropology and adopted a monistic apprehension of the nature of man[42]. Teilhard's anthropology has found a very extensive response in Christian philosophy of man[43]

Still, Teilhard's anthropology provokes objections both essential and methodological. The latter result from the fact of the ontologicalization of the idea of evolution through which he attempted to explain everything. Indirectly, he spoke for the unity of the scientific method which he identified with the methods of empirical sciences. Such methodological elimination seems controversial because the method should correspond to the object examined. Man's world differs from the world of plants and animals, and for that reason the biologicalization of anthropology deforms the image of man.

The empiricism-inspired current is also clearly discernible in the writings of Alfred N. Whitehead († 1947), a physicist and philosopher. Although he acknowledged the autonomy of philosophy in respect to pure sciences, in fact he borrowed from them a number of methodological principles in his philosophical analyses. This is especially true about the two explicative principles, namely, the process and the organism. His conception of being was dynamic-monistic, so that he accepted the process of constant transformations as the essence of being[44]. According to him, the whole reality is an unceasing evolutionary process from which there emerge ontic structures, called by him "actual beings". The latter also include man who is an integral part of the cosmic organism. The "philosophy of organism" is the second explicative principle in the philosophy of the English scholar. The universe is a cosmic organism which is an eternal process of self-becoming. "The process of creation is a form of the unity of the universe"[45]. Whitehead questioned the existence of substantive-independent beings, opting for dynamic monism in interpreting the nature of the world. This monism was so radical that it was not undermined by the conceptions of man and God. Man exists in the world, and the world exists in him.[46] The claim was not meant as a highlighting of the immanene of man, but it was rather man's monistic-pantheistic interpretation. Human nature is understood by Whitehead in accordance with his process philosophy and that is why he described man as a "stability of perception" and a series of successive actual occasions[47]. The human person is a set of experiences, sensations, decisions, acts of cognition etc. Hence, this led to a desubstantialization of man. Sometimes the author called man a "community" of historical experiences, actual beings, multiple elements of the cosmos. In this way the human person was interpreted as a resultant of

---

[42]*Du cosmos à cosmogénèse* [in:] *Oeuvres*, Paris 1964, vol.7, pp.266-267.

[43]Cf. T.Wojciechowski: *Wybrane zagadnienia z filozoficznej antropologii* [Selected Problems of Philosophical Anthropology], Kraków 1985.

[44]A.N.Whitehead: *Process and Reality*, New York 1969, pp.28,53-54.

[45]A.N.Whitehead: *Adventures of Ideas*, Cambridge 1939, p.231.

[46]A.N.Whitehead: *His Reflections on Man and Nature*, New York 1961, p.27.

[47]*Adventures of Ideas*, p.263; *Process and Reality*, pp.125-126.

cosmic-biological and historical-social forces. In such a case it is hard to speak about man's personal identity, his individual autonomy and permanence. Although Whitehead used personalistic terminology, in fact he questioned the ontically stable personhood of man. In further perspective, the process theology does not allow for individual responsibility for one's acts or for individual immortality.

Whitehead's anthropology was shaped in the circle of the influences of natural sciences, especially physics and the biological theory of evolution. The theology which he has initiated, unavoidably leads to man's de-individualization, and, thus, to his de-subjectivization. It undoubtedly implies a naturalistic apprehension of the human person, totally incorporated in the evolving cosmos. It was a consequence of the extrapolation of the methods of natural sciences to the domain of metaphysics, so that as a result the human person was analysed exclusively on the basis of natural theories or hypotheses. Whitehead's thought, so controversial from both methodological and essential points of view, still finds its followers both in the United States and in Europe[48]

The three predominant currents discussed above do not exhaust the whole richness of trends in modern philosophical anthropology[49]. For instance, the survey has completely omitted Marxist philosophy of man, since the the present chapter concerned primarily the presentation of personalistic reflections.

LITERATURE

BARBOTIN, E.: *Humanité de l'homme. Etude de philosophie concréte*, Paris 1970.

BOGLIOLO, L.: *La verita dell'uomo*, Roma 1969.

BUBER, M.: *Das Problem des Menschen*, Heidelberg 1954.

BRÜNING, W.: *Philosophische Anthropologie*, Stuttgart 1960.

CORETH, E.: *Was ist der Mensch?*, Innsbruck - Wien 1973. *De homine. Studia hodiernae anthropologiae. Acta VII Congressus Thomistici Internationalis*, vol.2, Romae 1970-1972.

DONCEEL,J.F.: *Philosophical Anthropology*, New York 1967.

DUFRENNE, M.: *Pour l'homme*, Paris 1968.

GOGACZ, M.: *Wokół problemu osoby* [Concerning the Problem of Person], Warszawa 1974.

GUARDINI, R.: *Welt und Person*, Mainz 1988.

HENGSTENBERG,H.E.: *Philosophische Anthropologie*, München 1984.

JAROSZEWSKI,T.M.: *Osobowość i wspólnota* [Personality and Community], Warszawa 1970.

JOLIF, J.Y.: *Comprendre l'homme. Introduction à une anthropologie philosophique*, Paris 1967.

KOWALCZYK, S.: *Człowiek i Bóg w nauce św. Augustyna* [Man and God in the Teaching of St. Augustine], Warszawa 1987.

KRAUS, B.: *Blickpunkt Mensch. Menschenbilder der Gegenwart aus christlicher Sicht*, München 1983.

KRĄPIEC, M.A.: *I - Man. An Outline of Philosophical Anthropology*, New Britain 1983.

[48]J.Van der Veken: "Whitehead's God is not Whiteheadian Enough" [in:] *Whitehead und Processbegriff*, München 1981, pp.100-311.

[49]Cf. S.Kowalczyk: "Personnalisme polonais contemporain", *Divus Thomas* 88 (1985) no.1-3, pp. 58-76.

LANDMANN, M.: *Philosophische Anthropologie*, Berlin 1969.

LOTZ, J.B.: *Der Mensch im Sein*, Freiburg im Br. 1967.

MARCEL, M.: *Homo Viator. Introduction to a Metaphysics of Hope*, New York 1962.

MARITAIN, J.: *True Humanism*, New York 1938.

MASCALL, E.L.: *The Importance of Being Human. Some Aspects of the Christian Doctrine of Man*, New York 1958.

MÖLLER, J.: *Zum Thema Menschsein. Aspekte einer philosophischen Anthropologie*, Mainz 1967.

PRZYWARA, E.: *Mensch. Typologische Anthropologie*, vol.2, Nürnberg 1958.

ROYCE, J.E.: *Man and His Nature. A Philosophical Psychology*, New York 1961.

SCHAFF, A.: *Marxismus und das menschliche Individuum*, Wien 1965.

SCHELER, M.: *Vom Ewigen im Menschen*, Bern 1954.

SUCHODOLSKI, B.: *Narodziny nowożytnej filozofii człowieka* [The Birth of the Modern Philosophy of Man], Warszawa 1963.

SUCHODOLSKI, B.: *Rozwój nowożytnej filozofii człowieka* [The Development of the Modern Philosophy of Man], Warszawa 1967.

TEILHARD de CHARDIN, P.: *Le groupe zoologique humain*, Paris 1956.

TISCHNER, J.: *Świat ludzkiej nadziei* [The World of Human Hope], Kraków 1975.

WCIÓRKA, L.: *Filozofia człowieka* [The Philosophy of Man], Warszawa 1982.

Współczesna filozofia człowieka [Contemporary Philosophy of Man], collected work ed. by J. Majka, Wrocław 1973.

ZIMMERMAN, A.: *Der Mensch in der modernen Philosophie*, Essen 1975.

ZUBIRI, X.: *Il problema dell'uomo. Antropologia filosofica*, Palermo 1985.

Chapter 3

From the Phenomenology to the Metaphysics of Man

In some respects the previously discussed currents in anthropology are opposed to each other, although this does not exclude a possibility of their approximate synthesis. Attempts of such a synthesis have been undertaken, among others, by two authors, S. Strasser and K. Wojtyła. They both perceived the lasting value of classical philosophy, especially that related to St. Thomas Aquinas, yet at the same time they thought it necessary to take advantage of the phenomenological method. Such an undertaking was possible because the medieval thinker often referred to the achievements of St. Augustine whose influence, in turn, is clearly evident in many phenomenologists. At any rate, the writings of St. Thomas contain various descriptions of the human person. Some of them (e.g. man is a rational person, an incommunicable individual, something most perfect in nature) have an objective - ontological character, while others (e.g. man is a subjectiveness, consciousness, freedom and so on) have a subjective-subjectivist character[1]. The ontological conception of man, typical of Thomism, may be supplemented with elements of the philosophy of the subject.

Stefan Strasser opted for phenomenological anthropology, but he also recognized the need for a metaphysics of man[2]. In his interpretation, phenomenological cognition has a hermeneutical, intuitionist, and dialectical character. The noetic value of the phenomenological method makes it possible to stress man's subjectiveness. Although Strasser called phenomenology a fundamental philosophy of man[3], he also affirmed metaphysical anthropology, its methods and theories (among others, hylomorphism)[4]. Beginning with phenomenology, in his considerations he reached to classical philosophy in his conclusions. He was an advocate of methodological pluralism in description and in interpreting the human being, so in consequence he also referred to empirical psychology. Both metaphysics and empirical psychology speak about man, although they employ different methods of cognition, so that the "I" described by psychologists is by no means

---

[1]J.B. Metz: *Christliche Anthropozentrik*, München 1962, pp.60-61.

[2]S.Strasser: *Phénoménologie et sciences de l'homme. Vers un nouvel esprit scientifique*, Louvain 1967, p.282.

[3]Ibid., p.318.

[4]S.Strasser: *The Soul in Metaphysial and Empirical Psychology*, London 1957, p.116.

identical with the philosophical category of soul. However, man's psychical life is deeply seated in his material body and for that reason descriptive-empirical psychology indirectly reveals the spiritual dimension of man[5]. Psychology describes man in his somatic and psychic activities, in this way uncovering an externalization of the inner-ontic self. The subject of metaphysical psychology is the personal-spiritual "I" which Strasser called a transcendental act. This agent transcends biological and social determinants and for that reason it can be discovered only in a philosophical analysis. Strasser is an advocate of cooperation between philosophical anthropology and empirical sciences in examining man. The latter rely on scientific experience but in their final theories they pertain to philosophical problems[6]. A converse dependence is also true, i.e. the philosophy of man must take into account scientific data about the human being. Strasser was called "a man of confrontation"[7] but, strictly speaking, he was an advocate of a dialogue between phenomenology and metaphysics, as well as between philosophy and empirical sciences in the analysis of the human being. His propositions did not lead to a methodological obliteration of differences between various disciplines, but to an integration of all kinds of knowledge about man.

Another adherent of a reconcilement between classical anthropology and phenomenological anthropology is Cardinal Karol Wojtyła, the author of Osoba i czyn [The Person and the Act]. He combines Thomism, called a philosophy of being, with phenomenology. Thomism is openly declared - and even more often assumed - in a number of crucial philosophical theories, such as hylomorphism, act and potentiality, autonomy of soul, existential apprehension of human nature, description of man as person etc.[8]. The thinker did not aim at a global presentation of Thomistic anthropology but at its re-interpretation so as to make it more accessible to the modern reader. It is undoubtedly Thomism, but enriched with elements of phenomenology. Cardinal Wojtyła, today John Paul II, did accept phenomenology, though not in E.Husserl's or M.Scheler's understanding of it. He stated quite openly that he did not aim at a doctrinal synthesis of the philosophy of being and the philosophy of consciousness[9]. He did not intend to create a single meta-philosophy. At the same time he confessed to "an attempt of fusing two philosophical currents, in a sense - even two philosophies"[10]. It is easy to explain the apparent contradiction between these two statements. Cardinal Wojtyła did not undertake an attempt to integrate Thomism and phenomenology in the maximal sense, that is, the metaphysics of both trends. As an ethicist, however, he was interested

---

[5]Ibid., pp.28 ff, 236-240.

[6]*Phénoménologie* ..., p.195.

[7]P.Ricoeur: *Introduction to Strasser's Phénoménologie* ..., op.cit., p.7.

[8]K.Wojtyła: *Osoba i czyn* [The Person and the Act], Kraków 1969, pp.30,66 ff, 216.

[9]K.Wojtyła: *Ocena możliwości zbudowania etyki chrześcijańskiej przy założeniach systemu Maksa Schelera* [An Evaluation of the Possibility of Constructing a Christian Ethics on the Assumptions of Max Scheler's System], Lublin 1959, p.125; also his: "Conclusion" in *Analecta Cracoviensa* 5-6 (1973-1974) p.249.

[10]*Osoba i czyn*, pp.22-23.

primarily in man. In respect to such an object of cognition, which is an ontic subject, he saw the need to enrich Thomism with the phenomenological method. Thus, although he questioned phenomenalism and phenomenology as metaphysics, he nevertheless accepted the phenomenological method. Such a method "facilitates the analysis of ethical facts on the phenomenal and experiental levels" and it also "makes it possible to discover this particular regularity of experience which results from it when it is directed at moral values"[11]. His book *Osoba i czyn* employs a nomenclature borrowed from phenomenology, e.g. the phenomenological criterion, the phenomenological insight, the phenomenological experience, the phenomenological reduction, the phenomenological method etc. Phenomenology plays here an instrumental role; it is a heuristic method of explaining the nature of man, and especially man's dynamism. Perceiving the complexity of the human being, Cardinal Wojtyła also saw the necessity of applying various languages and methods[12]. He was convinced that the languages of Thomism and phenomenology do not exclude but rather complement each other.

The writings of Strasser and Wojtyła confirm the possibility of integrating some elements of Thomism and phenomenology or, speaking more broadly, of ontological-systemic anthropology and existential-subjectistic anthropology. Analogically, one may make use of elements of Augustinianism and existentialism in Thomistic philosophy of man.

St. Thomas's *Summa Theologiae* begins with the metaphysical category of soul and only in subsequent parts of considerations does it characterize man's cognition[13]. In modern philosophical anthropology the point of departure is more and more often the phenomenology of man. However, the notion of phenomenology is by no means unequivocal; it was differently understood by Kant, Hegel, Husserl, Scheler, Heidegger, Edward von Hartmann or Sartre[14]. Particularly interesting is the phenomenology initiated by Husserl and Scheler. In their considerations, phenomenology has several more meanings: (a) the metaphysics accepting the transcendental ego of objective idealism; (b) the eidetic science dealing with consciousness and its data; (c) a method understood as a perception of essence, based on immediacy (and reaching beyond sensible experience) [15]. Husserl combined the phenomenological method with idealism, but Scheler re-interpreted the method of phenomenological description on the basis of epistemological realism (though he was not ultimately consistent till the end). The phenomenological method is particularly useful in anthropology because it breaks the

---

[11]*Ocena możliwości* ..., pp.122-123.

[12]Conclusion, op.cit., p.259; cf. also *Osoba i czyn*, pp.67,188.

[13]St.Thomas's epistemology of realism is undoubtful but in spite of that the empirical-experiential foundation of his anthropology is restricted.

[14]W.L.Reese: *Dictionary of Philosophy and Religion*, New York 1980, pp.428-429.

[15]S.Strasser: *The Soul* ..., op.cit., pp.2-3; A. Półtawski: *Świat, spostrzeżenie, świadomość* [The World, Perception, Consciousness], Warszawa 1973, pp.443-444.

barrier between the subject and the object, while simultaneously respecting man's subjective dimension in its description[16].

The question of the usefulness of phenomenology in philosophical anthropology is connected with the way in which anthropology is understood: whether philosophy of man is only an extension of general metaphysics or an autonomous philosophical domain. The followers of existentialistic Thomism admit that philosophy of man cannot be viewed as a particularization of ontology (in its Thomistic understanding). Yet, at the same time they claim that general metaphysics and anthropology, although their points of departure vary in their scopes, do not differ in their formal object and the applied method[17]. In such an interpretation the philosophy of man loses autonomy and becomes a treatise on a general philosophy of being. It is our conviction that anthropology, although it takes over from ontology some notions and methods of justification, still differs from it in some significant aspects, such as, the point of departure, object, terminology, and, partly, in its method. The axioms of general metaphysics are insufficient for particular philosophical disciplines, for philosophy of nature, anthropology, ethics, the philosophy of God etc.[18]. The variety of objects of the philosophy of being and the philosophy of man makes any identity of their methods and terms impossible. The formal object of anthropology is not man as a being but as a rational and free being[19]. And thus neither the material nor the formal objects of both disciplines are quite identical.

What constitutes the point of departure of philosophical anthropology? Obviously, it is the world of man. It is often suggested that a convenient starting point of this discipline is the fact of man's rationality. Man as the ***animal rationale*** is the datum of the generally accepted, pre-scientific experience[20]. It is undoubtedly true, but can rationality constitute a sufficient foundation of philosophical anthropology? Aristotelianism and Thomism concentrated their attention on external experience, underestimating the scope and function of inner experience. The point of departure of the philosophy of man should be double: the perception of the external world and inner experience. The latter was known to Thomas Aquinas[21], but it was used by him only in a very small extent in his anthropology. In external experience man is apprehended as an object, whereas in inner experience it is possible to grasp him in the role of the subject. Here one can see the

---

[16]In Husserl's understanding the world is an intentional configuration of the cognizing subject, not an objective datum. Such an understanding of the phenomenological method results from the thinker's idealism but it does not belong to the essence of phenomenological description.

[17]S.Kamiński: "Antropologia filozoficzna a inne działy poznania" [Philosophical Anthropology and other Domains of Cognition] [in:] *O Bogu i człowieku* [On God and Man], Warszawa 1968, vol.1, pp.162-164.

[18]Cf. M.Molski: "Zdania pierwotne w nauce św. Tomasza z Akwinu" [Original Propositions in the Teaching of St. Thomas Aquinas], *Collectanea Theologica*, 28 (1957), pp.14 ff.

[19]The identification of the formal object of ontology and anthropology blurs their specificity and distinctness.

[20]M.Krąpiec: *I - Man*, op.cit., pp.33 ff.

[21]*Summa Theologiae*, I, q.76, a.1.

necessity of adopting phenomenology as a foundation of the philosophy of man. The fact of man's rationality is evident but one should also take into account the broad range of facts connected with man's nature. Anthropology should therefore take into consideration various facts, psychological, historical, social, ethical, religious, cultural[22]. These facts are described by the humanities and sociological sciences which provide a rich informative, descriptive material about the human world. Anthropology cannot ignore the humanities and restrict itself to pre-scientific experience.

Another problem that demands consideration is the question of the relation between the philosophy of man and natural sciences. One should undoubtedly be careful when exploiting natural theories and hypotheses since they frequently entail controversial philosophical assumptions, e.g. connected with idealism or subjectivism. But it would be hard to ignore the factual material of these disciplines or to treat them as conventions, mere possibilities, working hypotheses etc. At any rate, many achievements of empirical sciences have become permanent elements of common (pre-scientific) knowledge[23]. But it would be a mistake to ontologicalize natural theories (or, for that matter, physical, cosmological, biological theories) which, unfortunately, occurs in the writings of Teilhard de Chardin and A.N.Whitehead.

Philosophical anthropology is organically connected with the conception of experience. The role of experience in philosophy is underestimated by all variants of idealism and rationalistic apriorism which depart from the realities of being and get entangled in futile speculations. Although in philosophy the fundamental role of experience is quite commonly recognized, the scope and way of understanding it often provoke controversies. There are many concepts of experience, among others, in extreme empiricism, existentialistic Thomism or phenomenology[24].

Extreme empiricism, related to D. Hume († 1776) and today accepted by neopositivism, understands by experience exclusively sensible perception. Only the latter has been accepted as a source of scientific cognition and that is why propositions regarded as cognitive and meaningful include exclusively statements that are empirically verifiable. The principle of empirical verification, accepted especially by the so-called Vienna Circle, arbitrarily excludes classical metaphysics from the domain of objective scientific knowledge[25]. In this interpretation the philosophy of man is reduced to a systematization and integration of the results of natural sciences.

---

[22]J.Majka: *Metodologia nauk teologicznych* [The Methodology of Theological Sciences], Wrocław 1981, pp.80 ff.

[23]Cf. S.Kamiński: *Antropologia filozoficzna* ..., op.cit., p.163. The author acknowledges the derivative character of anthropology in relation to the philosophy of nature.

[24]Cf. S Kowalczyk: *Drogi ku Bogu* [Roads towards God], Wrocław 1983, pp.53-89.

[25]The principle of empirical verification has been repeatedly reinterpreted and today it is also differently understood by representatives of logical empiricism. Cf. A.J.Ayer: *The Central Questions of Philosophy*, New York 1974, pp.3 ff.

The concept of experience as defined in extreme empiricism is controversial for many reasons. First of all, at its basis one may uncover the a priori epistemological-methodological assumptions: sensualism, scientism, methodological exclusiveness, sometimes also materialism. This understanding of experience is too restricted, breaking the unity of sensible and intellectual cognition in man and ignoring his personal dimension. Man constitutes an integral whole and that is why it is unjustified to narrow down the category of experience and scientific cognition to the sensory level.

The Aristotelian-Thomistic current in philosophy emphasizes the personal dimension of man but in the field of epistemology it presents a restricted conception of experience. Human experience is to include sensual perception and the cognition of the inner "I"[26]. Hence, the main domain of experience is therefore the cognition of a singular being, determined in the space-time continuum, apprehensible by cognitive - sensual faculties. The followers of existentialistic Thomism suggest that direct contact with experience, entailing no assumptions, is secured by existential propositions[27]. Yet, the way of understanding those propositions is differentiated, since some understand them as reflective acts while others - as totally spontaneous and pre-reflective acts. The conception of experience in existentialistic Thomism, though far from the extreme position of the adherents of extreme empiricism, still defines the category of experience too narrowly. After all, sensible cognition and self-consciousness do not exhaust the whole range of human experiences. This conception is lacking in sufficient consideration of, and stress laid on, inner experience; no distinction is made between experiencing things, values and persons. Epistemological realism certainly does not demand such reductionism in the description of human experience and cognition.

In this context, particularly inspiring is the conception of experience in phenomenology, contained in the writings of E.Husserl, M.Scheler, H.Bergson († 1941) and J.H.Newman († 1890). According to the phenomenological interpretation, the intuitive insight into the essence of the thing, or the so-called eidetic perception, constitutes an integral part of human experience[28]. On the other hand, when speaking about the experience of values, Scheler formulated the theory of emotional intuitionism. The introduction of axiological experience into philosophy is precisely the contribution of this thinker. Bergson was an advocate of a broad understanding of experience, including in its range the following phenomena: sensible perception, emotions, aesthetic feelings, ethical experience, desires, drives, interpersonal experiences[29]. Scheler and Bergson have convincingly demonstrated that sensible and intellectual cognitions do not exhaust the whole range of human potential in this field. Man's emotional sphere, mainly

---

[26]A.M.Krąpiec: "Doświadczenie i metafizyka" [Experience and Metaphysics], *Roczniki Filozoficzne*, 24 (1976), no.1, pp.5-16.

[27]E.Gilson: *L'etre et l'essence*, Paris 1948, chap.IX.

[28]E.Husserl: *Ideen zu einer reinen Phänomenologie und phänomenologischer Philosophie*, Den Haag 1950, vol.1, pp.23-25, 63-69.

[29]H.Bergson: *Essai sur les données immédiates de la conscience*, Paris 1944, pp.1-15, 23 ff.

connected with the world of values, also plays the cognitive function, though in a way which has not always been clearly specified. The monistic understanding of man does not legitimize the global and aprioristic denial of the cognitive value to the emotional sphere. Man's experience undoubtedly goes beyond sensible perception (*Erfahrung*) and covers a wide range of personal experiences (*Erlebnis*).

The construction of a philosophical conception of man requires the foundation of the realities of experience. Yet, sober epistemological realism does not demand a renunciation of those forms of human exprience which are integrally connected with the subjectiveness of person. For that reason, apart from empirical-sensible experience, in anthropology one should also dinstinguish and take into consideration such other forms of experience as mental-cognitive, personal and axiological[30]. After all, the human world is not the world of things-objects, and even less the world of material beings. At his disposal man has various forms of cognition, sensible and intellectual, discursive and intuitive, external and internal. A characteristic feature of the conception of cognition accepted here is the revalorization of various domains of inner experience. This conception, referring to the thought of St. Augustine[31], concentrates attention on man as a person. The world of the human person includes such phenomena as consciousness and self-consciousness, intellectual cognition, ethical and aesthetic sensitivity, religious faith, interpersonal relations, experience of community. There is no rational reason to regard one form of experience, e.g. empirical experience, as exclusively objective and valuable, while rejecting other forms of experience. The cosmological experience of the world of material beings is necessary for anthropology and for that reason it takes advantage of the achievements of natural sciences and the philosophy of nature. However, the construction of an adequate conception of man demands the acceptance as a point of departure also other forms of experience, personal, axiological and social. Man's experience is, first of all, a cognitive contact with oneself as a person[32]. It is possible through the exploration of the data of internal experience. An important aspect of human experience is the sensitivity to the world of values, of truth, good, beauty, Sacrum etc.; moral experience is the experience of good and evil; religious experience concerns values connected with the recognition and acknowledgement of God; interpersonal values are connected with the phenomenon of social life. A restricted conception of experience may constitute a serious mistake when constructing a correct conception of man. Man cannot be perceived merely as an owner of the receptors of sensible cognition but he is also a person living within the realm of his proper values. Naturally, the experience of one's self, personhood of other people and a variety of values have all a subjective-subjectivist and

[30]J.Mouroux: *L'expérience chrétienne. Introduction à une thélogie*, Paris 1952.

[31]S.Kowalczyk: *Człowiek i Bóg w nauce św. Augustyna*, op.cit., pp.43-48. The role of the experience of values in the philosophy and theology of the old-Christian thinker is emphasized by John Paul II in *Redemptor hominis* nr.18.

[32]K.Wojtyła: *Osoba i czyn*, op.cit., pp.5 ff, 11-12; also his: "Problem doświadczenia w etyce" [The Problem of Experience in Ethics], *Roczniki Filozoficzne* 17 (1969) nr.2, pp.5-24.

individualized character. Yet subjectiveness is not identical with subjectivism[33]. Emotional experiences, even most intimate, do not exclude man from the domain of the objective world and cognition. Only negative feelings (hatred, jealousy etc.) deform the objectivity of human cognition.

Yet, even the most broadly understood experience is merely the point of departure of philosophical anthropology. The accumulated material requires now a rational analysis and certain methods of examination. The methods employed in the philosophy of man are highly varied. One should first of all distinguish their two kinds, phenomenological and metaphysical. One cannot always determine a precise and constant borderline between them. The phenomenological method consists in the fact of perception and then of a description of all that is immediately given to us and of the manner in which it is given[34]. Naturally, the phenomenological method has no codified formula, so its understanding is partly different in individual writers. In addition, it also depends on the discipline, e.g. epistemology, axiology, philosophy of religion or philosophy of man. The characteristic elements of the phenomenological method include: intuition, hermeneutics, specific dialectic, introspection and retrospection, reduction.

Intuition is the crucial component of the phenomenological method. If Aristotelian - Thomistic philosophy restricted the cognitive role of intuition to the apprehension of the basic laws of being and thought (to the so-called primary principles), then modern philosophy approaches the function of intuition much more broadly[35]. Phenomenologists speak about the intuitive perception of the essence of the thing - individual features, generic characteristics, sense, value, social interconnections etc. Extreme intuitionism questions the value of intellectual-discursive cognition, thus undermining the cognitive role of notions (nominalism). Yet, the dangers of extreme intuitionsim do not disqualify intuitive cognition which cannot be substituted by anything else in respect to the domain of personal values. Such values cannot be correctly recognized and understood by apprehending man as an object. Only intuition, experienced subjectively and individually, is capable of identifying the values of the human person. Obviously, intuition is not restricted to intellectual cognition but it also covers the domain of impulses and emotions. One can therefore speak of the intuition of the will and feelings whose object of discernment is, for instance, another person, that person's attitude, the spiritual-moral values represented by that person etc. The role of intuition should not be overestimated, but it is also a mistake to underestimate or even to ignore it. The element of intuitive recognition, it seems, constitutes a component of discursive-rational cognition. The intuitive-eidetic perception is realized in the phenomena

---

[33]D. von Hildebrand: *Über das Herz*, Regensburg 1967, pp.17-19, 29-33, 41-43.

[34]Cf. O.Muck: *Die transcendentale Methode in der scholastischen Philosophie der Gegenwart*, Innsbruck 1964.

[35]S.Kowalczyk: *Drogi ku Bogu*, op.cit., pp.175-225.

of universalization and inductive thinking[36]. The transition from concrete, single observations to a universal conclusion demands the participation of intuition.

Many phenomenologists combine the phenomenological method with hermeneutics. An example of such a combination of the phenomenological description and hermeneutical explanation may be found in M. Heidegger († 1976) who discovered a sense of human existence by applying linguistic analysis[37]. In this case the understanding of man takes place through the explanation of the sense of the spoken and written word. The word becomes a coded sense, while its logic reveals the sense of human existence.

Although it aims at apprehending the supra-individual self, the phenomenological method takes as its point of departure the observation of concrete beings and situations. The existentialistic character of this method requires a constant confrontation with the realities of the object examined. For this reason many followers of this method combine it with a specific dialectic[38]. This is not a dialectic understood ontologically but epistemologically. Its point is to take into consideration in the philosophical analysis various horizons of beings and of situational perspectives, which should enrich our knowledge about the world. It is precisely such a procedure that is indispensable when approaching the poly-faceted human being. The dialectic method does not imply cognitive-axiological relativism but it protects one from reductionism when looking at the world of the human person. The dialectic thus understood cannot be realized without dialogue and encounter. It is therefore by no means accidental that many phenomenologists practise "the philosophy of the encounter"; among others, they include M.Buber and E.Levinas. At any rate, dialogue belongs to the very idea of philosophy whose development requires a creative confrontation of various opinions and attitudes. The dialectic cannot turn into either a monologue or a simulated dialogue, because all monopolization of truth leads unavoidably to its impoverishment and deformation.

The inner experience, so important in the phenomenological method, is connected with the method of introspection. It is a well known method in many humanistic sciences and often applied[39]. The method is frequently criticised, mainly because of a possibility of subjectivisation in describing the data and explicating them. Still, introspection undoubtedly enables an insight into our personality and its experiences, while through analogy it partly conditions the cognition of other people. At any rate, it should be applied together with other methods, while man himself should be apprehended in the totality of the external world and social life. In examining the human person the method

---

[36]K.Wojtyła (in *Osoba i czyn*, op.cit., pp.20, 192) includes intuition in phenomenological-philosophical methods. The description of this cognitive undertaking is in agreement with the phenomenological conception of sight.

[37]M.Heidegger: *Sein und Zeit*, Halle 1941, pp.37-38; S.Strasser: *Phénoménologie et sciences de l'homme*, op.cit., pp.220-229, 240 ff.

[38]S.Strasser: *Phénoménologie* ..., op.cit., pp.156 ff, 265 ff.; comp. *Rencontre - Encounter - Begegnung*, Antwerpen 1957.

[39]R.McCall: *Preface to Psychology*, Milwaukee 1944.

of introspection should be connected with the method of retrospection[40]. The human ego is stable and that is why an examination of its current state should be confronted with an analogical examination carried out in the past. The combination of introspection and retrospection should allow an elimination of mistakes in description and interpretation of the human self.

The phenomenological method is also related to the category of reduction[41]. It consists in "bracketing" (epoche) the contingent elements of being, also including its factual existence. Husserl claimed that everything can be epistemologically questioned, with the exception of one's self, i.e. the one's who doubts. In this way phenomenological reduction indicates the necessity of the "I". The realistically re-interpreted method of reduction departs from Husserlian solipsism, namely, the acts of human consciousness have an intentional character, being always directed towards determined objects (beyond the domain of our ego). Man's consciousness is neither empty nor exclusively egocentric. The phenomenological description of man apprehends him in various contexts, ontological, axiological, social and so on. And then anthropology cannot turn into an "egology"; it will rather speak about the "egotic I", the "axiological I", the "agatological I" etc.

The phenomenological methods of the philosophy of man must naturally be supplemented by metaphysical methods. As has already been mentioned, the borderline between the two types of methods is not always easy to grasp, nevertheless they should be distinguished. There are two significant exploratory stages of scientific methods, a description of a fact and its explanation. The phenomenological method provides a relatively good description and a partial interpretation of facts connected with man's world. The phenomenology of man makes it possible to formulate a number of statements on this subject[42]. Here are some of the most significant of such propositions: (1) man is a subject but he also exists as a semi-object through his body; (2) he is a single being, but multiple in his actions and manifestations; (3) he is active and passive; (4) he is an owner of an inner "I", stable and identical in spite of the stream of experiences; (5) he consists of a bodily-material element and of a psychic-spiritual element; (6) he is sensitive to higher values. This is not a closed list of propositions justified by a phenomenological description of man. In fact, it is a description of the phenomenon of man, though already containing its initial explication. That is why one may agree with K.Wojtyła's claim that "The phenomenological method does not stop on the surface of the [human] reality but makes it possible to reach down to its depth. It gives not only a sight but also an insight"[43].

---

[40]S.Strasser: *The Soul ...*, op.cit., pp.83-92.

[41]Ibid., pp.155-175.

[42]Ibid., pp.102 ff.

[43]*Osoba i czyn*, op.cit., p.189. Similar remarks may also be encountered in the writings of S.Strasser.

What is actually the basis of the metaphysical explanation of man's world? Many authors (and especially the followers of existentialistic Thomism) apply the method of the so-called systemic explanation. It consists in explaining the human person in the context of general metaphysics and philosophy of nature. In this way the human being would become merely a particularization of being in general. This method has its good and bad sides. The former concern a possibility of constructing philosophical anthropology as a system in agreement with a philosophical vision of the totality of the universe. This method also has the advantage of the unity of the philosophical method, worked out by ontology[44]. Unfortunately, the method of the "systemic context" also has some drawbacks. They include the deductive and as if "downward" look at man. The exclusive application of general ontological terminology for the metaphysical explication of the human being unavoidably means an impoverishment, bordering on reification. The philosophy of man must undoubtedly use the language of ontology, that is, of such categories as being, act and potentiality, substance and contingency, essence and existence, transcendental properties (unity, truth, good) and so on. Still, it cannot be the only terminology in the philosophical interpretation of the human being. General metaphysics does not have at its disposal a description of man as a subject and person or an axiological description, without which man's ontic specificity becomes obliterated. The analogical understanding of philosophical categories does not solve the problem because ontology simply does not contain a personalistic and axiological language. These languages appear in the phenomenological description of man, that is why it would be detrimental to renounce them in metaphysical explication.

The essence of the metaphysical method is the reference made to the primary logical-ontological principles. The principle of non-contradiction is the most operational and therefore the explanation of the human being is identified with the search for its ultimate, ontical reasons entailing no contradiction. The principle of non-contradiction provides a basis for the principle of a sufficient reason which, in turn, constitutes a foundation for the principle of causality. Philosophical anthropology attempts to explain the phenomenon of man by indicating his ultimate ontic causes, both internal and external. This is the so-called reductive method, occurring, among others, in the domain of the philosophy of God. Metaphysical reduction (as different from Husserl's understanding of reduction) means an explanation of the ontical bases of man, among others, by indicating and characterizing the personal "I", its indispensable attributes, structure, faculties, potentialities, sense etc. The reductive method is based on the philosophical adage: ***agere sequitur esse***. Yet, if traditional Thomism explained man's ***agere*** through his ***esse***, then Thomism applying the phenomenological method explains man's ***esse*** through his ***agere***. The nature of human actions indicates the nature of their subject-person, and that is why it is such an important matter to attain a possibly

[44]The methodology of the philosophy of man is variously explained even by the Thomists. Comp. J.Owens: "The Unity in Thomistic Philosophy of Man", *Mediaeval Studies*, 15 (1963) pp.56 ff.; A.Pegis: *St. Thomas and the Problem of the Soul in the Thirteenth Century*, Toronto 1984.

complete description of man's activities. It is precisely here that man's ontical specificity and structure become revealed. The method of metaphysical reduction means an "excavation" of the ontical foundations of the phenomenon of the human person. The systemic context of the totality of being is obviously desirable and important, but it does not constitute the essence of the metaphysical method applied in the philosophy of man.

LITERATURE

ANDERSON, J.F.: "On the Demonstration in Thomistic Metaphysics", *The New Scholasticism*, 32 (1958) pp.474-494.

BALTHASAR, M: *Le méthode en metaphysique*, Louvain 1943.

BOCHEŃSKI, I.: *Logik der Religion*, Köln 1968.

BRAITHWAITE, R.B.: *Scientific Explanation*, New York 1960.

EMMET, D.M.: *The Nature of Metaphysical Thinking*, London 1945.

GEIGER, O.: "Abstraction et séparation d'aprés S. Thomas", *Revue des Sciences Philosophiques et Théologiques*, 31 (1947) pp.3-41.

GILSON, E.: *Le réalisme méthodique*, Paris 1937.

GILSON, E.: *The Unity of Philosophical Experience*, New York 1937.

HENLE, R.J.: *Methods in Metaphysics*, St. Louis, Missouri 1950.

HESSEN, J.: *Die Methode der Metaphysik*, Bonn 1955.

HERBUT, J.: *Hipoteza w filozofii bytu* [Hypothesis in the Philosophy of Being], Lublin 1962.

KAMIŃSKI, S., KRĄPIEC, M.: *Z teorii i metodologii metafizyki* [Selected Problems in the Theory and Methodology of Metaphysics], Lublin 1962.

KLUBERTANZ, G.P.: *Introduction to the Philosophy of Being*, New York 1955.

MANSION, S.: "Philosophical explanation", *Dominican Studies*, 3 (1950) pp.197-219.

MUCK, O.: *Die transcendentale Methode in der scholastischen Philosophie der Gegenwart*, Innsbruck 1964.

OWENS, J.: "The Unity in Thomistic Philosophy of Man", *Mediaeval Studies* 15 (1963) pp.54-82.

PEGIS, A.: *St. Thomas and the Problem of the Soul in the Thirteenth Century*, Toronto 1984.

POPPER, K.R.: "Über die Möglichkeit der Erfahrungswissenschaft und der Metaphysik", *Ratio*, 2 (1958) pp.1-16.

STĘPIEŃ, A.: *Wprowadzenie do metafizyki* [Introduction to Metaphysic] Kraków 1964.

PART II

THE PHENOMENOLOGY OF MAN

Chapter 1

Corporeity

We live in the world of material bodies and we have bodies, too. The Cartesian saying "I think, therefore I am" can therefore be rephrased into "I have a body, therefore I am". The phenomenon of corporeity surrounds us everywhere but we seem to be most fascinated by the puzzle of our own corporeity. I have a body which I am using in my life; I am walking, running, stopping, sitting down, working and so on; I have a body, therefore I have a face, hands, head, heart, nervous system. Not only do I have a body, but in a sense I am a body. But am I only a body and nothing else? What is my body for me - a parental home, an uncomfortable, temporary lodging, or a prison cell? What obligations have I in respect to my body and what are its obligations towards the whole of my person? The role of the body is significant for the totality of the human person, i.e., everyday life, work, social bonds, love, suffering, death, ethos.

Human body was an object of interest of many thinkers, such as Plato, Aristotle, St. Augustine, St. Thomas Aquinas, Descartes, Kant, Husserl, Scheler, Heidegger, Marcel, Merleau-Ponty, Sarte[1]. Since it would go beyond the scope of current considerations to sketch out their metaphysics of the body, let us present merely some elements of the phenomenology of human corporeity[2]. The thematicalization of topics concerning the human body involves many problems, of which we shall mention the following: the possibility of knowing man's body, deforming and alienating approaches to corporeity, functions and sense of corporeity, the ontological status of corporeity; the latter problem occurs already on the borderline between phenomenology and metaphysics.

(i) The Knowledge of Corporeity

When characterizing human body it should first be separated from the cosmos as a set of material properties. The difference between the two was emphasized by M.Scheler,

---

[1]R.M.Zaner: *The Problem of Embodiment. Some Contributions to a Phenomenology of the Body*, The Hague 1971.

[2]Cf. W.A.Luijpen: *Existential Phenomenology*, Pittsburg 1960, pp.180- 195; G.Haeffner: *Philosophische Anthropologie*, Stuttgard 1982, pp.88- 105.

who employed the German terms, ***Leib*** for man's body, and ***Körper*** for body in general[3]. Although human body is immanent in respect to the cosmos and biocosmos[4], its nature is specific. This is a consequence of the fact of its bonds with the totality of human nature, including also the rich domain of psychic life. Human body can be apprehended in two ways, through external experience and through internal experience[5]. In the first case, the body is an object of pure, especially natural, sciences. On the other hand, internal experience makes it possible for man to apprehend his own body in its subjective aspect. And thus these two types of knowledge of the body, objective and subjective, complement each other.

Human body is an object of both pre-scientific and scientific cognition. In the first case, in everyday life one observes obvious differences between human bodies on the basis of such factors as age, sex, state of health, skin colour, race etc. Natural sciences examine various aspects and sectors of human body, biological, physical, chemical, electrical, neurological, physiological etc. Contemporary naturalistic knowledge undergoes far reaching specialization, so in consequence there appear ever new disciplines dealing with particular organs of man's body - cardiology, ophthalmology, laryngology or pulmonology; even formerly there existed such fields as anatomy, physiology, histology etc. The whole of the naturalistic knowledge about man is concentrated in medicine[6]. It is not always remembered that human body is a whole which is something more than just an accumulation of its constituent parts. That is why the apprehension of the human body, and, even more so, of the whole of the human person, exclusively through the prism of the somatic aspect constitutes a fundamental error. Such an error is committed precisely by adherents of behaviorism, Freudianism and all kinds of naturalisms. Man "lives like plants and feels like animals do"[7], but he is neither a plant nor an animal. Man's immanence - physico-chemical, biological and physiological-vegetative - in respect to the world does not detract from his transcendence. Man's specificity is also imparted to his body so, in consequence, one cannot speak about him as about a quasi-object. The human body differs from the world that surrounds it in both static-structural and dynamic orders. The cosmos does constitute his horizon, but his internal organization and inseparable links with the psychic factor designate it in an inimitable manner. The difference is even magnified in the dynamic aspect since man's body is an active agent of actions both within the human person and beyond it.

External experience, both commonsensical and scientific, apprehends man observed or examined as an object. Such relations occur precisely between a physician and a

---

[3]*Vom Ewigen im Menschen*, Bern 1954, p.309.

[4]S.Kowalczyk: "Transcendencja i immanencja człowieka w świecie" [Man's Transcendence and Immanence in the World] [in:] *Powołanie człowieka* [Man's Calling], Poznań 1982, vol.5, pp.111-126.

[5]G.Marcel: *Etre et avoir*, op.cit., p.226.

[6]Fr.Hartmann: *Ärztliche Anthropologie. Das Problem des Menschen in der Medizin der Neuzeit*, Bremen 1973; A.Faller: *Der Körper des Menschen*, Stuttgart 1980.

[7]St.Augustine: *Sermo* 43,3,4 PL 38,255.

patient, between a seller and a customer, between a teacher and a pupil etc. The tendency towards a depersonalization of interhuman relations is spontaneous, though, obviously, detrimental. That is why the cognition of the human body, similarly to that of the whole man, should take into account the data of inner experience. This subject was considered with a particularly perceptive and deep insight by existentialists, such as G.Marcel, M.Merleau-Ponty († 1961) and J.P.Sartre († 1980). Although they laid particularly great emphasis on the role of man's consciousness and subconsciousness, they did not ignore the co-participation of the body. And thus, Sartre described man as embodied consciousness, which implies that the body actively participates in construing images, emotional experiences, actions etc.[8]. On the other hand, Marcel called man "an incarnate being" in which the personal-spiritual "I" is incorporated in the material body[9]. Man is "an organo-psychical presence"[10]. Such designations clearly present the body as an integral component of the human kind.

How does man experience his own body? The relation between man's integral "I" and his body is described in two ways, in terms of owning and of being. We are conscious of the fact that we have a body; we experience it from the inside; we feel its vigour and health; we also feel pain and symptoms of impending old age; we suffer the effects of stresses and so. Other material beings we observe from the outside; it is only our body that we get to know from the inside. We have a body but we own it in a different way than we possess, for instance, tools or clothes. The body is "mine" but in a way different than a pen, a book or a field are mine. We can pass over a thing to somebody but we cannot renounce our own body because we are not bodiless beings. The category of possession does not describe the whole relation that we have with our body. That is why we also say that we are a body. Only when both categories, of possession and of being, are combined, can we grasp the specificity of the ties between the body and the human nature[11]. The body cannot be an object for me, since I myself am a body. At the same time one cannot completely identify the body and me as a personal subject, since I am something more than my material body.

Our inner experience shows us the body in two aspects, as bound with the external world and as grasped in itself. Consciousness tells us that our body is tied with thousands of bonds with the cosmos, through laws of nature, climate, nutrition, atmospheric conditions etc. Yet, at the same time we are also aware of the fact that the body we have is a specific separate wholeness. The body is an expression of the inner "I" and partly also its complementation. The body participates in our experiences and psychic-spiritual states; it even affects them. Health, illness or suffering, directly connected with the state of the body, co-create man's everyday life.

---

[8]J.P.Sartre: *Being and Nothingness*, tr. by H.Barness, New York 1966, pp.374-414.

[9]G.Marcel: *De refus* ..., op.cit., pp.30-33.

[10]Ibid., p.33.

[11]G.Marcel: *Etre et avoir*, op.cit., p.225-226; R.Zaner, op.cit., pp.1-56.

The knowledge of the human body requires the application of both ways of cognition, of inner experience and external experience. The two ways of cognition do not always correspond. Often science speaks about something that our consciousness does not inform us about and the opposite situation is also true - inner experience shows us regions of our corporeity which natural sciences are silent about. The two types of knowledge, both subjective and objective, have their limitations. Self-consciousness is fugitive and subjective, whileempirical-scientificcognition depersonalizes man and is incapable of grasping values. Thus, it would be a mistake to restrict oneself to any single mode of fragmentary cognition, subjective or objective; at any rate, the former need not always be arbitrary, and the latter - always absolutely certain and reliable.

(ii) Deforming and Alienating Approaches to Corporeity

The conceptions which deform the role of corporeity are varied; in some it is disparaged; in others it is absolutized; in still others it is alienating. The first two kinds have strong philosophical or ideological foundations; the third one is an existential-social attitude rather than a generalized theory.

Disparagement of corporeity occurs in many currents of both Eastern and Western thought, e.g. in Hinduism, Platonism, Neo-platonism, Manicheanism, deformed variants of mysticism. It is an attitude of angelicization, i.e. apprehending man as a spirit only temporarily incorporated in the world of matter. It is sometimes claimed that in Western philosophy the body is apprehended too passively, namely, as a source of negative sensations (suffering, death)[12]. It would be difficult to share this opinion since it is precisely in the Far East that many philosophical-religious trends pejoratively interpret the material world, including man's body. A confirmation of this view can be found in the sacred books of Hinduism, the Upanishads, speaking about the identity of the absolute being (Brahma) and the deepest element in man (Atman). The Absolute is described in terms of immanence and non-personal being in which man loses his identity[13]. The visible being is to be merely an illusory manifestation (maya) of the Absolute Being. The goal of man's mystical experience is an integration with the universal-absolute "I" to the point of the loss of one's identity. Similarly to the whole material world, the human body is neither permanent nor particularly worthy of attention. Such an interpretation of corporeity and the material world has consolidated the attitude of passivity towards everyday tasks of life in many adherents of Hinduism. This could partly explain their apathy towards chance accidents and striking social disparities.

The angelical interpretation of man is also typical of the Platonic and Neo-platonic thought. Charaterizing the role of the soul Plato called it a helmsman of the body which

---

[12]E.Levinas: *Otherwise than Being or Beyond Essence*, The Hague 1981, p.110.

[13]Cf. G.Parrinder: *Mysticism in the World's Religions*, New York 1976, pp.36-40.

he compared to a ship[14]. In another place he called the soul a prisoner of the material body[15]. The body is compared by him to unruly horses, bridled by the charioteer, i.e. rational soul. The pejorative evaluation of the role of the material body is determined by Plato's ontological idealism. The seventh book of the Republic contains the famous simile of the cave. People sitting in the cave and turned with their backs to the source of light can see only the shadows - silhouettes of things and persons on the wall. The sense of the metaphor is unequivocal: the material reality is merely a reflection of the invisible ideal being. Man's body is also merely a "shadow", that is, an illusion. It has no sense in itself; its reality is only temporary; and its function for the immortal soul is negative. The depreciation of the body in Platonic thought has a double character, both moral-religious and ontological[16].

The angelical-Platonic interpretation of man is unacceptable. This kind of anthropology ignores the evident fact that man is incorporated in a material body. Hence, his disincarnation cannot be accomplished because man's structure is psycho-physical. Christian anthropology revalues the role of the body also in the theological aspect, speaking about its future resurrection. It is precisely this thought that sounded so strange in antique Greece and for that reason St.Paul - speaking about resurrection in the Athenian Areopagus - received such a cool reception (Acts 17,16-34).

On the pole opposite to Platonism and angelicalism there is modern civilization whose characteristic feature is the absolutization of the body and the values connected with it[17]. Man's body is in the centre of attention not only of businessmen, tradesmen, physicians etc., but also of men of letters, artists, entertainers, ideological propagandists. This tendency also has some philosophical sources since its roots can be traced back to Nietzscheanism and Freudianism. In his polemic with the Christian conception of man Nietzsche described man as "a tamed animal"[18]. Accepting the assumtpions of materialism and biologism, he shifted the factor of man's corporeity to the foreground. The human person was reduced by him mainly to the fact of having a body. He called the body "the grand reason", that is, the source of man's fundamental values, physico-biological and moral-spiritual[19]. "The creative body created spirit for itself, as

---

[14]Plato: *The Laws XII*, 961 e.

[15]*Phaedo* 65 b-e, 82 e. Cf. R.Schaerer: *Dieu, l'homme et la vie d'après Platon*, Neuchâtel 1944; C.A. van Peursen: *Le corps - l'âme - l'esprit. Introduction à une anthropologie phénoménologique*, The Hague 1979, pp.28-40.

[16]C. van Peursen (op.cit., p.39) thinks that Plato diminished the role of the body primarily because of his moral assumptions.

[17]Cf. N.Elias: *Über den Prozess der Zivilisation*, Frankfurt am M. 1976; G.Böhme: *Anthropologie in pragmatischer Hinsicht*, Frankfurt am M. 1985, pp.126-138.

[18]F.Nietzsche: *Thus Spoke Zarathustra*, p.279.

[19]Ibid., p.61.

a hand of its will"[20]. The animal sphere was thus recognized as the most primeval source of man's life and all his values. It is from this sphere that the whole richness of psychic life, the phenomenon of consciousness, moral culture, mental cognition etc. are to be derived. From this proposition Nietzsche drew the logical conclusion that biological life should be given utmost care. It is an aim in itself, not merely a means[21]. The human body is not a blind machine but the very creator of the human being.

An analogical conception of man, though more closely connected with biological-medical sciences, was accepted by S.Freud. The main assumptions of his theory include: anthropological biologism, determinism of psychic life, priority of the subconscious over consciousness, and a reduction of human life to the play of instincts[22]. Man's body, the seat of biological drives, was accepted as the fundamental and, practically, the only reality of the human being. The biological-deterministic conception of the human person finds its continuators even today. By way of example, let us mention the book On Human Nature in which Edward Wilson attempts to explicate mankind exclusively by means of biological categories[23]. Man's whole spiritual life, including the phenomena of ethics and religion, has been accepted by the writer as a specific continuation of biological-genetic evolution. The history of humanity is exclusively a genetic history.

The absolutization of human corporeity, typical of the last two centuries, is usually postulated for the sake of noble slogans, of science, progress, culture, humanism etc. Under the banner of such ideals a specific "levy" is being recruited of the followers (not always fully aware) of such phenomena as moral license, "liberation" from moral-religious codes, abortion, addictions, moral perversities. The erroneousness of the ideologies which absolutize corporeity is evident and may be described as the error of the synecdoche or pars pro toto. The body is not the whole of the man-person since around it - to use Marcel's phrase - there persists "an existential orbit"[24]. The latter consists of conscience and the sense of responsibility, caring about others, interpersonal solidarity, the sense of life, aesthetic and religious sensitivity. The body deserves respect since it participates in the dignity of the human person. Yet, its functions and sense cannot be separated from the context of the calling of the wholeness of humanity. If this humanity is being destroyed, then the reference to the grand slogans becomes a patent lie.

The absolutization of corporeity means in fact its alienation because the place of its natural functions is to be taken by aims hitting at the integrity of the human person. Thus, for instance, regardless of the proclaimed slogans, pornography destroys fundamental human values. A similarly destructive role is played by drug addiction and alcoholism. It

---

[20]Ibid., p.62.

[21]F.Nietzsche: *Der Antichrist*, Berlin 1941, pp.23-25, 40, 49.

[22]S.Kowalczyk: *Bóg w myśli współczesnej* [God in Contemporary Thought], Wrocław 1982, pp.89 ff.

[23]*On Human Nature*, London 1978.

[24]G.Marcel: *De refus ...*, p.30.

is also possible to speak of another form of the alienation of the human body, connected with the fact of its emaciation; the latter may take place in various ways and on various occasions, for example, through tortures, individual and mass murder, purposefully fomented conflicts (tribal, racial, national, class wars), through too exhausting work (hard labour was actually regarded as a means of extermination in special camps), lack of medical care, causing or tolerating hunger. Obviously, this is not a complete list of the forms of man's extermination through the destruction of his body. The phenomenon of turning corporeity into an absolute and its alienation are often contiguous, so that, for example, the luxury of privileged individuals breeds in them impassiveness to the material needs of other people.

(iii). Functions and Sense of Corporeity

We have a body which is our integral part. But does it always constitue a positive value? Sometimes they speak about "the drama of corporeity"[25]. The term "drama" denotes the role of the body in a way too wholly negative so it would perhaps be better to speak about the ambivalence of the body. The body is perceived in a dual way, positive and negative. Both ways of interpreting the body may in turn concern two levels of human life, biological and spiritual. Undoubtedly, the body is a source of positive experiences, of good health, strength, vigour, pleasure, and it is a condition of founding a family. Man's body is a subject of literature, arts, natural sciences, as well as of philosophical and theological reflection[26]. The body enables the realization of such values as labour, sports, and entertainment; in its own way it also participates in the prayer. Man's strong body, combined with courage, makes it possible for him to defend the weak. The healthy body of the physician is a blessing for the patient.

Yet, there is also a negative, and often tragic, dimension of the human body. It is unavoidably bound with the experience of hunger and thirst, of pain and suffering, of old age and death. We have a body and therefore we feel tired after hard work; we are exposed to heat and cold, to accidents and crippledom. Every hospital and every hospice are constant witnesses to the agonies of the human body[27]. It is also a source of moral evil in all its various forms. This is the subject of the old Greek myth of Oedipus which shows the connection of the human body and the sin of incest. In Biblical language the body (Hebr. ***basar***) quite often has a moral-pejorative meaning, namely, it implies man's ethical weakness[28]. The body simply means the condition of sin in man's life (*Ezekiel* 16,26; 23,20). It is that meaning that often appears in St. Paul, who wrote: "So I say, live

[25]J.Tischner: "Dramat cielesności" [The Drama of Corporeity], *W Drodze*, (1985), pp.63-71.

[26]Cf. the theology of the body contained in the speeches by John Paul II.

[27]The fragility of the human body is often mentioned in the Holy Scripture; cf. *Isaiah* 40,6-7.

[28]C. van Peursen, op.cit., pp.78-85; A.Gelin: *L'homme selon la Bible*, Paris 1968.

by the Spirit, and you will not gratify the desires of the sinful nature. For the sinful nature desires what is contrary to the Spirit, and the Spirit what is contrary to the sinful nature. They are in conflict with each other, so that you do not do what you want" (*Galatians* 5,16-17). It is the conviction of the Apostle that "the law of the body" means "the law of sin" (*Romans* 7,23). Yet, it should be remembered that the negative evaluation of the body in the Bible has an exclusively moral-religious sense. It does not imply the questioning of the ontic value of the body, which is confirmed by the theological truth about the resurrection of the bodies.

The ambivalence of corporeity requires an integrated approach to the functions that the body may play in man's life. These functions are highly differentiated but the most important ones are of three kinds, epistemological-pragmatical, ontological, and moral-religous.

The epistemological-pragmatic function of the human body is realized in two ways: it connects man with the world of things and with the world of persons. The body is not a "prison" but a "bridge" between our "I" and the external world. By having a body, we can be incorporated in the material-biological world through it. The body is a continuation of our individual subjectivity, while simultaneously including us in the objectivity of the external world. In this way the body (animated by the psychic factor) places man in the totality of the cosmos. As beings with material bodies we are in communion with the world of nature, while as rational and free beings we are resposible for this world. Fellowship with the plant and animal world, resulting from our corporeity, was perfectly demonstrated by St. Francis of Assisi († 1226).

There is also the other form of realizing the epistemological function of the human body. The body contains a set of receptors and faculties of sensory cognition, the nervous system, the emotional domain and the locomotor system. All this, naturally in combination with the psychic-spiritual "I", makes it possible to establish contact between people[29]. The body is a manifestation of human consciousness, of acts of cognition, feelings, sensations, decisions, choices of various kinds etc. The introspective knowledge of oneself and observations of the behaviour of other people, combined with reasoning based on analogy, make it possible to come to know the world of persons. It is an objective knowledge, though undoubtedly restricted and not free of errors[30]. Man's interior is only partly uncovered in the somatic expression and for that reason the knowledge of another man acquired through observation and analysis of his behaviour is inadequate. Between the spiritual subject and his body there always persists some non-identity, a certain distance, which makes it impossible to determine man's spiritual interior in an unequivocal way. Man is not a biological machine and that is why there are limits to his knowability. Nevertheless, the body is not a wall separating people, but an

---

[29]W.Luijpen, op.cit., pp.180-185.

[30]This was mentioned by J.P.Sartre. More optimistically was the possibility of knowing another man evaluated by M.Scheler, formulating the so-called theory of empathizing (*Einfühlung*).

intermediary between them. In a direct way, it is an instrument of sensory cognition, while indirectly it is an instrument of mental cognition, too.

The second important role of corporeity is the ontological function. Man's body, as an integral component of his personality, has its ontic calling. Particular elements of the body, its external and internal organs, directly serve the good of its totality. Indirectly, however, one may speak of their "dialogic" relation. Such is undoubtedly the character of the face, eyes, mouth, hearing, hands, the nervous system. It is thanks to them that man makes contact with the external world, so their ontological role is evident. The body serves man but not only him. The elementary activities of man include labour, creation of the values of culture, entertainment, hobby etc. Such activities are impossible without the participation of his body. Yet, in addition, all the values man creates have a social dimension. Such is also the character of man's body and its multiple activities. Man does not work only for himself; he learns from and with somebody; he wants to share his fun.

Speaking about the dialogical sense of the human body E.Levinas refers to the phenomenon of fertility[31]. He even expresses an opinion that it is precisely this phenomenon that makes it possible to speak about the specific transcendence of the human body. The bestowal of life requires an overcoming of the egocentrism of one's own "I", becoming involved in the life of another person, looking for harmony with that person. In this way the human body reveals its property of being directed towards another man. A man becomes a father thanks to a woman, and she becomes a mother thanks to a man. One person becomes integrally connected with another in order to create a family. An embodiment of such an attitude can be found in Biblical Abraham who perceived God's blessing in the possibility of bestowing life. Still, husband and wife do not live only for each other but also for hildren. The latter, in turn, also live for their parents and siblings, and some time in the future they will in turn live for their own children. Hence, the ontological function of the body is not egocentrically closed within the individual but it is open to other people and their good.

The dialogical and subservient character of the human body is particularly evident in the domain of morality. The body is an instrument of action and cooperation which, by their nature, have a social goal. Common good lies at the foundations not only of man's labour but also his joy and fun. It is in community that, at least potentially, man experiences his work, acquisition of knowledge, professional skills, and even suffering. We do have a body but not only for ourselves. The body makes it possible for us to participate in the community, so, of necessity, it must have a social-subservient bias. Even suffering and the atrophying of the body acquire sense when placed in relation to others[32].

[31]*Totalit é et Infini*, La Haye 1968, pp.236 ff.

[32]G.Marcel: *Etre et avoir*, op.cit., pp.165-167.

(iv). The Ontological Status of Corporeity

In the conclusion of this analysis of the phenomenology of corporeity we shall attempt a determination of its ontological status, i.e. an explanation of its connections with the spiritual factor of man. The solutions existing so far are very diversified, although the major ones can be reduced to four, namely: materialistic monism, idealistic-spiritualistic monism, extreme dualism and moderate dualism.

In the history of human thought materialistic monism occurred in many varieties. In contemporary thought three of them seem to predominate, namely, the mechanistic materialism of B.Russell and C.Lévi-Strauss, the vitalistic materialism of F.Nietzsche and S.Freud, and, finally, the sociological materialism of Marxism[33]. The common feature of all these trends is the reductionistic interpretation of man whose nature is perceived to contain only one factor, namely, the material body. Human thought is explained as a function of a specifically organized matter. This is to be proved by the fact of the dependence of higher psychical processes on the normal functioning of the nervous system. The body and the psychic-spiritual factor are to constitute not only a functional unity, but also a structural-ontic unity. The adherents of materialism do speak about spiritual life, and humanism, psyche, freedom, thought, sometimes even about soul, but such terminology has exclusively pragmatic-psychological aims, without undermining their declared materialistic monism. The material body is apprehended as the only element with real and stable existence; the "soul" is merely a function, an expression or culmination of the processes taking place in this body.

Materialistic monism usually refers to empirical sciences, natural or economic-social. Such a procedure is not methodologically justified because the philosophy of man differs significantly from the empirical sciences about man. For that reason the naturalistic and sociological knowledge about the human body does not yet constitute a philosophy of the body[34]. Anatomy, physiology or empirical psychology do not provide an adequate knowledge about the humankind whose ontical richness goes far beyond empirical-descriptive methods. The body is a part of man and therefore it cannot be identified with the totality of the human person. Hence, the unity of the body and the psyche should not be interpreted as their identity. Man has a body but his internal "I" cannot be reduced to his body. Materialistic monism identifies the body and the psyche. Critically evaluating anthropological materialism Marcel states:

> *"This supposed identity is a nonsense; it can be confirmed only under the condition of performing the act of annihilating the "I", and then it turns into a materialistic statement: my body is myself, only my body exists. But such a statement is absurd: the property of my body is the fact that it does not exist by itself because around it there appears an 'existential orbit'"*[35].

---

[33]Cf. S.Kowalczyk: *Bóg w myśli współczesnej*, op.cit., Parts I and II.

[34]Cf. Bruaire: *Philosophie du corps*, Paris 1968, pp.216-226.

[35]*De refus ...* , op.cit., p.30.

The body is not the only reality or a mysterious creator of the human being. The body is "for" psychic-spiritual life, being subordinated to it both functionally and ontologically.

The theory of immaterialism is on the opposite pole in relation to materialistic monism. It was created by George Berkeley († 1753). He referred to J.Locke's extreme sensualism, regarding the totality of human experience as a set of sensations. On this basis he concluded that the existence of things can be reduced to subjective sensations (esse = percipi). His next conclusion was the thesis about the unreality of the whole material world. Bodies, including the human body, are only subjective ideas. In this way Bishop Berkely combines immaterialism with spiritualism, claiming that only spiritual beings, God and human souls, have existence[36]. The theory of immaterialism is an example of extreme subjective idealism which questions man's connection with material body. This position ignores the evident fact that man is a consciousness incorporated in the visible world through his corporeity[37]. Authentic personalism has an existential character, i.e. it shows man's personality placed in the visible world through its material body. Thus, personalistic spiritualism is by no means identical with idealism; it can even be opposed to it. That is why we cannot treat ourselves as if we were lacking in corporeity.

As we have seen, the ontological status of the human body is quite differently explained by materialistic monism and by idealistic monism. The former reduces the totality of human kind to corporeity, while the latter altogether questions its reality. Still differently is the role of the body in human nature interpreted by dualistic trends. Most often philosophers distinguish extreme dualism and moderate dualism, although such a classification is not quite satisfactory[38]. Extreme anthropological dualism was accepted by Platonism, Neoplatonism and Cartesianism.

Describing the relations which combine man's body and soul, René Descartes († 1650) showed himself as an evident proponent of radical dualism. Taking the phenomenon of the human thought as his starting point, he concentrated on the phenomenon of consciousness: "Descartes' method locked consciousness up in itself"[39]. The French thinker distinguished and separated two kinds of substances in the world, material and spiritual. Material beings, characterized by extension and an ability to move, constitute complexes of mechanically acting forces. Such a conception made Descartes infer that all material bodies - including animals - are machines. And then he had to face the problem of man who is both an extensive substance and a thinking being. In his *Meditations on First Philosophy* we read:

[36]A.Luce: *Berkeley's Immaterialism*, London 1945.

[37]G.Marcel: *Etre et avoir*, pp.10-12.

[38]We shall return to the problem of dualism in the last part of this study, when undertaking an attempt to characterize in greater detail the dualism of Christian anthropology.

[39]W.Luijpen, op.cit., p.181.

> *"My essence consists solely in the fact that I am a thinking thing. [...] And although [...] I possess a body with which I am very intimately conjoined, [...] it is certain that this I is entirely and absolutely distinct from my body, and can exist without it"*[40]

On the one hand, this entails a depreciation of the role of the body in human nature, while on the other - a separation of psychic and bodily elements. Since all body is merely a machine, it cannot affect the domain of the human soul. Such extreme conclusions resulted from the assumptions of Cartesian ontological dualism. Yet, this thinker also shows a different approach to the problems of the nature of man, a more existential approach, taking into account the realities. He then acknowledges that consciousness is more closely connected with the material body than the helmsman with the ship. The phenomena of pain or hunger prove that consciousness (soul) is most closely connected with the body, forming a unity with it[41]. The fact of the mutual influence of the body and the soul, perceived by the thinker, was not solved by him on the plane of metaphysics. His conception of the body, regarded as a machine, from which consciousness is completely removed, proved too great an obstacle.

Cartesian dualism erronously apprehends the role of both the body and of consciousness. Man's body is not some kind of a general body but a concrete human body. This humanized body participates in man's psychic-spiritual life, realizing his aims, and itself affects the character of man's activity[42]. That is why even the functions and actions of the body are identified with our "I", for instance when saying "I am running", "I see", "I feel pain". Corporeity is neither a machine or a strange body in man; it is his integral part.

A continuation of Cartesian dualism is encountered in Husserl's phenomenological conception of consciousness. In the second volume of his work *The Ideas of Pure Phenomenology* he presented his egological conception of consciousness, explaining the whole reality as a projection of the transcendental ego. In this conception of the world, objective reality is being constituted by man's consciousness and, ultimately, by trascendental consciousness. Cartesian assumptions led to the problematization of the role of the human body[43].

There still remains the position of moderate dualism that should be mentioned. The notion of dualism is ambiguous and hard to define univocally[44]. One may speak about extreme and moderate dualism, ontological and axiological dualism, static and dynamic dualism. The difficulties are further compounded when the position of a certain thinker

---

[40]Descartes: *Meditations on First Philosophy* [in:] *The Philosophical Works of Descartes*, rendered into English by E.Haldone and G.Ross, Cambridge 1967, vol.I, p.198.

[41]Ibid., p.102. Cf. C.Peursen, op.cit., pp.14-27.

[42]W.Luijpen, op.cit., pp.185-188.

[43]At the end of his life Husserl took closer interest in the animated world (*Lebenswelt*) which made his conception of the body more real.

[44]J.Seifert: *Das Leib-Seele-Problem in der gegenwärtigen philosophischen Diskussion*, Darmstadt 1979, pp.120-163.

is classified as radical or partial dualism. It is generally assumed that moderate dualism was accepted, among others, by Aristotle, St. Thomas Aquinas, Scheler, Marcel, Hildebrand. The first two thinkers explained the relation between the body and the soul on the basis of metaphysics, and that is why they will not be discussed at this point. We shall restrict ourselves to some remarks on the phenomenological interpretation, taking advantage of the analyses by the authors representing the phenomenological-existentialistic trend.

The complexity of man's personality requires primarily a questioning of the extremes of each monism, both idealistic and materialistic. The unity and integrity of human being, in turn, demands a rejection of extreme dualism, and therefore, the theories of parallelism and occasionalism. In interpretations of this kind man's life becomes something like "the theatre of illusion". The dualistic explanation of human psycho-physical person requires a recognition of the mutual non-reducibility of the soul and the body. They are undoubtedly differentiated, both structurally and dynamically, but this differentiation does not necessarily mean the lack of ontological unity[45]. They are different in nature, while together creating one man. The human person is one being, but not a simple being. The psychic-spiritual factor is interiorized in our personality, while the material-bodily factor constitutes its exteriorization. The body is an expression of the soul, while the soul is its "I" endowed with the ability of reflection. To some extent, the unity of the soul and the body has an antinomial, yet also complementary character. Both components of man are different, yet correlative to each other. Man has a material body and in part he is this body, but our internal "I" cannot be reduced exclusively to corporeity. The body is for mental-spiritual life but the latter is neither a product of the body nor does it exist exclusively for its sake. The human person is immanent to the world through its coreporeity, but at the same time - thanks to the soul - it transcends the visible world. The complete explanation of the relation which connects man's body and soul is regarded as impossible by many thinkers. Therefore, St.Augustine, H.Newman and G.Marcel speak about man's mystery. The current of Aristotelian-Thomistic philosophy refers to the theory of hylomorphism, describing the soul as a substantial form shaping the medium of the material body. The phenomenological description of man does not allow an unequivocal explication of the character of the relations between the body and the soul. We experience their unity existentially with the same intensity as their antinomy. Man is a unity but he is not a uni-dimensional being. He is a unity of the psycho-physical person - subject.

[45]S.Strasser: *The Soul ...*, op.cit., pp.102-105.

LITERATURE

ARMSTRONG, D.M.: *A Materialist Theory of the Mind*, London 1968.

BICKEL, L.: *Aussen und Innen. Beitrag zur Lösung des Leib-Seele-Problems*, Konstanz 1960.

BRUAIRE, C.: *Philosophie du corps*, Paris 1968.

CHENG, C.Y.: *Philosophical Aspects of the Mind-Body Problem*, Honolulu 1975.

CHIRPAZ, F.: *Le Corps*, Paris 1963.

FALLER, A.: *Der Körper des Menschen*, Stuttgart 1980.

HENRY, M.: *Philosophie et phénoménologie du corps. Essai sur l'ontologie biranienne*, Paris 1965.

LASKEY, D.: "Embodied Consciousness and the Human Spirit", *Analecta Husserliana* 1 (1971), pp.197-207.

LINGIS, A.: "Intentionality and Corporeity", *Analecta Husserliana* 1 (1971), pp.75-90.

LORSCHEID, B: *Das Leibphänomenon*, Bonn 1962.

LOTZ, J.B.: *Die Identität von Geist und Sein*, Rome 1972.

MAIER, W.: *Das Problem des Leiblichkeit*, Tübingen 1964.

MARCEL, G.: *Etre et avoir*, Paris 1935.

MULLIN Mc E. [ed.]: *The Concept of Matter*, Notre Dame 1963.

PEURSEN, C.A.,van: *Le corps - l'âme - l'esprit. Introduction à une anthropologie phénoménologique*, The Hague 1979.

PLUEGGE, H.: *Der Mensch und sein Leib*, Tübingen 1967.

RUYER, R.: *La Conscience et le corps*, Paris 1950.

SEIFERT, J.: *Das Leib-Seele-Problem in der gegenwärtigen philosophischen Diskussion*, Darmstadt 1979.

ZANER, R.M.: *The Problem of Embodiment. Some Contributions to a Phenomenology of the Body*, The Hague 1971.

Chapter 2

Consciousness and Selfconsciousness

The claim that "man is a rational being" (*animal rationale*) was already known in ancient Greece. Man's rationality was apprehended in two ways, extensive-technocratic or contemplative-interioristic. The former view on the development of the human mind is typical of natural sciences and technology, while the latter - of the practice of the humanities, philosophy, art and the domain of religion. In the latter case rationality means man's capability of reflection, especially the phenomena of consciousness and self-consciousness. Animals possess a sensory-spatial consciousness, i.e. they can place themselves in the surrounding world and in their actual situation. Man's unique specificity consists in his reflective-mental consciousness and in self-consciousness. The latter phenomena are unknown in the non-human world and they find no adequate explanation in the evolution of the biocosmos explained naturalistically. Only man experiences his being subjectively, i.e. his sensations and actions have their source in consciousness. Consciousness reflects man's nature and, at the same time, it enables its further self-development. Man is a being who not only knows much but also knows that he knows. His nature is self-reflective and self-conscious of itself.

(i) Description, Structure and Types of Consciousness

The conception of consciousness in Latin (con-scientia), understood in the ethymological sense, denotes knowledge shared with somebody else[1]. The actual sense of the term somewhat departs from this meaning, for consciousness may also be called a cognition of cognition or the knowledge of knowledge. A specific feature of man's consciousness is found in the interiorization of experiences, connected with the ability of self-cognition. An almost synonymous term is the category of reflection and the two notions are sometimes used interchangeably. However, it does not seem valid because consciousness and self-consciousness condition intellectual reflection.

The notion of consciousness is one of those conceptions which escape exact definition. The category is central in phenomenological analyses, yet even there it is hard to find a

---

[1]Comp. St.Thomas Aquinas: *Summa Theologiae*, I q.79, p.13 c; DeVeritate q.17, p.1 c.

precisely formulated definition. It is not provided by Roman Ingarden († 1970) although he mentions various forms of consciousness[2]. He seems to understand consciousness essentially as a continuum, i.e. a stream of reflexioned experiences of man. An integral element of human nature is the state of "being conscious"[3], i.e. having some knowledge about oneself. Other beings are "dumb", because they are deprived of the consciousness of their existence and its sense. Consciousness is that which self-explains and self-reveals itself to man. The difficulty of describing it results from the fact that whole human cognition - if it is true cognition - is connected with consciousness. At this point we may refer to the classical distinction: although man's act (actus hominis) may be unconscious or half-conscious, then human act (actus humanus) is always conscious. Lack of consciousness makes authentic human cognition impossible.

Speaking about consciousness, one should further distinguish various connotations and denotations of this category[4]. First of all, consciousness is a specific knowledge which accompanies every psychic activity due to which man becomes aware of his own experiences and actions. Phenomenologists usually speak about the "stream of the consciousness" of acts. Consciousness may also denote particular acts - moments during which man becomes aware of the opposition between his own "I" and the rest of the world. Consciousness may also be apprehended as a permanent disposition, faculty or power, thanks to which man feels to be a consciously operating doer. In its meaning consciousness thus understood is close to the notion of self-consciousness. Finally, consciousness, in the broadest sense, means all direct cognition which requires no discursive justification.

Every conscious act of human cognition has a bipolar structure, for it concerns an object being perceived and a perceiving subject. The unity of the subject and object is emphasized by Thomistic philosophy[5], while simultaneously recognizing the primacy of the former. Conscious cognition is always a cognition of something, of a certain object, transcendent in respect to our "I" (although it does not mean that the object is always external, e.g. in the case of the experience of pain). In phenomenological language the subject and object are called the "noema" and "noesis": the act of conscious cognition is the noesis, while the object perceived is the noema. In this way one may speak of two integrally connected aspects or functions of the acts of consciousness. First, as in any cognition, consciousness intentionally reflects objective reality. Consciousness does not create being but reconstructs it in a way proper for human mental psyche. However, man is not passive in his acts of cognition, in a way analogical, for instance, to photographic film. Consciousness reveals man's subjective and personal dimension; it is its egotic

---

[2]*Spór o istnienie świata* [Controversy about the Existence of the World], Warszawa 1961, vol.1, p.476.

[3]R.Ingarden: *U podstaw teorii poznania* [The Foundations of the Theory of Cognition], Warszawa 1971, p.368.

[4]P.Foulquié: *Dictionnaire de la langue philosophique*, Paris 1962,pp.122-123.

[5]St. Thomas Aquinas: *I Sent.*, d.10. q.1, p.5, ad.2; *Summa Theologiae*, I, q.93, a.7, ad 4; I, q.87, p.3, ad 2.

function, to use the language of the phenomenologists[6]. If Thomism acknowledges the primacy of the objectivized aspect of consciousness, then the philosophy of the subject lays greater stress on its subjective aspect. In this way Husserl created the category of "pure consciousness" which he understood as a subjective-intentional being, deprived of reality[7].

Consciousness appears in many varieties. First of all, one may distinguish pre-reflective and reflective consciousness[8]. Pre-reflective consciousness, also called simple, spontaneous or co-occurring, means a cognitive apprehension of an object. It is the experiencing of a certain state, situation or an act of perception of objective reality; it constantly accompanies man in his life. On the other hand, reflective consciousness is directed at man himself (his concrete acts, properties or personality), so it is already self-consciousness. Every consciousness of an object is virtually also a consciousness of a subject. In another respect one may also distinguish a consciousness which has the character of an act and the consciousness which has no such character. The former is directed at a certain object, e.g. the perception of a tree or thinking about something concrete. The consciousness which has no character of an act includes, among others, the experiencing of a certain mood, perceiving the general "background" etc. The act-like consciousness is actualized and has an evident intentional character. The non-act-like consciousness has a potential character, constituting an intermediation for concrete cognitive acts. Man's psychic life is a constant transformation of moments of reflective attention and latent consciousness. The act-like consciousness has a thetic character, i.e. ascertaining something (an object), while the non-act-like consciousness has a non-thetic character.

The common distinction between spontaneous and reflective consciousness has an equivalent in Scholastic philosophy, namely, the latter distinguishes ***reflexio in actu exercito*** and ***reflexio in actu signato***[9]. The former is a spontaneous-coocurring consciousness, while the latter is a fully reflective consciousness. The above classical distinction is somewhat differently interpreted by H.Bergson. He also distinguished direct and reflective consciousness, stressing their ontological and epistemological oppostition[10]. The immediate consciousness has a dynamic and "deep" character, constituting an expression of the primeval, unexplored levels of the human psyche. On the other hand, reflective consciousness is inspired by the activity of discursive intellect and that is why it has a

---

[6]Both aspects of consciousness are emphasized by K.Wojtyła: *Osoba i czyn* [The Person and the Act], Kraków 1969, pp.41-42,47-49.

[7]R.Ingarden: *Spór* ..., op.cit., vol.2, pp.474 ff.

[8]J.Maritain: *Distinguer pour unir ou les degrés du savoir*, Paris 1948, pp.173 ff; W.Luijpen, op.cit., pp.74-78.

[9]Cf. W.Chudy: *Refleksja a poznanie bytu. Refleksja "in actuexercito" i jej funkcja w poznaniu metafizykalnym* [Reflection and theCognition of Being. The Reflection "in actu exercito" and its Functionin Metaphysical Cognition], Lublin 1984.

[10]H.Bergson: *Essai sur les données immédiates de la conscience*, op.cit., pp.53-55,97-99,111 ff.

"superficial" character. Man's authentic self is articulated through the spontaneous consciousness, separated from the categories of quantity, time and space. "Deep" consciousness has a qualitative and personal character. Another characteristic division of consciousness is proposed by J.P.Sartre[11]. Under the influence of Descartes and phenomenology he emphasized the phenomenon of consciousness in the human being. Yet, at the same time, he opposed the passive understanding of consciousness, typical of Hume's empiricism. For that reason, as an object of his analysis he chose the imaginative consciousness, opposed in its nature to the purely perceptual consciousness. The latter is passive, reconstructing intentionally the object which is being apprehended. Imaginative consciousness has an active character and creates a world of purely intentional beings.

Self-consciousness is a variety of consciousness. It is a reflective consciousness, i.e., thinking about oneself. Due to it man discovers himself as a subject. Man's conscious existence is organically connected with the fact of being conscious of existing. However, self-consciousness should not be identified with the Cartesian cogito which has a purely formal character (thought is not an immediate apprehension of man's subjectiveness). Nor is the fact of self-observation identical with self-consciousness. When observing ourselves visually or mentally, we unavoidably become an object, whereas self-consciousness is an egotic experiencing of one's own subjectivity. The phenomenon of self-consciousness takes place completely in the realm of the immanence of our individual-personal psyche[12]. Karol Wojtyła, in turn, distinguished consciousness and self-knowledge. An analysis of his description of consciousness indicates that he has self-consciousness in mind. It is a kind of experiencing oneself as a subject, devoid of direct cognitive functions. On the other hand, when we apprehend ourselves as an object, even when characterizing our own personality and its appropriate mental activities, we are dealing with self-knowledge[13]. Self-knowledge has an objective and intentional character, whereas self-consciousness has an existential-experiential character. This distinction by the author of Osoba i czyn is connected with the separation of reflectiveness and reflexivity[14]. Reflectiveness is a property of objective cognition, therefore, of self-knowledge. Reflexivity, on the other hand, concerns the domain of consciousness; it is a more egotic experience than the process of cognition.

Self-consciousness, connected with man's capability of self-perception, is not a uniform phenomenon. Introspection and retrospection were traditionally distinguished, but today, under the influence of phenomenological analyses, the following forms of self-consciousness are usually recognized: experiencing, inner perception, immanent

[11]L'imaginaire. *Psychologie phénoménologique de l'imagination*, Paris 1940, pp.13-29.

[12]J.Tischner calls self-consciousness "con-scientivity"; cf. *Świat ludzkiej nadziei* [The World of Human Hope], Kraków 1975, p.119.

[13]*Osoba i czyn*, op.cit., pp.38-44.

[14]Ibid., pp.45-47.

perception, recollection[15]. Experiencing, which is an equivalent of what R.Ingarden calls Durchleben in order to distinguish it from sensing or feeling (Erleben), denotes a consciousness of the occurrence of a certain act or psychic state. It is still only a virtual self-consciousness, since the object is grasped in an indirect way - through existentially experienced situations. It is only introspection, also described as inner perception, that can be called self-consciousness in this strict sense. The foregrounded object of such a perception concerns us ourselves: our acts, mode of perceiving, mood, faculties, and our inner "I". We then become conscious, for instance, of the character of our personality, attitude towards life, experienced joy or sadness, undertaken efforts etc. Naturally, inner perception of this kind should not be confused with inner sensory perception, for instance, the experiencing of pain in the internal organs of our body. In contradistinction to animals, man has a faculty of actively remembering past events in his life. It is the ability of retrospection.

The domain of man's self-consciousness is connected with the so-called immanent perception, widely discussed by phenomenologists[16]. In fact it is a derivative form of inner perception but interpreted in the context of the phenomenological method. An integral part of the latter is phenomenological reduction (epoche) which means a procedure of bracketing the connection of the psyche with the psycho-physical totality of man's organism. The stream of consciousness loses then its ties with man's life activity but is apprehended as an independent whole. In immanent perception the objective-informative sense disappears, since the object of interest is exclusively the very stream of consciousness - its course, structure, intentional-subjective contents. What is being experienced is referred exclusively to the subject himself. Phenomenologists usually call this subject "pure consciousness", "pure I", or "transcendental I". Immanent perception is variously understood by phenomenologists themselves; Husserl explicates it according to his transcendental idealism, while Ingarden reinterprets this category realistically.

(ii) Conceptions of Consciousness

The category of consciousness, so important for the comprehension of the human person, has been variously understood in the history of philosophical thought. The variety of the conceptions of consciousness is strictly connected with a multiplicity of the conceptions of man. As a result there are several classifications of the conceptions of consciousness. Some of them seem to indicate a variety of the functions of consciousness

---

[15]R.Ingarden: "O niebezpieczeństwie "petitionis principii" w teorii poznania" [On the Danger of "petitionis principii" in Epistemology] [in:] *U podstaw teorii poznania* [The Foundations of Epistemology], Warszawa 1971, pp.368 ff.

[16]Cf. Ingarden: *Spór* ..., op.cit., vol.1, pp.19-25.

rather than taking into account the ontology of consciousness[17]. The following ontological conceptions of consciousness can be distinguished: objectivistic, subjectivistic, naturalistic, pantheistic, negativistic, psychological, and functional-pragmatic[18].

The subjectivistic - realistic conception of consciousness is typical of Aristotelian-Thomistic philosophy[19]. It recognizes the fact that consciousness is the ontological datum of the human self viz. the subject. Thus, consciousness is not shaped by the external material world, but it is actualized by it in its cognitive dispositions. Man is not a disembodied spirit, and that is why in his cognition and actions he is directed towards the external world. The cognitive contact with the world evokes man's mental reflection and then makes it possible for him to understand his subjectiveness in acts of self-consciousness. The objectivistic conception of consciousness, while not questioning the ontological autonomy of the human person and its self-consciousness, recognizes the priority of being over reflection on the epistemological plane. Consciousness is a "response" to the contact with the world of objects, and that is why it is always intentionally directed towards this world. Man's consciousness is not a closed monad, but an opening of oneself to objective reality and its ever better comprehension[20]. In its actualization and operation consciousness is extrovertic, connected with the external world.

The objectivistic conception of consciousness well illustrates man's ontic and epistemological relations with his surrounding world, while rather poorly revealing the phenomenon of self-consciousness. Using the language of Scholasticism, one may say that Thomism stresses ***reflexio in actu exercito*** more strongly than ***reflexio in actu signato***. And it is precisely this aspect that is stressed by the subjectivistic conception of consciousness which asserts the priority of consciousness over the objective world, ***resp.*** the priority of epistemology over ontology. This trend was initiated by Descartes whose thesis ***cogito ergo sum*** asserts the priority of self-consciousness over real being. A leading continuator of the subjectivistic conception of consciousness and the creator of phenomenology, Edmund Husserl, oscillated between realism and idealism in his philosophical conceptions and that is why they are now subject of highly varied interpretations[21]. In the first volume of *The Ideas of Pure Phenomenology and Phenomenological Philosophy* he distinguished consciousness in the strict sense and consciousness in a broad sense. The latter covers all

---

[17]A.Stępień: "W poszukiwaniu istoty człowieka" [In Search for the Essence of Man] [in:] *Aby poznać Boga i człowieka* [To Know God and Man], vol.I: *O człowieku dziś* [Of Man Today], Warszawa 1974, pp.78-83.

[18]B.Mijuskowi (*Contingent Immaterialism: Meaning, Freedom, Time and Mind*, Amsterdam 1984, pp.90-93) distinguishes three conceptions of consciousness: behavioral, intentional and reflective.

[19]Cf. J.Maritain: *Distinguer pour unir ou les degr és du savoir*, op.cit., passim.

[20]Some authors describe the conception of consciousness intraditional philosophy as a combination of the intentional conceptionand mirroring or reflective.

[21]Cf. A.Półtawski: *Świat, spostrzeżenie, świadomość. Fenomenologiczna koncepcja świadomości a realizm* [The World, Perception, Consciousness. The Phenomenological Conception of Consciousness and Realism], Warszawa 1973, pp.7-24.

conscious experience, whereas consciousness in its proper sense denotes the Cartesian *cogito*[22]. Other writings by Husserl make it possible to distinguish a triple conception of consciousness: (1) a stream of psychic experiences, i.e. the so-called phenomenological "I"; (2) inner perception; and (3) the totality of psychical acts[23]. In the phenomenological literature one may find still other classifications of the forms of consciousness in Husserl[24].

The differences between particular divisions of the varieties of consciousness are of secondary importance; much more relevant is the question of the interpretation of the nature of consciousness. The analyses of the founder of phenomenology reveal an evident subjectivistic-idealistic implication. He accepted the *cogito*, which on some occasions was called by him pure consciousness, transcendental consciousness or internal perception, as a significant form of consciousness. The object of such consciousness is the immanent world of the subject. Even if we speak about the consciousness of something, in fact it is the experiences of the subject or his intentional creations that are the point. Ultimately, Husserl could state:

> "*Everything that exists for me in the world of things is in principle only a supposed reality; that it is just to the contrary, that I myself, for whom this thing exists [...] resp. my experiential actuality is the absolute reality*"[25].

This is a subjectivistic-subjective conception of man's consciousness. The "pure I" or the "transcendental I" is not identified with man's real, psycho-physical "I". Husserl apprehended consciousness in an immanent way; his "pure I" is the transcendent immersed in immanence[26]. The *cogito* was thus transformed into a monad closed to the external world, while consciousness became exclusively an egotic self-consciousness. The object of consciousness lost its ontic autonomy and was reduced to the role a subjective moment of the experience of the subject.

There is also a naturalistic interpretation of the phenomenon of human consciousness. This conception occurs in a variety of types; among others, it is represented by the adherents of dialectical materialism and behaviorism. Although Marxism acknowledges the functional variety of consciousness and biological processes in the human being, yet it still identifies them in the genetic and ontological respects[27]. Reflective consciousness is interpreted as an epiphenomenon of biological-neurological structures. In Marxism, and

---

[22]*Ideen zu einer reinen Phänomenologie und phänomenologischen Philosophie*, Haag 1950, vol.1, p.67.

[23]A.Półtawski, op.cit., pp.39-43; the author refers to Husserl's *Logical Analysis*.

[24]Cf. J.Tischner: "Strukturalne zagadnienia refleksji i spostrzeżenia immanentnego w świetle niektórych tez E.Husserla" [The Structural Problems of Reflection and Immanent Perception in the Light of some Theses by E.Husserl], *Studia Philosophiae Christianae*, 1(1966) nr. 1, pp.209 ff.

[25]Ideen ..., vol.1, p.108; see also pp.91-110.

[26]A.Półtawski, op.cit., pp.196 ff, 415-444. The author presents acritical evaluation of Husserl's conception of consciousness.

[27]S.Kowalczyk: *Z problematyki dialogu chrześcijańsko-marksistowskiego* [On the Problems of the Christian-Marxist Dialogue], Warszawa 1977, pp.55-63.

especially in V.Lenin, this reductionistic-materialistic explication of consciousness is combined with the conception of human cognition as a "mirroring" of the external world[28]. Psychical processes of cognition are here explained as a reflection of the material world and of social environment. Consciousness is therefore to be a kind of a mirror in which external reality is reflected.

Man's consciousness finds an extreme naturalistic explanation in the trend of behaviorism. This current is a combination of the epistemology of sensualism and the ontology of vitalistic materialism. In a peremptory manner it questions the value of internal experience and intellectual cognition, so that thinking is explained as "a play of impressions". Consciousness is interpreted as a biological-physiological reaction to stimuli from the external world. A good example of a contemporary adherent of behaviorism is Gilbert Ryle[29], although he also has adopted some elements of analytical philosophy. The existence of consciousness, of the human "I", man's psychic-spiritual domain, are all called a myth by him.

Regardless of the differences between these trends, in the interpretations of behaviorism and dialectical materialism consciousness is not so much explained but rather questioned ontologically. Materialistic monism leads to anthropological reductionism, and the latter, in turn, provides no foundation for the recognition of the ontical and cognitive autonomy of consciousness. It means a biologicalization of consciousness, which is characteristic of behaviorism, while in Marxism consciousness is reduced to the fact of "mirroring" the external world. In both interpretations there is no place for the owner of consciousness, the being self-conscious of his own "I".

Ontological character can also be perceived in two other conceptions of consciousness, typical of pantheism and of J.P.Sartre's theory. Oriental pantheism, characteristic of some currents of Hinduism, questions the reality of both the external world and man's empirical "I". Real and permanent existence is granted only to the non-personal Absolute, placed beyond the sphere of the visible, illusory being. The way to the unification with the absolute being leads through a loss of individual identity, including the self-consciousness of one's own "I"[30]. Depersonalization and de-individualization of human consciousness are components of every pantheism, also in Europe, for instance, in Spinoza and Hegel. Man's subjective-individual consciousness was explained by Hegel († 1831) as a moment in the growth of the consciousness of the Absolute, as its expression and, simultaneously, as its dialectic transformation. Man's consciousness of himself is actually the self-consciousness of the deity. A significant drawback of pantheistic conceptions of consciousness is the questioning of individual personality, which undermines its ontological and epistemological sense. In this interpretation, the self-consciousness of

---

[28]N.Łubnicki: *Teoria poznania materializmu dialektycznego* [The Epistemology of Dialectical Materialism], Lublin 1946.

[29]*The Concept of Mind*, London 1973, pp.264-301.

[30]S.Kowalczyk: *Drogi ku Bogu* [The Roads to God], Wrocław 1983, pp.154-170.

oneself is an illusion. And if there is no individual owner of consciousness, then its cognitive function loses its foundation.

The survey of the conceptions of consciousness should also include one more conception, namely, the proposition of J.P.Sartre. He distinguished two forms of being, namely, being in itself and being for itself. The latter being is precisely consciousness, i.e. the subjective being of man. Man has the consciousness of the existence of both the external world and of his own consciousness[31]. Consciousness always implies duplication because it concerns what we still are or what we are no longer. A conscious being does not stand still, in the contingency of its existence, but it searches for new situations and is directed towards the future. The privilege of transcending the present is however connected with the perception of lacks, limitations, unrealized intentions, and, finally, with one's own finiteness. And that is why in the very heart of the human being there is nothingness[32]. As a constant property of human consciousness, nothingness is also connected with the attribute of freedom and the risk it entails. The Sartrean conception of consciousness has a negativistic character, since it stresses only the element of annihilation in its nature. Still, it is a mutilated conception of consciousness, whose ontic foundations contain, after all, a positive element, namely, the ontic identity of the new "I"[33]. Consciousness is always bipolar: I - subject and object; the "I" perceives its own limits, but it is not submerged in nothingness.

Another conception of consciousness, called a psychological one, was presented by George Berkeley. It is an extremely subjective understanding of consciousness because it is regarded as the only source of knowledge about the world. Obviously, subjective idealism and the theory of immaterialism make it impossible to speak about the real world; it is exclusively a world of human impressions and ideas. For the English thinker, consciousness, separated from the material body, was an artifact of the subjective-imaginary world.

There still remains the pragmatic-functional conception of consciousness whose leading representative was William James († 1910). He was opposed to the atomistic-associationistic conception of consciousness and saw in it an uninterrupted stream of acts. The a-metaphysical attitude of the American thinker did not allow him to affirm a constant subject of these acts of consciousness and that is why he only saw a function in it rather than substantial beingness[34]. The last two conceptions discussed above no longer have any major following in contemporary philosophical thought.

---

[31]J.P.Sartre: *Being and Nothigness*, op.cit., pp.97 ff.

[32]Ibid., pp.126-128, 52-54.

[33]W.Luijpen, op.cit., pp.112-116.

[34]James's treatise entitled *Does Consciousness Exist?* was published in 1914.

(iii) The Noetic Function of Consciousness

The phenomenological description of man's consciousness makes it possible to distinguish two of its important aspects, noetic and ontological. Consciousness is a fundamental kind of mental cognition, while simultaneously constituting the subjectiveness of the human person[35].

The noetic role of intellectual reflection and consciousness was strongly emphasized by Descartes. Looking for effective methods of overcoming skepticism, he referred to the intuitive obviousness of the fact of human thought. He accepted the truth of "I think, therefore I am" as unquestionable[36]. The Cartesian *cogito* is a turning point in the history of philosophy because it shifts the starting point of the analysis from the external world to man's inner world. The epistemological realism of Thomistic philosophy is turned into rationalism; the minimization of the role of sensory cognition is connected with the acknowledgement of the priority of the phenomenon of thought in the domain of philosophy. The human self was not reduced by Descartes to the plane of thought, for he acknowledged the richness of man's psychic experiences[37]. He was also far removed from anthropological phenomenism because he recognized the reality of the body and the substantiality of the "I". Descartes described man as "A substance the whole essence or nature of which is to think"[38]. Yet, this description also confirms the fact that thought was accepted as the most important sector of humankind. To the question "What is man?" Descartes answers that he is thinking. The author loses the intentional character of consciousness. "I think, therefore I am" meant for him: I think about myself, I am conscious of my own consciousness[39]. It was a completely immanent understanding of the process of human cognition. However, in such a situation, the cognition of the objective world, including man himself, becomes problematical. Isolated from the external world, consciousness cannot secure sure knowledge about it. Hence, cognition turns into a manipulation of subjective ideas. In Descartes there also occurs a vicious circle. The human "I" is an object of conscious cognition but at the same time it is practically apprehended as a criterion of that cognition. But can one be one's own judge? Skepticism turned out to be a trap for Descartes and the *cogito* proved unable to overcome it.

The adage "I think, therefore, I am" also provokes other doubts, namely, is thought really man's primary act? Paul Ricoeur is of the opinion that Freud's psychoanalysis has undermined the self-obviousness of human thought. He thinks that the gap between the *ego* and the *cogito* is too large to speak about their direct relation. The Cartesian starting

---

[35]Phenomenological epistemology is discussed by R.A.Mall: *Experience and Reason. The Phenomenology of Husserl and its Relation to Hume's Philosophy,* The Hague 1973, especially pp.111-126.

[36]Descartes: *Discourse on the Method of Rightly Conducting the Reason* [in:] *The Philosophical Works of Descartes,* op.cit., vol.1,p.101.

[37]*The Principle of Philosophy* [in:] *The Philosophical Works...,* op.cit., vol.1, pp.209-210.

[38]*Discourse on the Method,* op.cit., p.101.

[39]W.Luijpen, op.cit., pp.81-83.

point ignores the rich world of symbolism, myths, irrational desires, sensitivity to values, and, first of all, the phenomenon of subconsciousness. Although Ricoeur was not an adherent of Freudian biologization of man, he still recognized the priority of the sphere of subconsciousness over reflective thought[40]. Man's authentic existence is not restricted to thought since man is also "a desire and an effort". It is important that man is, but ***what*** he is is even more important. The reflective *ego* emerges from the mysterious domain of subconsciousness and unconsciousness, although it cannot be reduced to them. The *cogito* is not absolutely primordial in the human self because it is preceded by the domain of irrational-subconscious life, although this fact does not imply the absence of conscious thought in the human person. At any rate, the statement "I think, therefore I am" contains the error of a simplification of the complex human being. Contrary to Descartes's suggestions, the epistemological function of the *cogito* is restricted, and therefore controversial.

The Cartesian *cogito* found its continuation in Husserl's transcendental idealism. As has already been remarked, in the evolution of this thinker one can perceive certain stages which mark his gradual departure from idealism[41]. Still, this development was neither unequivocal nor consistent. Characterizing the phenomenon of man's consciousness, the German writer perceived its intentional nature. He recognized that consciousness is always directed at something, at some object. But his understanding of the object was far from epistemological realism[42]. Thus, he did not mean the external-transcendent object in respect to the perceiving man, but a correlate of his acts of consciousness. Husserl acknowledged the connection of the *cogito* and *cogitatum*, but the latter did not refer to the objective world[43]. At any rate, in his understanding, the "pure I" is not identified with the psycho-physical person of a real man[44]. The *cogito* refers to an object, but it is an intentional-conscious relation. Obviously, both Cartesian and Husserl's understandings of the *cogito* provoke objections from the point of view of epistemological realism. Man's consciousness is always intentional, i.e., directed at an object. Our consciousness is not only consciousness but a consciousness of something, of an object. It excludes the immanent interpretation of consciousness. Man's ***ego*** is not an arbitrary creator of the experiences and acts of consciousness, since it is always connected with the external world. Man is not a closed monad, although he is not a passive reflection of his surroundings, either[45]. Man is sovereign in his consciousness and

[40]P.Ricoeur: *Le conflit des interpr étations. Essai d'herm éneutique*, Paris 1969, pp.118-120, 171-175.

[41]The second volume of *Ideas*, published posthumously, is undoubtedly closer to realism than volume 1.

[42]J.Tischner (op.cit., pp.240 ff) distinguishes four meanings of thecategory of the "object" in Husserl, but in fact none of themcorresponds to consistent realism.

[43]Husserl: *Ideen* ..., vol.2, Haag 1952, pp.120-123.

[44]W.Luijpen's (op.cit., pp.95-98) interpretation of Husserl's thought is controversial because it obscures its transcendental idealism.

[45]Cf. S.Strasser: *The Soul in Metaphysical and Empirical Psychology*, op.cit., pp.47-50, 92-99.

reflective thought, in whose context he discovers his inalienable subjectiveness. Human consciousness does not constitute the world of objects, yet it is not its own epiphenomenon, either.

While Cartesianism and Husserlian transcendental idealism deform the noetic role of consciousness, detaching it from the totality of man's cognitive faculties, there is also a reverse tendency, which undermines any cognitive value of reflection and self-reflection. As a rule, the point is to negate the method of introspection[46]. The opponents of the method bring forth many objections, such as, a static apprehension of psychic life, the objectivization of the human "I" - subject, departure from the empirical-biological view of man etc. The latter objection is raised by the adherents of behaviorism who attempt to replace completely the method of introspection by that of extrospection. They are of the opinion that in its essence the human psyche consists in a physiological-neurological reaction to external stimuli. Hence, if one wants to know man, it would suffice to appropriately dose out the stimuli and thus, to determine his attitudes in this way. If one accepts such an anthropological perspective, the human world would turn into a world of mechanically controlled robots. The behavioristic interpretation of man entails his depersonalization and, in fact, dehumanization. The method of introspection out of necessity implies the recognition of the spiritual dimension of the human person. Behaviorism reduces man's beingness to the role of passive reflecting of the external world and its stimuli. But then man would be merely an automaton, a self-controlled machine.

The objective value of reflective mental cognition is recognized by many leading thinkers, both past and contemporary. St.Thomas Aquinas quite unequivocally confirms the value of self-consciousness when referring to the assertion of our self[47]. Descartes's position has already been discussed above. Husserl regarded internal experience as a direct and reliable source of knowledge about ourselves. In his *Ideas* ... he wrote that "I can experience myself 'directly'"[48]. Also H. Bergson acknowledged the intuitive-reflective cognition of oneself as a fundamental source of knowledge of man. Still, he also added that one should not forget the constant dynamics of psychic life[49]. He distinguished between man's surface and deep "I", noticing that it is only that latter that provides a real knowledge of man.

The opponents of introspection claim that it de-subjectivizes man; since he becomes a direct object of the acts of consciousness, he automatically loses the status of a subject. This is a misunderstanding resulting from the lack of distinction between the ontological and epistemological planes. The objects of human cognition are ontologically

---

[46]The method is questioned by L.Brunschvieg: *De la connaisance desoi*, Paris 1931; G.Ryle, op.cit., pp.301-311.

[47]"Experitur enim unusquisque seipsum esse, qui intelligit", *Summa Theologiae* I, q.76, a.1, c; comp. *De Veritate*, q.10, a. 8,c.

[48]Ideen ..., vol.2., p.200.

[49]H.Bergson: *Essai* ..., op.cit., pp.57-59, 98-104.

differentiated; some of them are merely something, while others are somebody. The self-reflective perception of oneself does not destroy our subjectiveness but, to the contrary, it affirms it. Self-consciousness makes it possible to experience oneself as a thinking and free "I"[50].

The phenomenon of consciousness is qualitatively different from other forms of cognition. That is why St.Thomas Aquinas remarks that the cognition of a stone differs from the fact of the consciousness of such cognition[51]. The difference of the cognitive levels in both cases is obvious. At the same time, this thinker repeatedly stressed the unity of the acts of cognition of the subject and the object. Since we consciously apprehend a certain object, we simultaneously become indirectly aware of our own cognitive possibilities[52]. We are those who apprehend something as well as those who are conscious of this fact. Thomism recognizes the priority of the cognition of the object over the subject, while Cartesianism makes just an opposite claim. The problem of the priority of either the cognition of the object or of the cognition of the subject is more speculative than existential. After all, every accompanying consciousness is potentially a reflective consciousness. Therefore, summing up, we may perhaps conclude that reflective consciousness, i.e. self-consciousness, is an unquestionable source of knowledge about man as a person. It is also an irreplaceable source, since internal experience cannot be substituted by either sensory perception or discursive thought.

The main object of reflective consciousness is our individual "I". But is it the only object of internal experience? Can we speak about an intuitive cognition of the psyche of another man (*alter ego*)? There are different opinions about this question; some allow the possibility of direct cognition of the "interior" of other people, while others question such a possibility[53]. Four theories are most often presented, namely, those of analogy, association, imitation and "empathizing". In one way or another they all refer to internal experience which is then confronted with the observations of other people and explained on the basis of certain theoretical assumptions. The cognizability of the psyche of another person is much more controversial than the exploration of our own "I".

---

[50]*Summa Theologiae*, I, q.79, a.4,c; *De Veritate*, q.10, a.8.

[51]*Summa Theologiae*, I, q.88, a.4, ad 2.

[52]"Ex obiecto enim cognoscit suam operationem, per quam devenit adcognitionem sui ipsius", *De anima* 3, ad 2; "Eadem operatione intelligointelligibile et intelligo me inteligere", *I Sent.*, d.1, q.2, a1, ad2; comp. *I Sent.*, d.10, q.1, a.5, ad 2.

[53]R.Ingarden: *O poznawaniu cudzych stanów psychicznych* [On Cognizingthe Psychic States of Others] [in:] *U podstaw teorii poznania*, op.cit., pp.407-427.

(iv) The Ontology of Consciousness

Consciousness, spontanenous and reflective, serves not only the noetic function but it also ontologically constitutes man's subjectiveness. It is precisely this aspect that we shall now consider, taking advantage of the analyses of consciousness carried out by phenomenologists, especially by Roman Ingarden. In the psychological structure of the person he distinguished three levels: stream of consciousness, dispositions and faculties, and the "I" - subject of these psychic acts and dispositions[54]. The Polish thinker was opposed to the atomistic conception of consciousness, since its consequence would entail a loss of the internal unity of acts of consciousness. Man's consciousness is a process, a change, the "happening of something". One can therefore speak of the "stream of consciousness", although the term "stream" should not be taken too literally. The common feature of the flowing river and the stream of human consciousness is the fact of changeability, of impermanence. The river contains the already existing particles of water, while the acts of consciousness are constantly coming into being and passing from the present to the past[55]. There are no ready-made structures - elements of consciousness; they are constantly appearing and interpenetrating. Obviously, consciousness should not be understood passively, either. Thus, it is not a mirror mechanically reflecting external impulses in itself. Although it constitutes the core of human subjectiveness, consciousness is actualized in contact with its surroundings on the principle of action and reaction. Ingarden distinguished two main states of consciousness, experiences and sensations. By the former he meant the consciousness of subjective acts of experience while by the latter - consciousness of certain contents[56].

Characterizing man's consciousness one should perceive both its differentiation and unity. The multiplicity of the acts of consciousness does not mean a multiplicity of "temporal objects" but "one should regard the stream of consciousness as one object, as one restricted whole"[57]. Man's conscious experiences not only occur one after another but they co-create an organic whole. The stream of consciousness is not an aggregate of sensations and acts, but one process of the same object. The abundance of experiences does not undermine the unity of man's consciousness. Acts of consciousness are spatially localized or extensional and that is why material beings cannot constitute their foundation[58].

Man's original experience is the continuity and unity of the stream of consciousness. Naturally, there are pauses in experiencing this consciousness but they cannot be

---

[54]Cf. Półtawski, op.cit., pp.381-414.

[55]R.Ingarden: *Spór o istnienie świata* [The Controversy about the Existence of the World], Warszawa 1961, vol.2, pp.478-479.

[56]Ibid., p.11.

[57]Ibid., p.485.

[58]Ibid., p.541.

identified with the destruction of human personality[59]. The phases of sleep or temporary loss of consciousness (in exceptional cases such states may last very long) do not mean a destruction of one human "I" followed by the appearance of a new one. Man's characteristic feature is his memory of the past stages of his life, the ability of actively remembering them, taking advantage of past experiences etc. The unity of experiences is a constitutive feature of man's consciousness. He lives his life as a continuum, as a whole covering the past, the present and the future[60]. The unity of the stream of consciousness is not an illusion but a continuously experienced reality.

The phenomenological analysis of the stream of human consciousness finds its equivalent in the considerations of St. Thomas Aquinas. In *Summa Theologiae*, when constructing his philosophy of man, the philosopher frequently referred to the realities of psychic life: acts of sensible and intellectual cognition, emotional experiences and appetitive-volitional acts[61]. Still, it should be admitted that this rich psychological material was not sufficiently exploited in the philosophical anthropology of the thinker.

The second level of man's psychic life includes dispositions, powers and faculties. St.Thomas clearly wrote about the powers of the human soul among which he mentioned intellect and will[62]. Trying to remain within the limits of phenomenological reduction, phenomenologists are usually more cautious in their formulations. In the second volume of *Ideas...* Husserl speaks about the "I" as the subject of powers. At the same time, he remarks that "power is not an empty capability but a positive potentiality"[63]. An analogical motif was taken up by R.Ingarden who perceived the existence of "real powers" which endow man's stream of the experiences of consciousness with directionality and dynamics[64]. The writer did not identify them with the category of psychic powers in the undestanding of classical philosophy, since he saw rather individual-flexible factors in them. The Polish phenomenologist is very cautious in his use of terminology and that is why he speaks about "properties and attributes" of human soul. The mentioned powers and properties inhere in the human being and that is why they lose their natural foundation when they are separated from it. The stream of consciousness and the set of properties do not exhaust the ontical structure of man. It is Ingarden's conviction that "our soul cannot be merely regarded as a simple set of this kind of 'spiritual' or 'vital' powers"[65]. The phenomenological analysis has led this thinker to the conclusion about

---

59 Ibid., pp.488, 492-493.

60 Ibid., pp.490-493.

61 *Summa Theologiae*, I, qq.81 and 85; I-II, qq. 22-48.

62 *Summa Theologiae*, I, qq.77-82.

63 Husserl: *Ideen...*, vol.2, p.255; cf. also pp.253-256.

64 Ingarden: *Spór* ..., vol.2, pp.514-519. The author makes areservation that the problem of the reality of the "properties ofhuman soul" cannot be solved on the plane of ontology.

65 *Spór* ..., vol.2, p.515.

the existence of the subject - self of man[66]. Such a conclusion, however, still remains in the realm of ontology, without yet turning into a metaphysical thesis.

The existence of acts of consciousness and their internal unity are logically explained through the unity and identity of the human "I"[67]. Yet, which "I" is the point here - phenomenological, real-concrete, personal, or axiological-I? Phenomenologists are not always in agreement on this point. E.Husserl concentrated his attention on the "pure I", also called "pure consciousness". The "pure I" is directed at itself and is identical with itself; it is nontransitional and indestructible[68]. It is not a part of the real-objective world, being autonomous in respect to it. Moreover, the "pure I" intentionally constitutes every object which appears in human consciousness[69]. Husserl's conception of the "pure I" is neither unequivocal nor - as Ingarden observes - uniform. Initially, the German thinker accepted the existence of one, absolute "pure I" in which he saw the exclusive source of all acts of consciousness. Yet, later on he seemed to be in favour of a multiplicity of pure subjects, and in his interpretation of "pure consciousness" he approached the idea of the human person[70].

The Polish thinker argued against the extremely subjectivistic conception of the "pure I". He showed that the phenomenological analysis suggests the necessity of the existence of the ontical foundation of the stream of human consciousness; namely, the "I" surpasses the level of acts of consciousness as the *transcendent*. The acts of consciousness derive from the subject much like a stream of water from a spring[71]. This internal "I" is cognizable for us directly, and not in opposition to other people. The category of "I" is ambiguous. Ingarden distinguishes three of its meanings: (1) "I" as a performer of the acts of consciousness; (2) "I" as a centre of the human person; and (3) "I" as the totality of human being[72]. The differentiation of the meanings of the "I" does not abolish the common property of the three enumerated designates of this category, namely, the ontical identity of subject - man. It is not an additive being, a sum of sensations and experiences, a succession of temporal moments, but a unity and identity of the same subject. Man is a real-ontic "I", a doer of psychic acts and an owner of psychic and somatic properties.

The culmination of Ingarden's anthropology is the theory of the person. He argued against the positivistic conception of individual being, reducing the subject to a sum of

---

[66]Ibid., p.516.

[67]Ibid., p.497.

[68]E.Husserl: *Ideen...*, vol.2, pp.101-104.

[69]*Ideen* ..., vol.2, pp.102-104; A.Półtawski: *Świat, spostrzeżenie, świadomość*, op.cit., pp.186-189.

[70]Ingarden: *Spór* ..., vol.2, pp.474-475. The author's suggestions find confirmation in volume two of Husserl's Ideas, especially in Part III, entitled "The Constitution of the Spiritual World", pp.197, 289,347, 352.

[71]*Spór* ..., vol.2, p.502.

[72]Ibid., p.504.

equivalent features deprived of a stable factor[73]. Even more, he questioned the asubstantial and apersonal understanding of man, so that he regarded the psychology "without soul" as senseless[74]. Ingarden recognized the need of a theoretical-methodological distinction between the categories of pure subject and of person, but he accepted their ontical-real identity. In the interpretation of this phenomenologist, the "I" - the *transcendent* of the stream of consciousness, the pure subject and a person (resp. soul), constitute one and the same reality[75]. His conception of the person was not quite unequivocal; sometimes he identified it with the soul, at other times - with the totality of the psycho-physical being of man. Yet, undoubtedly the person was not for him a secondary and theoretical category, but a factor organizing and controlling human reality[76]. Thus, man is a unity of the stream of consciousness, the "I" - their subject, and the person (soul). Ingarden's personalistic conception of man in principle belongs to the phenomenologically understood ontology, yet in fact it "opens way to metaphysical considerations"[77].

As Ingarden persuasively demonstrated, the ontology of man's consciousness is connected with the ontology of the person. An analogical ascertainment, though included already in the metaphysical analysis of the human being, may be found in St. Thomas Aquinas. His consistent genetic empiricism made it impossible for him to recognize the possibility of the direct cognition of the human soul[78]. The soul cognizes itself indirectly, through an exploration of the acts of mental life, including also the phenomenon of consciousness. Intellectual cognition and reflection have an immaterial character. Hence, St. Thomas thinks that "the soul apprehends itself" and, due to that, it also partially apprehends the nature of immaterial beings[79]. The self-reflective cognition of oneself is for man a recognition of his partly immaterial personality.

The analysis of consciousness carried out by phenomenologists undoubtedly possesses a great cognitive value (in spite of the limitations of the phenomenological method). The "I", shown in the context of acts and sensations of consciousness, denotes an existential experiencing of our subjectiveness and personhood. Consciousness uncovers the personal "I", and, at the same time, it ontically constitutes it. In opposition to the deformations of idealism, consciousness does not absorb the real being, either the external reality or man. Consciousness creates the human personal being in its very essence. Thanks to it, we feel we are autonomous subjects and factual performers of actions. In the course of the

[73]Ibid., vol.1, pp.462 ff.

[74]Ibid., vol.2, pp.511-512.

[75]Ibid., pp.521-523.

[76]R.Ingarden: *Książeczka o człowieku* [A Booklet about Man], Kraków 1987, p.119.

[77]Ibid., p.128; comp. *Spór* ..., vol.1, pp.63-64.

[78]*Summa Theologiae*, I, q.87, a.1.

[79]*Summa Theologiae*, I, q.88, a.1, ad 1; I, q.87, a.1, ad 1 and ad 2; I, q.87, a.3, c; *III Sent.*, d.23, a.1, ad.2, ad.3.

functioning of consciousness, our personal "I" shows itself as self-obvious and undeniable. Reflective consciousness is also an existential experiencing of the spiritual dimension of the human person, in both cognitive and appetitive-moral spheres. Hence, consciousness is not merely a mirror in which we can see ourselves. The phenomenon of consciousness is an expression of the psychic interpretation of the human person, since, in a sense, it is a possessing of oneself in what appertains to man in his personal internal "sanctuary". As a being capable of reflective thought, man does not look at himself from the outside nor does he objectivize himself. Self-consciousness means a presence in oneself and possessing oneself. And this is the role of its ontological function. Thanks to consciousness and self-consciousness man is a person, i.e. a subject capable of cognitive, appetitive, axiological and social autonomy.

LITERATURE

ADLER, M: "Intentionality and Immateriality", *The New Scholasticism* 41 (1961), pp.312-344.

BERGSON, H: *Essai sur les données immédiates de laconscience*, Paris 1944.

BRUNSCHVIEG, L.: *De la connaissance de soi*, Paris 1931.

CHUDY, W.: *Refleksja a poznanie bytu* [Reflection and theCognition of Being], Lublin 1984.

DEC, I.: "Ontyczne racje danych samodoświadczenia człowieka w ujęciu św. Tomasza z Akwinu" [Ontic Rations of the Data of Man's Self-Experience as Apprehended by St. Thomas Aquinas], *Colloquium Salutis* 16 (1984) pp.293-337.

FINANCE, J. de: *Cogito cartésienne et réflexion thomiste*, Paris 1946.

GILSON, E.: *Réalisme thomiste et critique de laconnaissance*, Paris 1947.

HUSSERL, E.: *Ideen zu einer reinen Phänomenologie und phänomenologischen Philosophie*, vol.2, Haag 1950-1952.

INGARDEN, R.: *Spór o istnienie świata* [Controversy aboutthe Existence of the World], vol.2, Warszawa 1960-1961.

INGARDEN, R.: *U podstaw teorii poznania* [The Foundations of the Theory of Cognition], Warszawa 1971.

LUIJPEN,W.A.: *Existential Phenomenology*, Pittsburgh 1960.

MARITAIN, J.: *Distinguer pour unir ou les degrés du savoir*, Paris 1948.

MARITAIN, J.: *Réflexions sur l'intelligence*, Paris 1938.

MERLEAU-PONTY, M.: *Phénomenology de la perception*, Paris1945.

MOHANTY, J.N.: *The Concept of Intentionality*, St. Louis 1972.

SARTRE, J.P.: *L'imaginaire. Psychologie phénoménologique del'imagination*, Paris 1940.

STĘPIEŃ, A.: "Rodzaje bezpośredniego poznania" [Types of Direct Cognition], *Roczniki Filozoficzne* 19 (1971) nr.1, pp.95-126.

WOJTYŁA, K.: *Osoba i czyn* [The Person and the Act], Kraków 1969.

Chapter 3

Intellectual Cognition - Language - Truth

The phenomenological description of man makes it possible to distinguish various ontical levels, such as those of existence, of biological life, of animal sensations and of thinking. The latter phenomenon is connected with the domain of intellectual cognition which opens for man the possibility of using significative - symbolic language and the cognition of truth. Animals, which are capable only of sensible cognition and have only an impulsive-instinctual sphere, feel no desire to acquire knowledge; they ask no questions and look for no truth. Only man wants to learn and to know the nature of reality; only man searches for a sense of life and perceives higher values. Already Aristotle, in the introduction to Metaphysics, stated that all people desire knowledge. Such questions as "How? Where from? Why?" constantly accompany human history. Thought, language as a vehicle of sense, and truth are the criteria of the human world, distinctly separating it from the rest of the cosmos.

(i) Intellectual congnition

Because of the universality of its scope and strict connection with man's being, the conception of cognition is difficult to define. Nevertheless, descriptions of this category are possible, though only partial and entangled in the systemic complexities of the philosophy practised. Cartesianism identifies the phenomenon of cognition with consciousness which is a one-sided approach to the problem. At the same time, it would be difficult to perceive the foundation of human cognition in existential propositions understood as pre-reflection acts[1]. Every cognition constitutes some relation between a subject and an object[2]. Speaking more precisely, cognition becomes factual by the subject becoming aware of the object. If there is no co-participation of consciousness, there is no authentic cognition. Therefore, the full cognitive process in man always involves a subject and an object, and then the cognitive act itself and its determined effect. ***Human***

[1]The role of existential propositions in epistemology was stressed by E.Gilson: *L'être et l'essence*, Paris 1948, pp.250-270.

[2]St.Thomas Aquinas: *I Sent.*, d.3,q.1,a.2.

cognition is not reduced, obviously, to the physiological process of a reaction to external stimuli or even to a neurological process; the latter are initial phases of the proper psychic act of cognition.

Apprehended realistically, human cognition is not closed within the circle of its own "I". It is a psychic-immanent act but at the same time, in its essence, it is directed towards the external world. It is a "reading" of the nature of being, its sense and truth. The act of cognition has both a passive and active character. It is a passive processs in so far as the conception of "cognizance" means: to accept some message or information about an object[3]. Obviously, it is not a spatial-material perception of an object by a subject, but a psychic-immaterial one. Explaining the phenomenon of human cognition J.Maritain distinguished a double existence of an object, real and intentional[4]. A concrete object has only one real being but it may also have a multiplicity of intentional beings. It is precisely the latter that are connected with the act of cognition: one object may constitute an object of cognition by many people. Thus, cognition means a specific existence of an object in a subject, namely, a psychic-intentional existence[5]. Aristotelian-Thomistic philosophy, connected with the philosophy of hylomorphism, describes cognition as a combination of two forms, of a subject and of an object. The form of a subject, the soul, acts through the power of intellect which is psychically connected with the substitutive form of the thing-object[6]. Even this very brief analysis of human cognition makes it possible to ascertain its double nature, immanent and transcendent. Cognition is a vital-immanent process, but it also goes beyond the sphere of materiality and biological life. The transcendence of human cognition is connected with its immateriality.

Human cognition occurs on two levels, sensory and intellectual. Sensory cognition always constitutes an initial stage and also a basis of contents for the analysis of the intellect[7]. Sensory perception concerns concrete-material beings as objects which man recognizes in their external-quantitative aspect. It is on the basis of the material of this cognition that intellect operates and creates notions, propositions and inferences. The distinction of sensory and intellectual cognition does not mean a separation of the two since they constitute one integral whole. The holistic understanding of man's cognition results, among others, from the fact that already in sensory perception the influence of mental reflection is evident. That is why man's sensory cognition differs from the analogical cognition in animals, although the latter usually possess better receptors (e.g. the senses of hearing and smell in dog are many times more sensitive than in man).

As has previously been stated, cognition is an immaterial connection of a subject and an object. Thus, in its essence the cognitive process transcends the sphere of materiality.

---

[3]St.Thomas: *De Veritate*, q.8,a.8, ad 2; q.2,a.1.

[4]*Distinguer pour unir* ..., op.cit., pp.215-223.

[5]Sometimes the intentional being is described as an incomplete or"diminished" being.

[6]*De Veritate*, q.8,a.11.ad 3.

[7]*Summa Theologiae*, I,q.78,a.3-4.

St. Thomas Aquinas even claimed that materiality is the root of cognition[8]. This can be understood in two ways, subjective and objective. The degree of the immateriality of the subject decides about the scope and quality of cognition. That is why the world of plants possesses no cognition, not even the sensory one. The animal world is already endowed with the phenomenon of sensory cognition which, however, has an exclusively vital-pragmatic character. Human sensory cognition leads to the creation of impressions and images which refer to certain determined individual beings. The image of a lake, though narrowed down in its object, does not yet mean the physical existence of water in the human brain. The full extent of immateriality is realized only on the stage of intellectual-conceptual cognition which, though relativized at the starting point in respect to the material world, already has a universal and internalized character. The conceptions of a lake, a man or a book are intentional beings, not pieces of matter. Thomism also speaks about the immateriality of cognition in the objective sense. Namely, the point is to distinguish two fundamental elements of being, the medium of matter and the immaterial form. An important object of intellectual cognition is precisely form, i.e. a set of qualitative-generic characteristics. Humankind, though connected with the material-bodily world, goes beyond this world. Specifically human characteristics include immaterial values, such as thought, freedom, spiritual values, conscience etc.

Man's intellectual cognition is first of all a phenomenon of thought. The phenomenon includes the process of abstraction, universalization, creation, heuristics, mental valuation, estimation, judgement, inference etc. The enumerated cognitive-intellectual processes cannot be apprehended in material categories of quantity, space, time[9]. In its essence thinking is an immaterial process, although functionally it is connected with man's nervous system, especially with the state of his brain. The immateriality of the processes of thinking requires an immaterial basis - a disposition, a power and a subject. A completely material self cannot act in an immaterial way, since then the ontic result would qualitatively differ from the cause. This, in turn, would break the principle of noncontradictability as the fundamental law of being. The brain is a condition and an instrument of thinking, but it is not its causal-principal cause. It is not the the brain that thinks, but man by means of the brain. Thinking is not an epiphenomenon of biological life and the nervous system, but an expression of the personal subject - the human "I"[10].

The distinction between sensible cognition and intellectual cognition becomes particularly evident when we pay attention to their final effects. Concrete things always have an individual character, analogically to impressions and images. On the other hand, concepts, the products of human intellect, have a completely different character - they are

[8] *Summa Theologiae*, I,q.14.a.1,c; I,q.84,a.2,c.

[9] J.Maritain: *Approches de Dieu*, Paris 1953, pp.81-90.

[10] Human thinking should not be confused with the "thinking" ofelectronic machines and computers. The latter surpass man in the speedof the processes, but they are incapable of heuretics. Machines "know"a formal-syntactical language but they cannot work with a semantic andsymbolic language. Sense and value are not known in the world of eventhe most perfect machines.

universal and unchangeable[11]. It does not mean that they are arbitrary-aprioristic products. After all, they are products of the power of intellect which is capable of reading (*intellectum* = *intus* - *legere*) the contents apprehensible in the sensory perception of individual objects. The concepts of a man, a table, or a book are abstract in so far as they do not exclusively refer to any concrete men, tables or books. A universal idea of man differs from an individual man and that is why it omits his idiosyncratic attributes which distinguish him from other people. An idea-concept has an exclusively intentional existence, constituting a psychic product of the human mind. Yet, at the same time the concept of man has not only an exclusively abstract character, because in a psychic-mental way it reproduces the generic features of all the men, whether encountered in life or not. Intellectual-conceptual cognition has as its object the essence of individual things (*quidditas*), i.e. what they are internally and generically. The first object of human intellect is the nature of material things[12]. Man is a psycho-physical whole and for that reason even his intellectual cognition is initiated in the material world. But the world of matter does not exhaust the scope of human cognition and that is why, on the next stage, we create ideas of immaterial beings - cognitive, moral, religious values. A concept, genetically derived from the world of individual beings, is not identical with the quantitative summing up of sensory pictures (impressions and images). The qualitative difference between concepts and sensory perception is obliterated by the adherents of sensualism. That is the reason why Hume reduces the universal concept to the role of an impoverished version of the sensory picture of apprehended individual objects. The idea of man is to be only a specific image of a concrete man. The error of extreme empiricism results from its simplified conception of the human nature in which it recognizes sensory consciousness as the only reality. Intellectual consciousness is supposed to derive from it. It also means an obliteration of the significant difference which separates sensory image from universal idea. Epistemological sensualism, questioning this difference, provokes ontological materialism as a further consequence. Since intellectual-conceptual cognition does not differ qualitatively from sensory perception, the spiritual dimension of man is no longer necessary.

Man's mental-cognitive activity indicates the existence of intellect as an ontical foundation and, in further perspective, the presence of the personal subject. Intellectual-conceptual cognition is impossible without a specific power, different from and qualitatively higher than the powers of sensory cognition. Reflective cognition implies the existence of an apprehending individual endowed with appropriate faculties or powers, to use the terminology of classical philosophy[13]. The immateriality of mental cognition is realized in two ways, structurally and objectively. Such cognition bears fruit in the form of concepts, i.e. universal ideas. Genetically they derive from the perception of concrete-individual beings, but later on they undergo the processes of abstraction and

[11]Comp. W.Luijpen, op.cit., pp.120-137.

[12]St.Thomas Aquinas: *Summa Theologiae*, I,q.84,a.7; I,q.85,a.8.

[13]St.Thomas Aquinas: *Summa Theologiae*, I,q.79,aa.1-11.

universalization. The concept of triangle is abstracted from any material properties and that is why it differs from an image of a concrete triangle. The essence of a geometric figure, grasped in a concept, is therefore immaterial. A universal, immaterial concept demands the presence of an immaterial power, i.e. intellect.

The immateriality of human mental cognition also concerns its object. Man creates ideas of immaterial beings: God, spirit, conscience, freedom etc. The mental realm is also connected with the sphere of personal values: cognitive (truth), moral (good, justice, love etc.), aesthetic (beauty), religious-ultimate (holiness, grace). Values of this kind transcend the world of matter and the properties of its parameters.

The existence of intellect is also indicated by other reasons. Man has a capacity of reflection, self-control of his cognitive processes, correction of his opinions and avoidance of committed mistakes etc. Phenomena of this kind go beyond the passivity of sensory cognitive faculties, concentrated on determined material objects. Human intellect is a revealing power which penetrates both the microcosm and the macrocosm. Man can discover the fundamental laws of being, laws of nature and moral norms connected with axiological sensitivity. Attention should also be paid to the potential infinity of human intellect which enables the constant progress of humanity in science, civilization and technology. The human mind is not a closed monad in which nothing new can be incorporated. Obviously, it is not an actual infinity (the latter is impossible in human nature), yet it evidently transcends the plane of sensory cognition. In its structure, scope and possibilities, human thought is really immaterial. Therefore, at its ontical basis there must exist an immaterial disposition or power.

In turn, intellect, the mental cognitive faculty, demands the existence of a subject - person. This inference is not accepted by everybody; for instance, it is rejected by adherents of materialism and behaviorism. It is precisely in this spirit that the Neopositivist, Gilbert Ryle, has written his book *The Concept of Mind*. In man's personality he finds nothing but a sum of habits, physiological-neurological reactions, acquired modes of behaviour etc. He questions the existence of the internal "I", subject, person, intellect as man's faculty[14]. This behavioristic interpretation of the realm of mental cognition is an offshoot of a reductionistic conception of man. An analogical apprehension of the human being can be found in the founder of structuralism, Cl. Lévi-Strauss, according to whom man's "I" is a semantic and psychological fiction. Man is a structure similar to an ant, deprived of personality and self-consciousness. A similar tone can be discovered in Burrhus Skinner[15]. What is most surprising in this attitude is the curious fear of man - person, his subjectiveness, consciousness, conscience, laws, sense of moral obligations etc. Separated from the foundation of the person as a subject, mental-intellectual cognition is left hanging in the air.

---

[14]G.Ryle: *The Concept of Mind*, pp.269-274, 308-311.

[15]*Beyond Freedom and Dignity*, New York 1971, pp.184-215.

(ii) The Significative-Symbolic Language of Man

Man's characteristic properties also include the ability of intelligible speech. H.G.Gadamer, a leading representative of contemporary hermeneutics, is even of the opinion that human language goes beyond the category of an instrument. Language is to be a kind of an environment which surrounds us and in which we are immersed[16]. An analogical view is expressed by Paul Ricoeur, who claims that language is organically connected with the fundamental ontical attributes of man, as a rational and social being. "Speech remains within all these functions - as an environment of all human actions"[17]. Language grows out of the very core of man's being; it is an expression of his personhood and its development, at the same time. *Homo sapiens* is a being capable of a linguistic articulation of a discovered truth and of making contact with other people by transmitting some message.

The structure and function of human language are not always explained in a proper and correct way. A controversial interpretation of the origin and role of human language can be found in behaviorism and radical materialism. Behaviorism questions the controlling role of consciousness in man's psychic life, reducing it to neurological centripetal-sensorial impulses and to a set of habits and drives. The negation of the realm of thought reduces human language to the role of signalling sensory sensations and emotional agitations. This "extinction" of spiritual life, connected with behavioristic anthropology, completely obliterates the difference between man's language and the "speech" of animals.

Somewhat differently is the phenomenon of human language explained by dialectical materialism. Although it acknowledges the difference between human and animal psychism, it still interprets human thought as a function of the material neurological system, especially of the brain. The acceptance of man's ontological-structural unity, reduced to the dimensions of materiality, greatly hinders the apprehension of the specificity of human language. For that reason Marxism derives the origin of human language from sound and kinaesthetic signalling (e.g. facial expressions, gestures) of animals[18]. The formation of human nature is connected by dialectical materialism with the phenomenon of work and as result labour is perceived as a cognitive instrument and source of significative speech. If the proposed explanation is problematical it is because the sound-mimical signalling of pre-human beings is ascribed the function of a significative vehicle[19]. This seems unacceptable because the "language" of animals is an emotional expression rather than a medium of meaning and verbal sense.

---

[16]H.G.Gadamer: *Hermeneutik I. Wahrheit und Methode*, Tübingen 1986, vol.1, pp.442-460.

[17]P.Ricoeur: *Le conflit des interpretations*, pp.80-96.

[18]F.Engels: *Ludwig Feuerbach*, Wien-Berlin 1927, pp.35-37.

[19]A.Spirkin: *Pochodzenie świadomości* [The Origin of Consciousness], pp.103-106.

The minimization of the distinctness of human language is particularly evident in the structuralist theory of Cl. Lévi-Strauss. The methods applied in the linguistics of the Prague School were transferred by him to the domain of ethnology. He recognized the leading role of language in human life and saw in it a phenomenon separating man from the world of animals. However, if classical philosophy treated human language as the effect of reflective thought, structuralism questioned this claim. The mentioned scholar showed that there is no significant difference between the mentality of primitive and modern peoples, that is, between pre-reflective and reflective thought[20]. Explaining the world that surrounds them, primitive peoples referred to myths, symbols and other semantic measures. They did not exclude cognitive universalization and that is why there is no essential difference between scientific cognition and symbolical cognition. Thinking is not autonomous in respect to life but it constitutes its reflection[21]. Ultimately, Lévi-Strauss concludes:

> *"Linguistics places us face to face with the dialecticaland totalizing myth which, however, is external to (orlower than) consciousness and will. Language - anonrelfective totalization - constitutes a certain humanbrain which has its reasons, but in fact man does not knowthem"*[22].

In this interpretation, the fundamental phenomena of man's mental life, including language, are placed on the level of non-reflective thinking.

Although structuralism justly re-valued thestructuralist-synchronic method in the domain of linguistics, at the same time, in an unjustified manner it questioned the priority of reflective thought over the word. Post-structuralistic linguistics revalues the semantic aspect of language, i.e. the co-participation of thought in formulating sentences, possibilities of multiple linguistic innovations, the communicative function of the identified message, the determinacy of the sense of the terms used etc.[23]. At the basis of man's verbal language there is undoubtedly reflective thought, and, hence, ultimately, a thinking subject - person. A separation of language from the person spells its death.

Behaviorism, Marxism and structuralism obliterated the difference between the language of animals and that of man which constitutes a fundamental error. Many distinguished linguists, among others E.Sapir, recognize and accept this difference[24]. The language of animals is thought to be an expression of the emotions they experience, e.g. satisfaction, satiety, hunger, fear etc. The kind of sound (its pitch, frequency and similar features) is a perfect message about the emotional state of the individual and the situation of the environment. Thus, for example, the characteristic "dance" of the honey bee carries information about the distance to the objects sought. Higher animals

---

[20]Cl. Lévi-Strauss: *Le pens ée sauvage*, Paris 1964, p.355.

[21]Ibid., pp.348-350.

[22]Ibid., p.334.

[23]P.Ricoeur: *Le conflit* ..., op.cit., pp.89-95.

[24]E.Sapir: *Language. An Introduction to the Study of Speech*, New York 1921. Comp. E.Cassirer: *An Essay on Man*, New York 1954, pp.142-175.

"understand" the human voice and its commands, but this is achieved exclusively through the kind of sound. They have been accustomed, usually through training, with a correlation between concrete sounds and concrete modes of behaviour; thus, the dog "knows" its name; the horse obeys the commands of the coachman etc. However, animals are incapable of reading the ***meaning*** of the words and, even less, the sentences they hear. They react exclusively to the phonetic-emotional aspect of the human voice. Some animals, e.g. parrots, have the "equipment" necessary for articulation. They can be trained to emit certain sounds but they are incapable of independently formulated judgements, because they do not understand what they pronounce. They have nothing to say.

The human language is completely different since two dimensions can be distinguished in it, namely, emotional and semantic-significative. The language of feelings connects man with the world of animals, although here too the operation of mental faculties becomes evident (mental memory, intellect). Specifically human language is characterized by the ability of formulating judgements-statements, whose sense is revealed only through comprehending the whole; it is not particular phonemes (or syllables) that are carriers of meaning but sentences. Another characteristic feature of the human language is its creativity thanks to which it is capable of providing an abundance of formulations and a potentially infinite possibility of creating new ones. That is why literary creation is possible. Another significant aspect of the human language is the fact that the sound signal (or writing) is a ***sign*** and a vehicle of sense. The speaker and the listener identify the meanings of particular words or whole sentences. The word "man" phonetically sounds different in various languages, and yet people knowing these languages unmistakeably read the mental sense of this concept. The human language is a language of concepts whose both connotations and denotations go beyond the material-sensory domain. The meaning of concepts is immaterial and universal, but the sounds - as their signs - have a physical-material nature. Animals hear only sounds, whereas man reads mentally the sense of words and statements. The consciousness of the sense is inaccessible to the world of animals and that is why their "language" is entirely restricted to the sphere of sense perception. The human language contains statements of a definite logical-syntactic structure which are carriers of some truths. The latter value is completely closed to animals and goes beyond their comprehension.

Human language is connected with the utilization of universal concepts and symbols. Man's speech is a system of symbols[25]. Only man is capable of creating symbols since it requires many faculties: abstracting and universalization, comparison, genetic thinking, foresight. A symbol has a double aspect, a physical being (a certain sound, inscription, drawing etc.) and a universal meaning. It is an artificial sign, created by man. Signs can be of two kinds, indexical and allegorical-symbolical[26]. An indexical sign, for instance, concerns such a category as "a tree". The sign which is a symbol has a double sense, original and derivative. The original sense is literal, e.g. an image of a dove. The

---

[25]E.Cassirer, op.cit., pp.174-175.

[26]G.Durand: *L'imagination symbolique*, Paris 1964, pp.4-14.

derivative sense is the proper symbolical sense; in this case the dove may be the symbol of peace[27]. A symbol has a universal sense, though narrowed down to certain groups, social, national, religious, professional etc. Symbols have their own fates; they are born and they die; when for some people they are still actual, for others they are already unintelligible. The symbolic language occurs in many domains of man's spiritual culture - in mathematics, arts, ethics, philosophy, religion. A good example of a religious symbol may be an ikon - a physical painting which implies man's psychic bond with the Transcendence. A symbol is usually plurisignative, so that it can be interpreted in many different ways. Carl Gustav Jung († 1961) connects the symbol with the category of the archetype as its psychic origin. In fact, the langugae of symbols does differ from the language of sound signals and that is why it is unintelligible for animals. Animals react to signals but they are deaf to meaningful symbols. The latter demand reflective thinking and, usually, sensitivity to higher values, which goes beyond animal psychism.

A symbol is semantically so constituted that it requiresa transition from the original (literal) sense to the derivative (spiritual) sense. A symbol is a sign which hides a truth to be discovered through the work of thinking. "A symbol makes one think"[28], i.e. it demands attentive reflection. Paul Ricoeur distinguishes three stages of explaining symbols, phenomenological, hermeneutical, and philosophical[29]. The phenomenological stage concerns primarily the ability of understanding a symbol which demands placing it in the context of a concrete epoch, cultural circle, religion etc. The hermeneutical explication of a symbol requires an existential involvement in the theme or domain of values connected with it. That is why, for instance, religious symbolism is fully comprehensible for believers. The last, philosophical stage of explaining a symbol is most complicated. Two dangers may occur on this stage; a too literal understanding of a symbol leads to a "dogmatic methology", while a too allegorical explication brings about the disappearance of the truth of the symbol. Hence, one should recommend neither an excessively literal explication of a symbol nor its extreme irrationalization. At the basis of any symbolism there is always hidden some truth although its articulation is different from that of a monosignative-conceptual language. Every human language, both conceptual and symbolical, is a transmission of the Logos - meaning, sense, truth. And this qualitatively distinguishes the human language from the phonetic-emotional speech of animals.

(iii) Truth

Intellectual cognition enables man to discover the truth about himself and the world while language makes it possible to transmit this truth. But what is truth? There exist

[27]E.Cassirer, op.cit., pp.214 ff.

[28]P.Ricoeur: *Le conflit...*, op.cit., p.295.

[29]Ibid., pp.292-297.

highly varied descriptions of truth. The most common one is the so-called classical definition of truth which first appeared in Aristotle and was then expanded by St. Thomas Aquinas[30]. Speaking most generally, truth means correspondence between propositions of the human intellect and the objective state of things. The category of truth presupposes the presence of two elements, subjective and objective. The former denotes the mentally cognizing subject-man, the latter - the objective reality as an object of cognition. Between the two elements of truth there occurs a specific "conformity", "adjustment", "correspondence" (*conformitas, adequatio*). Naturally, this is not a complete conformity because reality is always richer than man's cognitive potentials. Hence, the acquired truth is not an exhaustive and ultimate truth. Both elements of truth, a subject and an object, are integrally combined. For that reason the questioning of one of them unavoidably leads to a distortion of truth, to its depersonalization or subjectivization.

Truth is always a result of adjusting the formulated judgements to reality. It is the truth of human cognition, also called a logical or epistemological (gnoseological) truth. Such a truth means a discovery of the sense-logos contained in reality, called the truth of being (the ontological truth). In its essence the truth of cognition amounts to the affirmation of the existing object (resp. its contents) or a negation of the absent being.

The value of truth has its opponents among representatives of such trends as nihilism, agnosticism and relativism. The motif of nihilism appeared in the philosophy of F.Nietzsche who wrote: "There is no spirit, or reason, or thinking, or consciousness, or soul, or will, or truth; all these are fictions good for nothing"[31]. Such an utterance should be interpreted in the context of Nietzsche's whole system - his sensualism, scientism, vitalism and pragmatism. He totally questioned the truth discovered and formulated by human intellect. The scientistic model of knowledge proposed by the German thinker amounted to a rejection of the truth of metaphysics, psychology, classical theory of cognition and theology. As a proponent of epistemological relativism, he was in favour of the Pontius Pilate's attitude towards truth[32]. He rejected the existence of universal-permanent truths and, in their place, he acknowledged exclusively subjective-temporal truths. Such relativism was combined with the Nietzschean philosophy of life according to which there is no objective and disinterested cognition. Man is not an impartial observer of the world since he is one of the constituent elements of this world and that makes him dependent on it. Even the distinction between the categories of the subject and object was questioned by him since it was seen as leading to a cognitive falsification of the world[33]. Human cognition is merely "a tool of power"[34], hence it

---

[30]Cf. Aristotle: *Metaphysics* IX 1051 b; St. Thomas Aquinas: *Contra Gentes* I, 59; *De Veritate*, q.1,aa.1-2; M. Krąpiec: *Realizm ludzkiego poznania* [The realism of Human Cognition], Poznań 1959, pp.134-154.

[31]F.Nietzsche: *Der Wille zur Macht. Gesammelte Werke*, München 1926, vol.19, p.12.

[32]F.Nietzsche: *Der Antichrist*, pp.71-72.

[33]*Der Wille* ..., op.cit., pp.12-13.

[34]Ibid., pp.19-23.

has been interpreted instrumentally and utilitarianly. It is a combination of nihilism and pragmaticism, so in consequence one may speak about a vitalistic-activistic truth in Nietzsche's case. Truth is created and selected rather than discovered.

Epistemological relativism occurred repeatedly in the history of human thought. Its classical form may be found in ancient and modern skepticism which questions the existence of absolutely true propositions[35]. Yet, classical skepticism is internally contradictory because - if everything is to be relative - its doctrine must be relative, too. Most often relativism occurs in a moderate form, i.e. it amounts to a claim that truth is changeable and depends on a variety of factors, such as time, man's biological or psychic structure, culture, religious beliefs, socio-economic conditions[36]. The absolute character of truth is recognized in classical philosophy, although it does not exclude the idea of the development of truth and its historical nature[37]. Reasons for the supposed relativity of truth are to be found in imprecision of propositions, vagueness of the terms used, incompleteness of formulated statements, use of subjective criteria of truth etc. Even the very concept of truth is variously understood: (a) as an objective truth; (b) as an absolute but partial truth; (c) as a complete and exhaustive truth. Of these concepts, the first two meanings of the existence of truth seem to be acceptable. What is authentic truth will be regarded as such always and by everyone. That is why the truth accepted today will also be the truth of tomorrow although undoubtedly it will then be enriched. The acquisition of truth is a continuous historical process and therefore it is possible to speak about the historical nature of truth. While in principle recognizing the permanence of truth, phenomenology speaks about its subjective and relative dimensions[38]. Yet, it does not imply a subjectivization or relativization of truth. Man discovers truth in a determined form, degree and scope, and that is why truth is subjective and partial.

The category of truth implies the co-existence of a subject and an object. There are several controversial conceptions of truth which depreciate or neglect either the subject or the object. These are non-subjective or non-objective conceptions of truth; the former are connected with sensualism, the latter - with idealism.

The Cartesian formula "I think, therefore I am" strongly emphasized the presence of the subject discovering truth. In modern philosophy, however, there appeared a trend of non-subjective epistemology whose leading representatives were John Locke († 1704) and

---

[35] I.Dąbska: *Sceptycyzm francuski XVII i XVIII wieku* [French Skepticism in the 17th and 18th Centuries], Toruń 1958.

[36] A variant of relativism is dialetical materialism which underminesthe autonomy of science and philosophy. Still, Marxism does notexclude the existence of universal truths which include its owninterpretation of the world.

[37] Comp. K.Twardowski: "O tak zwanych prawdach względnych" [On theso-called Relative Truths] [in:] *Rozprawy i artykuły filozoficzne* [Philosophical Papers and Studies], Lwów 1927, pp.64-66, 80-81.

[38] W.Luijpen, op.cit., pp.163-166. Some phenomenologists stress therelative nature of truth more radically.

David Hume († 1776)[39]. Although they both connected the process of human cognition mainly with the activity of sensory faculties, they ultimately acknowledged subjective impressions as the object of cognition. Since human consciousness was reduced by them to sensual consciousness, one may speak about phenomenalism in their case. The English empiricists omitted the active co-participation of man's intellect and his reflective consciousness. Finally, their sensualism made them lose man's substantiality, i.e. his personality as a subject of cognition. The subject of cognition became an idea formed as a result of habit, that is, practically a fiction. In this way the scientistic-sensual apprehension of cognition and truth led to the undermining of man's subjectiveness. The discovery of truth without a discovering man - subject becomes an absurd misunderstanding. If there is no personal subject, then who makes the discovery and for what purpose? The world of reflective cognition and truth is the world of man. Only a rational being is sensitive to the value of truth, perceiving in it the sense of his life.

Sensualism is a non-subjective conception of cognition and truth. On the philosophically opposite pole there is idealism which, to a larger or smaller extent, reduces the object of cognition to the apprehending subject. In fact, it is a non-objective conception of truth. Modern idealism was initiated by Descartes who accepted the self-consciousness of the subject expressed in the *cogito* as the only undoubtful fact[40]. This thinker still recognized the reality of the world - object, but subsequent continuators of idealism more and more renounced the conviction about of the existence of objective reality. Their only reality was to be the subject (or subjects), that is, they reduced everything to his sensations, ideas, consciousness, will etc. Berkeley reduced the external-material world to the fact of the perception by the subject. A classical example of epistemological and ontical immanentism is the idealism of J.G.Fichte († 1814). He wrote: "Everything you perceive beyond yourself is always you yourself. This consciousness has very perceptively been called an insight. Every consciousness consists in the fact of always seeing yourself - because I am I. Subjectively, for the person becoming aware, this is an insight. And what is objective, what is seen and perceived is also I myself"[41]. The subjective-idealistic understanding of cognition amounts to closing oneself within one's subjectiveness whose borders cannot be crossed. Man is the creator of the external world and, hence, also the creator and the criterion of truth. Idealism accepts subjectivistic criteria of truth: clarity and obviousness of concepts, systemic coherence, agreement with the laws of logic etc. The criteria of this kind ignore the existence of the object and its objective obviousness. Elements of subjectivism and idealism also appear in representatives of existentialism. And thus, for instance, Heidegger apprehends truth as

---

[39]Ibid., pp.84-88,117 ff; A.Siemianowski: *Człowiek i prawda* [Man and Truth], Poznań 1986, pp.77,108,117 ff.

[40]A.Siemianowski, op.cit., pp.113-116.

[41]J.G.Fichte: *Die Bestimmung des Menschen*, Leipzig 1976, p.64.

a personal choice and decision[42], which clearly diminishes the objective dimension of truth.

The idealistic, i.e. non-objectve, apprehension of cognition and truth spells alienation from the world of reality. Human thought is only a part of the real world and it cannot obscure its totality. According to the interpretation of idealism, thought as if "absorbs" external reality, and yet truth makes sense only as a cognitive apprehension of this world. Truth is a manifestation of that which is. The human mind discovers truth but it does not create it arbitrarily. Idealists reject the world of objects as a source of truth, thus undermining the truth's possibility and sense. Human consciousness is intentionally directed at the world of objects rather than being closed within itself. The authentically experienced consciousness is therefore a consciousness of something or somebody, and not an empty, object-less consciousness[43]. Cognition is a "dialogue" of the subject and the object, and for that reason authentic truth includes both subjective and objective elements. The non-objective conception of truth, suggested by idealism, means a deformation of this value and its self-destruction.

The objective-realistic conception of truth makes it possible to perceive its ontical sources. The truth of human cognition is not autonomous but it constitutes the discovering of the logos of being[44]. The heuretics of truth indicates its objective character. The human mind recognizes the truth of things: their internal logos, sense, structure, purposefullness. Reality is comprehensible, intelligible, sensible (it is "intelligible" in the sense of the Thomistic philosophy). Thanks to the perceptible logos of the world, man is capable of identifying the forces and laws that govern it, the generic nature of things, mechanisms of action, ontical structures and possibilities. The "architecture" of being is therefore sensible which implies the priority of sense of its giver. The human mind recognizes the truth of being but does not create it. The ontical truth of things indicates therefore the presence of the Creator of the world. The sense and the truth of being are not autonomous, and that is why they demand the ultimate primordial source - the absolute sense and the absolute truth, i.e. God[45]. Every truth is a conformity of mind and reality. Epistemological truth is a conformity of mental statements and identified reality. On the other hand, ontical truth is a conformity of being and the intention-aim of its maker. Man is not a creator of the observed world and therefore he is not a source of its ontical truth, either. Such a primordial source of the truth of being may only be God as the giver of existence.

---

[42]Comp. B.Rioux: *L'être et la vérité chez Heidegger et saint Thomas d'Aquin*, Paris 1963, pp.10-16.

[43]W.A.Luijpen, op.cit., pp.95-97. J.D.Robert: *Approche contemporaine d'une affirmation de Dieu*, Bruges 1962, pp.157-174.

[44]Cf. S.Kowalczyk: *Podstawy światopoglądu chrześcijańskiego* [Foundations of the Christian Worldview], Wrocław 1986, pp.172-176.

[45]The organic connection of the truth of being and the reality ofGod are recognized even by J.P.Sartre, and that is why - opting foratheism - he questioned the existence of ontical truth.

The truth of being and the truth of cognition oblige man to a loyalty towards this value in his personal and social life. The logos of truth requires therefore the ethos of truth. Truth is not a theoretical-speculative value but an existential-personal one. The authenticity of being is a natural consequence of recognized truth. There are numerous dangers to the ethos of truth, both individual and social. The former include, among other, the attitudes of dogmatism and integralism, skepticism, nihilism, loss of external or internal freedom. The social ethos of truth also encounters many dangers - propagation of lies and half-truths, sophistry and demagogy, fanaticism, and primarily various forms of dictatorship (political, ideological, cultural and educational, psychological and moral). Truth is a fundamental value of man as a person and that is why all depreciation or destruction of truth amounts to a destruction of man. Without truth there can be no humanism, and even less so, personalism. Man discovers truth and desires to live in truth. Faithfulness to truth is the calling of the human person.

LITERATURE

AYER, A.J.: *Language, Truth and Logic*, New York 1936.

CASSIRER, E.: *An Essay on Man*, New York 1954.

CORETH, E.: *Grundfragen der Hermeneutik*, Freiburg-Wien 1969.

GADAMER, H.G.: *Hermeneutik I. Wahrheit und Methode*, Tübingen 1986.

GILSON, E.: *Le réalisme thomistique et critique de laconnaisance*, Paris 1947.

KRAFT, V.: *Erkenntnislehre*, Wien 1960.

KRĄPIEC, M.A.: *Realizm ludzkiego poznania* [The Realism of Human Cognition], Poznań 1959.

LUIJPEN, W.A.: *Existential Phenomenology*, Pittsburgh 1960.

ŁUBNICKI, N.: *Nauka poprawnego myślenia* [The Science of Correct Thinking], Warszawa 1965.

MALL, R.A.: *Experience and Reason. The Phenomenology of Husserl and Its Relation to Hume's Philosophy*, The Hague 1973.

MARITAIN, J.: *Les degrés du savoir*, Paris 1940.

PEIPER, J.: *Wahrheit der Dinge*, München 1951.

RICOEUR, P.: *Le conflit des interpretations. Essaid'herméneutique*, Paris 1969.

SAPIR, E.: *Language. An Introduction to the Study of Speech*, New York 1921.

SCHAFF, A.: *Z zagadnień marksistowskiej teorii prawdy* [Selected Problems of the Marxist Theory of Truth], Warszawa 1959.

SIEMIANOWSKI, A.: *Człowiek i prawda* [Man and Truth], Poznań 1986.

Chapter 4

The Emotional Sphere - Love

In man's psychic life an important role is played by the affective-emotional domain. The anthropology which neglects it may be exposed to the danger of slipping into the paths of Platonism or rationalism. Obviously, the overestimation of the role of feelings would be unjustified, too, because the functions of intellectual cognition and of will would then be obscured. St. Thomas Aquinas discussed the problems of emotions repeatedly and in detail[1], although somewhat one-sidedly he connected them with the biological-sensual component of the human being. Contemporary Thomists, such as for instance Dietrich von Hildebrand, distinguish three spiritual centres of man, namely, the mind, the will and the heart[2]. The latter concerns precisely the realm of emotional experiences, growing out of vital-sensual life but then entering the higher levels of man's psychic life.

(i) A Description of the Emotional Domain

The understanding of the emotional domain is not uniform because it again depends on the general conception of man. Yet, it seems worthwhile to note a triple interpretation of feelings, connected respectively with materialistic biologism, Thomistic philosophy and phenomenology. The trend of anthropological naturalism has many representatives in contemporary philosophy. One of them is F. Nietzsche who accepted the biological-animal domain as the primordial source and main centre of human life. It is from this domain that the whole psychic life is to grow, including consciousness, mental-cognitive culture, social life etc. For that reason biological life should be placed under particular care: good is everything that develops it, while whatever limits it is evil[3]. Animal life and health constitute man's most important goal rather than being merely means for the realization of higher aims. The acceptance of the autonomy of the spirit is interpreted as succumbing to "fictions"[4]. The category of soul denotes only biological-instinctual life, since man is

---

[1]Cf. *Summa Theologiae*, I-II, qq.22-48.

[2]*Über das Herz*, Regensburg 1967, p.122.

[3]F.Nietzsche: *Der Antichrist*, op.cit., pp.27,36.

[4]F.Nietzsche: *Der Wille zur Macht*, op.cit., pp.12, 15-18.

merely "a civilized and tamed animal"[5]. Mental life constitutes exclusively a product of the nervous system and therefore animal life is the basic component of the human being.

S. Freud is also a classical representative of biological materialism. In man's personality he distinguished three elements, the "id", the "ego" and the "superego". The first one is to be the primordial and most fundamental component of humankind, and it concerns the impulsive-instinctual domain. This is a mysterious realm of biological impulses, instincts, unconscious desires etc., all derived from the material body[6]. Human conscious "ego", although commonly regarded as man's distinctive feature, is reduced to subconsciousness. The Austrian psychiatrist questioned the existence of man's mental-spiritual needs, whether cognitive, moral or religious[7]. Even the fundamental emotions of love and hatred were regarded by him as secondary expressions of the sexual drive[8]. For him man is not the ***ens cogitans*** or ***ens amans*** but a field of the activation of biological drives. They co-create the "id", i.e. a kind of a bridge between the body and psychic life. Two of the drives in particular, sex and death, determine man's behaviour and his whole life. Man's spiritual culture, including his social and religous life, is to constitute an expression of both these drives. In this way man is explicated as a being controlled by drives, while man's culture is reduced entirely to nature.

Freudian interpretation of man is tainted with his materialism and metaphysical biologism[9]. In an anthropology of this kind man is not a person - a subject of conscious and free activities; he is to be merely a knot of drives all serving the search for maximum pleasure. The error of the Austrian psychiatrist appears to consist in his confusing a part of man with the whole of man. Methodologically, he carried out an extrapolation of empirical methods, which he accepted as a sufficient and the only valid approach, to the examination of man's psycho-physical person. In fact, man's sensuality, through its connection with the mental domain (intellect, will), can by no means be reduced to the mechanisms of the instinctual domain. And, analogically, man's emotionality should not be reduced to the sensual domain, either, because its character is more psychical than biological. In spite of its rootedness in biological drives, man's emotional domain is experienced by him in a responsible way. And this, in turn, implies the participation of consciousness. The mythicization of the category of unconsciousness, which is evident in the writings of the founder of psychoanalysis, distorts the picture of human affective life. Still, naturalistic apprehensions of man's psychic life, though presented in a somewhat more objective manner, are quite frequent in the literature[10].

---

[5]F.Nietzsche: *Zur Genealogie der Moral*, Leipzig 1922, pp.334-334.

[6]S.Freud: *Beyond the Pleasure Principle*, tr.by J.Strachey, New York 1961, pp.13-14,45.

[7]Ibid., pp.33-35.

[8]Ibid., pp.46 ff.

[9]Cf. P.Ricoeur: *Philosophie de la volonté*, Paris 1949, pp.361 ff.

[10]Cf. H.Plessner: *Die Frage nach der Condition humana*, Köln 1976; E.O.Wilson: *On Human Nature*, London 1978.

The second conception of man's emotional life is connected with the current of Aristotelian-Thomistic philosophy. St. Thomas Aquinas accomplished a kind of ontologicalization of the emotional domain since he accepted general ontological categories as his starting point. The crucial concept here is the term "appetitus", which can be translated as appetite, desire, wish, urge, agitation, inclination, aspiration. The first term seems perhaps the most accurate, since "desire" usually has a somewhat pejorative overtone. In the Thomistic interpretation appetite is an attribute of every being. Every activity is an actuation of the potentials contained in being. The variety of beings is a cause of a differentiation of activities. In turn, every activity is directed towards some aim, i.e. some good[11]. St. Thomas distinguished natural and induced activities[12]. The "natural appetite" (*appetitus naturalis*) is determined by the structure (i.e. the substantial form) of every being. It is a property even of inanimate beings and of plants.

The "induced appetite" (*appetitus elicitus*) is a higher form of aspiration, connected with the possession of certain faculties and powers. Activities of this type can be further divided into two kinds, sensual and mental. The "sensual appetite" (*appetitus sensitivus*) concerns precisely emotions. The "intellectual appetite" (*appetitus intellectivus*), in turn, is a higher form of man's activity connected with the will. St. Thomas Aquinas employed still another name to describe the emotional domain, namely, the term ***passio*** which corresponds to passion, inclination, lust, affectation, feeling, emotion. It is characteristic that in his treatise on man's emotional life he uses the latter term. What is emotion for St.Thomas Aquinas? His considerations make it possible to formulate the following definition: emotion is an act of the sensual appetite which is accompanied by bodily changes[13]. In the phenomenon of emotion one may distinguish three elements: (a) a sensory perception of an object; (b) a feeling which produces certain sensory activities; and (c) a somatic-physiological change. The object evoking emotions appears as a good (real or regarded as such) which naturally creates a desire to win it or a yearning after it. It is usually accompanied by a reaction of the body, e.g. in experiencing pleasure, fear, danger, joy etc. Emotion implies a cognitive moment but its essence inheres in sensual agitation, i.e. a reaction to an object.

In fact, St.Thomas Aquinas narrowed down the affective-emotional domain to man's sensory side. That is why he claimed that there are no higher spiritual feelings. Such emotions as love, joy and others constitute in fact man's acts of will[14]. This separation of emotional life and the mental - appetitive domain, propagated by traditional Thomism, is often questioned today[15]. It really seems that one should not separate emotional

[11]*Contra Gentes* III, 16.

[12]*Summa Theologiae* I, q.81, a.1.c; *Contra Gentes* II, 47.

[13]*Summa Theologiae* I-II, q.22, a.1.

[14]*Summa Theologiae* I, q.81, a.1.c; I-II, q.22, a.3,c and ad.3.

[15]F.Sawicki: *Bóg jest miłością* [God is Love], Kraków 1949, p.34. Although St. Thomas Aquinas seemed in principle to negate the existence of spiritual emotions, yet he frequently seemed to acknowledge their presence in man's internal life; cf. *Summa Theologiae* I-II, q.26, a.2. We can find there a distinction of two

experiences from the realm of sensual appetites. It is from the latter that emotions derive, although they are not limited to it; sensual appetites are caused by certain stimuli, whereas emotions can have no object; the former have an active character, while the latter are, in principle, passive-receptive experiences. The holistic understanding of man also makes it possible to speak of emotional life in respect to the mental domain.

The third conception of emotions, today very popular, was initiated by phenomenology. This trend actually goes back to F. Brentano († 1917) who broke away from the Aristotelian division of man's psychic life into the realm of cognition (senses, intellect) and that of appetites (will). The German thinker distinguished representations (concepts), judgements and emotions. He claimed that all these psychic experiences have an intentional-cognitive character, i.e. that they refer to certain objects. Therefore, the domain of emotions cannot be reduced exclusively to sensations and sensory experiences[16]. Emotions constitute an integral element of man's internal experience and imply a reference to an object. Such an object is apprehended in terms of good or evil, i.e. on the plane of values. In this way the realm of emotions became strictly connected with axiology, also including ethics. Emotional experiences can be exemplified by the feeling of love which makes it possible to characterize the phenomenon of good and classify its qualities. In Brentano's Ethics we read: "We call something good when the love concerning it is right"[17]. The description indicates that the domain of emotions is comprehended very broadly, i.e. as a combination of emotions and will, for only then can one speak of "right" love. Emotions always have a subjective character, although this cannot be identified with subjectivism.

The phenomenological conception of emotions was presented much more fully by Max Scheler († 1928), the author of *Wesen und Formen der Sympathie*. Although he did not develop there his theory of emotions in a systematic way, still he ascribed to them a crucial role in man's life. The emotional domain is the "sym-pathizing 'heart'" of man[18], and the core of his personality. Some commmentators even speak about Scheler's pan-emotionalism[19]. Although it is perhaps too extreme an interpretation of his philosophy, nevertheless emotions do play a very significant role, both epistemological and existential-personal, in his conception. The German thinker separated two important kinds of human cognition, sensory-intellectual, directed at the world of things, and emotional, directed towards the world of values. Intellect is to be insensitive to the realm of values, because it separates values too radically from man's experiences. Only emotions have

---

forms of love: (1) emotional-appetitive, and (2) the act of the will. The unity of the phenomenon of love makes it possible to speak about love as a spiritual-emotional experience.

[16]F.Brentano: *Vom Ursprung sittlicher Erkenntnis*, Hamburg 1955, pp.18 ff; H.Buczyńska-Garewicz: *Uczucia i rozum w świecie wartości* [Emotions and Reason in the World of Values], Wrocław 1975, pp.77-114.

[17]*Vom Ursprung sittlicher Erkenntnis*, p.17.

[18]M.Scheler: *Wesen und Formen der Sympathie*, pp.144-148.

[19]K.Kanthack: *Max Scheler. Zur Krisis der Ehrfurcht*, Berlin 1948.

therefore been accepted as capable of apprehending values. Thus, Scheler demonstrates here emotional intuitionism, a theory which endows the realm of emotions with cognitive exclusiveness in respect to the world of values. In this respect the author accepts the "obviousness" of emotional-appetitive experiencies[20]. Values are apprehensible in emotions and only in them. Such an interpretation of the emotional domain stands in contrast to the positivistic-sensualistic understanding of emotions. Although connected with the domain of senses, emotions are not restricted to it. They play both cognitive and existential roles, developing man's personality by incorporating it in the world of values.

The phenomenological conception of emotions was continued and expanded by Dietrich von Hildebrand († 1977). He was opposed to the naturalistic interpretation of emotional life, i.e. its reduction to the biological-sensual plane. The author distinguished and discussed various forms of emotions: passions, moods, sensations, impressions, experiences of values etc.[21] The richness of emotional life makes it impossible to reduce it exclusively to the plane of sensual impressions and reactions; some emotions undoubtedly have a bodily character, while others are psychic-spiritual. The former cover, first of all, the passions, i.e. feelings connected with man's somatic side. They have an irrational character and, to a large extent, are beyond the control of intellect and will. This concerns primarily pre-reflective moments of the functioning of exceptionally strong passions[22]. Yet, many other emotions have a psychic-mental and spiritual character; they are usually inspired by higher values - first of all, moral and religious[23]. Man's emotional response to perceived values is connected with the recognition of existential obligations, also including ethical duties.

The phenomenological conception of emotions was criticized on many occasions. This also holds true about Scheler's theory of emotionalism which is accused of irrationalism, especially as concerns the conception of love[24]. The criticism is justified in so far as Scheler's emotional intuitionism is in fact anti-intellectualistic to some extent. However, the phenomenologist justly questioned the traditional view that man's emotional domain plays no cognitive role. After all, the subjectivity of emotional experiences cannot be identified with individualistic arbitrariness and subjectivism, either epistemological or axiological[25]. Emotions constitute an integral part of humanity, so it is difficult to negate a priori their existential and cognitive functions. Nor can they be reduced to the plane of biological-sensual sensations. An evident advantage of the phenomenological

---

[20]M.Scheler: *Der Formalismus in der Ethik und die materiale Wertethik*, Halle 1921, pp.61 ff; H.Buczyńska-Garewicz, op.cit., pp.181-280.

[21]D. von Hildebrand: *Über das Herz*, pp.52-60.

[22]Ibid., pp.64-65, 100-101.

[23]Ibid., pp.76-77.

[24]Cf. K.Kanthack, op.cit.; R.J.Haskamp: *Spekulativer und phänomenologischer Personalismus*, München 1966.

[25]D. von Hildebrand: *Über das Herz*, pp.87-91.

conception of emotional life may be found in the recognition of the variety of emotions, their personal character, and their cognitive function.

(ii) A Typology of Emotions

The classifications of emotional experiences correspond to the abundance of the conceptions of man. The naturalistic-biological anthropology has not developed any interesting typology of emotions since it reduces man's whole psychic life to the sensual-animal dimension. The Thomistic philosophy distinguished in man's emotional life two components, "concupiscent" feelings (*concupiscibilitas*) and "irascible" feelings (*irascibilitas*)[26]. Such a division takes into account the subjective criterion or, strictly speaking, the relation of an object to man's sensations. The domain of feelings connected with desire covers various forms of man's yearnings after things or values which he finds precious. Within the scope of feelings of this kind St.Thomas distinguished the following types: love and hatred, desire and dislike, joy and sadness. The other component of emotional life concerns the feelings of anger whose objects are either a good which is hard to obtain or an evil which is hard to overcome. Feelings of this kind include the following experiences: hope and despair, courage and fear, and anger (the latter has no paired equivalent). This classification of emotions is commonly accepted in Thomistic psychology and anthropology. It also provides a reference point for traditional aretaics, because the arrangement of virtues corresponds in Thomism with a classification of emotional experiences.

As has already been remarked, Thomism combines the emotional experience with man's sensual domain. This procedure amounts to the negation of spiritual emotions. Yet, the problem is by no means so clear in the writings of St. Thomas Aquinas. He distinguished two types of pleasures (delectatio), sensual and mental. The former are common to man and to animals, whereas spiritual pleasures are analogical both in man and in angels[27]. Much like the experiences of joy, sadness, love or hatred, pleasures occur on two levels, sensual and mental-spiritual. Not every emotion must be accompanied by a somatic-physiological reaction. And even if the latter does occur, it still does not justify the claim that these are sensual emotions. The questioning of the existence of spiritual emotional experiences does not seem justified. At any rate, the phenomenon of love, which constitutes the centre of emotional life, evidently transcends the sensual-animal dimension. The presence of spiritual emotions enables a sublimation of lower emotions, i.e. diverting them towards personal values.

An interesting classification of emotions has been proposed by M.Scheler. His interpretation of emotional life is interrelated with the domain of values. He distinguished four types of the latter: sensual, vital, spiritual and religious. This typology of values

[26]*Summa Theologiae*, I, q.81, aa.2-3; I-II, q.23, aa.1-4.

[27]*Summa Theologiae* I-II, q.31, a.4, ad.3; II-II, q.84, a.4.

corresponds with his classification of emotional experiences which also occur in four forms, namely, as sensual, vital, psychic and spiritual feelings[28]. Sensual feelings are placed in the human body and are connected with the contents of material-sensual stimuli. They exist only at the moment of the occurrence of the stimulus and for that reason it would be difficult to speak about "sym-pathizing" or imitating this kind of experiences. Such feelings include: pain, hunger, thirst etc. Vital (bodily) emotions are exemplified, for instance, by the feelings of fatigue, weakness, good health or illness. They have no precise localization because they concern the whole human organism. If sensual feelings have a rather passive character, the vital feelings have an intentional and functional character[29]. Their objects are some determined life-serving values.

The third form of emotional experiences includes psychic feelings, directly connected with man's self. These are emotions of joy or sadness, which help to create a certain mood of the internal "I". Such emotions can be intentionally directed and transmitted to others. But the highest form of emotional life concerns spiritual emotions which are already the experiences of man as a person. These are the emotions of joy, despair or happiness. They do not merely constitute a mood (as in the case of psychic emotions) but they are conscious acts of the human person. They express man's spiritual attitude, which is autonomous in respect to organic-sensual conditions. Spiritual emotions grow out of the personal being and they are directed towards this being. The typology of emotions proposed by Scheler has an anti-positivistic and anti-sensualistic orientation. It reveals the richness of aspects and levels in the emotional life of the human person, which cannot be reduced exclusively to the biological-sensual domain.

Scheler's typology of emotions has, in turn, served as a reference point for D. von Hildebrand who attempted to integrate it with the Thomistic conception of man. His main distinction is the dichotomic division of emotions into bodily and psychic[30]. The bodily feelings include, for instance, pain, physical exhaustion, the pleasure of a walk or a swim. These are experiences directly connected with the body, although they cannot be reduced to purely physiological processes. For that reason man's bodily feelings cannot be identified with the analogical feelings in animals, because, for instance, pain, is actualized differently in the psyche of a man and of an animal.

A specific variety of bodily feelings is found in passions, especially those connected with the domain of instinctual-sexual life. In addition, they play an important role in the functioning of a marriage and a family, both of which are founded on the phenomenon of love. However, the somatic-biological origin of love does not undermine the fact that in its essence it is an emotion concerning the whole of the human person, so it also has a psychic-spiritual dimension.

The second form of feelings includes psychic emotions which can be extremely differentiated in man's life. Some psychic emotions result from the experiences of the

---

[28]M.Scheler: *Formalismus in der Ethik und die materiale Wertethik*, pp.352-356.

[29]In this question Scheler's opinions underwent certain modifications.

[30]*Über das Herz*, pp.52-55.

body, e.g. depression, sense of vitality, the euphoria after alcoholic intoxication etc. Spiritual emotions constitute a still higher form, e.g. the joy resulting from conversion, sympathy, love of one's neighbour, religious faith etc.[31]. Still another kind of psychic feelings covers artistic and poetic emotions, connected with the experience of beauty. Between bodily and psychic feelings there occurs a significant difference: the former are genetically derived from the domain of the human body, while the latter are inspired by higher values. Hildebrand further distinguished intentional and nonintentional emotions[32]. Intentional emotions are directed towards some determined objects or values; such is also the character of all psychic emotions, e.g. the love of beauty, good, man. Nonintentional emotions have no direct connection with a given object, as, for instance, in the case of a good mood or depression.

A specific type of feelings covers passions of extremely strong dynamics, intensity of occurrence and mysterious depth. The German phenomenologist distinguished four forms of emotions connected with the domain of passions[33]. The first form concerns passions in the strict sense of the term, e.g. ambition, desire of power, greed, lust etc. Some emotions, for instance, anger, often escape any control of the intellect or will and that is why they can frequently turn into ungovernable passions. The third form of passions concerns uncontrolled instincts, for instance, those of an alcoholic or a gambler.

Finally, there are emotions which, although inspired by higher values, can lead to a violation of obligatory moral and social norms, because of their strength and explosiveness. Such is frequently the character of love between a man and a woman, when the emotion turns into an irrepressible passion.

In man's life emotions constitute a domain which is extremely complex, multiform, often difficult to be subjected to any moral classification. Still, a fundamental error is committed when all feelings are being reduced to lower emotions, i.e. to bodily sensations. A classification of the forms of emotional life may take into account various criteria, for example, ontological, social, or axiological. Having in mind the ontological criterion, one may distinguish three levels of emotions: somatic-organic, sensual-instinctive, and psychic-spiritual. Somatic-organic emotions are in principle connected with the domain of the human body, as e.g. the feelings of hunger, fatigue, health, vigour, pain etc. Sensual-instinctive emotions derive from the functioning of biological drives: fear of death, prolongation of the species, aggression etc. Finally, psychic-spiritual emotions are directly connected with man's psychic-mental life, e.g. joy, friendship, hope, love of man and of God.

The above typology of emotional life takes into account the ontological status of particular emotions, while refraining from their moral evaluation. Actually, somatic-organic feelings are morally neutral, though existentially they can undoubtedly be experienced in a positive or negative manner. The remaining two categories of

[31]Ibid., pp.58-59,65-66.

[32]Ibid., pp.75-77.

[33]Ibid., pp.53-54,57,71-73.

emotions are also morally neutral in themselves, but their actualization is never morally neutral. The domain of drives may be experienced in a personal-humanistic manner or in an anti-personal and anti-moral way. Thus, for instance, sexual life may constitute a realization of the tasks of the human person and then it has a positive character. Emotions ontically higher are not always morally positive, e.g. hatred, envy, ambition etc. The primitive character of emotions is not a privilege of the biological-animal domain since it may equally well concern mental life[34]. Every domain of human life, both body and soul, may be emotionally experienced and realized in a manner morally positive or negative.

The typology of emotional life may also take into consideration two other criteria, social and axiological. In the former case we may distinguish emotions connected with the individual dimension of man or with the social-communal aspect of his life. The feeling of joy, for instance, undoubtedly has an individual character, while, for example, friendship has a social character. Bearing in mind the axiological criterion, we may distinguish emotions that are cognitive, moral, aesthetic, religious. The richness of emotional life corresponds to the richness of man's psycho-physical personality.

(iii) The Value and Role of Emotions

Man's emotional life is not evaluated univocally. Among opinions about the role of emotions one may distinguish three predominant views: an exaltation of the atrophy of feelings, an excessive glorification of feelings connected with sentimentality, and a cultivation of the sensitivity of emotions.

The postulate of the "extinction" of emotional life appears among the Stoics for whom ataraxy, i.e. emotional indifference, was an ideal. The Stoics postulated an attenuation of all feelings, both lower and higher. That is why they negatively evaluated all forms of love, perceiving in it a danger of an enslavement of man by his body. In some people the atrophy of feelings may be connected with an excessive cult of intellect and cognitive values, i.e. a specific hypertrophy of the mind[35]. People of this type are satisfied with the attitude of an examiner or a detached observer, consciously renouncing any heart throbbing and emotions. Such an attitude may actually lead to emotional coolness and then to moral indifference. Emotional atrophy may also result from ethical cynicism, although then it is at the same time connected with lack of moral principles.

Emotional atrophy does not always have an unrestricted character. The history of man and his philosophical thought contains records of the phenomenon of selective atrophy. A classical example may be found in the theory of immoralism postulated by F.Nietzsche.

---

[34]Some writers distinguish three classes of feelings: archaic- primitive (satisfying personal needs and needs of the species), higher emotions (erotic values serving the family), and the highest values (altruism, ascesis etc.).

[35]*Über das Herz*, pp.101-103.

He questioned the existential role of man's positive emotions, such as love, good, charity, ethics etc.[36] At the same time, however, he glorified negative emotions: fight, hatred, cult of violence, biological drives etc. His critique of positive feelings was connected with materialistic biologism, which reduces man's being to the level of animal life. Since man is described as "a civilized animal", the emotions which favour ethics are treated as spurious luxury. Nietzsche's philosophy finds many adherents, among others, in cynics, in people ashamed of demonstrating benevolence, in people indifferent to the fate of others, in egoists etc. Yet, these same people feel no shame when manifesting negative emotions, e.g. anger, contempt or antipathy.

Emotional indifference may also have its sources of philosophical character. Some representatives of traditional philosophy consciously diminish the role of emotions in man's life, because they are afraid of subjectivism and emotionalism[37]. The category of feelings is associated with the attitudes of irrationalism, anti-intellectualism etc. In fact, however, it is a kind of anti-personalism since the domain of emotions constitutes an integral part of the human being. Struggle against excesses and abuses of emotions does not necessarily justify the questioning of their positive role.

Emotional atrophy is not the only danger to man's spiritual life[38]. Equally dangerous is emotional hypertrophy which assumes various forms and sources. Excessive predominance of feelings is particularly dangerous when emotion is excluded from the control of intellect and will. In such a case, even feelings positive in themselves may bring about catastrophic consequences, e.g. religiosity experienced only emotionally may lead to fanaticism. Another form of emotional hypertrophy is excessive emotionalism or sentimentalism which is accompanied by a depreciation of everyday life, intellectual cognition and self-discipline. Superficial people are frequently exposed to the dangers of sentimentalism and auto-sentimentalism which lead to egocentrism. The object of attention does not then concern objective universal values but the individual "I". Another negative symptom of excessive sentimentalism is the separation of emotions from other components of the human person, because then the emotional "discharge", e.g. in the form of regret for committed evil, is deprived of any deeper influence on man's real behaviour. Finally, there is also a possibility of the so-called "tyranny of the heart" whose symptom is a disordered love of man[39]. In this case, for example, a man is unable to refuse money to a notorious drunkard, parents spoil their children, the superiors tolerate lack of discipline in work etc.

Man's proper attitude is neither sentimentalism nor atrophy of emotions, but emotional sensitivity. Emotions constitute an integral component of the human person

---

[36]S.Kowalczyk: "Konsekwencje zanegowania miłości i miłosierdzia w myśli Friedricha Nietzschego" [Consequence of the Negation of Love and Charity in the Thought of Friedrich Nietzsche], *Chrześcijanin w świecie* 15 (1983) nr.11, pp.69-77.

[37]*Über das Herz*, pp.82-83,88-91.

[38]Ibid., pp.93 ff.,117-120.

[39]Ibid., pp.117 ff.

and that is why they accompany his thoughts, decisions and actions. Emotions play multiple roles, for instance, theoretical-cognitive and existential-social. The cognitive function of emotional experiences was particularly emphasized by Max Scheler, especially in respect to the ethical and religious domains of man's life[40]. Generally, it is assumed that feelings constitute a "reaction" to perceived values. In this sense it is possible to speak of their cognitive function, at least in respect to the individual person. A special part in emotional life is played by broadly understood love which cannot be said to have no participation in the process of getting to know people and values connected with them. Naturally, emotional cognition cannot replace intellectual-theoretical cognition, but the latter does not exclude the former, either. Scheler's emotional intuitionism is controversial in its schematism, yet today it is hard to totally question the participation of emotions in the cognition of many values. Intellect reads values in their quantitative and essential aspect, while emotional experiences constitute a kind of existential cognition. The same values play various roles in the lives of different people, depending on their conditions, situations, needs etc. In this respect emotional intuition is irreplaceable.

To a large extent, emotions derive from the biological-instinctive domain which is ruled by its own laws. There is a natural logic (ratio) of biological-animal life which man cannot ignore, yet neither can he blindly yield to it[41]. Personally experienced emotions should obey the logic of man as a rational and free person. Emotional sensitivity should correspond with internal-moral zeal, since only together can they lead to man's spiritual greatness. The emotional domain plays an important existential-personal role in many domains of human life, in the perception of art, study of literature, in interpersonal relations, social and religious life, in making plans and fulfilling duties. By way of example we may refer to eroticism and eudemonism. Love, which is a fundamental dimension of the human being, is unthinkable without the participation of emotions. The love which is ultimately rationalized is not an authentic love which, naturally, does not exclude some rational premises of love. Besides many other things, every man is also looking for happiness, yet in choosing it he is determined to a large extent precisely by his experiential-emotional domain. Moderate eudemonism cannot be identified with hedonism and for that reason the right to emotional satisfaction does not mean an approval of the principle of pleasure as a guide line in one's life (even less so of sensations restricted to animal life). The heart, a symbol of emotional life, is an integral part of the human person; without it man would not be a unique individuality.

The function of emotions is not limited to the individual dimensions of man although it is most evident there. Emotional sensitivity is also necessary in social life, especially when it is understood as a community of persons. Anonymity and the sense of being lost in the crowd constitute serious dangers to social life, especially in large metropolises. Traditional societies respected the individuality of its every member; even if they limited

---

[40]M.Scheler: *Der Formalismus* ..., pp.10 ff., 263 ff.

[41]*Über das Herz*, pp.126-128, 160.

his freedom, they did so for the sake of the good perceived in a longer perspective. A multi-generational family provides an emphatic confirmation of this statement. Contemporary societies are characterized by atomization and disruption of individual-personal ties. As a result, social relations lead to the objectivization and reification of man, which is connected with the disappearance of emotional elements. Totalitarian models of state and society go still further and refuse individual men their right to personal emotional evaluation[42]. The captivity of mind in such a social situation is thus connected with the captivity of the heart. Therefore, it is not surprizing that the feeling of love is depreciated for the benefit of the a-personally realized categories of social equality and justice.

(iv) Love

The emotional-affective domain finds its culmination in love which is commonly recognized as a distinctive feature of human life. St.Augustine's words are characteristic in this context: "My love is my burden; it carries me wherever I go"[43]. The author of the Confessions referred to Aristotelian physics according to which every thing has its natural place. Such a place is designated for man by love which is both his natural destiny ("the burden") and the driving force of life. That is why a man, incapable of love and lacking it, would be "dead"[44]. Love endows man with the dynamics, necessary for life and human activities; it reveals their sense and direction.

The approval of love is almost universal, although even here there are some exceptions. It was particularly the nineteenth century that proved exceptional in this respect when the cult of empirical knowledge and social-economic progress concealed to some people the value of love. F.Nietzsche, the eager propagator of vitalism and immoralism, consciously renounced love. The glorification of biological-vitalistic values and of "the will of the power" logically led to the questioning of moral-religious values, also including love. The German materialist was quite right in perceiving in love an opposition to egoism and that is why he maintained that "a love of thy neighbour means a bad love of oneself"[45]. Altruistically inspired love requires a surpassing of biological-animal life and taking into account moral-spiritual criteria. Such a perspective could not find its place in Nietzschean vitalism.

A critical evaluation of love also occurred in the founders of Marxism, especially in F.Engels. The idea of love clashed with historical materialism whose leading motifs included the slogans of the class war, revolution, and the dictatorship of the proletariat.

---

[42]Ibid., pp.88,105.

[43]*Confessiones* 13,9,10 PL 32,849.

[44]*De bono viduitatis* 21,26 PL 40, 448.

[45]F.Nietzsche: *Thus Spoke Zarathustra*, p.86.

Such an interpretation of human history left no room for man's love as a leading principle of social life. Hence, it is not surprizing that Engels repeatedly mocked at the apotheosis of love in Feuerbach[46]. The Christian idea of the love of one's neighbour could not be accepted by him, either, because it was thought to constitute an obstacle on the way to an effective universal social revolution which, in turn, was to be the ***condition sine qua non*** for the realization of justice.

The negative attitude of Nietzsche and the founders of Marxism towards the idea of love resulted from their conviction that this value demands a recognition of the leading role of the ethos in human life. It was a valid conviction, though it was not shared by everybody. Love is frequently interpreted exclusively as a fundamental law of nature serving the purpose of the extension of life and prolongation of the species. Biologicalization of the phenomenon of love is typical of S.Freud. He questioned the autonomy of spiritual culture, morality and religion, perceiving in them merely a specific expression of biological drives. Two drives, those of the ***eros*** and ***thanatos***, were accepted by him as the main ones. They "constitute the cause of the whole richness of psychic life"[47]. Even the fundamental emotion of love was regarded by him merely as a channelling of the sexual instinct, although the Austrian psychiatrist admitted a possibility of the sublimation of the erotic domain[48].

The somatic-biological aspect of love, connected with the functioning of the sexual instinct, is an integral element of the human being. For that reason Manichaeism and Platonism constitute a falsification of man's psycho-physical nature. Yet, it is not the only dimension of love because it covers the totality of the human being. That is why we can speak about the ontological sense of love. Love is a synthesis of human life: of man's desires, experiences and actions. "Everything is evil, when love is evil; everything is good, when love is good"[49]. St. Thomas Aquinas described love as man's fundamental act of will and a basis of the whole appetitive-affective life[50]. Love is an activating-creative power; it is a pre-act of all desire; it is at the basis of the operation of emotions and will. Deeply rooted in man's beingness and in his emotional domain, love is also a conscious act of will[51]. In this way the ontological-psychological aspect of love is combined with its personal dimension.

There are various languages which can be used to characterize the phenomenon of love. It can be a biological-vitalistic language, or the languages of psychology, ontology, phenomenology, personalism, axiology, ethics, theology, or of literature. The ontological-psychological character of human love implies its personal dimension. Love

---

[46]F.Engels: *Ludwig Feuerbach*, op.cit., pp.37,47.

[47]S.Freud: *Beyond the Pleasure Principle*, pp.38 ff.

[48]S.Freud: *Die Zukunft einer Illusion*, Leipzig 1927, pp.6 ff.

[49]St.Augustine: *De civitate Dei*, 14,7,2 PL 41,410.

[50]*Summa Theologiae* I,q.20,a.1,c; I, q.60, prologue; *Contra Gentes* IV, c.19.

[51]St.Augustine: *De Trinitate* 15,10,38 PL 42,1087.

apprehended exclusively on the bodily-biological plane is characterized by the phenomenon of lust. At its basis there is the desire of "possession", while the leading principle is the search for pleasure. Yet, man is also a subject and that is why personalistically experienced love must take into consideration the personal "being". Love is therefore a subjectivity of a subject, a sanctuary of individuality and the shaping of the spiritual aspect of the human person. Thanks to love the world of things and persons becomes our fatherland in which we can feel at home[52]. Without love the world is alien and hostile for us. Individual and social life, when deprived of love, becomes unbearable. Love is a communion of persons, that is, an interpersonal relation[53]. The biologicalization of love reduces it to quantitative relations of the type which unites particular specimens of a given species. Personally apprehended love is a relation between "you-and-me", i.e. a relation between persons who are free subjects. Their relation expresses rationality and free choice, an effect of maturity and accomplishment of common good. Love treated as an attribute of a person has many forms. It may be friendship, Platonic love, pre-marital and marital love, parental and brotherly love, the love of one's neighbour, and, finally, the love of God.

Freud reduced love to the functioning of the sexual instinct. He did not see (or did not want to see) that man is a person inspired by values. This axiological dimension of human love was strongly emphasized by phenomenology. Authentic love means a yearning after values, also including trans-sexual values[54]. One can say that love is a response to values. The axiological character of love implies its moral dimension. That is why St.Thomas Aquinas described love as a fondness of desirable good and, at another time, as wishing somebody something good[55]. Obviously, benevolence alone does not yet mean love since the latter introduces the element of unification. Morality implies the existence of man's internal faculties, i.e. virtues. Their synthesis is love[56].

The multiplicity of the conceptions of love is a consequence, among others, of the great variety of forms of this phenomenon. There have been many attempts to classify love. One should first of all distinguish human and God's love. The former is love as a need, while the latter is love as a gift[57]. Man is incapable of totally altruistic love, although he needs love for his physical and spiritual growth. God's love is a disinterested gift to man.

At the moment we are interested in human love, i.e. the love to man as a psycho-physical person. It can have a natural and religious (supernatural) character. Natural love is usually identified with broadly understood erotic love. Yet, man's natural

---

[52]W.A.Luijpen: *Existential Phenomenology*, pp.215 ff., 230-231.

[53]K.Wojtyła: *Miłość i odpowiedzialność* [Love and Responsibility], Lublin 1986, pp.119 ff.

[54]M.Scheler: *Wesen und Formen des Sympathie*, München 1973, pp.179-187, 198-199.

[55]*Summa Theologiae* I-II, q.26,a.2.,c; I, q.20, a.2,c.

[56]St.Augustine: *De civitate Dei* 15, 22 PL 41, 476.

[57]C.S.Lewis: *The Four Loves*, London 1963.

love may assume a variety of forms; its object may be both another man or nature. In the latter case we sometimes speak about cosmic love[58]. It is a natural reaction of the human heart to love nature, both inanimate (the seas, mountains, native land etc.) and animate (the world of plants and animals). A classical example of such love was St.Francis of Assisi whose humanism was connected with his fascination with nature. He was not an adherent of pantheism. His love of nature constituted an expansion of his love of people and, especially, of his love of God.

The authenticity of the love of nature does not negate the fact that the phenomenon of love usually has an interpersonal character, i.e. that it is a bond between two persons. Interpersonal love in turn covers two realms - it is either connected with the domain of eroticism or it has a non-erotic character. Love connected with eroticism is by no means uniform, because its actualization depends on man's psychological-moral attitude. That is why it is possible to distinguish three major forms of love connected with man's sexuality: instinctive-sexual, erotic-emotional, and personal. Properly speaking, the instinctive-sexual love does not deserve the name of love because it is restricted to man's biological-physiological plane. It is simply an actualization of the sexual drive, separated from the psychic-spiritual dimension of the human person. In such a case it is a man's act but it is not an authentic human act. Sexuality does constitute an integral part of man but it is only a part. Physiology alone does not yet mean a love between two persons. The falsity of the Freudian conception of love resulted from the restricted perspective which reduced man to non-personal biological drives. The bodily dimension of love should not be allowed to obscure its personal dimension.

In respect to sexual differentiation, a higher form of human love is the erotic-emotional love. The differences between the *eros* and sex have justly been emphasized[59]. Sexualism treats man instrumentally and turns him into an object, whereas erotic love recognizes the personality of the loved person. However, the fullness of authentic love is reached only in personal love which also activates the rational-volitional domain. It is a love of a person to a person, a responsible love, respecting the obligations it entails. Personally experienced love cannot assume the forms of "free love", "trial love", "partnership love" etc. The lower forms of love constitute some kind of possessing man, hence, they entail his captivity and destruction of personal dignity. Personal love reaches to the depth of man's "being". Its object is the personal "you" rather than any individual properties of that person or, even less, social-economic worth. The final act of personal love is the pre-marital (betrothal) love and marital love. Thus experienced love respects the ethical-social requirements and that is why we can speak of the ethos of love[60].

---

[58]M.Scheler: *Wesen* ..., op.cit., pp.105-134.

[59]J.Pieper: *Über die Liebe*, München 1972, pp.139 ff.

[60]Cf. K.Wojtyła: *Miłość i odpowiedzialność*, op.cit.; John Paul II: *Mężczyzną i niewiastą stworzył ich* [Man and Woman Created He Them], Lublin 1987; T.Ślipko: *Życie i płeć człowieka* [Man's Life and Sex], Kraków 1978.

Interpersonal love may also be abstracted from the domain of sex or at least it need not directly refer to it. First of all, it will include love within the family circle, such as fatherly and motherly love, children's love to parents, love between siblings and cousins. These are important forms of love without which man's psychical development would be impossible[61]. Another form of non-erotic love may assume the form of Platonic love and friendship. Platonic love, in fact, has a purely psychical character, being based on a shared fondness of higher values or ideas. Friendship may be connected with erotic love but in most cases the latter element is absent here. Thus, it is a new form of love whose basis consists of a community of goods rather than an erotic bond.

Natural love, in spite of a variety of its forms, does not yet exhaust the abundance of the phenomena of love. The second basic form of love is the love experienced in the context of religious life, called ***caritas*** or ***agape***. Such love takes into consideration man's supernatural calling and the eschatological goal of his life, i.e. apprehending everything in respect to God. Religious love may have a triple object: one's own person, another person, or God. Most often we speak about the love of one's brother and the love of God.

History of philosophy has recorded many conceptions of love. Among them, two have won a predominant position; their quintessence is the old Greek idea of love - ***eros***, and the Christian idea of love - ***caritas***. The two ideas are sometimes perceived as mutually excluding each other. It is claimed that the ***eros*** is a natural love, egoistic, based entirely on lust. The Christian understanding of love is to be totally opposed to the ***eros***, since this is a totally altruistic love, based on disinterested benevolence. The ***eros*** is an exclusive domain of the body, while the ***agape*** is an exclusive domain of the spirit[62].

Undoubtedly, the opposition between the old Greek conception of love and the Christian conception of love is quite real, but one should not speak of their permanent contradiction. Natural love and religious love are in fact different but they do not exclude each other. The contradiction concerns the existential attitudes of people but there is no doctrinal and axiological contradiction. Attempts to integrate both forms of love have been undertaken from the beginnings of the Christian thought. St. Augustine distinguished two forms of love, good and bad, that is, the love of the world and the love of God[63]. Good love is the love of both God and the creation, yet it always has an orderly and responsible character. Bad love means a disorderly desire of the creation to the point of contempt for God. The thinker of early Christianity did not totally condemn erotic love but only its egoistic form.

A similar division of the forms of love was presented by the second classical thinker of Christianity, St.Thomas Aquinas. He distinguished two kinds of love, desire and

---

[61]E.Fromm: *The Art of Loving*, New York 1962.

[62]A.Nygren: *Eros und Agape*, Lund 1930.

[63]*In Joan. ad Parthos* 2,8 PL 35,1993; *De civitate Dei* 14,28 PL 41,436.

fondness (also called benevolent love)[64]. The desirous love is connected with the phenomenon of sexuality, while the benevolent love is a wishing and realization of some good for somebody. The two forms of love can clash but they do not have to. The attributes of the human being include contingency and finiteness. A confirmation of this statement is found in the biological domain where man's sexual differentiation also constitutes his limitation. This fact produces a desire of physical and psychical complementation, which is characteristic of natural love. However, desire need not mean exclusively sensual lust, and that is why the desirous love is not limited to the bodily plane. Its natural complementation is a desire of good for the beloved person. In this way the desirous love can be harmoniously combined with the benevolent love. The thesis about their natural contradiction is a mistake, although it does not amount to their axiological-existential identity.

Love is a foundation of man's emotional-affective domain, being a pre-act of life. The multi-sidedness of the human being gives birth to a multiplicity of forms of love and, indirectly, of conceptions of love. Love combines man's bodily-sensual domain and psychic-spiritual domain into one unity. Speaking about natural love one should neither turn it into a fiend or into an absolute. The acceptance of the eros as autonomous in respect to the totality of the human person and its tasks is a mistake. Sexuality is man's integral part but it has to be integrated with his psychic-mental life, otherwise it may play a destructive role. Thus, the basic requirement of natural love is its humanization and personalization. The eros is neither a superior good nor an aim in itself, but only a means to man's full growth.

The personalism of love, in turn, demands a respect of the ethos. Man is not an animal driven by instincts but a person attracted by values. Love is to serve values, beginning with vitalistic values up to moral and religious values. The axiological and moral context of love endows it with the properties of responsibility and spiritual maturity. The destiny of love is the service to life, and that is why an opposition to life, both natural and internal, is a confirmation of the deformation of love. Love's spontaneity does not cancel out the need of man's self-control, control of the domain of drives, and thus also respecting of the demands of modesty and purity. Cynicism and hedonism destroy authentic love. In turn, biologicalization means a trivialization of the emotion of love. Love is an interpersonal relation and therefore it must respect the dignity of the beloved person. Hence, true love is accompanied by the ethos and conscience.

Emotional life, culminating in the phenomenon of love, is a fundamental dimension of man's life. It is not an opposition to spiritual life, just as the eros is not an enemy of love. The instictual-emotional domain is neither morally good nor morally evil, but its employment may be good or evil. There are two equally false conceptions of love, hedonistic-apersonal and angelical-puritan. Christianity represents an integral-personalistic conception of love, emphasizing the need of combining it with the psycho-physical totality of the human person. The separation of love from the person spells a degradation of love.

---

[64]*Summa Theologiae*, I-II, q.26, aa.1-2.

LITERATURE

BAKER, R.D.: *The Thomistic Theory of the Passions and Their Influence on the Will*, Notre Dame 1941.

BUCZYŃSKA-GAREWICZ, H.: *Uczucia i rozum w świecie wartości* [Emotions and Reason in the World of Values], Wrocław 1975.

DUNBAR, H.: *Emotions and Bodily Changes*, New York 1954.

FROMM, E.: *The Art of Loving*, New York 1962.

HILDEBRAND, D. von: *Das Wesen der Liebe*, Regensburg 1971.

HILDEBRAND, D. von: *Über das Herz*, Regensburg 1967.

HUFTIER, M.: *La charité dans l'enseignement de saint Augustin*, Paris 1960.

JOHN PAUL II: *Mężczyzną i niewiastą stworzył ich* [Man and Woman Created He Them], Lublin 1987.

LEONARDY, H.: *Liebe und Person*, Den Haag 1976.

LEWIS, C.S.: *The Four Loves*, London 1963.

OLEJNIK, S.: *Katolicka etyka seksualna* [The Catholic Sexual Ethics], Warszawa 1966.

PIEPER, J.: *Über die Liebe*, München 1972.

REYMENT, M.L. (ed.): *Feelings and Emotions*, New York 1950.

SAWICKI, F.: *Bóg jest miłością* [God Is Love], Kraków 1949.

ŚLIPKO, T.: *Życie i płeć człowieka* [Man's Life and Sex], Kraków 1978.

WOJTYŁA, K.: *Miłość i odpowiedzialność* [Love and Responsibility] Lublin 1986.

Chapter 5

Freedom

The problems of freedom appear in the very centre of philosophical anthropology. If the latter is not to be exclusively a philosophy of nature or a philosophy of being, it must contain a philosophy of freedom. For, after all, what is man? Is he a passive product of his biological and social environment or is he an active being realizing himself and his calling? Is he only a mirror of the external world or a self-controlled free being? Freedom is not merely a recognition of his human nature but also a vehicle of the sense of his life. Without freedom man would not be a person. The problem of freedom concerns both an individual man and social life. The history of humankind is a history of an unceasing struggle to conquer and broaden the borders of its freedom, although often it is also a history of the betrayal of the idea of freedom, of enslaving others or of an escape from freedom[1]. Freedom is a meeting point of existential and social problems concerning ethics, politics, religion and philosophy.

What is man's freedom - a reality, a duty, a social utopia, or a moral ideal? The category of freedom is ambiguous, hence it has been interpreted in a variety of ways in the history of human thought. Many of itsconceptions are radically opposed to each other. Perhaps one should first separate the disciplines which deal with the analysis of the idea of freedom. There are several connotations of the concept of freedom - commonsensical, ontological, psychological-moral,jurisprudential, social-political, theological. This variety of domains gives birth to a variety of classifications of the types of freedom. One of the most important divisions concerns a distinction between freedom as a possibility of choice of one of several alternatives and freedom as an internal-moral autonomy. Introducing this division, St. Thomas Aquinas distinguished ontological freedom and moral freedom[2]. Dietrich von Hildebrand separated the freedom of self-determination (i.e. of choice) from the freedom as an ability to act[3]. At any rate, the typologies of freedom are quite

---

[1]E.Fromm: *Escape from Freedom*, New York 1971, pp.17 ff.

[2]*Summa Theologiae* I,q.83,a.2,ad.3; J.Maritain: *Freedom in the Modern World*, London 1935, pp.9 ff.

[3]*Christian Ethics*, New York 1953, pp.328 ff.

numerous which is connected with a multiplicity of conceptions of man[4]. In the considerations below we shall distinguish four forms of freedom: (1) freedom as self-determination or the possibility of choice (the ontological sense); (2) freedom as autonomy or self-perfection (the psychological-moral sense); (3) freedom as activity or self-realization (the existential sense); and (4) freedom as a human right or self-responsibility (the social sense). The ontological sense of freedom is most fundamental, while the other forms of freedom constitute its actualization and development.

(i) Freedom as Self-Determination

What is freedom apprehended in its ontological sense? It is not a univocal conception; for instance, we speak of animals living in freedom, of a free fall of a material object, of the functioning of the free market in economy etc. However, when freedom is connected with man's nature, this category is understood in quite a different sense. Classical philosophy speaks about man's freedom as of a natural attribute of his nature. Christian thinkers usually use the phrase "freedom of the will" (*liberum arbitrium*), having in mind a permanent attribute of man. A description of this freedom covers two aspects, negative and positive. Freedom of the will in the negative sense denotes lack of an external or internal compulsion[5]. External compulsion means a physical cause restricting man's actions and making any choice impossible. Internal compulsion is connected, for instance, with drug addiction or a psychic disease which destroys man's freedom. Although the opposite to freedom is compulsion, it does not concern the necessity as such[6]. Man is subject to the necessity of the laws of nature, of logic and of real being, the laws of social life etc. A desire ofhappiness and yearning after values constitute an "inner necessity". But necessities of this kind do not destroy freedom because they do not impose on man a specific mode of behaviour. He still sees many ways of action open to him and then chooses one of them. Hence, man's freedom does not mean indeterminism, i.e. his isolation from the world of nature and humanity. The attribute of ontical freedom cannot be identified with a lack of psycho-physical predisposition, the influence of social groups, acquired habits, inherited inclinations, the pressure of drives etc.[7]. Man is certainly included in the mechanisms of the cosmos, its laws and forces, which clearly narrow down

---

[4]Cf. B.H.Loomer: *Dimensions of Freedom* [in:] *Religious Experienceand Process Theology*, ed.by H.J.Cargas and B.Lee, New York 1976,pp.323-339; M.Adler: *The Idea of Freedom*, Westport Conn. 1958, vol.1,pp.164-172,256 ff.,400 ff.

[5]*Summa Theologiae* I, q.83,a.2,ad.3.

[6]*Summa Theologiae* I, q.82,a.1,c; *De Veritate*, q.22,a.5,c; J.E.Royce: *Man and His Nature*, New York 1961, pp.175-220.

[7]J.Maritain: "The Conquest of the Freedom" [in:] *Freedom. Its Meaning*, ed.by R.N.Anshen, London 1942, p.212.

the limits of his freedom. Yet, the fact of multiple influences does not mean lack of freedom since dependence does not necessarily mean enslavement.

Man's ontological freedom also has a positive sense and it means then a possibility of choosing one of many alternatives[8]. The fact of choice is not identical with lack of dependences, empirical (physical and biological), social, moral etc. Man is not a monad closed to the external world. However, all the multiple influences and determinants do not exclude man's self-determination whose confirmation is precisely the fact of choice. The choice is an epiphenomenon of freedom but it is not its root. The phenomenon which is ontologically and personally deeper concerns the ability of taking a decision whose natural background is man's mental life. The liberty of decision and of choice constitutes a positive sense of man's freedom. The choice does not only concern the object - value, but, indirectly, it is also a choice of oneself, or, speaking more precisely, a choice of a determined model of life and behaviour. And this is precisely self-determination, i.e. the determination of one's self, taking decision about oneself, determining one's direction. Freedom means placing oneself within a certain system of values and creating a bond with a given community. Hence, choice is not a mechanical fact but a commitment combined with self-direction towards something. St. Thomas Aquinas thought that the choice concerned only the means to an end, not the end itself[9]. Speaking about the necessity of an end, he had in mind a natural inclination of human will towards good and happiness. Today the object of choice is usually understood much more broadly, namely, as a choice of both the means and the ends[10]. St.Thomas took it for granted that man looks for the highest good as the ultimate aim of his life. However, since in everyday life man encounters goods that are limited and mutilated, he is forced to make choices. Man chooses life goals, ideals, values, existential models, modes of realizing his aims etc.

Ontological freedom, understood as a possibility of free decision and choice, is actualized in various ways[11]. First of all, it is an ability of saying "yes" or "no", i.e. of affirmation or negation. Secondly, freedom makes possible the choice of a determined object; it is a freedom of specification. Finally, freedom means a possibility of choosing certain mechanisms of realizing the accepted aims. Therefore, the freedom of choice and of self-determination concerns many directions and many levels. It is an exclusive privilege of man and, in further perspective, also his obligation.

Man's freedom is a truth accepted quite generally, although there appear differences in ways of justifying it. Classical philosophy deduces freedom from the nature of the human being, while modern philosophy (Descartes) and contemporary philosophy

---

[8]*Summa Theologiae* I,q.83, a.3,ad 2 and ad 3; *II Sent.*, d.23, q.1, a.1; L.B.Geiger: *Philosophie et spiritualit é*, Paris 1963, vol.2, pp.42-57.

[9]*Summa Theologiae* I,q.82,a.1,ad 3.

[10]D. von Hildebrand: *Christian Ethics*, p.310-311.

[11]St.Thomas: *De Veritate*, q.22, a.6. Cf. D.Welp: *Willensfreiheit bei Thomas von Aquin*, Freiburg 1979, especially pp.15,25,99-122.

(Bergson, existentialism) infer about man's ontic character from the fact of freedom. This difference in points of view causes differences in the argumentation for the existence of ontological freedom. It is perhaps worthwhile to pay some attention to the argumentation of both trends.

The main argument for man's freedom is inner experience[12]. Materialism and extreme empiricism interpret man's activity in the spirit of radical determinism, analogically to the functioning of the mechanism of physical causes and effects. Such an interpretation is contradicted by inner experience whose part concerns the awareness of taking decisions and making choices. Self-consciousness and reflection tell us that we are active-efficient causes of our actions. Before taking a decision we carry out an analysis of the situation and perceive, as a result, a multiplicity of possible solutions. While taking a decision, we are conscious of the existing internal and external circumstances[13], and yet we do feel ourselves to be the doers of certain deeds. The final choice and the action that follows constitute precisely man's self-determination and self-designation. Even after the moment of choice we experience reflectively our freedom, whose externalization and consequence may occur as pricks of conscience or moral satisfaction. The convictionabout inner freedom is reflected in everyday speech which distinguishes between "I will" and "I want". The adherents of determinism explain the phenomenon of the awareness of freedom as a subjective illusion. Errors often accompany inner experience but they also occur in sensual experience. The peremptory undermining of the cognitive value of inner experience, including the affirmation of ontical freedom, leads to scientistic apriorism.

The consciousness of decision and of choice constitutes a datum of man's inner experience, which proves the existence of freedom as an ontical attribute of the human person[14]. The term "consciousness of freedom" requires a closer explanation. Bergson and Scheler are justified when they admonish us against the rationalization of the emotional-volitional domain[15]. Freedom means an action of the whole person as a subject; it is a continuous action, interiorized, passing beyond empirical and conceptual cognition. That is why the consciousness of freedom is an authentic cognition but evading a univocal verbal explanation. It is an intuitive cognition, to some extent also an existential-pragmatic cognition (the decision being, after all, contained in life realities). As has already been stated above[16], the phenomenon of consciousness may be

---

[12]*The Principles of Philosophy* [in:] *The Philosophical Works of Descartes*, op.cit., vol.1, pp.221,234; H.Bergson: *Essai sur les donn ées immediates de la conscience*, Paris 1944, pp.114-135; M.Scheler: *Zur Phänomenologie der Freiheit* [in:] *Schriften aus dem Nachlass*, Bern 1957, vol.1, pp.163-164; K.Wojtyła: *Osoba i czyn*, op.cit., pp.109-128.

[13]This moment is stressed by P.Ricoeur; cf. *Le conflit des interpr étations* ..., op.cit., pp.101-121.

[14]Some Thomists depreciate the role of psychic facts while simultaneously perceiving the essence of arguments for freedom of the will in systemic premises. Such an approach departs from realism in which facts constitute the most important criterion of truth.

[15]H.Bergson: *Essai* ..., pp.165-171.

[16]Comp. Part II, Chapter 2 of this study.

understood in many ways. Speaking about the consciousness of freedom we have two moments in mind: (1) the consciousness which accompanies the acts of taking a decision and making a choice; and (2) the consciousness reflectively returning to the choices made in the past. The element of intellectual cognition, as an initial condition of conscious choice, is something else and we shall discuss this aspect later on.

The second type of motivation of man's freedom refers to the domain of social-moral life. For I.Kant freedom is only a postulate and a premise demanded by the observation of moral rules. But this is an extreme view. It seems, however, that ethical, legal, social and state norms imply man's ontical freedom. The "should" with which man is confronted presupposes his "can". Only a free person has the conscience which, in turn, justifies the imposition of social-moral demands. A free man is responsible for his actions and therefore he can be both rewarded andpunished. Responsibility without freedom is absurd and for that reason legal norms and the commands of social life can find no explanation on the basis of the philosophy of determinism[17]. Without the ontical "can", the moral-legal "should" swerves away from the laws of being and thought. Ontological determinism is contradictory with the idea of social-moral obligations.

The anthropology of St.Thomas Aquinas contains yet one more argument for man's freedom[18]. Namely, freedom is a logical and necessary consequence of man's rationality. Animals act on the basis of biological instincts, whereas man employs his mental discernment in his actions. The important role of intellect should not be identified with its domination and that is why extreme intellectualism, explaining good and evil as attributes of cognition, is also a mistake. The intellectual discernment of a situation is very significant but it does not determine the taking of a decision. The latter is an act of will. Man is, after all, attracted by values. His individual sensitivity and preferences evade any intellectual-conceptual schemes. The intellect signalizes a multiplicity of finite goods and that is why their selection is necessary. The act of choice, connected with the preference of one value over others, is a privilege of free man. Thus, the general inclination towards values does not cancel out the possibility (and, in fact, the necessity) of individual choice. The choice of a particular good is an act of man's free will.

There still remains the mechanism of the functioning of free will in the totality of the human being to be explained. Freedom of decision and freedom of choice, attributes of man - the person, cannot be reduced to the domain of irrational drives and affects. Their influence is unquestionable but not exclusive nor determining the final decision. Therefore, St.Thomas Aquinas rightly observes that "reason is the root of all

---

[17]The thesis that "Obligation presupposes possibility" is questioned by some writers who point to man's moral weaknesses. The Christian should be a saint, but can he always become one? Cf. R.B.Edwards: *Freedom, Responsibility and Obligation*, The Hague 1969, pp.103-115. Acritique of this kind confuses the ontological plane of the humanbeing with the psychological-individual plane.

[18]*Summa Theologiae* I,q.82, a.2,c; I,q.83, a.1,c; I-II, q.10, a.2; *Contra Gentes* II,c.48; J.Maritain: *Freedom in the Modern World*, pp.5-10.

freedom"[19]. Only a rational being can be free. Intellect enables man to recognize the nature of things and values, to evaluate their usefulness for the tasks undertaken, to make conscious choice of means and ends. A truly free action is preceded by acts of intellectual deliberation, such as a discernment of the existing situation, scale of feasible possibilities, postulated tasks, priority of values etc. But even the best intellectual-cognitive analysis does not yet become a choice for which the participation of will is necessary. St.Thomas explains the cooperation of the cognitive and desirous domains, or, speaking more precisely, of intellect and will, in the following way:

> "*Choice is the attribute of free decision and that is whywe speak of ourselves that we have freedom of choice, thatwe can accept one thing while rejecting another, and thisis precisely an instance of choice. For that reason thenature of free decision can be considered from the pointof view of choice. And choice consists of something of the cognitive faculty and of something of the desirousfaculty. The cognitive faculty provides advice whichdetermines what should be prefered to something else,while the desirous faculty in choice causes that,desiring, one accepts what the advice has decided. [...]Free decision is a desirous faculty*"[20].

In the quoted statement some doubts may be raised by the last fragment which implies a decisive influence of intellect on will. Yet, on another occasion St.Thomas recognizes a mutual influence of intellect and will, and, hence, the influence of cognition on choice - and the other way round[21]. Will suggests specific epistemological solutions.

The cooperation of intellect and will is an object of attention of Thomists who, taking advantage of the propositions of St.Thomas and his whole metaphysics, present a detailed scheme of the interconnections of the two faculties. The operation of intellect covers such elements as idea, design, deliberation, command, judgement. The activity of the will is expressed through: fondness, intention, permission, choice, active performance, and satisfaction[22]. These schemes are not quite satisfactory because they do not take into consideration the influence of the instinctual-emotional domain on man's final decision. Man's choice of a specific value is an effect of both objective and subjective factors, and, among the latter, one should not omit the emotional-affective domain. Intellectual cognition prepares the act of choice but the act itself is governed by the will. The choice is preceded by reflection concerning the circumstances of an action, its aims and motives, but the cognitive-mental analysis does not yet constitute a decision. Self-determination is a domain and a decision of the will, which still constitutes a mystery of the human being. Hence, the irrationalization of the idea of freedom is a mistake but its excessive rationalization and schematization would also depart from truth. The decision of the will should not be depersonalized, either, because it is the whole man that thinks and takes

---

[19]*De Veritate*, q.24,a.2,c. D.Welp, op.cit., pp.186 ff.,191-192; G.Verbeke: "Le développement de la vie volitive d'après saint Thomas", *Revue Philosophique de Louvain* (1958), pp.5-34.

[20]*Summa Theologiae* I,q.83,a.3,c.

[21]*Summa Theologiae* I,q.82,a.4,c. and ad 1.

[22]These are representatives of both traditional and existentialistic Thomism.

a decision about something. Rational man does not act without motivation, but an adequate verbal explanation of this motivation does not seem possible. The decision and the choice constitute man's privileges but also his mystery.

Man's freedom is collateral with his ontical status, hence it is a relative freedom. Man's psycho-physical beingness indicates the limits of his freedom, connected with the existence of a variety of determinants. Self-determinism does not mean indeterminism. In his life and activity man is included in the functioning of the cosmos, and is subject to physical, biological, psychological, social-economic and other laws. The laws of nature and of social life are obligatory for man who, along with his progressing recognition of their mechanisms, frequently perceives a decreasing range of the possibilities of choice. In spite of all barriers, man's freedom still constitutes a breach in the causality of nature. Human activity is not exclusively a mechanical result of the pressure of his biological and social environment. It is therefore right to point out the significant differences which separate man's conscious act from the spontaneous-instinctual action of animals[23]. First of all, the initiator of human action is the internal-personal "I", whereas the movements of animals are wholly explained by a set of external and internal stimuli. Obviously, man is also subject to the pressure of the biological-instinctual domain but in his action he also takes into consideration higher values, cognitive, moral, religious, social etc. The activity of the human person is not merely a physiological reaction to stimuli but a planned action, flexible in its course, frequently corrected and improved. Another significant difference concerns the sensitivity to altruistic values and ideals whose realization demands a restraint of the sensual-instinctual domain. An animal knows only training but it is incapable of self-control and self-perfection. The animal spontaeous activity is totally subjected to the immanent determinism of biological organism, whereas man's free activity goes beyond the mechanism of various kinds of determinants. In spite of its external and internal limitations, man's freedom is nevertheless a capacity of taking autonomous decisions and making choices. That is why human activity can be called not only bio-dynamics but also noo-dynamics.

When questioning man's freedom, the proponents of radical determinism usually refer to empirical sciences, natural or social. The repertory of their arguments frequently contains information about such facts as: somatic-psychic anomalies in the human world, hypnosis and suggestion, various types of drugs, the demoralizing effect of some social circles, the dependence of consciousness on subconsciousness, the pressure of the animal-instinctual domain on man's psychic life. All these factors actually do restrict or even suspend man's internal freedom. Yet, the scope and force of the pressure of particular determinants have not been fully explained so far. At any rate, one thing is certain: the enumerated factors depart from the normal state of the human person and for that reason psychic and social pathological conditions cannot undermine freedom as

[23]D. von Hildebrand: *Christian Ethics*, pp.295-301.

man's general attitude[24]. The margin of anomalies and pathologies does not justify the questioning of man's ontological freedom.

The rejection of determinism, however, should not be identified with the questioning of the determinants affecting the activity of man's will. The determinants are of various kinds, subjective and objective. The former include the influence of the emotional-affective domain[25]. Emotions arise in man's psycho-physical personality spotaneously and they affect consciousness and subconsciousness. They penetrate the whole domain of appetites and that is why they are strictly connected with the functioning of the will and its decisions. In a sense, one can even say that an emotional response often constitutes man's pre-decision. The strict connection between emotions and the will is a reason for comprising their activity under one name, such as love or hatred, courage and fear, benevolence or antipathy etc. St.Thomas Aquinas emphasizes the connection between the emotional domain and man's animal-sensual life[26]. Modern philosophy, also including phenomenology[27], concentrates its attention on the so-called higher emotions. They constitute a response to the perceived values and for that reason it is possible to speak about the intentional character of emotions. The axiological motivation of emotions makes them close to mental desire, that is, the will. Naturally, there are considerable differences between them. Emotions arise spontaneously, they fluctuate, they are impermanent and pre-reflective; whereas acts of will are consciouss, more stable, and they are products of the inner "I". In itself, the emotional domain is a-moral, and only the use of emotions may be good or bad. That is why the cultivation of the culture of emotions and their sublimation constitute an extremely important existential and social problem[28]. Although the actuation of emotions is often independent of the will, still an act of will can contribute to their "quality". Our internal "I" can neutralize the lower feelings, inspire the higher ones, direct them towards new values, include them in the relization of the undertaken tasks. Therefore, the emotional domain cannot be excluded from man's responsibility but it should be inspired and controlled by intellect and will.

The combination of the functioning of the will and the emotional domain constitutes an exemplification of its ontological determinants. Man is not an Absolute and that is why his freedom cannot be infinite[29]. The contingency of the human being finds its reflection in the appetitive-volitional domain: in the exertion of taking decisions, the uncertainty of choices, lack of consistency in the realization of the accepted aims etc. Man's contingency is connected with the complexity of his psycho-physical nature.

---

[24]Cf. J.E.Royce: *Man and His Nature*, New York 1961, pp.211-220; P.Chauchard: *Biologie et morale*, Tours 1959.

[25]Comp. Part II, Chapter 4 of this study.

[26]*Summa Theologiae* I-II, q.22, a.2, ad 1; q.22, a.3, ad 3.

[27]D. von Hildebrand: *Christian Ethics*, pp.334-336.

[28]*Summa Theologiae* I-II, q.24, a.2, c and ad 1; q.56, a.4; *De Veritate*, q.20, a.2.

[29]*Summa Theologiae* I, q.83, a.1, ad 1.

Although they derive from the personal "I", acts of will are included in man's somatic side. The latter undoubtedly exerts some influence on the will, on its axiological orientation, range of aims, manner of their realization etc. Man's freedom has not a purely spiritual character, for man is neither God nor an angel. That is why love, friendship, hope, anxiety etc., the phenomena connected with the domain of will and emotions, find their expression on the somatic plane.

The ontological determinants of man's freedom are not the only ones. The world in which man lives also covers the realm of values. For that reason it is possible to speak about the axiological context of the functioning of the will. This problem will be discussed in greater detail when analysing psychological-moral freedom, so we shall restrict ourselves here only to some remarks. Man's free activity is not a noncausal activity. However, the reasons which affect the human personality do not function mechanically but they inspire and direct its activity. Such reasons include, first of all, values which exert a decisive influence on the choices made, though they do not compel them[30]. The choice is a selection of certain values which legitimize the decision taken. Man chooses various values, lower and higher, individual and social, economic and moral. Freedom ensures a free choice of all values but their quality and character may either develop freedom or diminish it. Not all the values are appropriate to man's personal dignity and therefore freedom should be combined with a sense of responsibility.

(ii) Freedom as Internal Autonomy

Freedom, apprehended in the ontological sense as a freedom of will, is an attribute of every man. It is simply a part of the human nature, it is "given" to it. But there is also another form of freedom which is "imposed" on man as his moral calling. Lack of compulsion and a possibility of choice do not exhaust the meaning of the idea of freedom. Self-determination is actualized when man achieves internal autonomy through moral effort. It is precisely the freedom of moral-spiritual autonomy that constitutes the second significant form of man's freedom.

The idea of internal freedom has been known to Christianity from the very beginning. In his letter to the Romans (6,20) St.Paul stressed the opposition between freedom and sin, and then (*Romans* 7,7-25) he distinguished three kinds of freedom: freedom from sin, freedom from death, and freedom from the law[31]. The overcoming of bad inclinations is a condition of freedom. This is the freedom of God's children, liberated from the slavery of evil through God's Spirit (II *Corinthians* 3,17).

Freedom from moral evil was a frequent motif in patristic thought. St.Augustine taught that a confirmation in good is a condition of true freedom. It amounts to becoming internally independent of moral evil. God is the source of all good. Yet, this fact leads

---

[30]R.Ingarden: *Książeczka o człowieku* [A Booklet about Man], Kraków 1987, pp.25 ff.

[31]Cf. S.Lyonnet: *Liberté chrétienne et loi de l'Eglise selon Saint Paul*, Paris 1954.

to a paradoxical situation: the more obedient man is to God, the more internally free he becomes: "he is free from sin, while remaining a servant of justice"[32].The old-Christian thinker warned that evil gives no real freedom but only slavery in respect to earthly gods and nature[33]. Freedom is a good and that is why it cannot be achieved or increased through moral evil.

The idea of internal-moral evil was continued by St.Thomas Aquinas when he spoke about freedom from guilt and moral misery (***libertas a culpa et miseria***)[34]. This kind of freedom was later on partly forgotten, because the theory of the freedom of choice was emphasized somewhat too one-sidedly. The freedom of moral autonomy was recalled anew by Jacques Maritain, who wrote: "Man has freedom of choice in order to reach that freedom of autonomy, the final freedom"[35]. That final freedom is sometimes called "the freedom of the sage"[36]. The idea of internal-moral freedom also appears in the documents of Vaticanum II. The pastoral constitution Gaudium et spes describes it as follows: "And such freedom is won by man when, freeing himself from all the enslavement of passions, he realizes his aims following the way of the free choice of good and when he effectively and urgently secures for himself appropriate aids. It is only with the assistance of God's grace that human freedom, wounded by sin, can make this inclination towards God fully effective" (GS 17). The conception of internal freedom also appears in a number of contemporary thinkers. Sören Kierkegaard made a distinction between the classical theory of free will and "positive freedom", perceiving in the latter the ability of a spiritual self-realization of one's own existence[37]. Another existentialist, Gabriel Marcel, interpreted freedom as a rootedness in values, especially in truth and goodness. Freedom without good will borders on the attitude approaching anarchism. "Our freedom is contained in recognizing our participation in the universe"[38]. Hence, freedom demands an interhuman brotherhood and its fullness is found in love. The interrelations between freedom and higher values were also discussed by Max Scheler[39]. In turn, Henri Bergson described freedom as "taking possession of oneself"[40], by which he meant an active co-creation of one's own personality and responsibility for life tasks.

---

[32]St.Augustine: *Enarr. in ps.*, 99,7 PL 37,1275.

[33]*De civitate Dei*, 19.15 PL 41,643-644. Cf. S.Kowalczyk: *Człowiek i Bóg w nauce św. Augustyna* [Man and God in the Teaching of St. Augustine], Warszawa 1987, pp.75-84.

[34]*Summa Theologiae*,I,q.83,a.2, ad 3.

[35]*Freedom in the Modern World*, p.30.

[36]L.B.Geiger: *Philosophie et spiritualit é*, vol.2, p.63.

[37]*Entweder-Oder*, Dresden-Leipzig 1927, p.523.

[38]*De refus...*, op.cit., p.36.

[39]*Zur Phänomenologie der Freiheit*, op.cit., p.164.

[40]*Creative Evolution*, tr.by A.Mitchell, London 1954, p.281.

A similar idea appears in Martin Heidegger who understood freedom as the authenticity of existence and faithfulness to oneself[41].

Freedom, understood as internal autonomy, is the calling of man as a person. The possibility of choice is a negative apprehension of freedom. Its positive supplementation is internal moral maturity. A truly free man is an integrated personality; he is somebody who has acquired the ability of self-possession and self-control. Through a moral act man discovers the scope of his own potentials, conquering himself and, at the same time, liberating himself spiritually. Permanent internal conversion, the Biblical ***metanoia***, means a broadening of the scope of freedom. In this way the idea of freedom is combined with the idea of the moral self-perfection of the human person. Free will should more and more turn into a good will[42].

The freedom of internal autonomy, postulated by Christian philosophy, is radically different from the liberalistic conception of freedom regarded as a strictly external autonomy[43]. The ideal of such freedom occurred in Kant who postulated man's ethical autonomy. The negativistic conception of freedom was propagated in a particularly radical way by Nietzsche and Sartre. Friedrich Nietzsche interpreted freedom as man's total liberation from all ethical, religious and social codexes. The superman is to be guided only by the "will of power", i.e. his own interest and the requirements of animal life, not by the idea of love. Finally, J.P.Sartre describes man as aconsciousness of freedom. Since freedom constitutes the very essence of the human being, the recognition of God is to mean a renouncement of freedom and responsibility. The believer self-degrades and annihilates himself. The French thinker was convinced that freedom cannot be reconciled with the acceptance of any code, either religious or social.

The liberal conception of freedom justly postulates respect for the fundamental right to freedom in social life. External-social freedom, however, is not the only variant of freedom, for it must be complemented by internal-moral freedom[44]. The autonomy may be of two kinds, authentic and apparent. The latter means merely an illusory liberation of man, propagated by Nietzscheanism, Marxism, and atheistic existentialism. Yet, history shows that the "liberation" from God is usually connected with becoming dependent on the gods of immanence, such as money, the collective, pleasures etc. Each attempt of turning man into an absolute ultimately leads to a threat to his personal dignity or to his intrumental treatment on an individual or social scale. Man's authentic autonomy is an internal freedom which can be achieved through a long-lasting moral effort. Freedom means first of all self-control, self-direction, and self-perfection.

---

[41]W.J.Richardson: "Heidegger and the Quest for Freedom" [in:] *New Themes in Christian Philosophy*, Notre Dame 1968, pp.37-59.

[42]St.Augustine: *De libero arbitrio*, 1,25-16 PL 32,1236.

[43]M.Scheler: *Zur Phänomenologie* ..., op.cit., p.164; J.Maritain: *The Conquest of Freedom...*, op.cit., pp.217,226-229.

[44]Cf. S.Kowalczyk: "Koncepcja wolności odpowiedzialnej J.Maritaina" [The Conception of Responsible Freedom], *Colloquium Salutis*, 16(1984)pp.279-291.

The liberal conception commits the error of the absolutization of freedom and its separation from responsibility. Man's freedom, although it is so organically connected with his nature, cannot be torn apart from the totality of his life tasks and the realm of values. Freedom means an opening of the human person to fundamental values, such as truth, goodness, brotherhood, solidarity, love, hope. The freedom which is egocentric, deprived of an object, and not directed at the realization of objective values, is an absurdity. Freedom is not an aim in itself, for its sense is subservient in respect to the value of the human person. That is why authentic freedom is expressed through activity in the world of values. Values, in turn, are connected with the existence of moral laws and duties. Nietzsche and Sartre suggested the existence of a contradiction between freedom and moral-social laws. It is a mistaken suggestion, arising, on the one hand, from a legalistic understanding ofthe law and, on the other, from the egocentric interpretation of freedom. Obedience to the law may be of two kinds, strictly external (often even enforced) and internal. The latter is connected with a conviction that man is "a being with principles". Ethical norms, encoded in man's rational nature and in his conscience, do not undermine man's freedom, provided however, that it is responsible freedom, affirming the values necessary for the moral shaping of the human person. The man who is internally free acknowledges therefore the existence of moral laws and duties, first of all, the law of love. Love means the fullness of internal freedom. Precisely such a freedom was meant by St.Augustine when he wrote: "Love and do whatever you want"[45]. As a quintessence of moral values, love protects freedom from anarchization.

Freedom of choice is an ontical attribute of human nature, constituting a foundation of any freedom. Still, it is not the only form of freedom, and therefore it should not be absolutized and separated from the totality of man's psycho-physical person. Ontological freedom is actualized and complemented by psychological-moral freedom which is an internal autonomy and spiritual maturity. It is a responsible and constructive freedom.

(iii) Freedom as Activity

Among the various meanings of the category of freedom it would be hard to omit the conception of freedom as activity and self-realization. It is an existential-pragmatic comprehension of freedom. It can further be subdivided into two kinds, pantheistic and personalistic. The pantheistic interpretation is typical of those thinkers who speak about the freedom of man but question the existence of the substantial self. Hegel is a classical example of such a doctrinal approach. His dynamic-idealistic pantheism reduced the individual human person to the role of a moment in the continuous process of the self-creation of the absolute spirit. Within the context of pantheism the German thinker could not acknowledge freedom of will, and had to reduce freedom to the fact of

---

[45] "Ame et quod vis fac". In epist. *Joan. ad Parth.*, 7,8 PL 35,2033.

self-development[46]. Freedom for him means self-creation, a continuous self-realization. Freedom means crossing the barrier of physical-biological needs, and therefore entering the world of the spirit. The growth of freedom takes place through the development of man's knowledge which makes it possible to deepen the recognition of oneself and to overcome his dependence on nature. Still, a result is to be "a discarding of one's own I"[47], since man discovers his finiteness incorporated in the inifinity of the deity. Individual-personal freedom is dialectically connected with the necessity of the development of humanity and, indirectly, it is an expression of the determinism of the self-creation of the Absolute.

In our times the pantheistic interpretation of man's freedom appeared in A.N.Whitehead. He accepted the dynamic-processual conception of being, also including the human being. Man is to be merely a continuous sequence of experiences, sensations, decisions, acts etc. Since the human person is not a substantial being, the power of free will is nonexistent. The English writer was even of the opinion that his nonsubstantial conception of man is a guarantee of authentic freedom because particular "actual occasions" and experiential acts are not determined by the cosmic and social environment. Freedom is merely a potentiality, a set of capabilities, self-causation and self-development, an ontical expansion etc.[48]. This is an ontological-pantheistic understanding of freedom, nonpersonal and nonsubstantial.

In Hegel and Whitehead the conception of freedom contains some elements of truth which in classical philosophy were treated marginally or even ignored completely. Freedom undoubtedly means a constant effort of liberating oneself from the pressures of external and internal limitations, of overcoming breakdowns and of self-development. Freedom-choice is to serve man's development. It is possible only at the price of a permanent external and internal effort. Such activism is therefore a necessary consequence of freedom. But there are also controversial elements in the pantheistic conception of freedom as self-creation. Its basic error is the depersonalization and de-individualization of man, reduced to the role of a moment in the self-creation of the deity or in a sequence of acts. Pantheistic language is nonpersonal and that is why it is incapable of expressing the specificity of the human person. The actualistic conception of man deprives him of a permanent substantial basis, and, hence, also of subjectiveness, autonomy, responsibility, and freedom. Freedom must have an ontological foundation, i.e. it is sensible as a freedom of the personal self[49]. The person cannot be merely a sum of acts and activities because they fail to explain moral categories (good and evil) and responsibility. The pantheistic understanding of man makes nonsense not only of his

---

[46]Z.Kuderowicz: "Heglowska dialektyka rozwoju" [Hegel's Dialectics of Development] [in:] *Antynomie wolności* [The Antinomies of Freedom], Warszawa 1966, pp.274-296.

[47]G.W.F.Hegel: *Phenomenology of Spirit*, tr.by A.Miller, Oxford 1977,p.137.

[48]A.N.Whitehead: *Process and Reality*, New York 1969, p.155; also his: *Religion in the Making*, New York 1926, pp.101-102.

[49]Cf. R.Ingarden: *Książeczka o człowieku*, op.cit., p.117; R.B.Edwards: *Freedom* ..., op.cit., pp.38-53.

biography but also of ethics, law, pedagogy, and religion. And then freedom becomes an empty word. Only a personal being, permanent in his internal "I", can love or befriend somebody. Freedom without a substantial person does not have its object, owner, manager, and causer.

Freedom is an activity of man - the person[50]. The ignorance of this variety or dimension of freedom in the past derived from a one-sided concentration on the element of the freedom of choice. Yet, decision and choice constitute a privilege of an active doer, but not an effect of a passive attitude. Free activity means an initiation of the internal or external activity. An internal act is often much more difficult than external activity, whether manual or mental. Freedom of autonomy enables the interiorized activity, cognitive, moral, religious, social etc. The pantheistic interpretation stressed external action more than internal-moral action. In this way man's act lost its personal-axiological character, going down to the level of mechanistic activity. The glorification of activity and labour, characteristic, for instance, of Marxism, cannot be identified with the recognition of the freedom of man as a person. It is a freedom apprehended exclusively in pragmatic terms, which may lead to an instrumental treatment of the human person. Labour does not create man's freedom because it is itself an act of human freedom. Creative activity and self-realization are forms of freedom, but they are not its ontical source.

(iv) Freedom as the Rights of Social Life

Man always lives in community and that is why his natural attributes, including freedom, should find their reflection in social life. There exist various conceptions of social life and, in consequence, interpretations of social freedom cannot be identical. As a rule, three basic conceptions of freedom are distinguished: liberal-individualistic, collectivistic-Marxist, and personal-Christian. The first conception concentrates on the right to freedom in social life which is apprehended maximalistically. The second conception recognizes the need of an institutional restriction of freedom, proclaiming the theory of the dictatorship of the proletariat. The last theory apprehends the right to freedom in conjunction with the obligations of social life.

The creators of the trend of liberal individualism explain social life as a consequence of "a social contract" whose aim is the security of private interests. It is the obligation of society to guarantee an unhampered activity of the individual. It also concerns the fact of acquiring and possessing material-economical goods. The right to broadly understood freedom constitutes the basis of the whole social life. Other rights - e.g. of equality and justice - are subordinated to it[51]. Radical individualism (as in Sartre) suggests the existence of an opposition between freedom and civil, ethical, religious and other codes.

---

[50]*Christian Ethics*, pp.284 ff; R.Ingarden, op.cit., pp.85-90; K.Wojtyła: *Osoba i czyn*, op.cit., pp.109 ff.

[51]Cf. M.Novak: *The Spirit of Democratic Capitalism*, New York 1982, pp.55-58, 82-91.

Liberalism impoverished the idea of social freedom because it reduced it to the postulate of the right to freedom. Social life is unavoidably connected with the existence of structures - legal, state, social, institutional etc. The right to freedom cannot ignore the common good of the community and therefore it should not be interpreted egocentrically. Freedom is an inalienable right of the human person but the maximization and absolutization of freedom may lead to a desintegration of social life[52]. Individualism questions the superiority of common good over individual good. The postulate of unrestricted freedom may constitute a threat to the demands of social justice whose realization is an integral element of authentic humanism. Man's freedom is always realized in the context of social life and that is why it is connected with participation in its duties and discomforts. The individual right to freedom demands an observation of social-moral norms which secure the freedom of others. In Catholic social teaching we can find many critical remarks about liberalism. A good example may be provided, for instance, by the following statement of Paul VI: "Philosophical liberalism in its foundations hides an erroneous claim about the autonomy of the individual in his activities, motivations and taking advantage of freedom" (*Octogesima adveniens* 35)[53].

A radically different interpretation of the freedom of social life is proclaimed by Marxism. Marx differentiated abstract freedom and concrete freedom; the former was a hypothetical theory of free will, while the latter required the abolishment of private means of production as a cause of the economical-social enslavement of man[54]. Marxism accepts the collectivistic conception of society and that is why it explicates freedom as a product of social life. Much like the whole man, freedom is created by the collective and it does not constitute the ontical datum of the human nature. Since community constitutes the primordial and fundamental being, it is also justified in restricting the limits of freedom of concrete men. The theory of the dictatorship of the proletariat postulates an institutional restriction of the freedom of social life, also including science, philosophy, politics and religion.

The theory of collectivism reduces man to an individual exemplification of society, which in itself questions the possibility and sense of his freedom[55]. This means an instrumental treatment of the human person, excluding his subjectivity and possibility of free self-determination. The theory of the dictatorship of the proletariat is controversial because all institutionalization of the restrictions of freedom is morally doubtful. At the basis of this theory there is the idea of the liberation of man but it is hard to speak about

---

[52]J.Maritain: *Freedom in the Modern World*, p.41; *La personne et lebien commune*, Paris 1947, pp.71-76.

[53]R.Coste: *Evangile et politique*, Paris 1968, Chap.XI; also his: *Pour une charité libératrice*, Paris 1974.

[54]Cf. T.Jaroszewski: "Wyzwolenie i rozwój osobowości ludzkiej w filozofii Karola Marksa" [The Liberation and Development of Human Personality in Karl Marx's Philosophy] [in:] *Antynomie wolności*, op.cit., pp.340-358; *Problem wyzwolenia człowieka* [The Problem of the Liberation of Man], Rome 1987.

[55]J.Maritain: *True Humanism*, pp.39-40, 123 ff.

the liberation of man when the means which enslave him are at the same time justified. The excessive restriction of the freedom of social life may lead to totalitarianism which in turn violates man's fundamental rights.

The Christian conception of social freedom is opposed both to liberalism and to collectivism. The dignity of the human person causes that man's internal "I" is autonomous in respect to community. Freedom is not licensed by the community and therefore it cannot be taken away by it. Human community is not an "organism" but a community of persons. Social life may function correctly only in conditions of freedom and that is why state authorities should not infringe upon man's inalienable rights. Social life means a conscious participation in the community and a voluntary acceptance of the duties connected with it. "The human person is and should be the principle, subject and aim of all the social establishments" (GS 25). The Second Vatican Council postulated respect for the right to freedom in various domains of social life, religious (GS 8), scientific and cultural (GS 59) and political (GS 76). A call for the respect of human rights and the rights of nations can also be found in the encyclical *Redemptor hominis* of the Pope John Paul II (RH 17). Human rights are not the rights of an egoist but the rights of a person involved in social life[56]. It is possible only on the basis of common good, which is a set of recognized and voluntarily accepted values of a given community. Authentic community is experienced as a community of persons and "a brotherly community"[57]. Common good sometimes requires many sacrifices, in exceptional cases including those of health or even life. However, it can never mean a renouncement of the dignity appertaining to a person, of an accepted truth, judgements of the conscience, of religious convictions. The defence of social freedom demands the acceptance of broadly understood pluralism, cultural, ideological, political, social etc. The opposite to pluralism is discrimination which is condemned by the Council constitution about the Church in the modern world: "One should [...] overcome and remove all forms of discrimination concerning the basic rights of the human person, whether social or cultural discrimination, whether based on sex, race, skin colour, social position, language or religion" (GS 29). The freedom of social life should be connected with the sense of responsibility. For that reason the Council admonishes that freedom is not to be understood as a liberty of "doing anything one wants, also including evil" (GS 17).

Integral elements of the freedom of social life constitute the freedom of conscience and of convictions which enable a free choice of the worldview. This point is discussed in the Vatican *Council Declaration about Religious Freedom*[58]. We can read there: "God calls on men to serve Him in spirit and in truth; such calling is binding in their conscience but it is not coercion. For He observes the dignity of the human person, created by Him, who should follow his own discernment and take advantage of freedom" (DH 11).

---

[56]J.Maritain: *True Humanism*, pp.127 ff.; also his: *La personne et lebien commune*, op.cit., pp.52-53.

[57]*True Humanism*, op.cit., pp.128-129; J.Splett: "Freiheit im Lichtdes Unbedingten" [in:] *Wie frei ist Mensch?*, op.cit., pp.83-103.

[58]R.Coste: *Théologie de la libert é réligieuse*, Gembloux 1969.

Religious faith is to be a rational and free act of man, and therefore "nobody should be forced, against his will, to accept faith" (DH 10). Acknowledging the right to the freedom of conscience, the Council calls to respect this right in social life. "Thus state authorities, through just laws and other appropriate measures, should provide effective protection for religious freedom of all the citizens and create good conditions for the development of religious life" (DH 6). The religious life has a moral-social dimension. That is why "religious freedom [...] should [...] serve and lead to a situation in which people, when fulfilling their obligations in social life, will conduct themselves with greater responsibility" (DH 8). Religious freedom is also to serve the common good of society and for that reason one should avoid any deformation of it, e.g. in the form of fanaticism or discrimination of people of a different persuasion.

Freedom is both given and set to man. It is a constant element of human nature as the possibilities of decision and choice which are connected with freedom of will. The limits of freedom may be broadened or narrowed by man who can even completely renounce his freedom. Man's calling is a freedom of autonomy and internal maturity. Freedom constitutes a sanctuary of humanity and its mystery, thanks to which it can transcend nature. Freedom is an ontical richness of the human person and also its hazard. Therefore, one may speak about the ambivalence and dangers of freedom[59]. Within the reach of his possibilities man has both good and evil,love and hatred, brotherhood and fight. Authentic freedom should have a personal and dialogic character, i.e. the freedom of an individual man is to be connected with the common good of community. Deadly dangers to freedom are posed by both individualistic egoism and an ideological glorification of the collective. Freedom achieves its full sense through the realization of higher values, cognitive, moral, artistic and religious. That is why the appropriate horizon of freedom is love of man and, for the believers, also the love of God. Only in the context of the world of persons and personal values will freedom avoid turning into man's self-annihilation, physical or spiritual.

---

[59]B.Welte: *Determination und Freiheit*, Frankfurt am M. 1969, pp.123-140.

LITERATURE

ADLER, M.: *The Idea of Freedom*, New York 1958.

CRISTALDI, M.: *Libertà e metafisica*, Bologna 1964.

EDWARDS, R.B.: *Freedom. Responsibility and Obligation*, The Hague 1969.

FINANCE J. de: *La liberté créée et la liberté créatrice* [in:] *L'existence de Dieu*, Tournai 1961, pp.229-244.

Freedom. Its Meaning, ed.by R.N.Anshen, London 1942.

GABAUDE, J.M.: *Liberté et raison*, Toulouse 1970.

GEIGER, L.B.: "De la liberté" [in:] *Philosophie etspiritualité*, Paris 1963, pp.61-96.

GUILEAD, R.: *Etre et liberté*, Louvain 1965.

HAMPSHIRE, S.N.: *Freedom of the Individual*, London 1965.

JAKUBISIAK, A.: *La pensée et libre arbitre*, Paris 1936.

KOWALCZYK, S.: "Christian and Marxist Theory of HumanLiberation", *Dialectics and Humanism*, (1989) nr.3-4,pp.123-131.

La liberté et l'homme du XXe siécle, Paris 1966.

LEBACQZ, J.: *Libre arbitre et jugement*, Paris 1960.

LONERGAN, B.: *The Notion of Freedom* [in:] *A Study of HumanUnderstanding*, New York 1958, pp.607-633.

LUCAS, J.R.: *The Freedom of the Will*, Oxford 1970.

MARITAIN, J.: *Freedom in the Modern World*, London 1935.

Problemy wyzwolenia człowieka [Problems of the Liberation of Man], a collective work, Rome 1987.

MONTANARI, G.: *Determinazione e libertà in San Tommaso*, Roma 1962.

QUILLIUT, R.: *La liberté aux dimensions humaines*, Paris 1967.

REGNABY, H.: *Philosophy and Freedom*, New York 1970.

REITMEISTER, L.A.: *A Philosophy of Freedom*, New York 1970.

RICOEUR, P.: *Philosophie de la volonté*, Paris 1949.

SARTRE, J.P.: *Of Human Freedom*, New York 1967.

SCHELER, M.: *Zur Phänomenologie der Freiheit* [in:] *Schriften aus dem Nachlass*, Bern 1957, vol.1, pp.155-177.

SIEWERTH, G.: *Thomas von Aquin. Die menschliche Willensfreiheit*, Düsseldorf 1954.

SPLETT, J.: *Der Mensch in seiner Freiheit*, Mainz 1967.

STEENBERGHEN, F.: "Connaissance divine et liberté humaine", *Revue Théologique de Louvain* 2(1972), pp.46-68.

VERBEKE, G.: "Le développement de la vie volitive d'aprèssaint Thomas", *Revue Philosophique de Louvain* (1958) pp.5-34.

VERGEZ, A.: *Faute et liberté*, Paris 1969.

WELP, D.: *Willensfreiheit bei Thomas von Aquin*, Freiburg 1979.

WELTE, B.: *Determination und Freiheit*, Frankfurt am M. 1969.

WERNER, C.: *L'âme et la liberté*, Paris 1960.

Wie frei ist der Mensch?, Düsseldorf 1980.

Chapter 6

Activity - Labour

Classical philosophy focussed its attention on the structural-ontological aspect of reality. In consequence, the problems of activity and labour failed to appear in the centre of its interests. This led to a too static interpretation of the human world. Naturally, it was not always so because, for example, the trend of Augustinianism did emphasize the role of the will and activity. Still, the revaluation of the dynamics of the human being is characteristic primarily of modern and contemporary philosophy. A confirmation of this thesis may be found in Hegel who explained the genesis of man as a result of a variety of actions, internal-cognitive and external-manual. The latter motif was developed by Marxism in which the category of praxis constitutes the central point of philosophical reflection. The role of the act was also emphasized by the creator of pragmatism, William James, and by Maurice Blondel in his "philosophy of the act". The fundamental role of experience and activity is also stressed in existentialism, among others, by Gabriel Marcel in his "philosophy of the concrete". The praxiological aspect of human activity was analysed by Tadeusz Kotarbiński in his *Treatise about Good Work.*

Labour is a form of activity. The old-Greek culture, fixed on speculative theory, held labour in contempt (especially manual work). Therefore, it is not surprising that the latter failed to become an object of philosophical considerations. It is a paradox that they attempted to recognize and comprehend man's personality while ignoring the dynamic aspect of his being, namely, act, activity and labour.

(i) The Notion and Types of Activity

Dynamics is an attribute of any being, not only of the human one. Quantum physics has complemented the corpuscular conception of matter with the dynamic-energetic conception by proving that matter is condensed energy. Yet, man's activity has some specific forms, which are not known in the extra-human world or even in the animal world. Man's dynamism is described with such terms as activity, act, aspiration, desire, labour etc. In the philosophical reflection on human activity one may distinguish two basic trends, ontological-substantial and dialectical-processual. The former is represented by classical philosophy, which accepted the priority of being over activity[1]. It may be expressed by the adage: activity is an expression of being (*operatio sequitur esse*). Hegelianism, Marxism, partly atheistic existentialism and A.N.Whitehead all accept the priority of activity over the human being and that is why the latter is regarded as an effect of the dialectic of activity. Both currents mentioned above undertake a philosophical analysis of human activity. Naturally, human activity is also in the centre of attention of other disciplines, such as psychology, praxiology, technology, theology etc.

Characterizing man's activity the Aristotelian-Thomistic philosophy employs general ontological terminology. Two terms are used most frequently, namely, action (actio) and act (actus). Action is understood as one of the categories of the accidental being, corresponding with sensation (pati). Action is a positive activity, while sensation is a passive change. The reduction of activity to the role of accidentality means a degradation of its role. St.Thomas Aquinas was aware of that and for that reason he frequently described action as an attribute of the substantial being[2]. For action is to be the highest act of every being, predetermined by its form and existence. The concept of the act in Scholastic philosophy denotes both actuality and activity. Action is the highest perfection of the substantial being. Thomism explains action most often in conjunction with the category of movement, understood as a passage from the state of potentiality to that of the act. Action is an actualization of a potential.

The ontological-substantial explication of activity, typical of Thomism, has its positive and negative sides. Activity is explained as an expression of the potentiality of a substantial being, and that is why the hypothesis about the priority of action over being seems absurd (in such a case, being would be constituted only through action). The unity of action and the causal performer is a significant point in an adequate explanation of the specificity of human activity[3]. Activity is an actualization of the potentials of the human being and of the mental faculties connected with it. Materialism and pantheism undermined the differences separating the mechanisms of the cosmos from human activity[4]. A negative feature of the conception of activity in traditional Thomism may be found in its restriction to the language of general ontology. The categories of action, act, aspiration and movement are incapable of grasping the unique specificity of man's rational, free dynamics. The problem of action was also discussed in an interesting way by Joseph de Finance, a Thomist, but his exclusively ontological point of view did not allow him to reveal fully the richness of human activity. Man's activity does respect the immanent logic of being but at the same time it introduces its own logic of a personal being.

---

[1]J. de Finance: *Etre et agir*, Paris 1945, p.240.

[2]"*Omnis substantia est propter suam operationem*", *Contra Gentes* I,45; cf. also II, 81.

[3]St.Thomas Aquinas: *Summa Theologiae*, I,q.77,a.1,ad 5.

[4]J. de Finance: *Essai sur l'agir humain*, Rome 1962, p.18.

The psychic dynamism of man concentrates the attention of the adherents of existentialism and phenomenology. The latter trend is particularly evident in Cardinal Wojtyła who combined elements of the philosophy of being and the philosophy of the subject[5]. He was a professor of ethics and that is why he was interested in the category of the act. Action occurs in the extra-human world, whereas the act is exclusively an attribute of a rational free person. The writer analyses the human act by means of the phenomenological method, yet in the ontological interpretation he refers to Thomism. As a result, he regards the act "as a phenomenon or manifestation rather than an ontical structure"[6]. The act is an expression of the ontical and spiritual richness of the human person, and then an actualization of the potentials it contains. Explaining the structure of the act, Cardinal Wojtyła referred to the traditional theory of the act and potentiality. He thinks that it is precisely that theory and its typical semantics that allow the fullest explanation of the mechanism of any dynamism, including the human act. A conscious, free act (*actus humanus*) is a realization of everything that is potentially contained in man's psycho-physical being. The interpretation of the act by the Polish thinker concentrates on many aspects. Some of them are particularly interesting at this point. As a phenomenologist, he perceived a possibility of recognizing a person through an analysis of the act[7]. If traditional Thomism inferred man's activity (agere) from man's beingness (esse), Cardinal Wojtyła inferred from the act about the person. This epistemological re-orientation, however, does not infringe on ontological principles, among others, on the principle of ***operari sequitur esse***. Activity is a consequence of a certain structure of being. For that reason the human act implies a causal activity of man as a person[8]. Man is a unity of nature and a person and that is why his actions are so greatly differentiated ontically and axiologically. A person is a source of human dynamism, while simultaneously being transcendent in respect to it. The strict connection between man and his act makes it possible to speak about the "personalistic" value of this act. A human act is an act of conscience and the ethos.

Man's act is the exteriorization of his potentiality and also its actualization. The ontological function of the act makes possible man's constant enrichment, cognitive, moral, emotional, social, as well as ontical. Man is a permanent ***fieri***. In the process of self-realization a particularly important role is played by man's freedom through which he becomes actively involved in the world of values. He must determine himself in respect to values: he chooses some, while rejecting others. And then he discovers his freedom which is "the root of the man becoming good or bad through his acts"[9]. A moral act results in "self-possession" and "self-control", appertaining only to man as his task.

---

[5]K.Wojtyła: *Osoba i czyn* [The Person and the Act], Kraków 1969. Cf. also *Analecta Cracoviensa* 5-6 (1973-1974), pp.243-263.

[6]*Osoba i czyn*, p.32.

[7]Ibid., pp.14,189.

[8]Ibid., pp.70,77,119,189-190,288 ff.

[9]Ibid., p.104.

"Thus, on the one hand, a person is what rules and controls itself, while, on the other - what it itself rules"[10]. Self-determination is connected with internal and external acts which, in turn, lead to man's self-realization. In this way, Karol Wojtyła's analysis of human dynamism goes beyond traditional Thomism, because he perceives the perspective of the self-realization and self-creation of the human person. This motif has become quite evident in some encyclicals, among others, in *Laborem exercens* (no.9).

The role of activity was revalued in the domain of philosophy by Maurice Blondel († 1949). If Scholastic philosophy treated activity rather marginally, the French Catholic thinker perceived in it a crucial problem of reality, especially of the human being. Activity is a kind of a "clue" which enables a correct explanation of nature, man, and even God[11]. Descartes accepted the phenomenon of thought as a basis of philosophical reflection, while Blondel - the phenomenon of activity. It is not the ***cogito*** but the ***ago*** that conditions the correct reading of the nature of the human person and for that reason philosophy should become "the philosophy of activity". Philosophy is a reflection of the intellect of the acting man. The epistemological function of activity is a consequence of the fact that action is an ontological bond of thought and life, individuality and generality, immanence and transcendence. Activity is a substantial unity, the ***vinculum*** of the whole reality[12].

Revaluing activity epistemologically and methodologically, Blondel explained its role according to the assumptions of classical philosophy. This was evident in respect to anthropology, social philosophy and the philosophy of God. He perceived the task of philosophy in discovering the ontical determinants of human activity, its vital logic, directions and sense. First of all, "pure activity", deprived of an ontical subject - doer, is impossible[13]. Human activity is always conscious and free, constituting a specific play of motives, values, aims etc. It is not an effect of the determinants of nature but it constitutes a fruit of man's consciousness and freedom. Activity is also an expression of the unity between an individual man and various circles of social life. Man's activity is a set of interpersonal relations in consequence of which man is integrated with his family and with his fatherland, his nation[14]. Although the human person is transcendent in respect to the community, it is not a monad. As Blondel pointed out, spiritual atomicity is a false alternative in human life. Finally, activity plays an important role in man's existential road towards God. The awareness of the deepest ontical bases of activity makes it possible to discover the presence of the Infinity, that is, of God[15]. The

---

[10]Ibid., pp.110-111; cf. K.Wojtyła: "Osobowa struktura samostanowienia" [The Personal Structure of Selfdetermination], *Roczniki Filozoficzne* 29 (1981) nr 2, p.10.

[11]M.Blondel: *L'action* (1893), Paris 1950, p.XXIII.

[12]M.Blondel: *L'action*, vol.1: *Le probl ème des causes secondes et le pur agir*, Paris 1949, pp.55 ff; vol.2: *L'action humain et les conditions de son aboutissement*, Paris 1963, pp.153 ff.

[13]*L'action*, vol.1, p.94; vol.2, pp.15 ff.

[14]*L'action*, vol.2, pp.212,253-276,483.

[15]Ibid., pp.61 ff.,80,155 ff,334,347.

dynamism of the human person cannot be finalized in nothingness or in a finite being, but only in the Pure Act and the most perfect Person. Blondel did not explicitly formulate the eudemonic argument but, in fact, all his philosophy showed the direction of the ***élan*** of human activities and aspirations towards God. Man directs himself towards his Creator not only through an intellectual analysis of being but also, and primarily, through a personal discovery of truth inspired by love. Man cannot do without religious life and without God, and that is why his calling is to go towards God. Thus, activity is a mirror of the human person and its ontical calling.

Thomism and Blondel emphasized the personalistic character of human activity. A completely different cognitive and ontical point of view can be found in Marxism. In the centre of its interest there is a material-productive and social activity, called ***praxis***[16]. In contemporary Marxism, referring to juvenile writings of Karl Marx († 1883), there function several interpretations of the category of praxis: dogmatic - scientistic, subjectivistic - idealistic, and an intermediate one. It is also possible to distinguish broad and narrow interpretations of the ***praxis*** in the writings of Marxists. The broad understanding of practice is characteristic of those authors who use this term to cover both man's material activity and his social-political, ideological, scientific, educational and other activities[17]. The ***praxis*** means a totality of the human being and life, among others, man's psychic-mental life. This is an anthropological conception of practice within Marxism.

There is also a narrow interpretation of the ***praxis***, identified with the process of producing material goods. Here practice means primarily man's material activity, first of all, economic and social. Hence, practice does not include the theoretical-spiritual activities, such as cognitive reflection, contemplation of works of art or the beauty of nature, educational work, man's internal life. The proponents of the narrow understanding of the ***praxis*** justify their position by systemic-doctrinal reasons. "With such a broad apprehension of the category of the ***praxis***, all Marxist considerations about the verification of the theory by practice, about practice as the criterion of truth, lose all sense"[18]. It is easy to understand the cause of the Marxists' anxiety: if the ***praxis*** covers the theory, then there is no sense to speak about the priority of practice over theory, endowing it with the function of the verifier of truth etc. At any rate, Marxism acknowledges practice as the central philosophical category and ascribes to it various functions, epistemological, ontological, axiological. Material-manual activity was therefore accepted as a significant factor of the humanization of prehuman beings.

---

[16]S.Kowalczyk: "Teoria i praktyka w poglądach marksistowskich" [Theory and Practice in Marxist Considerations] [in:] *Kontemplacja i działanie* [Contemplation and Activity], Lublin 1984, pp.95-115.

[17]Cf. K.Martel: *Podstawowe zagadnienia marksistowskiej teorii poznania* [The Fundamental Problems of the Marxist Theory of Cognition], Warszawa 1961, pp.192 ff.

[18]T.Jaroszewski: *Rozważania o praktyce* [Considerations about Practice], Warszawa 1974, p.98; cf. also pp.108-109.

Activities are multiple and differentiated. First of all, one should distinguish the physico-chemical and biological dynamism of nature from the activity of man. The former type of activity is entirely determined, while the latter is not. Aristotle distinguished three types of human activities: cognitive-theoretical (*speculabilia*), practical-moral (*agibilia*), and productive (*factibilia*). This division, connected with the classification of sciences and contempt for physical work prevailing at that time, is often criticised today. Christian philosophy emphasizes the differences between man's internal act and his external-somatic activity. Yet, the internal act should not be identified exclusively with thought, because in this case an important role is played by the domain of will. The latter division is connected with the distinction between immanent activity and transitive activity[19]. The former perfects man himself and is closed within the limit of his individual being. On the other hand, transitive activity is initiated within the human person but finalized in an already different being. Physical work is precisely an example of the latter type of activity. Christian thought draws a line between "man's act" and a "human act"; the former can have a pre-reflective and unconscious character, while the latter is a conscious and free act of man. The latter distinction is apprehended somewhat differently by Karol Wojtyła who speaks about active and passive activity[20]. The former concerns the dynamism of man's psychic-mental domain, while the latter - the dynamism of the somatic-vegetative level. In other words, the division concerns two fundamental types of man's activity, connected with the body and with the soul. This two-level structure of the human being makes it possible to differentiate various forms of his activity: organic - biological, physical-manual, cognitive (discursive and contemplative), emotional, volitional, artistic, ideological etc. This abundance of human dynamism is sometimes obscured because all activities are interpreted as effects of some determinants. One can also distinguish individual and social activities, the latter being connected with the functioning of the family, nation, professional groups etc.

There still remains to be analysed the relation between the categories of activity and labour. The latter is undoubtedly a fundamental and universal form of human activity but can one say that every activity is labour? It is not labour when one is active practising some personal hobbies which, nevertheless, constitute a form of recreation necessary for man. It seems that many other forms of the activities of the human person could not be placed within the borders of the category of labour. Thus, one would not regard as labour acts of consciousness and self-consciousness, emotional sensations, impulses, reflexes, non-reflective thinking, processes of sensual and intellectual instinctive cognition, religious life, existential experiences of the beauty of nature or works of art etc. The dynamism of the human person goes in many directions beyond the domain of labour.

At any rate, a precise description of human labour constitutes a problem in itself. Its definition is difficult for many reasons: differences in subjective experiences, variety of social-economic systems, multiplicity of disciplines involved in looking for an integral

---

[19]J. de Finance: *Etre et agir*, pp.209 ff.

[20]*Osoba i czyn*, op.cit., pp.102 ff.

description, possible worldviews and social-political options, differentiation of forms of labour etc. Some authors define labour in a narrow way and perceive in it mainly a creation of material goods which are socially useful. An example of such a narrow understanding of labour may be found in Remy C.Kwant who perceives in labour a systematic human activity connected with a system of services[21]. There are also definitions that apprehend the phenomenon of labour very broadly, most often connected with some philosophical assumptions. Marxism describes labour as man's self-creation. Among Christian authors, the philosophical domain is employed by Czesław Bartnik. By labour he means "an activity which is connected with the shaping of the human being, individual and social, and, therefore, an activity which shapes this being, which supports, transforms and develops it"[22]. Another plane of description is accepted by Czesław Strzeszewski who writes: "Labour is a free, though, naturally, necessary activity of man, resulting from a sense of duty, connected with effort and joy, and aiming at creating socially useful, spiritual and material values"[23]. This description, connected with the domain of social philosophy, presents labour as an ideal. In existential experience, labour is not always experienced in this way. Elements of ethics and philosophy are combined in another description of labour: "Labour is an aspect of man's active behaviour towards the world, subjected to moral norms, and resulting from man's lack of self-sufficiency revealed in his needs; it is realized in the human act in order to conquer the world for an indirect satisfaction of his needs; it causes man's development and has an ambivalent character"[24]. The definitions of labour quoted above by way of example present its various aspects: its connection with man's ontical status, direction towards satisfying needs and creating values, its psychological, moral and social conditions. Labour may be understood in two ways: in a strict and in a broad sense. In the first case it will mean the creation of material or spiritual values which are socially useful. Labour understood broadly means the self-realization of man as a person. An adequate description of labour is probably impossible, but it is very important to apprehend man's labour in an integral-personalistic manner.

(ii) Christian Interpretation of Labour

In the Christian interpretation, labour is not a marginal problem but it appears in the very centre of human life. A close connection of the human being with labour is suggested by the Book of Genesis (1,28) which recalls God's command to people: "Be fruitful, and multiply, and replenish the earth, and subdue it". Early Christianity took up

---

[21]*Philosophy of Labor*, Pittsburgh 1960, pp.119-123.

[22]*Teologia pracy ludzkiej* [The Theology of Human Labour], Warszawa 1977, p.15.

[23]Cz.Strzeszewski: *Praca ludzka. Zagadnienia społeczno-moralne* [Human Labour. Social and Moral Problems], Lublin, 1978, p.19.

[24]J.Gałkowski: *Praca i człowiek* [Labour and Man], Warszawa 1980, p.182.

the topic of labour which can be confirmed by the treatise by St.Augustine *On the Labour of Monks*[25]. During the Middle Ages the problem of labour was brushed aside, though even then the recommendation of physical labour appeared in the rule of the Benedictines. The problem appeared again in the social teaching of the Church which culminated in the encyclical *Laborem exercens* by John Paul II in 1981. In this document we find a statement that "labour constitutes the basic dimension of man's life on earth". This is confirmed by "all the achievements of various sciences concerned with man - anthropology, palaeontology, history, sociology, psychology and others" (LE 4). Thus, labour is not an accidental phenomenon of the human being but it belongs to its essence.

Labour is an illustration of paradoxes connected with man's being[26]. First of all, the bipolarity of the human person brings about a differentiation of many kinds of labour; in some of them the somatic factor predominates, while in others - the psychic-mental factor. However, the distinction between manual and mental labour is relative because most often they do not occur in mutually exclusive forms. Physical labour demands a co-participation of intellect and the will, while mental labour, in turn, is conditioned by the health of the body. Man is a potential and finite being, yet, in spite of that, he is capable of actualization and opening to the infinity. The indispensability of labour is connected with the existence of many needs and with man's contingency. The aim of labour is precisely the satisfaction of the wants experienced, protecting one's existence from the threats of the environment, satisfaction of hunger etc. However, labour is also something more, namely, an internal need of the human spirit, a self-affirmation, a search for higher values, a road towards infinity. Another manifestation of the ambivalence of labour is the fact that it is an effect of both man's determinants and his freedom. Biological and social determinants bring with them an element of restriction, so for that reason the techniques and forms of labour are often imposed by the circumstances and the environment. Regardless of that, truly human labour demands respect of human freedom, for otherwise it would become a source of enslavement. Still another paradox of labour concerns its connection with a pair of opposed features, creativity and routine. Labour means a continuous creation of new values, a transformation of nature and even of man himself. Inventiveness is desirable in both mental and manual labour, while creativity constitutes a significant dimension of any labour. Yet, at the same time, it is a fact that everyday labour produces a sense of routine, monotony, dullness. It is worthwhile to point to another instance of the ambivalence of labour. It is a source of joy and satisfaction, but so often it produces fatigue, discouragement, and even suffering. To some extent, the briefly outlined paradoxical nature of the phenomenon of labour is unavoidable, since its source is man's ontical status. It constitutes a conjunction of opposed properties. In existential experience labour is placed between the poles of dialectically and mutually opposed properties, and for that reason it is possible to move towards one of these poles, usually temporarily. Labour is not a substantial being,

[25]*De opere monachorum* PL 40, 547-580.

[26]R.Kwant: *Philosophy of Labor*, op.cit., pp.1-27.

autonomous in respect to the human person. But at the same time neither is it something accidental. It is a natural state of the human being, an unavoidable necessity of normal man.

Speaking about labour, Christianity points to its strict connection with man as a cause and a subject. The subjective character of labour is extensively discussed and justified by John Paul II in the encyclical *Laborem exercens* (6-7). Labour is initiated in the human person but it is finalized beyond that person. Although in the scheme of the categories of Thomistic metaphysics labour is an accidentality, existentially it is a significant component of the human being. Labour is an actualization of the potentials contained in the human nature. That is why it is also a cause of man's development, ontical and axiological.

In the Christian interpretation the ontology of labour makes it possible to speak of various functions of man's labour. The ontological-creative function of labour is of primary importance. It should be properly understood: labour is not an initiating creation of man but his finalization and actualization. The demiurgic role of labour is implied in the Biblical description of the creation of man, made in "God's likeness" (*Genesis* 1,27). *Homo sapiens*, made in the likeness of the operating Creator, is at the same time *homo artifex*[27]. God ordered man to examine, "replenish", and perfect the universe. The earth requires human labour. Man must have dominion over it and must transform it creatively. In the Bible labour is understood as a continuation of the act of creation, and that is why St. Paul called people "God's fellow workers" (I *Corinthians* 3,9). The old-Christian thinker, St. Augustine, paid attention to the fact that God created many things in a germinal form and that is why the world was developing gradually and in an evolutionary way. This also concerns man, into whose nature God incorporated dispositions and powers which are actualized in consequence of activity. Thus, man continues the act of creation also in respect to himself. The Biblical suggestions provided a reference point for St. Thomas Aquinas who stated that labour is the essence of human life and for that reason it endows it with sense[28]. Man is a being which is actual only relatively. Labour means a perfection of man's nature - of its faculties, abilities, potentials, and values. That is why it is possible to speak of the self-realization of man as a person, not only functionally but also structurally. Perfection through labour, reaching in many directions, means a co-creation.

The ontological-creative function of labour is emphasized in contemporary Christian theology and philosophy. Jean Lacroix is of the opinion that "through labour man is a co-creator of the act of creation and a demiurge of his evolution in discovering, exploiting and spiritualizing of his own nature"[29]. A French Dominican, Marie-Dominique Chenu,

---

[27]Cz.Bartnik: *Teologia pracy ludzkiej*, op.cit., pp.56-79.

[28]*Summa Theologiae* I-II,q.3,a.2,ad 1; q.18,a.3,c. Thomas's philosophical conception of labour is criticised by R.Kwant (op.cit., pp.38-39) who, among others, objects against the lack of social motivation of labour.

[29]"La notion du travail", *La Vie Intellectuelle* (1952) nr. 6, p.23.

makes a similar claim. He understands labour as a complementation of the act of creation, as constant organizing and directing the universe. Thanks to that *homo artifex* becomes a demiurge in perfecting nature and himself[30]. Cardinal Stefan Wyszyński († 1981) also acknowledged the ontological function of labour when he wrote: "Human labour is a continuation of God's labour; it is a finishing of the act of creation"[31]. Obviously, man's labour does not mean a co-participation in the original act of creation by God. Nor is it self-creation in the understanding of Hegelianism or Marxism. It is a collaboration with God, a co-creation of the world and one's self. The creative function of labour was confirmed by John Paul II, when he wrote in the encyclical *Laborem exercens*: "Through labour man not only transforms nature, adapting it to his needs, but he also realizes himself as a man and, in a sense, he 'becomes more a man'" (LE 9). Through labour man becomes more and more a person; he develops ontically, deepens spiritually, becomes more closely connected with the society he lives in.

The role of labour in human life cannot be reduced exclusively to the ontological-creative function. Christian philosophy also points to other functions of labour - cognitive, moral, social, and religious-soteriological. In Marxism the epistemological function of human labour was connected with the thesis about the priority of the ***praxis*** over theory which, obviously, is hard to accept. After all, man's activity implies a cognitive penetration of a real existential and social situation. Labour is not realized in a cognitive vacuum but it is co-constituted by consciousness. Yet, on the other hand, it is a fact that labour broadens the scope of man's knowledge both about the world and about himself. Practical activity stimulates new directions of research; it allows a verification of the current state of knowledge; it broadens the research foundations. At any rate, labour is a valuable experience of man which, as any experience, is indispensable for theoretical knowledge. The epistemological value of labour is particularly precious on the existential level, where it constitutes a recognition of one's own personality and its possibilities.

Another function of human labour is personalistic-moral. Sometimes personalistic and moral values are separated, but they are undoubtedly interconnected. "The personalistic value consists in the person actualizing itself in the act and in this its structure of self-possession and self-control is being expressed"[32]. Personalistic values demand some activity. Their factual development is possible in the climate which is morally positive, and, hence, through the realization of moral values. Labour is an indispensable component of both types of values; it actualizes man's personal dimension, while simultaneously enriching him spiritually. The moral function of labour concerns many aspects; it shapes the personality and character of man; it facilitates the overcoming of doubts and hesitations; it reveals the scope of real obligations; it places him at the service for others. Labour is not the highest value but in contemporary world it is a universal and one of the leading values. Conscious renouncement of labour makes man's correct

---

[30]*Pour une théologie du travail*, Paris 1955, pp.29-30.

[31]S.Wyszyński: *Duch pracy ludzkiej* [The Spirit of Human Labour], Poznań 1957, p.57.

[32]K.Wojtyła: *Osoba i czyn*, op.cit., pp.290-291.

development impossible, turning him into a moral cripple and a social parasite. Without labour such higher moral values as justice, love, or peace, are turned into fictions and mere verbosity. Labour does not directly create such values, yet it is nevertheless their indispensable exteriorization and confirmation.

The next function of labour is its social value. Man is not a closed entity but he lives and realizes himself in a society. This is why labour cannot have an exclusively private-individual character but it should also take into consideration social aims[33]. Labour is usually undertaken in order to satisfy one's own needs (of the individual and of the family), but it also means a creation of the values necessary for the society (nation, state, humanity). Labour means a production of common good, thus becoming a source of social ties. It is an encounter of people who are unified by common toil, demanding solidarity and partnership. Under the conditions of responsible or hard labour man's experiences his insufficiency with greater intensity and becomes aware of the need of the assistance of others. Thus, labour becomes an experience of brotherhood and solidarity, initiating the attitude of mutual respect and lasting friendships. All this leads to the formation of real community. People are bound not only by shared joys and recreations, but also - even more strongly - by common toil and the risks it may involve. Labour is a social obligation, constituting a sacrifice for others. Thus, avoidance of labour means living at the expense of other people, exploiting their strength and toil. Social life means a reciprocal exchange of services, which inescapably implies mutual subservenience and work for others.

The social function of labour demands the involvement of an individual in the life of the society and its organization[34]. Labour not only has a social character but its realization most often involves the necessity of collectively working in a team. Classical examples are provided by a factory, a research institution, university, a designing office, a supermarket etc. Labour performed by a team is usually more efficient, quicker, and in some exceptional cases (e.g. natural disasters) quite indispensable. Efficient organization, in turn, demands a subordination of individuals to the leaders which is understandable in itself and therefore does not infringe on personal freedom. Common good often demands external restrictions.

For believers labour still has a religious-redemptive function. In God's designs labour plays an important role. Becoming involved in the human world, Christ displayed solidarity by participating in man's toil. That is why the directing and transforming of the cosmos, the satisfying of human material and spiritual needs, creating civilization and culture - all mean a co-participation in the mystery of Christ. Eschatological hope does not undermine the sense of labour but, just to the contrary, it confirms and complements it. Labour means an overcoming of egoism and the moral vices it entails; it means becoming rooted in a sacrificial service for others. Hence, labour constitutes an

---

[33]St.Thomas Aquinas: *Summa Theologiae* I-II,q.183,a.3,ad 2; E.Borne, F.Henry: *Travail et l'homme*, Paris 1937, pp.141 ff,228 ff.

[34]R.Kwant, op.cit., pp.128-131.

opposition to moral evil. All this makes it possible to speak of its religious and redemptive function. In the Christian interpretation labour as such does not mean a punishment for sins but only toil and suffering are connected with it. The Book of Genesis (2,15; 3,16-19) states explicitly that it is not labour (*labor*) but the toil it involves (*dolor*) that is a consequence of the fall of our original primogenitors. At any rate, the toil of labour is a purifying and redemptive punishment rather than the punishment of revenge. The religious sense of labour is significant, frequently even the only one. If social determinants undermine the natural-immanent sense of labour then the soteriological dimension of labour remains intact for believers.

An integral element of the Christian conception of labour is the idea of the humanism of labour. The various functions of human labour outlined above have a chance of realization only when the postulates of humanism are fulfilled. At the moment we are interested mainly in the anthropological conditions of such humanism. Labour is a significant value and that is why it deserves respect. This is true about every kind of work, also physical jobs. The value of labour derives from its connection with the doer who is a man - the person. "As a person, man is the subject of labour [...] Man, its subject, is the first and fundamental value of labour" (*Laborem exercens* 6). A subjective apprehension of labour is unavoidably connected with a depreciation of the working man, with disregard for his natural dignity. For that reason labour cannot be evaluated exclusively by the laws of the market. A just pay is man's fundamental right which can be claimed on the basis of appropriate laws.

The humanism of labour means mainly respect for work and its performer. In Greek and Roman antiquity labour and man were separated, which led to contempt for manual labour. Physical labour was regarded as appropriate for slaves whose legal-social situation was regarded as their natural state. Only Christianity restored respect to physical work. The Old and the New Testaments showed working men in a new perspective and the most emphatic example in this respect was the Person and teachings of Christ. He was personally a working man, thus restoring dignity to hard working people. Labour is man's right and also his duty. The quintessence of the Christian teaching in this respect can be found in these words of St.Paul: "The man who will not work, shall not eat" (2 *Thessalonians* 3,10). Labour is a part of the Christian calling and that is why laziness and social parasitism cannot be reconciled with the evangelical command of loving one's neighbour.

The humanism of labour is connected with its subjective dimension. This is stated by John Paul II when he writes: "The sources of the dignity of labour should not be sought first of all in its objective dimension but in its subjective dimension" (*Laborem exercens* 6). Although man is called to labour, he does not exist exclusively or mainly for labour. It is labour that is for man, not the other way round (LE 6). The working man has a right to have his dignity respected, but his dignity does not arise from the very fact of creating economic or cultural goods. Dignity inheres in the human person, not in the functions of a producer and consumer. The humanism of labour is realized through the *logos* and *ethos* of labour. The *logos* of labour demands that every worker - according to his scope of duties and responsibility - participate in programming his work. That is why the employees should have access to the information about the mechanisms and aims of their work, the technology of performing it, about the expected difficulties and efficiency. The *logos* of labour is destroyed by totalitarian systems, voluntarism of peremptory decisions, bureaucracy, lack of healthy competition, sluggishness of collective structures, lack of opportunities of advancement for capable workers etc. A rational organization of work always liberates energy and favours the *ethos* of labour. Reason should direct labour on a macro-social scale - competence, know-how, knowledge of social mechanisms, modern technology.

Labour has an ambivalent character: it may serve man but it may also destroy man. This was noticed by John Paul II when he spoke about the possibilities of both man's integration and disintegration through labour (LE 6-9). Although labour has its immanent sense, in a situation which is existentially or socially abnormal it may seem to be lacking any sense. The forms and causes of the alienation of labour are highly varied: technical-structural, social-moral, ideological. The former are typical of highly industrialized and technicised societies in which the worker is an "addition" to the assembly line. Consequences appear as people's frustrations, mainly as a result of the murderous speed of work. The absolutization of labour is also a form of its degeneration. The *ethos* of labour should not be artificially elevated by raising the quotas of work, excessive burdening of the workers, compelling them (psychologically or financially) to work during holidays etc.

Competitiveness of work should not be allowed to assume absurd forms, as it happened during the so-called "Stakhanovite movement" during the Stalinist period. The coercion of labour, especially a legal obligation, is also hard to be reconciled with humanism. It should be permitted only in very exceptional cases, for instance, in order to counteract natural disasters. The enslavement of labour may also be indirect, for instance, when the state becomes the only indirect employer. Still another form of the alienation of labour may appear as a consequence of the "ideology of production" when man is treated instrumentally. Summing up, it should be stated that authentic humanism of labour is impossible without respecting man's subjectiveness. Christianity accepts both the priority of labour over the capital and the priority of person over labour.

LITERATURE

ARVAN, H.: *La philosophie du travail*, Paris 1964.

BARTNIK, C.: *Teologia pracy ludzkiej* [A Theology of Human Labour], Warszawa 1977.

BLONDEL, M.: *L'action*. Vol.1. *Le problème des causes secondes et pur agir*, Paris 1949; vol.2. *L'action humaine et les conditions de son aboutissement*, Paris 1963.

BORNE, E., HENRY, F.: *Le travail et l'homme*, Paris 1937.

CHENU, M.D.: *Pour une théologie du travail*, Paris 1955.

FINANCE, J. de: *Etre et agir*, Paris 1945.

FINANCE, J. de: *Essai sur l'agir humain*, Rome 1962.

FISCHER, G.: *Mensch und Arbeit im Betrieb*, Stuttgart 1949.

GAŁKOWSKI, J.: *Praca i człowiek* [Man and Labour], Warszawa 1980.

JAROSZEWSKI, T.M.: *Rozważania o praktyce* [Considerations about Practice], Warszawa 1974.

JOHN PAUL II: *Laborem exercens*, Warszawa 1982.

KWANT, R.C.: *Philosophy of Labor*, Pittsburgh 1960.

LANGFORD, G.: *Human Action*, New York 1971.

PSZCZOŁOWSKI, T.: *Praca człowieka* [The Labour of Man], Warszawa 1966.

STRZESZEWSKI, C.: *Praca ludzka. Zagadnienia społeczno-moralne* [Human Labour. Social-Moral Problems], Lublin 1978.

SZEWCZYK, J.: *Filozofia pracy* [Philosphy of Labour], Kraków 1971.

VIALATAUX, J.: *Signification humaine du travail*, Paris 1953.

WOJTYŁA, K.: *Osoba i czyn* [The Person and the Act], Kraków 1969.

Chapter 7

Philosophical Concepts of Values

Every philosophical trend offers different interpretations of the nature of being and, in consequence, various visions of reality are proposed by idealists, personalists, materialists, pantheists, representatives of "reism" etc. Classical philosophy focussed its attention mainly on ontology, that is, the science of being. Modern and contemporary philosophy is increasingly concentrating on axiology, apprehending man and his world as values of a certain kind[1]. Regardless of the ontological interpretation of the world, every man distinguishes a rich realm of values. In particular, two types of values are recognized, objects and persons. The two types of values are not regarded as equal and, for instance, one does not greet a chair, while persons are not treated instrumentally as chairs.

The philosophical science of values, that is, axiology, concerns many aspects, such as ontological, epistemological, anthropological and theological. The considerations presented below will be limited to axiological ontology and will deal mainly with the problem of the inner nature and structure of values. Only at the end will the personalistic dimension of the theory of values be briefly outlines.

Axiology constitutes not only an integral part of realistic metaphysics but also a plane shared by several humanistic sciences, theological, philosophical, legal-ethical and those concerning man's artistic activities[2]. Thus, for instance, ethics cannot be treated as an arbitrary codification of norms but should be explained on the basis of a hierarchy of values. Axiology cannot be irrelevant in psychology and sociology which, while analysing the world of man, cannot ignore the fundamental values of personality.

(i) Description of Values

The category of "value" has an analogous character in both subjective and objective senses. The very term "value" (Latin *valor*) is derived from the verb "to be valuable" (*valere*). The concept of value is used in mathematics, economy, ethics, aesthetics,

---

[1]A.Forest: "L'expérience de la valeur", *Revue Néoscholastique*, 43 (1940) p.16.

[2]L.Lavelle: *Traité des valeur*, vols.1-2, Paris 1951-1955; S.Kowalczyk: "Filozofia wartości" [The Philosophy of Values], *Zeszyty Naukowe KUL*, 3 (1960), no.4, pp.71-84; H.Buczyńska-Garewicz: *Uczucia i rozum w świecie wartości* [Emotions and Reason in the World of Values], Wrocław 1975.

sociology, religion and philosophy. In the latter domain value may mean, among others, a specific object evaluated by somebody, a formal reason of value, the idea of value or the experience of value. The first two meanings of the concept of value seem particularly relevant at the moment.

There are two main reasons for the difficulty in providing a definition of value. First of all, in its scope the category of value is as wide as the concepts of being, act etc., which makes a definition impossible in the classical understanding of the term (with a determination of the kind and generic distinction). Moreover, each value also involves an element of experience and evaluation, thus additionally complicating its description.

However, the difficulties indicated above have not discouraged scholars attempting to describe the concept of value. Some of the most characteristic results may easily be cited: Value consists in overcoming the indifference of a subject towards an object so that in consequence the significance and importance of the latter are perceived[3]; value is anything we seek and love[4]. The latter statement clearly refers to a description of the good as formulated by Aristotle in the *Nicomachean Ethics* where the good is defined as an object of human desire.

When describing value one should undoubtedly indicate the relation between the subject and the object. The descriptions of particular authors underline the role of either the subject or the object which leads, respectively, to the subjectivization or objectivization of the concept of value. The former case clearly occurs in the description of value proposed by Franz Brentano. According to him "we call good only that thing whose love is justified and valid"[5]. Thus, value is determined by the "valid" love of a subject. A more objective character may be found in the descriptions of value which refer to the Thomistic philosophy. Erich Przywara understood value as that which belongs to the essence of being and which, in consequence, is an inspiration to action[6]. Another description has a similar character: value is a being perfecting an object which is usually a cause of an action[7]. Both descriptions emphasize the role of the object rather than that of the subject.

Yet, most of the definitions attempt to avoid the extremes of either the reification or subjectivization of the category. Johannes B. Lotz reserves the term value for such a being which, although independent of actual human experience, is nevertheless a cause of the subject's experiences[8]. Another author employs the term value to name the good which is particularly useful for a subject[9]. Value is also described as objective perfection which

---

[3]L.Lavelle, op.cit., vol.1, p.3.

[4]P.Siwek: "Problem wartości" [The Problem of Values], *Przegląd Powszechny*, 41 (1938), pp.3-4.

[5]F.Brentano: *Vom Ursprung sittlicher Erkenntnis*, Hamburg 1955, p.18.

[6]E.Przywara: *Religionsbegru¨ndung*, Freiburg im Br. 1923, p.91.

[7]E.Gutwenger: *Wertphilosophie*, Innsbruck 1952, p.70.

[8]J.B.Lotz: "Sein und Wert", *Zeitschrift für katholische Theologie*, 57 (1933), pp.600-605.

[9]J.Santeler: "Rezension", *Zeitschrift für katholische Theologie*, 70 (1948) p.114.

is an aim of one's aspirations[10]. Some descriptions of value are evidently too narrow as, for example, the following statement: "Value is everything which affects the emotional and volitional faculties of man and makes them tend towards that which brings pleasure and joy, which satisfies the aesthetic taste or religious and moral feelings, or, more generally, which fulfils some demands of human nature"[11]. It is too subjective an understanding of values since it neglects the role of intellect in the perception and experience of values. Much happier is the following description: "Value is a quality of being in so far as the latter is an object of intentional cognitive-volitional acts"[12]. The latter definition of value is almost literally taken over from the Thomistic theory of the transcendental attributes of being.

Each of the quoted definitions of values leaves some dissatisfaction because it impoverishes the abundance of meanings of the concept of value. Moreover, every description is fully understandable only within the context of its philosophical system. Undoubtedly, value is any kind of being perceived in relation to the cognizing and experiencing subject, that is, a personality; in some way value develops man by opening him up to the Infinite.

Characterizing value one should also explain its relation to the concept of the good. The problem acquires different interpretations in the Platonic and Aristotelian trends in philosophy. Plato regarded the good as the highest of ideas, so he consistently acknowledged the superiority of the good over being. The influence of Platonism is evident in this trend of phenomenology in which being and value are distinguished as two different realms of reality. Ontological dualism was accepted by Max Scheler and Johannes Hessen. The latter recognized the priority of value over the good, suggesting that the good is constituted by value[13]. Such an understanding of the relation between value and the good is connected with the acknowledgement of the priority of axiology over ontology which, in turn, reveals an idealistic element in phenomenology.

The philosophy inspired by Thomism differently interprets the relation between value and the good. Value is usually identified with the broadly understood good, while at other times the good is defined as one of the values. Both statements need not be mutually exclusive because the good can be understood in two aspects, ontological and ethical. The ontological good is a being which corresponds to the desire[14], particularly to the model idea of its creator. Thus understood good is interchangeable with being - *ens et bonum convertuntur*. The essence of all the good contains an ability of awakening appetites

---

[10]G.F.Klenk: *Wert - Sein - Gott*, Rom 1942, p.75.

[11]W.Granat: *Personalizm chrześcijański. Teologia osoby ludzkiej* [Christian Personalism. The Theology of the Human Person], Poznań 1985, p.380.

[12]M.A.Krąpiec: "Filozofia bytu a zagadnienie wartości" [The Philosophy of Being and the Problem of Values], *Znak*, 17 (1965) p.430.

[13]J.Hessen: *Lehrbuch der Philosophie*, vol.2: *Wertlehre*, München 1948, pp.47-48.

[14]"Convenientiam ergo entis ad appetitum exprimit hoc nomen bonum": St.Thomas Aquinas: *De Veritate* q.1,a.1,c.

(*appetibilitas*) which, in turn, are differentiated according to the nature of beings. The ethical good appears only in the realm of rational beings, aware of the agreement or disagreement between their actions and a moral norm. As these considerations indicate, the ontological good does not differ in scope from value, although the two differ in meaning: the good emphasizes more strongly the element of being, that is, of the object, while value clearly implies the participation of a subject. The good is a being comprehended in relation to the volitional area, while values also cover the domain of human cognition. That is why it has rightly been noted that the concept of value goes beyond the domain of the strictly understood good. After all, there are multiple values, cognitive, ethical, artistic, religious, economic etc. The difference between the concepts of value and the good becomes sharper when we speak of the moral good. Then it is merely one of several categories of values. Still, the feature shared by both is the dynamic aspect, connected with their ability to provoke desire.

The category of value has several, almost synonymous, terms such as aim, idea, perfection, significance, advantage etc. When constituting an objective and real attribute of being, value usually becomes somebody's aim[15]. The concepts of value and aim, though close in meaning, cannot be totally identified. Aim is an actual object of one's desire while value is only a potential object of desire. Quite frequently value is identified with idea. However, this is not fully justified since the category of value implies more emphatically the fact of reality. Ideas need not be objective and real, while values are esteemed precisely because of their objective and real character. Although values are not always actually real, nevertheless they have a potential reality.

Characterizing values one cannot neglect their structure. Most likely they have no substantial character, that is, they do not exist separately from being. They are objective and real because they are "embodied" in the being of an object. Value is not isolated from being but it penetrates it. In their structure values are not homogeneous and simple; inherent in an object they fascinate a subject and usually have a creator[16]. Especially the first two elements, the object and the subject, are organically connected with the category of value. The loss of an object unavoidably leads to the subjectivization or relativization of values, while the neglect of the role of a subject practically neutralizes value as such. Value separated from an object loses its sense. A thing may be of value only for somebody. This fact explains the unavoidable changeability of the criteria of estimating values, which is not identical with their relativization. Value individually experienced by man is a confirmation of his personal dimension. Subjective experiencing of values does not undermine their objective character, because axiological experience is based on real foundations.

A great majority of values have a qualitative rather than quantitative character. That is why values are described as "lower" or "higher" rather than "smaller" or "greater". Values have a bipolar nature, that is, each positive value has a corresponding negative

[15]J.B.Lotz, op.cit., p.602.

[16]L.Lavelle, op.cit., vol.1, pp.185-246.

value. Thus, we perceive the opposition between truth and falsehood, good and evil, beauty and ugliness, and so on. The ontological structure of an anti-value is usually explained in the context of its positive value, among others, by means of a theory about the negative nature (privatio) of falsehood and evil. The genesis of anti-values is a complex problem, often approaching the border of mystery[17].

(ii) Subjectivistic concepts of value

The ontological status of values is an object of endless controversies. Indeed, the very classification of approaches in this respect is already difficult enough. Johannes Hessen distinguished the following four attitudes: psychological approach, naturalistic objectivism, logical approach and ontological approach[18]. The psychological approach to the existence of values reduces human existence to a psychological fact. Aristotelian-Scholastic philosophy recognized the existence of objective values but connected them too strongly with the cosmos which resulted in their naturalization. Neo-Kantianism tended to logicize values and endow them with the status of merely mental beings. Finally, N.Hartmann speaks for axiological ontologism when he regards the existence of values as ideal beings.

The classification of the ontological concepts of values, quoted above by way of example, is neither exhaustive nor valid in all its suggestions. Perhaps it is impossible to design one exhaustive typology of axiological ontologies. For that reason it is probably better to distinguish simply such ontological concepts of values as relativistic and absolute, realistic and idealistic, subjectivistic and objectivistic, Thomistic and phenomenological etc. These considerations will be restricted to a brief account of the representatives of subjectivistic and objectivistic trends in axiology.

Moderate axiological subjectivism, represented among others by Kant and Brentano, is opposed to skepticism and relativism. Immanuel Kant († 1804) sharply objected against hedonistic subjectivism and he recognized the absolute moral value of man's acts[19]. The primary value in human life is not pleasure but the fulfilment of duty. Kant was therefore far from the axiological relativism of Protagoras, the Epicureans or even the Stoics. In his case subjectivism appears as a result of a sharp opposition between being (*Sein*) and value (*Wert*), theoretical or pure reason and practical reason. According to him, value is not comprehensible by means of theoretical reason, that is, by intellectual cognition. Value is only a postulate of the will, that is, an assumption. The inner relation between value and being, questioned by Kant, makes consistent axiological realism impossible. The

---

[17] S.Kowalczyk: "Zło - problemem czy tajemnicą?" [Is Evil a Problem or a Mystery?] [in:] *Studia z filozofii Boga* [Studies in the Philosophy of God], ed.by B.Bejze, Warszawa 1977, vol.3, pp.457-486.

[18] J.Hessen: *Wertphilosophie*, Paderborn 1937, pp.19-21.

[19] I.Kant: *Kritik der praktischen Vernunft* [in:] *Werke*, Berlin, no date, vol.1, pp.164 ff; also his: *Kritik der Urteilskraft* [in:] ibid., pp.39 ff.

source of values is found in the subject, in his responsibilities, desires and attitudes. As a carrier of values, the object is pushed down into background. Personally recognizing the objectivity of values, Kant has initiated the subjectivistic trend in the axiology of modern thought. He understood value primarily as an intentional correlate of human will. "The critical theories which refer to Kant recognize as a source of value the requirements posed to objects by the nature of subjects (for example, according to the Kantians the objective value of cognitive acts does not result from their agreement with an object but from subjective conditions necessary for an object to become for us an object of cognition)"[20].

Moderate axiological subjectivism found its continuators in such thinkers as Rudolf Lotze († 1881) and Heinrich Rickert († 1936). They distinguished two spheres of reality, beings and values[21]. Beings exist, while values possess "significance" (*gelten*). They are somehow interconnected, still, it is difficult to speak of the real existence of values as such. Values enrich personality, yet, at the same time, they "have significance" exclusively in relation to it.

Franz Brentano († 1936) is often classified as a follower of objective axiology[22], but it is hard to accept this claim. He won fame, among others, thanks to his thesis that the aspirational sphere - the will and emotions - has a significant function in respect to values. Intellectual cognition makes it possible to distinguish truth from falsehood, while "valid" emotions are helpful in identifying the categories of the good and evil. "We call something good when the love concerning it is valid"[23]. This description makes it possible to state that for Brentano it is not being (*Sein*) that is a source of values but emotional experience (*Erlebnis*). That is why one should speak of evaluating (*werten*) rather than of values (*Werte*). It is not the real thing that guarantees the good or evil but the psychic act and its quality. At any case, values do not exist autonomously, i.e. regardless of the subject. They exist only subjectively and are evaluated by means of emotions[24]. The hierarchy of values depends on predilections and man's love rather than on the inner richness of things. Nevertheless, man's emotions have an intentional aspect, that is, they are directed towards the external world. In spite of that, "values cannot be predicates of things, they only belong to acts of consciousness. And this is the essence of Brentano's subjectivism: one may speak of values only in the sphere of the phenomena of consciousness"[25].

---

[20]E.Bréhier: *Les thèmes actuels de la philosophie*, Paris 1961, chap.10.

[21]Cf. F.-J.Rintelen: "Die Bedeutung des philosophischen Wertproblems" [in:] *Philosophy perennis. Abhandlung zu ihrer Vergangenheit und Gegenwart*, Hrsg. von F.-J.Rintelen, Regensburg 1930, Bd. 2, pp.943-945.

[22]L.Lavelle, op.cit., vol.2, pp.100 ff.

[23]F.Brentano: *Vom Ursprung sittlicher Erkenntnis*, op.cit., p.17.

[24]J.B.Lotz: "Wertphilosophie und Wertpädagogik", *Zeitschrift für katholische Theologie*, 57 (1933) pp.1-43.

[25]H.Buczyńska-Garewicz: *Uczucia i rozum ...*, op.cit., p.92; cf. also pp.77-114.

Brentano's axiological subjectivism had its limits and that is why he did not question the objective dimension of the world of values. His ontological subjectivism is not identical with psychological subjectivism. The latter is connected with extreme individualism and relativism in the estimation of values. Ontological subjectivism merely claims that emotions do not so much identify values as they co-produce them. Love is a carrier of the good and evil. Therefore, there are no autonomous values but there is only "valid" or "invalid" love. Thus, Brentano's axiology raises a disturbing question: how can an axiologically neutral world (*wertfreie Welt*) provide a basis for sound estimation? The outlined concepts of value by Kant and Brentano, though dissociated from relativism, evidently explain the structure of the good in too subjective a way. The axiology of both thinkers is based on a psychological-epistemological foundation while lacking a sufficient ontological basis. In consequence, it entails a subjectivization of the phenomenon of values and indirectly there emerges the danger of relativism. The followers of subjectivism most often quote two arguments: (1) values do not occur beyond man's psychic experiences; and (2) values do not enrich the factual description of the object examined[26]. Neither of the arguments is entirely convincing. Naturally, similarly to the whole external world, values are accessible to subjective experience. Still, the fact does not prove that the object of these experiences is a product of a cognizing subject; otherwise, idealistic solipsism would be unavoidable. The other argument of the followers of axiological subjectivism does not seem valid, either. Values differ from categorial notions of the type "tall" or "round", but that does not prove their lack of content. Categorial notions differ from qualitative and transcendental concepts (understood in the spirit of classical philosophy).

Speaking of the "relativity" of values, one should bear in mind the multiple sources of different judgements in this field. Thus, for instance, Roman Ingarden distinguishes three causes of such a "relativity", namely, epistemological, ontological and situational[27]. The limitation of human cognition is not identical with the relativization of values, much like the fact of mistakes does not prove the falsity of all cognition. Identical values are differently estimated by man and by animal, which results from their different existential status. Finally, the fluidity of man's existential situations leads to a factual reshuffling of the hierarchy of values but does not imply their relativity. Axiological relativism is most often a consequence of a reductionistic concept of the world or man.

The controversy between the adherents of subjectivism and objectivism in the domain of the science of values often springs from semantic imprecision. The very terms "objective" and "subjective" have many meanings[28]. Here are some of them: (1) objective - occurring in the object; subjective - real in the subject; (2) objective - existing autonomously; subjective - existing, for instance, as a correlate of an act of consciousness (an intentional being); (3) objective - existing regardless of man's

---

[26]T.Czeżowski: "Czym są wartości?" [What Are Values?], *Znak*, 17 (1965) pp.408-410.

[27]R.Ingarden: *Przeżycie - dzieło - wartość* [Experience - Work - Value], Kraków 1966, pp.68-74.

[28]Ibid., pp.184-186.

experiences; subjective - constituted by such an experience. Naturally, semantic distinctions of this kind will not suffice to overcome axiological subjectivism but they indicate the vagueness of many of its claims.

(iii) Objectivistic concepts of values

Objectivistic axiology has many representatives but the following considerations will be limited to two trends, Thomism and phenomenology. Although initially Thomism did not use the term "value", one may nevertheless speak of Thomistic axiology. It is based on the thesis about the mutual conversion of being and the good. St. Thomas Aquinas († 1274) wrote: "Each being, if it is a being, constitutes the good. For each being as such appears in the act, is perfect in a sense, because each act constitutes perfection. Perfection in itself contains the notion of desirability and the good [...]. Therefore, each being as such is the good"[29]. On the basis of Thomism the conversion of being and the ontological good makes it possible to infer a strict unity of being and values. Thus, there is no such being which would constitute no value (the good) or such value that would not constitute a being[30]. Value does not exist beyond being but within being itself. It is simply its new apprehension by a subject. Axiology is not autonomous but it constitutes an integral element of metaphysics.

In modern Thomism the philosophy of values is based on the theory of the transcendental properties of being. According to this interpretation, particular transcendentals - unity, truth, the good, probably also beauty - are really identical with being, though at the same time they differ from it in meaning. Between being and transcendental attributes there occurs a difference in connotation and not in denotation. Truth, the good and beauty add nothing new to being, though they are really identical with it. They differ from it only mentally and constitute being's references to man's faculties, mind or will. In their characterization of values modern Thomists distinguish transcendental and categorial values[31]. The former are not "qualities", that is, accidental features which really differ from substantial being. They are only new aspects of being distinguished in respect to the subject's faculties, cognitive or emotional-volitional. Among others, transcendental values include truth, the good and beauty. In modern understanding the realm of values goes beyond the scheme of transcendental properties of being as such. The Thomists are aware of that and therefore they speak of categorial values. They describe them either as a "particularization" of transcendental values or as a "superstructure" of content, distinct from substantial being. The former concept is questionable because, for instance, economic or life values evidently cannot be included in any of the transcendental features of being. They are really distinct from being itself,

---

[29]St.Thomas Aquinas: *Summa Theologiae*, I,q.5,a.3,c.

[30]J.B.Lotz: *Wertphilosophie* ..., op.cit., p.4.

[31]M.A.Krąpiec: "Filozofia bytu ...", op.cit., pp.424-433.

introducing new, categorially restricted content. Thus, they are not only a particularization of the attributes of all being because they create new ontological categories. These values may be designated as a "superstructure" of being, even though the term is not precise enough, either.

The Thomistic interpretation of values possesses an undoubtedly desirable element of realism. The foundation of value is unquestionably the real existence of an object, especially its essential and existential act[32]. The substantial form of being and the act of existence are important "carriers" of all values and therefore the separation, or even more, the opposition, of being and value would be unjustified. However, traditional ontology is not yet an axiology because it neglects the relation between the being and the subject. The ontological language is not identical with the axiological language which reveals the multiple interrelations between value and the subject. Being becomes a value only when the subject's active attitude is manifested as cognitive, aspirational, emotional etc. In the Thomistic interpretation values are not reducible to facts of behaviour or the subject's attitude. That is why in this understanding of values the error of relativization does not occur[33]. Values are the intentional correlates of man's cognition and choice, although they are not arbitrarily shaped by him. The essence of values does not consist in actually fulfilling man's needs but in their potential connection with his mental-aspirational life. Traditional Thomism perfectly stresses the realism of the realm of values but it does not fully reveal the multiplicity of ontological and axiological languages. In many writers of this trend there occurs a tendency to reduce the language of values to that of being.

A German thinker, Dietrich von Hildebrand, combines Thomism with elements of phenomenology. While being essentially a Thomist, he also recognizes the objective and absolute character of values, founding them on being. The influence of phenomenology becomes evident in the subjectivistic starting point in his analysis of the problem of values. Value is primarily the "importance" of being[34]. In human cognition "importance" is understood in three ways, as strictly subjective, objective ("internal", "in itself"), and as "good for a person". Values are apprehended by different types of the cognitive faculties, but especially by the "heart"[35]. Values are real and concrete properties of an object, possessing a definite nature (*quidditas*)[36]. They are the objective "importance" of being, regardless of the fact of human cognition. One may, therefore, infer that values are autonomous in respect to man's feelings and experiences in the sense that they cannot be

---

[32]This is emphasized by L.Lavelle, op.cit., vol.1, p.29.

[33]However, this objection was raised by R.Ingarden in a discussion organized by the editors of the monthly *Znak*; *Znak*, 17 (1965) pp.466- 467.

[34]D. von Hildebrand: *Christian Ethics*, New York 1953, pp.34-59; M.H.Szymeczko: "Koncepcja wartości u Dietricha von Hildebranda" [The Concept of Value in Dietrich von Hildebrand], *Roczniki Filozoficzne*, 12 (1964), vol.2, pp.43-55.

[35]D. von Hildebrand: *Über das Herz*, Regensburg 1967, pp.122-129.

[36]D. von Hildebrand: *Christian Ethics*, op.cit., p.88.

reduced to them. Value is the "core of being"[37]. It is a primordial phenomenon (*ein Urphänomenon*), analogous to essence, being or truth[38]. Value is even prior to the good because the latter may only be an already valuable being. Moreover, value is not the very experience of man or the moment of cognition.

The foundation of value is existence due to which it is realized. The ontological value of the human person results from the fact of man's reality[39]. Yet, at the same time, value is not to be equated with existence alone. Value possesses an internal unity, content and a set of attributes, and that is why it itself constitutes the very essence (*echte Wesenheit*). Value even possesses its own existence, namely, an ideal existence (*ideale Existenz*)[40]. The realization of value does not change its nature but only its mode of being. The depreciation of the role of existence, typical of Hildebrand's axiology, is clearly a consequence of the influence of phenomenology connected with the essential concept of being[41].

The German axiologist by no means continues Plato's idealism and that is why he does not approach values as pure possibilities. Values simultaneously constitute protoelements of reality because they have their ultimate reality in God[42]. Without God values would be merely "a sheer kingdom of shadows"[43]. God is "the highest Value" and a fusion of all values[44]. He is "the Good itself" and "the good of all the goods"[45].

Dietrich von Hildebrand distinguishes such kinds of values as formal, of the created being, ontological and qualitative[46]. Formal values are connected with being itself, when apprehended, for instance, in opposition to nothingness; these are, among others, the values of essence and existence. The values of the created being are the effects of God's omnipotence Who has endowed His creatures with a certain dignity and significance. The ontological values are not connected with the Thomistic theory of transcendentals but they reveal the nature of particular beings. Thus, for instance, man's ontological value is

---

[37]Ibid., pp.72,78.

[38]Ibid., p.95.

[39]Ibid., pp.137,154; comp. also his: "Die Idee der sittlichen Handlung", *Jahrbuch für Philosophie und phänomenologische Forschung*, 3 (1916), pp.194 ff.

[40]D. von Hildebrand: *Der Sinn philosophischen Fragen und Erkennens*, Bonn 1950, p.57.

[41]M.H.Szymeczko, op.cit., pp.51 ff.

[42]"But in God they [values] have the ultimate substantial reality": D. von Hildebrand: *Christian Ethics*, op.cit., p.160.

[43]D. von Hildebrand: *Die Menschheit am Scheideweg*, Regensburg 1955, p.45.

[44]Ibid., pp.225-226; also his: *Christian Ethics*, op.cit., p.162.

[45]Ibid., p.160.

[46]Ibid., pp.146-152; also his: *Über das Herz*, op.cit., pp.170 ff.

the fact that he is the *imago Dei*. Finally, qualitative values are connected with human activity and that is why we speak of cognitive, moral or artistic values[47].

Thomistic axiology emphasizes the unity between value and being, while phenomenology entails a dualistic - heterogeneous conception of values. One of the founders of phenomenology, Max Scheler († 1928), accepted ontological dualism, when he distinguished things and values. They are interrelated but not identical. Values are not the relation itself or an emotional experience of a subject[48]. This makes it possible to speak of an objective-absolute character of values. They are independent of the subject's evaluation because they are not his arbitrary creation.

Scheler has not offered a definition of values, characterizing them in a negative rather than positive manner. Value is not a physical attribute of things, nor is it a power or a real disposition. Value is an object comprehendible by intuitive-emotional cognition. Value is a kind of a "material quality" (*materiale Qualität*), that is, it has an objective and real character[49]. Values imply the obligation or duty of realization but they cannot be reduced to obligation alone. "The very existence of a positive value is in itself a positive value. The very existence of a negative value is in itself a negative value"[50]. This means that positive values should be realized, while negative values - rejected. The above probably does not imply that values are exclusively ideal qualities. Therefore, the idealistic interpretation of values, accepted by Hanna Buczyńska-Garowicz[51], seems doubtful. After all, Scheler did acknowledge the autonomy of values. He saw in them "independent phenomena" for which things are merely "carriers"[52]. Among values the good assumes the predominant position since it contains all the other objectively existing individual values.

Scheler's ontological dualism was related to epistemological dualism. The world of things is an object of intellectual cognition, while the world of values is comprehendible only through emotional intuition[53]. The German philosopher has achieved a "rationalization" of emotions, that is, he endowed them with the cognitive function, and even exclusiveness, in respect to values. Emotions are an intuitive "view" of values and in this domain they remain autonomous in respect to intellect and will. The primary category of emotional experiences is love, "the most elementary act which provides a basis for all other acts"[54]. Scheler acknowledged the priority of love over cognition when he

---

[47]D. von Hildebrand: *Christian Ethics*, op.cit., pp.154 ff, 158-160. Comp. Wahrheit, *Wert und Sein. Festgabe für Dietrich von Hildebrand zum 80. Geburstag*, Hrsg. von B.Schwarz, Regensburg 1970.

[48]M.Scheler: *Der Formalismus in der Ethik und die materiale Wertethik*, Halle 1921, pp.248-255.

[49]Ibid., p.12.

[50]Ibid., p.79.

[51]H.Buczyńska-Garewicz: *Uczucia i rozum ...*, op.cit., p.228.

[52]M.Scheler: *Der Formalismus ...*, op.cit., pp.12-13.

[53]Scheler distinguished usual emotions (*Gefühle*) and emotional experience of values (*Wertgefühl*).

[54]M.Scheler: *Moralia*, Leipzig 1922, p.143.

wrote: "Love is therefore a stimulus for cognition and will, even more, it is the mother of spirit and reason itself"[55]. Man is, first of all, the ens amans.

Max Scheler's concept of love clearly contains controversial elements which have been pointed out, among others, by Bishop Karol Wojtyła[56]. For instance, the actualistic concept of person is unacceptable since it diminishes the causality of person in respect to values. Scheler also questions the norm of the "duty to one's brother" perceiving in it a threat to man's autonomy. Still, it would be hard to describe all love as an irrational act and deny it a cognitive function[57]. Scheler clearly endows love with an ability to "discover" the world of values. As he wrote: "Values cannot be created or destroyed. They exist quite independently of any organization of certain spiritual beings"[58]. His conception of values is not idealistic but theistic, i.e., it perceives their ultimate ontological basis in God.

A well known contemporary axiologist, the Rev. Johannes Hessen, combines, in turn, elements of Augustinianism and phenomenology. He accepts a triadic structure of reality and distinguishes in it three elements, essence, existence and value[59]. Values have "significance" and they constitute ideal beings. Real beings have no normative character and this indicates the difference between being and value. Values always imply an obligation, yet they undergo no change even if their carriers are destroyed[60]. His ontology of values Hessen describes as "reduced Platonism"[61]. Following Scheler he perceives the only manner of recognizing values in emotional intuition which is a kind of experience[62]. He does not speak for extreme emotionalism since he indicates mutual interrelations between three forms of intuition, namely, intellectual, volitional and emotional. Their synthesis is to be found in the so-called total intuition which makes it possible to discover the presence of God[63].

The philosophical thought of a Polish scholar, Roman Ingarden, is also related with the phenomenological trend. He indicated the complexity of the structure of values which

---

[55]M.Scheler: "Ordo amoris" [in:] *Gesammelte Werke*, vol.10, *Schriften aus dem Nachlass*, Leipzig 1923, p.356.

[56]K.Wojtyła: *Ocena możliwości zbudowania etyki chrześcijańskiej przy założeniach systemu Maksa Schelera* [An Evaluation of the Possibility of Developing Christian Ethics on the Assumptions of Max Scheler's System], Lublin 1959, pp.91-96.

[57]H.Buczyńska-Garewicz (op.cit., p.277) interprets Scheler's concept of love in a too irrationalistic manner. Her thesis would be hard to reconcile with Scheler's own statements quoted by her in her work.

[58]M.Scheler: *Der Formalismus ...*, op.cit., p.268.

[59]J.Hessen: *Religionsphilosophie*, München 1955, vol.2, p.160.

[60]J.Hessen: *Im Ringen um eine zeitnahe Philosophie*, Nürnberg 1959, pp.84 ff.

[61]Ibid., p.87. Comp. A.Nossol: *Cognitio Dei experimentalis. Nauka Jana Hessena o religijnym poznaniu Boga* [The Teaching of Johannes Hessen about the Religious Cognition of God], Warszawa 1974, pp.23-33.

[62]J.Hessen: *Erkenntnistheorie*, Bonn-Berlin 1926, p.90.

[63]J.Hessen: *Lehrbuch der Philosophie*, vol.1: *Wissenschaftslehre*, München 1947, p.249.

have an objective character and which are not "factual" properties of things[64]. They are also a relation, but not only; they imply obligation but cannot be exclusively reduced to it. Value is "a kind of a superstructure", though at the same time "it grows out of its foundations"[65]. Ingarden separated aesthetic and ethical values: the former have an intentional character, while the latter are created by man at the moment of realizing an undertaken act. Consequently, the Polish phenomenologist was of the opinion that value cannot be unequivocally classified as "an ideal being, real being or intentional being"[66]. Thus, agnosticism was his last word although he also acknowledged that the "significance" of values presupposes some kind of their existence.

The latter concepts of value share a common ground, namely, they accept their objective character. Still, the nature of values is explained differently in particular trends, Thomism and phenomenology. The complex problem of the ontological status of values is most often solved in two ways, ontologically or personalistically. The first way was taken by traditional Thomism, the latter - by D. von Hildebrand and some phenomenologists (including Scheler). In principle, the two approaches are not mutually exclusive and that is why they should be integrated. In our opinion, values are not merely man's subjective experiences or exclusively potential beings. Values have an objective character, while their reality has two aspects, ontological and personalistic. Ontological reality is dependent on the act of existence of a being as a carrier of values. At the same time, however, there is an evident fact of the connection of values with the world of persons as rational and free causes of values. One may therefore say that values are real thanks to persons - formally as a result of man's activity and, fundamentally, due to the causative power of God. The affirmation of the reality of the world of values is not identical with granting them an existence of a substantial being, that is, an autonomy in respect to the "carriers". Values are anchored in being, they inhere in it, they are its immanent "quality". At the same time, one may speak of a new degree of the reality of the phenomenon of values when they are seen, approved of, or realized by a person. Only in this context may one speak of values as such, especially of higher cognitive, ethical or sacral-religious values. Man's death or his infidelity to values of this kind do not mean their annihilation since they are always fundamentally real - in the Prime Cause, that is, in God. The problem of the ontological status of values is very complex and still poses many questions. The attempt to solve this problem presented above could be described as "personalistic ontology". On its basis it seems possible to undertake another difficult problem of the relations between value and person, but it would require a separate analysis.

---

[64]R.Ingarden: *Przeżycie* ..., op.cit., pp.83-127.

[65]Ibid., p.100.

[66]Ibid., pp.108,112.

LITERATURE

BRENTANO, F.: *Vom Ursprung sittlicher Erkenntnis*, Hamburg 1955.

BUCZYŃSKA-GAREWICZ, H.: *Uczucia i rozum w świecie wartości* [Emotions and Reason in the World of Values], Wrocław 1975.

FOREST, A.: "L'expérience de la valeur", *Revue Néoscholastique* 43 (1940).

GUTWENGER, J.: *Wertphilosophie*, Innsbruck 1952.

HESSEN, J.: *Lehrbuch der Philosophie*, vol.2: *Wertlehre*, München 1948.

HESSEN, J.: *Wertphilosophie*, Paderborn 1937.

HILDEBRAND D. von: *Christian Ethics*, New York 1953.

HILDEBRAND D. von: *Der Sinn philosophischen Fragen und Erkennens*, Bonn 1950.

INGARDEN, R.: *Przeżycie - dzieło - wartość* [Experience - Work - Value], Kraków 1966.

KLENK, G.F.: *Wert - Sein - Gott*, Rom 1942.

KOWALCZYK, S.: "Philosophical Concepts of Values", *Collectanea Theologica* 57 (1987), fasc. specialis. 115-129.

KRAUS, O.: *Die Werttheorien. Geschichte und Kritik*, Berlin 1914.

LAVELLE, L.: *Traité des valeur*, vols.1-2, Paris 1951-1955.

LOTZ, J.B.: *Sein und Wert*, Paderborn 1938.

RINTELEN, J.: *Das philosophische Wertproblem*, Halle 1923.

SCHELER, M.: *Der Formalismus in der Ethik und die materiale Wertethik*, Halle 1921.

SCHELER, M.: *Moralia*, Leipzig 1922.

ZNANIECKI, F.: *Zagadnienie wartości w filozofii* [The Problem of Value in Philosphy], Warszawa 1910.

Chapter 8

Moral Experience - Conscience

Although man is so deeply rooted in nature, in the material world, he becomes more specifically human only through the world of culture. It is primarily an internal-moral culture. To use the language of I.Kant, man is a being that perceives a moral imperative in himself. This ontological imprint of the moral law is a privilege and an obligation of the rational, free person. The world of persons is inescapably bound with the world of morality. Ethical experience, connected with the categories of good and evil, always constitutes a part of human experience.

(i) Explanation of Basic Concepts

History of humankind makes it possible to find out a variety of attitudes towards the phenomenon of moral values. Some of them include: amoralism, immoralism, conventionalism, reductionism, utilitarianism, emotivism, legal rigorism, ethical personalism[1].

Amoralism occurred in several varieties; the Greek sophists and adherents of hedonism (among others, Aristippus of Cyrene), were propagators of ethical relativism and they rejected unchangeable and universal moral laws. Another form of amoralism was accepted by the followers of extreme individualism (M.Stirner, J.P.Sartre) who expressed a conviction that an individual man establishes for himself his rights and obligations. A similar attitude towards the realm of morality was accepted by F.Nietzsche who described himself as an immoralist. He questioned traditional morality and regarded it as harmful for the "supermen", so he subordinated ethics to the command of "the will of power". Moral is that which serves the biological-pragmatic development of man. Conventionalism is accepted by the adherents of naturalism who interpret ethics as a specific consensus of people, based on historical knowledge, ethnology, science about religion etc. In Poland moral norms were interpreted in this way by Maria Ossowska. Ethical reductionism is

---

[1]Cf. J.de Finance: "La notion du bien", *Gregorianum*, 39 (1958), pp.5-42; W.Tatarkiewicz: "O bezwzględności dobra" [On the Absolute Nature of the Good] [in:] *Droga do filozofii* [The Road to Philosophy], Warszawa 1971, pp.211-290; W.Bartuschat: "Gut" [in:] *Historisches Wörterbuch der Philosophie*, Basel 1974, vol.3, pp.937-977.

accepted by the adherents of biologism, psychologism, and sociologism, who reduce moral phenomena to more fundamental categories, such as biological-material, psychological or economic-social structures. Among others, reductionism occurs in Freudianism and Marxism[2].

A specific attitude towards morality is assumed by the followers of utilitarianism (J. Bentham, J.S.Mill) who subordinate moral categories to the demands and interests of social life. This clearly means moral relativism, though motivated by reasons of the good of social groups. A mild variant of relativism appears in the form of emotivism, an attitude especially popular in the circles of the followers of Neo-Positivism (R.Carnap, A.J.Ayer, and, in Poland, I.Lazari-Pawłowska). Emotivists reduce moral norms exclusively to the sphere of emotional sensations and personal convictions, so that their rational justification becomes impossible. Hence, for them, moral norms have no cognitive value because one cannot justify the passage from the descriptive language to the evaluative and normative language. The enumerated interpretations of moral life are unsatisfactory because instead of an explanation they in fact propose an abandonment of normative ethics. The undermining of the autonomy and universality of moral categories destroys their immanent sense and personal function.

Positive attitudes towards ethics are doctrinally differentiated in evaluating the character of its norms, manner of motivation, distribution of emphasis etc. The history of moral doctrines makes it possible to distinguish in this respect intellectualism, voluntarism, emotionalism and pragmatism. A good representative of intellectualism was Socrates who identified virtue with adequate knowledge. An evil man is the one who does not know the truly real good. Moderate intellectualism is characteristic of the Thomistic interpretation of conscience. Ethical voluntarism occurs in the trend of Augustinian thought, among others, in St. Bonaventura who connected both the genesis of moral norms and their realization mainly with the sphere of the will. A radical variety of voluntarism is Kantian rigorism (also called legalism) which interprets moral values as a fulfilment of duties. Ethical emotionalism is characteristic of phenomenology, especially of Max Scheler, a propagator of axiological intuitionism.

Christian thought is permanently related with personalism and that is why it speaks, among others, about ethical personalism. There are many varieties and domains of Christian morality. Theologians distinguish three main concepts of ethics, nomological, teleological and Christological. The followers of the first one describe the moral good as a realization of God's will; the adherents of the second one interpret the good as an actualization of the human being according to its ontological perfection; while the proponents of the third concept combine morality with the fulfilment of Christ's commands. The latter trend already has a theological character.

---

[2]Marx and Engels questioned the autonomy and universality of ethical norms, whereas some contemporary Marxists (among others, M.Fritzhand) affirm the existence of elementary moral judgements common to most people.

Christian ethics is organically connected with the recognition of absolute moral norms, although this should not be identified with their static understanding. The opposition to ethical absolutism is found in relativism which may occur in two forms, subjectivistic and objectivistic. The former is usually connected with individualism, e.g. emotivism or atheistic existentialism. Objectivistic relativism is typical of the historical materialism of Marxism, in whose interpretation moral categories are secondary and dependent on economic and social structures. Bearing in mind the manner of justifying moral norms, one may distinguish three conceptions of the good, phenomenological, ontological and axiological-psychological. The former is typical of Aristotle who described the good as an object of human desire. St. Thomas Aquinas was not satisfied with a description of the good by pointing to psychological effects, i.e. to a desire of winning it, and he searched for its ontical sources. The good is that which constitutes it ontologically, namely, the form and real existence. The axiological-psychological conception of the good appeared in Brentano who defined the good as an object of the "right love". This conception was continued by M.Scheler who emphasized the moral good as a leading category in the world of values.

Man's personal experience demands the application of several languages, descriptive, evaluative and normative. Empirical sciences are in principle limited to description and interpretation, with the latter containing elements of explicating heuretic. Ethical propositions do not constitute a description of facts (only the sociology of morality has a descriptive character), but they have an evaluative-appraising and normative character. That is why there is much simplification in a proposition by David Hume († 1776) who claimed that the passage from declarative sentence of the "is" type to the prescriptive sentences of the "ought to" (resp. "ought not to") type is unprovable[3]. The English sensualist, in keeping with the assumptions of the scientistic conception, obscured the difference between humanistic and natural sciences. The philosophy of man belongs to the former and that is why an adequate description of the reality of human existence requires the application of the language of values and evaluation. In turn, the axiological language cannot provide a description of empirical realities because it concerns the world of the human person. Hence, its natural consequence is the normative language.

(ii) The Moral Good: Its Sense and Genesis

The idea of the moral good, if it is to function as a category epistemologically and existentially meaningful, must be apprehended in the context of ethical experience. A number of philosophical trends (logical empiricism, emotivism, dialectical materialism), in consequence of accepting the scientistic model of science, narrow down human

---

[3]N.K.Smith: *The Philosophy of D.Hume*, London 1941, chaps.6-9.

experience to sensual perception[4]. As a result they lose from sight the fundamental forms of human experience, including the moral experience. Such an experience has as its object a moral fact which constitutes a basic means of expression of the human person. The ethical datum appertains to every normal man and only to man (in the world known to us), constituting a natural culmination of his rational consciousness and freedom. The objects of moral experience include ethical values which appear to man as existential ideals, patterns of behaviour, inner commands, or obligations which demand realization. Moral values may be apprehended in two ways, as objective and subjective. Their classical understanding usually stressed the objective aspect, that is, their agreement with an objective norm of the law, natural or civic. Today, greater emphasis is placed on the subjective aspect of moral values, that is, their relation with the human person[5]. However, this cannot be understood as their subjectivization or, even less, as their relativization. Any adequate comprehension of moral values requires a consideration of three moments: man's personal dimension, his freedom, and values as objects of human activity.

The relations between ethics and philosophical anthropology have been repeatedly questioned. Tadeusz Kotarbiński propagated the so-called independent ethics[6]. Although he based it on the idea of "conscience", which was not clearly specified, he simultaneously acknowledged a possibility of separating the theory of morality from religion and philosophy. Some Marxists are also convinced that there is no significant relation between ethics and the philosophy of man[7]. Such a relation is questioned at least in the sense that moral principles cannot be deduced from anthropology.

The above position is controversial, while its motivation omits the essence of the relation between ethics and a philosophical theory of man. For, even if the former does not deductively result from the latter, one may take advantage of the method of reduction[8]. Moral norms are explained adequately only by bringing them down to the human nature as their ontical foundation. Such a rational and free person as man perceives in his nature certain moral obligations. By ignoring and breaking them in some significant way we provoke our own self-destruction. Man is a potential being and that is why he demands actualization and finalization. He actualizes himself through an act or, speaking more precisely, through a morally good act. Thus, ethics finds a natural foundation only in a philosophy of man, because only a person can be a subject and an

---

[4]K.Wojtyła: "Problem doświadczenia w etyce" [The Problem of Experience in Ethics], *Roczniki Filozoficzne*, 17 (1969), no.2, pp.5- 24; S.Ohe: "Wert und menschlicher Sein", *Revue International de Philosophie*, 28 (1974), pp.82-98; W.Ernst: "Zur Begründung christlicher Sittlichkeit", *Studia Moralia*, 14 (1976), pp.9-46.

[5]K.Wojtyła: *Osoba i czyn*, op.cit., pp.14-16.

[6]*Sprawy sumienia* [The Matters of Conscience], Warszawa 1956; *Medytacje o życiu godziwym* [Meditations on Worthy Life], Warszawa 1967.

[7]Cf. *Etyka* (1970), no.6, pp.51-79.

[8]K.Wojtyła: *Osoba i czyn*, op.cit., pp.19 ff.

object of a moral obligation. At its ontical foundation, the moral fact is connected with the personal being which, in the direct perspective, is human, while, in further perspective, is God's.

Man exists but at the same time he is also becoming, that is, developing. This is achieved as a result of the ontical faculties of taking decisions about the shape of one's own life. The moral good and evil are consequences of self-determination, i.e., of freedom. Therefore, the ethical good is not only a consequence of obligations, but also of freedom. Without real freedom the category of obligation, so strongly stressed by Kant, loses its ontological sense. Moral responsibility is conditioned by man's internal freedom.

Another component of the moral good is found in the category of values. This problem has already been discussed above, nevertheless, two points should again be made. Thanks to his rationality and freedom, man is responsible for the realization of higher values. Due to them he develops internally, while when he opposes them - he undergoes disintegration. Secondly, being himself a subject, he is the central value of the world. Since he is responsible for values, he must, first of all, be responsible for himself. There is never any moral good where the value of the human person is disregarded. And there can be no full humanity when cognitive and moral values are endangered.

Moral experience is an integral part of man's experience as a person. But there arises a problem: how can one pass from existential experience to universal ethical norms?[9] How can one generalize individual moral impressions? There have been multiple attempts of justifying moral principles, ontological and extra-ontological. The latter occur in the ethical thought connected with the currents of phenomenology and empiricism.

Franz Brentano, author of *Vom Ursprung sittlicher Erkenntnis*, was a forerunner of the phenomenological current. Although he proclaimed an objective existence of values, yet, as their criterion he accepted the subjective feeling of love. The good is that which is worthy of love[10]. It was an emotionalistic interpretation of values, also including the moral good. Such a conception of ethics was connected with a conviction that feelings - and not only concepts and judgements - play a cognitive role in human life. The same line of reasoning is followed in Max Scheler's emotional intuitionism. Although emotional experiences most probably co-participate in broadly understood man's perception, the excessive ethical subjectivism of phenomenologists would be hard to accept. For if the moral evaluation of the good depends on man's subjective impression, then ethics, as a philosophical science, is deprived of objective criteria. What is accepted by the "right love" of one man, may be questioned by that of another man. The criterion of emotional "obviousness" is equally subjective and arbitrary.

---

[9]J.Pieper: *Die Wirklichkeit und das Gute*, Mlinich 1956; S.Olejnik: *Eudajmonizm. Studium nad podstawami etyki* [Eudemonism. A Study in the Foundations of Ethics], Lublin 1958; T.Styczeń: *Problem możliwości etyki jako empirycznie uprawomocnionej i ogólnie ważnej teorii moralności* [The Problem of the Possibility of Ethics as an Empirically Justified and Generally Valid Theory of Morality], Lublin 1972.

[10]F.Brentano: *Vom Ursprung* ..., op.cit., p.18.

In its radical variety, the phenomenological interpretation of axiology and ethics follows Plato who accepted the priority of ideas over reality. In consequence, he accepted the priority of ethics over metaphysics, of the *ethos* over the *logos*. Moral norms are not discovered in a being, even if it is a personal object - man. That is why it is suggested that moral experience is a consequence of an encounter with another man. Only the experience of another man is to be a moral experience. The above interpretation of axiology and ethics approaches very closely subjectivism and idealism. A rational passage from our "I" to the reality of another man, i.e., from individual consciousness to the external world, is lacking. On the one hand, they speak of the "axiological I" as man's primordial experience, but, on the other hand, moral experience is to begin only when encountering other people. Is it possible that moral norms do not inhere in the very subjectivity of the human person and did not refer to it? Without an ontology of the human person it is difficult to speak meaningfully about its *ethos*.

An extra-ontological motivation of normative ethics is accepted, among others, by Tadeusz Czeżowski. He derives universal moral norms from the so-called elementary original evaluations[11]. These are existential-concrete appraisals of values, formulated in an equally direct manner as perceptions. Judgements of this type are based on a specific obviousness of evaluations. Spontaneous axiological experience gives rise to general norms of human conduct, thus constituting a basis for an ethics. The proposition of the Polish philosopher is unsatisfactory since it reverses the fundamental course of reasoning. An existential evaluation of an encountered or realized value logically results from the accepted ethical pattern, hence it cannot constitute its justification. The evaluative-appraising judgement is not a description of the perceived reality, but a personal-moral attitude towards the situation that has occurred. Obviously, this does not lead to a conclusion that ethics does not refer to the axiological-moral experience. Ethical concepts and norms always grow out of man's personal experience.

The considerations presented so far prove the impossibility of justifying ethical norms in separation from the ontology of the human being. This is the way of Thomistic philosophy, referring to Aristotle. The old-Greek thinker accepted the teleology of the good, perceiving in it a natural actualization and perfection of human nature. Thomists agree with a conviction that only the beingness of man - person constitutes the natural foundation of the moral good. Yet, if in the past reference was made primarily to the category of natural law, today the category of human dignity is being emphasized.

The idea of the moral good is based on natural law by the Thomist, Jacques Maritain. He referred to St.Thomas Aquinas, who recognized the moral act as an integral element of the human being[12]. It is within man himself that every moral dilemma occurs, frequently turning into a drama. Human nature is a foundation of moral experiences but it is not their highest criterion. Man discovers in himself natural law, i.e. a set of

---

[11]"Etyka jako nauka normatywna" [Ethics as a Normative Science] [in:] *Odczyty filozoficzne* [Philosophical Lectures], Toruń 1958, pp.59-67.

[12]*De Veritate*, q.25,a.5.

universal, unchangeable and obligatory moral principles[13]. They should determine man's conduct. Speaking about the knowability of natural law, Maritain renounces the deductive-rationalistic method. Natural law is an expression of man's spontaneous dynamism, therefore it is being discovered in its existential realization. Experience and moral values express man's natural predilection. Obviously, there is a multiplicity of human predilections, biological and mental. The latter include inner imperatives of the type: "Do good"[14]. The identification of moral categories takes factually place in pre-philosophical reflection which should not be identified with an emotional-subjective impression or an irrational intuition. Natural law, "readable" in human nature, is not man's immanent work. Following St. Thomas Aquinas, Maritain states that it is a participation in the creation of a rational being in God's eternal law[15]. Human reason recognizes natural law but it does not create it. This is confirmed by the attributes of this law, that is, universality, permanence, normative character. Natural law is a basis of normative ethics.

There is also another version of the ontological explication of the sources of man's moral goodness. Karol Wojtyła speaks about the personalistic norm of morality[16]. Thus, moral action means an act of man as a subject and a person in respect to another man - person. All instrumental treatment of oneself or of another man is in disagreement with man's ontical structure, with his attributes, natural calling, immanent sense. Human dignity is therefore an ontical foundation of the moral norm, though it is not an ultimate criterion of differentiating between good and evil. The moral "ought to" is read by man in his inner nature. Ethical norms are as universal and permanent as humankind - its dignity, structure, attributes. Thus, the logic of the *ethos* is the logic of a person.

The Thomistic conceptions of the moral good, traditional and phenomenological, briefly presented above, are mutually complementary. The first conception claims that the moral good is a consequence of the agreement of a human act with an obligatory ethical rule, especially with natural law. The second conception describes the good as an agreement with the personalistic norm of morality. The structure of the human person is of such kind that the will accepts the norm discovered by reason. Man did not create his own nature and therefore he cannot arbitrarily establish moral norms. He identifies and realizes them, but he does not create them.

---

[13] *Summa Theologiae* I-II,q.94, aa.1-6; J.Maritain: *Moral Principles in Action*, New York 1952, pp.63-72.

[14] J.Maritain, op.cit., pp.63-65.

[15] Ibid., pp.65 ff.

[16] *Osoba i czyn*, op.cit., especially pp. 162 ff; cf. A.Rodziński: *Osoba i kultura* [The Person and Culture], Warszawa 1985, pp.29-32.

(iii) Conscience

An integral part of man's moral experience is the phenomenon of conscience. The category of conscience plays a crucial role in Christian thought, although it is not always interpreted identically. St.Thomas Aquinas explains conscience as, first of all, an act of reason and that is why one may speak about its intellectualistic interpretation in his case. Conscience, also called synteresis, is understood by St. Thomas as a cognition of the fundamental norms of conduct based ultimately on natural law[17]. If in the theoretical sphere man recognizes the fundamental laws of being and thought, in the sphere of moral action conscience points to rules corresponding to human dignity. In existential experience conscience is not restricted to a disclosure of general ethical norms but it is a practical judgement[18]. If natural laws command "Do good", conscience teaches the manner of realizing good under given circumstances. Conscience constantly accompanies man in his life, in his perturbations, decisions, choices, reflections. Moral norms have a general character, but reality constantly changes and we are acting in unique situations. Hence, there occurs a certain tension between general ethical principles and the specificity of the ever changing existential situation. The voice of conscience allows the proper choice to be made, although often it is not easy either in the theoretical moral evaluation or in the pragmatic choice of the way. Judgements of conscience are not restricted to the moment of moral evaluation, but they always imply a command to action.

The Thomistic analysis of conscience emphasizes in it mainly the co-participation of intellect. St.Bonaventura († 1274), in agreement with his voluntarism, stressed in conscience primarily the element of the will. Conscience means a dynamics of the will directed at moral activity. The role of the aspirational sphere in the activity of human conscience was also indicated by the English thinker, Cardinal John Henry Newman († 1890). He stressed the fact the conscience is an integral element of man's spiritual-mental sphere. "Conscience has a legitimate place among our mental acts; as really so, as the action of memory, of reasoning, or as the sense of the beautiful"[19]. The voice of conscience constitutes a constant factor of the human person. "It is a moral sense, and a sense of duty; a judgement of the reason and a magisterial dictate. Of course its act is indivisible"[20]. The nature of conscience is interpreted by Newman somewhat ambivalently; he calls it an "intellectual sentiment", perceiving the participation of intellect in it, but he also emphasizes the role of emotional experiences when he claims that "it is always emotional"[21]. It was not an irrationalization of conscience, although the

---

[17]*Summa Theologiae* I-II,q.94,a.1, ad 2; I,q.79,a.12; H.Eklund: "Das Gewissen des modernen Menschen", *Zeitschrift für systematische Theologie*, 14 (1967), pp.197-224; L.Szafrański: *Sumienie* [Conscience], Lublin 1958.

[18]Some Thomists call conscience a practically practical judgement.

[19]J.H.Newman: *An Essay in Aid of a Grammar of Assent*, New York 1947, p.80.

[20]Ibid.

[21]Ibid., p.83.

cognitive-mental factor has insufficiently been taken into consideration. The English thinker justly indicates the rich scale of experiences connected with conscience, both positive (e.g. deep peace, sense of security, trustfulness, joy) and negative (such as anxiety, fear, loneliness, condemnation of oneself etc). Conscience is a phenomenon which is universal historically, culturally, religiously, and it concerns men of every age (beginning from the early childhood).

The holistic interpretation of conscience is affirmed by K.Wojtyła who describes conscience as an internal act of the human person and as the fulfilment of the person through this act[22]. The axiology of conscience, connected with the differentiation of the moral categories of good and evil, derives from the ontology of conscience. Conscience is man's conscious action and that is why its natural aim is the recognition of a full truth about man and his calling. Truth is naturally complemented by the good which, through the voice of conscience, reveals itself as a "normative reality"[23]. Man's conscience is a synthesis of his mind and will, a finalization of his ability of recognizing the truth and of his self-determination. The Polish thinker warned against a strictly formal and intellectualistic apprehension of conscience, i.e. against restricting it to the stage of the final judgement. "When seen as a whole, conscience is a completely specific effort of a person attempting to apprehend a truth in the realm of values. It is, at first, a search for this truth and its examination, before it turns into certainty and judgement"[24]. Conscience is a normative voice of the truth which the human mind has recognized and to which the will feels subordinated. Although the mental faculties, intellect and will, play a significant role in the domain of conscience, yet in a personal experience it has a strong emotional impact. The latter factor is particularly active after a performance or avoidance of performance of a perceived moral obligation.

Conscience has a double function, evaluative and normative[25]. The former is connected with man's axiological consciousness, perceiving a multiplicity of qualitatively different values. Axiological consciousness is complemented by ethical consciousness, whose consequence is a sense of obligations connected with social-moral commands and prohibitions. One may also speak about prospective and retrospective conscience[26]. Prospective conscience informs man about the moral values of foreseen actions. Retrospective conscience concerns the consequences of the acts already performed: the good brings joy and peace, while evil - a sense of guilt and anxiety. In this way conscience is for man both a guidepost - before the deed, and a sanction - after the deed.

There still remains the problem of the genesis of human conscience. Herbert Spencer († 1903) was a follower of ethical evolutionism. He claimed that a long-lasting external

---

[22]*Osoba i czyn*, op.cit., p.160.

[23]Ibid., pp.163,167,174.

[24]Ibid., p.167; cf. p.169.

[25]J.H.Newman, op.cit., pp.80-81.

[26]G.Kalinowski: *Initiation à la philosophie morale*, Paris 1966, p.185.

compulsion (fear of a ruler, social group, punishment etc.) has led to the development of an inner compulsion, that is, of conscience. Freud interpreted conscience as an effect of the "social censor" on human personality, so that the individual "I" is to be a product of the social "super-ego". A decisive role of society is also stressed by historical materialism in whose interpretation the whole man - including his conscience - is shaped by the collective.

The above interpretations of the phenomenon of conscience do not so much explain it but rather neutralize its normative function. They lead to a depersonalization of conscience, reducing it to the role of a social mirror. Yet, conscience should not be trivialized by perceiving in it only fear of punishment or social opinion. Conscience is not a result of a training of man. It should not be separated from man's personal being, from his self-consciousness, sensitivity to values, freedom. Conscience is an ability of reading the truth about one's own life calling which cannot be justified by any social intervention or a mechanism of biological drives. Man is neither a "product of society" (as Marxism suggests) nor a being directed exclusively by instincts (as Freud maintained), but a person attracted by values and capable of directing itself by the voice of conscience. Biological and sociological interpretations of conscience lead to its deformation since they fail to perceive its anthropological foundation. The category of conscience loses all sense when it is separated from the ontology of the person and axiology connected with love.

Extra-ontological explications of the phenomenon of conscience do not explain anything and in practice, destroy it. The naturalistic-immanent interpretation of conscience omits its relation to natural law, universality of moral intuitions, unconditionality of norms, depth of personal experience. Conscience is a part of the human being, rational and free, and yet accidental in its existence. Man's cognitive faculties explain the knowability of moral categories, while the accidentality of being does not explain the genesis of conscience. The voice of conscience is a living sense of man's responsibility to the Person, omnipotent, omniscient and holy. Only God can be such a Person, the Creator of man and his highest Law-giver[27]. Speaking about eternal, universal and obligatory moral laws, conscience constitutes an existential bond between man and God. That is why an appropriate development of conscience leads - within the depth of our being - to an experience of Him, Who gave us our human face, both physical and spiritual. The loss of moral sensitivity and the stifling of the voice of conscience amount to man's spiritual self-destruction.

[27]J.H.Newman, op.cit., pp.83 ff.

LITERATURE

BOURKE, V.J.: *History of Ethics*, New York 1968.

BRENTANO, F.: *Vom Ursprung sittlicher Erkenntnis*, Hamburg 1955.

KALINOWSKI, G.: *Initiation à la philosophie morale*, Paris 1966.

MARITAIN, J.: *Neuf leçons sur les notions premières de la philosophie morale*, Paris 1950.

NEWMAN, J.H.: *An Essay in Aid of a Grammar of Assent*, New York 1947.

OLEJNIK, S.: *Eudajmonizm. Studium nad podstawami etyki* [Eudemonism. A Study in the Foundations of Ethics], Lublin 1958.

PIEPER, J.: *Die Wirklichkeit und das Gute*, Münich 1956.

REINERT, H.: *Gut und Böse*, Fribourg 1965.

RODZIŃSKI, A.: *Osoba i kultura* [The Person and Culture], Warszawa 1985.

SCHELER, M.: *Der Formalismus in der Ethik und die materiale Wertethik*, Halle 1921.

STYCZEŃ, T.: *Etyka niezależna?* [Independent Ethics?], Lublin 1980.

ŚLIPKO, T.: *Etos chrześcijański. Zarys etyki ogólnej* [The Christian Ethos. An Outline of General Ethics], Kraków 1974.

WITEK, S.: *Chrześcijańska wizja moralności* [The Christian Vision of Morality], Poznań 1982.

WOJTYŁA, K.: *Love and Responsibility*, tr.by H.T.Willetts, London 1982.

Chapter 9

Religious Experience

As history of humankind demonstrates, man has always been the homo religiosus and ens adorans. This is additionally confirmed by prehistory which reveals that the manner of burying the dead about three or four thousand years ago constitutes evidence of a belief in afterlife[1]. The universality of religious life is not only a historical fact. Religious experience is shared by a majority of humankind also today. The disregard of the religious dimension of man's life by philosophy is contrary to epistemological and ontological realism.

(i) Semantic explanations

The category of "religious experience" demands an explanation of the concept of religion. There are various kinds of descriptions of the phenomenon of religion, etymological, sociological, emotional-psychological, ethical, speculative, and, finally, integral[2]. The etymological description appears in St.Augustine who combined the term "religio" with the verb "reeligere", perceiving in religion a specific bond between man and God. There have also been frequent attempts to describe religion from sociological and psychological perspectives. Erich Fromm († 1980) used the term religion to denote "any system of thought and action which provides the individual with a frame of reference and an object of worship"[3]. Others define religion as "a quest of force in life" and a search for the sense which would make it possible to order one's whole life into a meaningful totality[4]. The sociologist, Émile Durkheim († 1917) defined religion as a community of believers in the existence of some sacrum who accept a certain ethics[5]. The above

---

[1]S.Kowalczyk: "Doświadczenie religijne" [Religious Experience] [in:] *Drogi ku Bogu* [Roads towards God], Wrocław 1983, pp.91-131.

[2]Z.J.Zdybicka and S.Kamiński: "Definicje religii a typy nauk o religii" [Definitions of Religion and Kinds of Sciences about Religion], *Roczniki Filozoficzne* 22 (1974), no.1, pp.103-160.

[3]*Psychoanalysis and Religion*, New Haven 1955.

[4]G.van der Leeuw: *Phänomenologie der Religion*, Tübingen 1956, pp.778-780.

[5]*Les formes élémentaires de la vie religieuse*, Paris 1912, p.65.

descriptions entirely omit the doctrinal element of religion and restrict themselves to indicate its psychological and social expression. This is too broad an understanding of religion, because it also covers pantheistic religions and even "lay religions"; the latter may include, for instance, the cult of a chief, race, state or the idea of social revolution.

Many definitions of religion offered today often emphasize one of its elements while neglecting others, equally or even more important. Following Friedrich Schleiermacher, Ludwik Feuerbach († 1872) understood religion as "a product of human instinct of happiness"[6]. It was a naturalistic and emotional explanation of the basis of religious life. On the other hand, characterizing religion, Immanuel Kant stressed its ethical functions. As he wrote, religion "is a recognition of God's command in all duties"[7]. On the opposite pole to this interpretation, there is the Hegelian conception of religion; namely, religion is understood as "a consciousness of the absolute truth"[8]. This, in turn, was a rationalization of religious faith, pushing aside its supernatural dimension and the element of mystery.

There have also been attempts to establish an integral definition of religion. Religious life possesses emotional, cognitive and aspirational factors; it plays ethical and social functions, but these factors, when grasped in isolation, do not constitute its essence. Johannes Hessen described religion as "the existential relation to the Sacrum"[9]. Louis Lavelle sees in religion a manifestation of the presence of God in Whose power man can participate ontically and ethically[10]. Sometimes religion is understood simply as "a sense of the Absolute"[11]. Religion always means an overcoming of man's loneliness[12]. Yet, it cannot be achieved exclusively on the psychological plane but through a discovery and acceptance of the extra-human reality. That is why religion can only be used in respect to the existential relation to the absolute "You", to the transcendental Sacrum. Such a description will, first of all, refer to monotheistic religions and, to some extent, also to polytheistic religions. But there also exist some pantheistic ideas of the deity (Neo-Platonism, Hegelianism) and even religions lacking any clear idea of the Absolute (Buddhism). It seems that in the latter case religion becomes an attempt of looking for an everlasting and eschatological sense of life through departing from the individual dimension of existence as a restrictive one.

Therefore, what is religious experience? The category of experience should be apprehended integrally and personalistically. Hence, the experience of the human person cannot be restricted to sensual perception but it ought to include a totality of man's

---

[6]*Das Wesen des Christentums*, Stuttgart 1960, p.13.

[7]*La religion dans les limites de la raison*, Paris 1913, p.183.

[8]*Phenomenology of Spirit*, tr.by H.Miller, Oxford 1977, p.483.

[9]*Religionsphilosophie*, München 1955, vol.2, p.27.

[10]*Traité des valeurs*, Paris 1955, vol.2, p.497.

[11]F.Ortegat: *Philosophie de la religion*, Paris 1937, p.23.

[12]Such a description has been proposed by L.Kołakowski.

experiences and impressions. Some speak about the "religious sensation" but this term does not seem very fortunate because it carries an implication of an emotional understanding of religion. Religious experience should not be understood exclusively as any one of the many sectors of man's psychic life. The point here is the "religious dimension of human experience"[13], i.e. referring its totality to God. In fact everything can be transformed into a religious experience - personal joy and sadness, suffering, a sense of a family or national community, admiration of nature, work etc. In consequence of religious experiences man's existence acquires a deeper, transcendental sense. Hence, religious experience may be understood in a strict or a broad sense[14]. The former concerns exceptionally intense experiences, manifestly referring to the idea of God, e.g. a conversion, mystical experiences, a revelation. Religious experience in the broad sense covers everything that is connected with the Absolute in whatever way: prayer, religious cult, acts of faith and love of God, offered sacrifices, construction of places of cult.

Verbal descriptions of religious experience are highly varied. Hessen describes such an experience as a sense of a transcendental axiological reality, occurring in the centre of personality, a reality which is a "***misterium tremendum***" and, at the same time, a "***misterium fascinosum***"[15]. In a similar way religious experience is characterized by Romano Guardini († 1968) who calls it "an impression of an element of the other, the holy, that ***numinosum***"[16]. Both descriptions are, in turn, based on the analysis of Rudolf Otto who, in his work *The Idea of The Holy* emphasized the ambivalence of religious experiences. Religious experience may therefore be described as: an internal encounter with God, consciousness of the presence of the deity and of one's participation in its internal life, experience of one's dependence on the transcendental Sacrum. The multiplicity of definitions of religious experience is a consequence of stress placed on different aspects of this phenomenon - ontological and axiological, subjectivistic and objectivistic, cognitive, emotional and ethical.

In the very centre of religious experience there is the act of faith. The conception of faith is also ambivalent since it is used in everyday life, as well as in social and even political realms. The element of faith occurs even in the domain of science where we lay our faith in historians, discoverers, travellers, experts etc. The point here concerns the religious faith in which one can still distinguish two senses, cognitive and existential[17]. In the cognitive sense faith means a belief in a given truth, usually formulated as a dogmatic system. This is a truth about the existence of God, about His attributes, about His relation to man. In its existential sense faith means man's attitude towards the

---

[13]J.E.Smith: *Experience and God*, Cambridge 1968, chap.II.

[14]C.H.Whiteley: "The Cognitive Factor in Religious Experience" [in:] *Religious Language and the Problem of Religious Knowledge*, ed.by R.E.Santoni, London 1973, pp.258-265.

[15]*Religionsphilosophie*, op.cit., vol.2, p.103.

[16]*Die Offenbarung. Ihr Wesen und ihre Formen*, Würzburg 1946, p.24.

[17]M.Buber: *Two Types of Faith*, London 1951, pp.9 ff.

acknowledged deity; it means believing or trusting in God. Both meanings of faith are mutually complementary, while their separation leads to a deformation of religious life. If experienced consistently, belief in God should be complemented by believing God, that is, showing him full trust in our personal and social life.

The religious sense of faith is a central element of Christianity. St.Thomas Aquinas characterized faith as "an act of mind accepting God's truth at the command of the will moved by God's grace"[18]. This description functioned in Christian thought for a long time, in fact, until the Vatican Council I. The Council then proclaimed that we believe in the revealed truth on the basis of God's authority who is infallible and cannot mislead anybody[19]. It was an intellectualistic and theoretical apprehension of faith. It emphasized the role of intellect and cognition, while the personal dimension of faith was pushed into the background. In our times there have appeared other definitions of religious faith - phenomenological, existential-functional, synthesizing. The dialogical and responsive characteristics of faith are also emphasized[20]. The culmination of the integral-personalistic trend in the description of faith has been Vaticanum II. The dogmatic constitution about God's Revelation (5) states: "To the revealing God one should show the 'obedience of 'faith' [*Romans* 16,26; II *Corinthians* 10,5-5], in which, out of his own will, man commits himself to God, in an attitude of 'complete submission of reason and will towards the revealing God' and voluntarily accepts the data revealed by Him". This description, while not renouncing the doctrinal element of faith, lays greater stress on its existential function. Faith means first of all a spiritual communion of man with God, which bears fruit in the realization of higher values in everyday life[21]. Faith means "knowledge born out of religious love"[22].

(ii) The Subjective Structure of the Religious Act

Religious experience, when perceived as a whole and especially in connection with monotheistic religions, has a double dimension, horizontal and vertical[23]. It takes place in man - the subject, yet, at the same time, it is strictly connected with the transcendental object of worship. Hence, it is possible to speak about the bipolarity of religious experience, about the dynamism of the subject and about the objective correlative, i.e. God. Both elements complement one another, while simultaneously constituting integral

---

[18] *Summa Theologiae* I-II,q.2,a.9. Comp. J.Hick: *Faith and Knowledge*, Glasgow 1975, pp.11-31.

[19] *Breviarum fidei*, Poznań 1964, 1,48.

[20] C.Cirne-Lima: *Der personale Glaube*, Innsbruck 1959.

[21] R.Guardini: *Welt und Person*, Mainz 1988, pp.145-160.

[22] B.Lonergan: *Method in Theology*, London 1972, p.115.

[23] G.van der Leeuw: *Einführung in die Phänomenologie der Religion*, Darmstadt 1961, pp.10-12.

components of religious experience. Authentic, personal religious experience occurs as a result of an internal-spiritual encounter of man with God in truth and love.

Philosophical anthropology is primarily interested in the subjective dimension of religious experience. Religion, apprehended as an expression of man's specific activity, may still be treated in two ways, as individual and as communal or social. The individual act of faith includes several factors, such as doctrinal-cognitive, aspirational-ethical, and emotional. On the other hand, religion, perceived as a social phenomenon, includes such elements as church organization, holy books, cult and a set of rites, observances, sacraments. At the moment we are interested in the individual-personal aspect of religious experience.

Religious experience contains elements which are cognitive, aspirational, ethical, emotional, pragmatic, sociological etc., although it cannot be reduced to them. It is a phenomenon irreducible to man's other experiences; it has a specific and unique character. However, the specificity of religious life does not mean that in the human person there exist some separate faculties or spheres reserved exclusively for religious acts. Religious life does not constitute a "ghetto" isolated from man's other experiences; it is an activity of the ***whole*** man, his personal involvement. This is generally recognized by psychologists of religion, philosophers and theologians[24]. For that reason the religious act is recognized as a function of man's whole personality (self) rather than of its peripheral sectors. The personal character of religious faith was emphasized by John H.Newman when he spoke about the "assent" of the whole human person to the existence of God[25]. Religious experience is a "junction" of acts in which the whole man participates. The personal dimension is perceived in acts of faith, of hope, love, loyalty and so on. That is why the Bible describes faith with such terms as "heart", "interior" etc.

Through a religious act man commits himself to God; with the faculty of his intellect he recognizes His existence; with his will, he entrusts to Him his whole life; he participates through his emotions; he wants to respect the moral norms obtained from Him; he prays. Religious experience therefore contains elements that are cognitive, aspirational, affective, ethical. Overestimation of one of those constitutive elements leads to some kind of deformation, to speculative intellectualism, voluntarism, or emotionalism in explaining religious life. Rationalism suggested that religious experience is primarily a cognitive-intellectual act. Religious ethicism perceived a particularly significant feature of religious experience in the will realizing moral obligations towards God. Finally, religious sentimentalism accepted the emotional sphere as a basis of religious life. The above trends isolate particular factors of religious experience from the totality of the experiences of the human person; they exaggerate some, and completely omit others[26].

---

[24]K.Girgensohn: *Der seelische Aufhau den religiösen Erlebens*, Gütersloh 1930; W.Gruehn: *Die Frömmingkeit der Gegenwart*, Münster 1956.

[25]Comp. A.Boekread: *The Personal Conquest of Truth according to J.H.Newman*, Louvain 1955.

[26]M.Scheler: *Vom Ewigen im Menschen*, Bern 1954, pp.240-258.

The cognitive-intellectual factor is undoubtedly a fundamental component of religious experience. Such an experience is verbalized by means of a religious language which, apart from many others functions, also plays the cognitive role, explicative and assertive. Although intellectual reflection does not yet create religious faith, still, the latter cannot ignore the mind which continues to function in religious experiences. It is not intellect that poses a danger to faith, but its excessive pretences, which may sometimes lead to "a belief in reason". Faith is primarily man's existential attitude but it cannot be based on doctrinal emptiness, for it is always faith in a certain truth. For the classics of Christian thought, for St.Augustine and St.Thomas Aquinas, belief in God means "a rational obedience" (obsequium rationabile) rather than "emotional obedience" based on a broadly understood tradition[27]. In religious experience reason plays a double role: it provides the motives of the belief in God and it performs a logical-essential systematization and verbalization of the deposit of faith. A rational explanation of the doctrinal contents of faith cannot, however, be identified with its rationalization and logicalization.

Religious experience is an object of studies of the philosophy of religion and also partly of the philosophy of God. The latter discipline analyses the fact of the existential fragility of the human being, its finiteness, and dependability in existence. Human reason, on the basis of the metaphysical principle of causality, demonstrates the indispensability of God as the Creator and Preserver of the human being. In religious experience itself the ontological relation between man and God is present, although most often it is not expressible in words. The trust in God presupposes His reality and ontological priority over man. Hence, the truth about God and man, which cannot be personally experienced without intellect, constitutes a constant element of the religious act. The religious cognition of truth, however, is not identical with a discursive-conceptual cognition, but rather an intuitive cognition combined with evaluation. Rationalization of religion, undertaken by numerous deists and by Hegel, significantly distorts the structure and sense of religious experience. In itself, thinking about God does not yet constitute a religious faith, while philosophical and theological considerations are not always accompanied by forming an existential relation with God. The verbal-doctrinal formulas expressing a truth about God are important, but still more significant is the internal choice of God as the deepest truth of human life.

The mental-cognitive factor of religious experience, although undoubtedly important, does not yet exhaust its subjective structure. Even the best codification of religious truths, if it is not confirmed by inner acceptance, can be turned into a specific reification of the deity. God is described with certain concepts and formulas but He is reachable only through the acts of commitment, entrustment and love. An assertion of God is an intellectual act, but the acceptance of God is a free act of choice by man seeking the highest good and sanctity. That is why love constitutes the most crucial element of religious experience. In the act of faith we accept God, we commit and entrust ourselves to Him. Here the elements of the will, conscience, personal "assent" to a perceived truth

[27]H.Fries: *Die katolische Religionsphilosophie der Gegenwart*, Heidelberg 1949, pp.347-355.

are activated. It is therefore right to speak about the ethical determinants of religious life[28]. Authentic religious life requires from man sensitivity to higher values, goodness, purity of heart, love, simplicity, humility, spiritual beauty, social justice, freedom etc. This is the ethical ***a priori*** in religious noetics. Intellectual-cognitive honesty and moral ascesis are necessary for the appearance of religious experience. God is apprehensible only on the way of spiritual values. The proper estimation of the aspirational-ethical factor in religious life need not mean an underestimation of other elements of this phenomenon. For that reason the views of I.Kant, who reduced religion mainly to the plane of morality, are controversial. Love is an inspiration of human life, but love itself must be directed by the light of the natural and revealed truth. Religious experience is finalized in the love of God and of people. Every real love is exteriorized in the form of morally righteous life, since faith without deeds is dead (*James* 2,26).

Another element of religious experience, apprehended from the point of view of the subject - man, is the emotional sphere. Its role in this respect was strongly emphasized by Rudolf Otto († 1937). According to him emotion "lives in every religion as something, which for itself is most deeply hidden and without which religion would not be religion at all. But with particular power it lives in Semitic religions, especially in the biblical religion"[29]. The foundation of religious emotion is perceived by Otto in the so-called feeling of being created[30]. In fact, this is a continuation of the Thomistic thesis about the accidentality of being which is experienced by man existentially - often even dramatically - in his life. Religious experience contains a rich variety of emotions and feelings. R. Otto particularly emphasized the role of two categories of feelings, fear and fascination[31]. On the one hand, the deity evokes in man fear, anxiety, sense of guilt, sometimes horror. But on the other hand, the Absolute attracts, evokes the emotions of fascination, and then a desire of friendship and love. In religious experience there often appear psychic tensions, sometimes also the experiencing of inner conflicts. The complexity and ambivalence of religious feelings were stressed by St.Augustine when in *Confessions* he wrote: "I recoil and I burn; I recoil in so far as I am unlike him, and I burn in so far as I am similar to him"[32]. When facing God, man experiences two kinds of emotions: he perceives his imperfection and sinfulness, while simultaneously he desires to meet Him. Religious life covers a rich scale of emotional feelings - faith, trust, entrustment, love, conversion, sorrow, intimidation etc. In fact, these are not purely emotional states because they involve man's whole personality.

As the above analysis has indicated, the abundance of religious experience is difficult to describe and express verbally. In such an experience there occur elements that are

---

[28]Comp. A.Nossol: *Cognitio Dei experimentalis*, Warszawa 1974, pp.50- 62.

[29]*The Idea of the Holy*, tr.by J.Harvey, London 1958, p.6.

[30]Ibid., pp.9-10.

[31]Ibid., pp.8 ff., 31 ff.

[32]*Confessiones*, 9,9 PL 32, 1773.

cognitive, volitional, ethical, emotional, communal. Yet, never can all these elements be regarded as a totality of what we call religious faith. That is why one cannot apply the term religious life to a purely speculative reflection about God, ethically just life, and, even less so, the experience of sublime emotional states. Religious experience is a personal act and an expression of the whole human existence; a rational acceptance of the revealed truth; the acceptance by the will of the values connected with the idea of the Absolute; an act of love of God and of people; and, finally, an emotional experience. The whole person of man goes towards God, and all the faculties and components are involved in religious experience. One can even speak about a specific intuition of God. Hessen calls it "a totalitarian intuition"[33], meaning by it the activation of the totality of the human person. The analysis of the subjective structure of the religious act, carried out so far, has not yet taken into account what is most mysterious in it, namely, the cooperation of God's grace. The values of religious life (truth, love, holiness, grace) do not undermine man's natural powers but they simultaneously transcend them. Faith is a supra-rational act, although it is not an irrational attitude.

(iii) Ontological and Psychological Foundations of Religious Life

The subjectivistic structure of the religious act outlined above indicates its integral-personalistic character. Religious experience involves the totality of the human being, naturally in believers. In this context one becomes conscious of the erroneousness of the thesis that religion is a marginal phenomenon in human life, or even its deformation and alientation[34]. The incorrectness of the negative interpretation of religion, pejoratively evaluating its individual and social functions, becomes still more evident when one points out the ontological and psychological sources of faith.

The fact of the universality of religious life has long intrigued historians, writers, philosophers, theologians, average men. It is among others the persistency and universality of religion that the traditional Christian thought referred to when proving the existence of God. In fact, Tertullian went so far as to claim that man is the "*anima naturaliter christiana*". Once even the so-called ethnological proof of the existence of God was formulated. In our times the philosophy of God renounces this argument in its classical form, i.e. based on the fact of the universality (historical, geographical, cultural) of the phenomenon of religion. Instead, it rather focuses its main attention on the ontological roots of religious experience[35]. Why does it occur in human life? Why does man recognize the indispensability of the existence of the absolute Sacrum? In both individual and social aspects, religious experiences contain an element of mystery. Yet, at the basis

[33]*Griechische oder biblische Theologie*, München 1962, pp.65,71 ff.

[34]Such a thesis was formulated by Marxism.

[35]J.Maritain suggests that religious faith is based on the so-called pre-philosophical cognition of God, which, among others, is connected with the experience of one's own accidentality by man.

of religious experience one may most frequently find an existential experience of one's own fragility, fascination with the greatness and beauty of nature, search for the sense of life, desire of sanctification and salvation, reflection on the history of humankind, experience of situations of extremities. In particular people there predominate different motives of faith which is dependent on individual psychic predispositions, conditions of the environment, historical and cultural traditions, as well as personal experiences.

At the foundation of religious experience in many people there may be contacts with nature, a perception of its greatness and majesty, overwhelming beauty or terror, one's own smallness in the context of the immensity of the cosmos. The "starry skies" - to use Kant's phrase - tell many people about the presence of God. Man's contact with nature often intensifies and deepens his religious life. Nature becomes then "the trace of God". It is not accidental that for many people in the past and today nature has been a kind of a hierophancy of the deity[36]. The contrast man feels between his own smallness and the immensity of the cosmos evokes the question about the Creator. That is why classical philosophy formulates cosmological arguments for the existence of God, on the basis of the principle of sufficient reason and the causality principle. Today nature is called a symbol or a cipher of the deity[37]. Another frequent foundation of religious life is the experience of one's own perishability and fragility of existence. This motive predominates in the sorrowful words of St.Augustine: "These days have no real existence; in fact, they are gone even before they come; and when they come, they cannot last; [...] Nothing returns from the past; and what is still to come is also something that will pass away"[38]. Experiencing his own accidentality, man spontaneously looks for a permanent basis of his own being and the being of nature. Ontological accidentality and moral weakness, that are man's lot, produce a desire of an encounter with a being that would be indestructible and holy. And this gives rise to religious experience, connected with the need of an ontical and moral support in something that is absolutely permanent, eternal, pure and holy. The experience of one's own accidentality, which is shared by every thinking man, prompts the thought about the indispensability of God as the original cause of our existence. We only have existence, whereas He - if this is to explain the reality of everything - i s existence. Religious experience is therefore a natural consequence of recognizing Him who, being nontransient and eternal, absolute and autonomous, is a foundation of human existence. He is our original beginning and our end, the cause and aim of our life and its sense. Religious experience is especially intense in the situations of extremities in our life, that is, in cases of utmost adversities, in suffering, great joy, spiritual conversion, taking decisions which may affect our whole lives etc. And then can we truly experience our own smallness and greatness, the great scope of possibilities and meagreness of achievements, direction towards the Transcendence and immanence in the world. Experiences of this kind spontaneously produce religious acts of faith. We then

---

[36]M.Eliade: *Traité d'histoire de religions*, Paris 1949.

[37]The theory of the symbol was developed by R.Guardini, while the theory of the cipher by K.Jaspers.

[38]*Enarr. in ps.* 38,7 PL 36, 419.

discover Him, Who is the Alpha and Omega of our life. Only in Him can we understand ourselves and survive.

Man's ontological accidentality directs him toward the world of spiritual values, including also religious values. The Thomistic philosophy of God formulated exclusively cosmological arguments, omitting the world of values. Undertaking attempts to justify the reality of God, the Augustinian trend (St.Augustine, St.Bonaventura) and, today, the phenomenological-existentialistic current (M.Scheler, M.Blondel, R.Guardini, J.Hessen, H.Bergson), formulate axiological arguments. As has already been stated above, values are not functions or products of emotional experiences but they co-create the objective world in which man is actualized as a person. Values are differentiated qualitatively, that is, they are lower and higher. The latter also include religious values. They are autonomous and irreducible to any other values. Despite his natural rootedness in the world of nature, man seeks and discovers the reality of the spirit, holiness, God. Man is "a seeker of God"[39]. Religious experiences have a personal character; they are not merely marginal and historical episodes in the history of humankind but they involve all the significant elements of man's personality, such as mind, will, emotions, the domain of action. Religious acts also have a dialogical and responsive character. They are not subjective-emotional phenomena but an intuitive recognition of an ontical-causal relation. Experiencing his accidentality, man discovers his ontological status, that of being a creature. In religious experience we perceive that we are incapable of ontical autonomy. That is why we recognize that we owe our existence to an independent being, that is, to God. The religious act means an intuitive cognition of the presence of God in creation, in man, analogically to the intuitive perception of a work of art in which we discover the artistic greatness of its creator[40]. Authentic religious life contains an element of the love of God. Every love is a response to somebody's love. The form of love that occurs in religious experience is man's spontaneous response to God's love towards him. In this way the act of religious faith becomes an intuitive experiencing of the presence of God as the highest Value - the giver of existence, the truth of love, grace. Summing up, it should be stated that, growing out of the depth of man's personal being, religious life points to the presence of the Absolute. If God did not exist, religious experiences would be incomprehensible and internally contradictory. The structure of the human being cannot be an existential nonsense. Being dialogical in its nature, the religious act cannot direct man to an absent God. If God did not exist, man, in a specific way, would be independent, yet he would still try to subordinate himself to Him by undertaking religious life. The rejection of the absurdity of the human being demands a recognition of the existential sense of religious experience. Axiologically it is an experiencing of man's ontological bond with God.

The ontological roots of religious life correspond with its psychological foundations. Many thinkers, mainly adherents of intuitionism, are of the opinion that atheism is

---

[39]M.Scheler: *Der Formalismus in der Ethik und die materiale Wertethik*, Halle 1921, p.302.

[40]M.Scheler: *Vom Ewigen im Menschen*, pp.162-163.

psychologically impossible. Descartes maintains that it is difficult to speak about atheism in the strict sense of the term but only of deism, agnosticism, skepticism etc.[41]. A similar position is taken by Sören Kierkegaard, Max Scheler, Maurice Blondel, Nikolay Berdaev, Michele Federico Sciacca, Henri de Lubac[42]. Karl Rahner claims that, apart from avowed atheists, there are also the so-called anonymous Christians[43]. Although verbally they question the existence of God, they still possess the sense of the mystery, they respect truth, they do good etc., thus discovering the Absolute in the transcendence of the human person. Scheler was convinced that religious acts constitute an indispensable element of man's spiritual life, since he must always believe in something. Man believes "either in God or in gods"[44]. Religiousness belongs to the essence of man. His right concerns only the choice of the object of his faith - the Absolute, "gods", or nothingness (the latter being the object of belief of an agnostic). A Dutch phenomenologist. Gerardus Van der Leeuw, also speaks about the necessity of the psychological attitude of faith. He argues for a broad understanding of the phenomenon of religion and, in consequence, distinguishes a number of its forms - the religions of detachment and of escape, of war and peace, of desire, of infinity and ascesis, of nothingness, of compassion, of will and obedience, majesty and humility, and of love (Christianity)[45]. Also Buddhism is regarded as a religion. Van der Leeuw also characterizes atheism in the psychological aspect and calls it "a religion of escape". His argument is as follows. "Even more evident is the religious character of the so-called atheism in its contemporary forms, as a supposed atheism of deism, naturalism, idealism. In all these cases the place of the former wearied gods is taken by another god: morality, nature, humanity, idea. But their essence is always power in the religious sense. In the atheism of today it is not different; the dream about God's Kingdom and the religion of humanity have been combined into a new religious ideal which is atheistic only in comparison with the old religion, while in itself it is more a search for God than an escape from him"[46]. The description of atheism as "a religion of escape" has become equally conspicuous and controversial[47].

Obviously, the attitudes of religious faith and of the negation of God are doctrinally and psychologically opposed. Still, Scheler and Van der Leeuw are quite right to perceive the need of faith in man's psychic structure. In turn, faith is connected with a search for some Absolute and reference point without which man's life loses sense. Therefore, it is

---

[41]*Meditations on First Philosophy* [in:] *The Philosophical Works of Descartes*, Cambridge 1967, vol.1, pp.136,139.

[42]M.Blondel: *La Pensée*, Paris 1948, vol.1, p.393.

[43]K.Rahner, op.cit.

[44]*Vom Ewigen im Menschen*, p.261.

[45]*Phänomenologie der Religion*, pp.669-749.

[46]Ibid., p.680.

[47]A.Vergote: "Analyse psychologique du phénomène de l'athéisme" [in:] *L'Athéisme dans la vie et la culture contemporaine*, Paris 1967, vol.1, part I., pp.216-219.

not surprising that verbal atheism is frequently connected with a specific lay religiousness. It is expressed on three planes: (1) psychological - the atheists deify natural values (science, morality, race, social model etc.); (2) semantic - they themselves employ the term "faith" or its synonyms; (3) doctrinal - they ascribe divine attributes to what is finite and accidental. Naturally, particular planes are mutually interpenetrating. Bearing in mind the doctrinal plane, one may also distinguish three kinds of atheistic "religiousness": individualistic, collectivistic, and axiological. The representatives of the first trend include, among others, Ludwig Feuerbach and Friedrich Nietzsche; those of the second trend - Auguste Comte and Karl Marks; and those of the third trend - Julian Sorell, Julian Huxley, John Dewey, George Santayana[48]. Obviously, there are considerable differences between them; some openly propagate an atheistic religion (Comte and humanity; Huxley and ideals common to all humanity), while others absolutize man and his values (Nietzsche and the superman; Marks and the collective and the idea of revolution). The phenomenon of "religious" atheism paradoxically confirms the indispensability of religious faith. As Mircea Eliade rightly states: "One cannot uproot the Absolute; one can only degrade it"[49]. Religious experience is a datum which cannot be questioned without simultaneously violating ontological and psychological realism.

LITERATURE

ELIADE, M.: *Le sacré et le profane*, Paris 1965.
ELIADE, M.: *Traité d'histoire des religions*, Paris 1949.
HEILER, F.: *Erscheinungsformen und Wesen der Religion*, Stuttgart 1961.
HESSEN, J.: *Religionsphilosophie*, vol.2, München 1955.
HICK, J.: *Faith and Knowledge*, Glasgow 1975.
KOWALCZYK, S.: *Drogi ku Bogu* [Roads towards God], Wrocław 1983.
LEEUW, G. van der: *Phänomenologie der Religion*, Tübingen 1956.
MENCHING, G.: *Die Religion*, Stuttgart 1959.
MILES, J.R.: *Religious Experience*, London 1972.
MOUROUX, J.: *L'expérience chrétienne*, Paris 1952.
OTTO, R.: *The Idea of the Holy*, tr.by J.Harvey, London 1958.
RABUT, O.: *L'expérience religieuse fondamentale*, Paris 1969.
SCHELER, M.: *Vom Ewigen im Menschen*, Bonn 1954.
VANCOURT, J.: *La phénoménologie et la foi*, Tournai 1953.
VERGOTE, A.: *Psychologie religieuse*, Bruxelles 1966.
WUNDERLE, G.: *Das religiöse Erleben*, Paderborn 1922.
ZDYBICKA, Z.J.: *Człowiek i religia. Zarys filozofii religii.* [Man and Religion. An Outline of the Philosophy of Religion], Lublin 1977.

[48]S.Kowalczyk: "'Religijność' w fenomenie ateizmu" ['Religiousness' in the Phenomenon of Atheism], *Communio* 1(1981) no.4, pp.75-90.

[49]*Le sacré et le profane*, Paris 1965.

PART III

THE METAPHYSICS OF MAN

Chapter 1

Man as The Substantial Self

A realistic metaphysics of man should be based on the rich material of human experience and therefore philosophical anthropology cannot have a deductive-aprioristic character, restricting itself to an exemplification of the accepted systemic premises. Yet, at the same time it cannot become a subjective monadicism, based exclusively on the experiences of self-consciousness. Christian personalism does refer to internal experience, but does not limit itself only to it. The human "I" is placed within the totality of the world and that is why the phenomenon of consciousness should be apprehended in the context of a total personal experience (cognitive, aspirational, axiological, interpersonal). The personal "I" cannot be correctly read in its ontical structure without reference to other people and the whole of the cosmos. Nor can the human self be explicated statically, either, because only in action can one grasp its ontical structure and richness.

(i) The "I" as the Ontical Foundation of Actions and Attributes

The category of the "I" (resp. "self") is by no means unequivocal and that is why at the beginning its fundamental meaning should be briefly outlined[1]. First of all, one should distinguish the phenomenological "I" from the ontological "I". Emphasizing the tie between the self and consciousness, phenomenology uses the term in its former sense. The theory of realistic personalism is interested in the "I" in its ontological sense, i.e. in the ontical structure of man. In an analogous sense one speaks about the epistemological "I" and the existential "I". Cartesian ***cogito*** is connected with the former meaning, whereas Thomism - with the latter one. The human "I" may also mean: (a) consciousness; (b) the totality of a person; (c) a biological organism. Still other meanings of the category include: a performer of actions, a subject, a set of human values. The latter sense is connected with the so-called axiological (ethical) "I". In further considerations we shall concentrate on the "I" which is ontological, personal and dynamic (a subject of actions).

In what way is the human "I" knowable? Certainly, not only through sensory perception, especially in its sensualistic understanding. In this respect external experience

[1] Cf. R.Ingarden: *Spór o istnienie świata* [The Controversy about the Existence of the World], Warszawa 1961, vol.2, pp.504 ff.

may only play a secondary role, but an essential function is served by internal experience. When speaking about the human "I", one should distinguish two of its aspects, existential and essential. The former concerns the very fact of man's existence, while the latter - his nature. Does there exist a stable "I"? The reality of the self is directly apprehensible in our internal experience. Especially the phenomenon of self-consciousness, characteristic of the human world, is organically connected with the recognition of the existence of our internal "I" as a centre of personality. The intuitive cognition of the self, connected with internal experience, is generally accepted in classical philosophy, among others, in Augustinian-existential and Aristotelian-Thomistic trends. Contrary to the propagated misconceptions, St. Augustine did not deduce man's reality from the fact of thought[2]. He acknowledged the simultaneity of cognition of three of his ontical levels, existence, life, and thinking. He did not infer man's existence from the phenomenon of thought, but perceived the fact of reality in the thinking subject. Obviously, his epistemological realism was not sensualism, but neither was it Cartesian nativism. Thomism, while focussing attention on sensory experience, does not exclude a significant role of internal experience in respect to the cognition of the self[3]. The existence of the "I" is the primordial datum of personal experience. Naturally, there occur psychological deviations which may cause, for instance, a dissociation of personality, pathological personality changes etc.[4]. But these are precisely abnormal states of psychic life which do not undermine the credibility of the intuitive cognition of our "I". At any rate, even in such cases the consciousness of the self does not disappear completely and only its picture is being deformed.

The existence of the "I" in the existential experience of self-consciousness is an undoubted fact. But the recognition of the presence of the self does not yet solve the problem of its nature. What is the human "I"? In our days some accept the actualistic conceptions of human personality. In their interpretation, man is merely a set of acts, impressions, experiences, decisions etc. All these acts are to constitute the object of consciousness, similarly to the reality of the "I". But there arises a question whether the "I" is not one of the experiential acts of man or whether it is not their sum.

Answering that question, one should notice the relation pertaining between the "I" and the acts connected with it. The acts may have a double character, passive-receptive or active-functional. Both imply the presence of the ontical foundation. There must be present someone who, for example, feels pains, perceives the green, hears the sound etc. Active experiences, i.e. activities, even more clearly demand the reality of the subject as their ontical reason. There is no action without an acting agent, that is, their causer and performer. Labour assumes the presence of the working subject. Classical philosophy proves the presence of the human "I" by referring to the principle of noncontradiction, namely, the real inner self makes the existence of experiences and activities ontologically

---

[2]S.Kowalczyk: *Człowiek i Bóg w nauce św. Augustyna* [Man and God in the Teachings of St.Augustine], Warszawa 1987, pp.46-48.

[3]*Summa Theologiae*, I,q.76,a.1,c.

[4]This is discussed in various standard textbooks in psychology and psychiatry.

noncontradictable[5]. Without such self no activity can find any rational explanation. Man's ontical dynamics proves the reality of the internal "I" and that is why it cannot be interpreted as a "pure object", that is, an exclusively mental being.

The "I" is immersed in acts of psychic life which accompany man. For it is this life that constitutes an axis of all the experiences and their ontical core. In this context, the opposition between the "I" and its accompanying acts of biological and psychic life is especially characteristic. The latter are fluctuating and they constitute a continuous stream of ever changing impressions. On the other hand, man's internal "I" is single, stable, and always identical. The unity of the human "I" cannot be reduced to the unity of the biological organism, even though the latter is only relative. The organism undergoes a physical "exchange" and yet man's individual unity is preserved. This unity is connected with the consciousness of the identity of the "I". In spite of all the changes caused by man's age, the external circumstances of his life, internal transformations and other similar factors, man preserves his individual identity. Gaps in the consciousness of existence, caused by sleep or loss of memory, cannot be identified with the disappearance of the internal "I". The latter is stable, though, obviously, only relatively so. Stability does not concern here man's ontological permanence (which is impossible in the case of the accidental being) but it is the permanence of humanity in existential being. As long as man exists, he always remains a man endowed with the ontical centre of the "I". The latter is a foundation of all the activities and attributes; it is their performer and manager. Hence, the "I" is not merely a succession of activities, their personification or symbol, but it is their ontical basis, their causer and their subject. The "I" is not one of the acts, because it is transcendent in respect to them. The transcendence of the self is revealed already in the semantic distinction between "I" and "mine"[6]. The "I" is superior in respect to what constitutes man's being, its attributes, activities, aspirations etc. We speak about our ("my") faculties, parts of the body, aims, means, thoughts, decisions, owned objects. "Mine" is the heart, will, conscience or emotion. They belong to me but they are not identified with the totality of my "I".

Therefore, what is our "I"? It is a totality of our being, although in a particular way it is expressed, among others, by consciousness and will. The "I" is not exclusively the material body, biological life, psyche, activity (labour), consciousness etc. The self covers the totality of the human being. It is a multiplicity of elements, organs, actions, acts, experiences etc., while simultaneously being indivisible. As a subject of all attributes and activities, the "I" is one indivisible whole. Man is one being, not a set of beings. Classical philosophy accepts the organic connection between the human self and individual existence. The "I" is logically and ontically prior to any social collective. The individual character of the "I" excludes the possibility of the existence of humanity beyond individual beings, as the Oriental thought and various kinds of pantheisms suggest. Hence, spiritual conversion, understood as a psychic loss of one's own individual identity, is impossible.

---

[5]Thomists call it a systemic proof of the reality of the human "I".

[6]M.Krąpiec: *I - Man* ..., op.cit., pp.90 ff.

Closing oneself in one's individual "I" is egoism, but a mental annihilation or an attempt of losing one's "I" would be contrary to human nature. The awareness of one's identity is the starting point of any altruism.

The next property of man's self is its relative autonomy. It is called by different names, such as self-existence, self-containment, independence etc. The term self-existence is not very fortunate because it obscures the difference between man and God. The human "I" is independent in the sense that it exists in its own subjectiveness. The "I" initiates a dialogue with the world and other people, but it is not their component, result or expression. The "I" is simply a subject.

The reality of the human self is confirmed in various ways, through internal experience (self-consciousness) and through systemic justification - the "I" is the ontical reason of any activity and property. The existence of the ontical "I" is also approved of by the social ***praxis***. Social life, including pedagogy, ethics, judicature and family, implies the existence of the human "I". It is generally treated as a subject and causer of its own actions, as a conscious and responsible being. Without the individual "I" - man, all social moral norms, reprimands and praises, persuasions and punishments would lose their sense. Humanity cannot be reduced to the external-superficial sphere, characterized by the transience of psychic or somatic acts. In the depth of the human reality there is the subjective "I": the centre of life activity, its motor and performer, the fastener of identity, and the carrier of attributes.

(ii) The "I" as a Substantial Self

The characterization of the human self carried out above makes it possible to refer now to the classical conception of substance. Man is not only a sum of impressions, experiences, sensations and decisions, but also a substantial being. The category of substance appeared first in Aristotle who distinguished several of its meanings. The main meaning is the so-called primary substance, which constitutes a reference point for all beings. As he writes in *Metaphysics*: "This substrate is a substance and an individual thing which becomes revealed when predicating of its various properties"[7]. An individual independent being is a substantial being, e.g. a concrete man, animal or plant[8]. This meaning of the conception of substance is commonly accepted in the literature[9], although it does not escape some objections. The latter are connected with the fact that

---

[7]Aristotle: *Metaphysics* Z(VII), 1,1028 a 27-28.

[8]The problem is more complicated in respect to the inorganic world. Aristotle recognized the four elements of matter as substance. Today there are controversies concerning this aspect; some speak about the totality of the inanimate world as a single substance, while others identify substance with smaller or larger complexes of matter or with energy.

[9]Cf. W.D.Ross: *Aristotle's Metaphysics*, Oxford 1958, vol.1, pp.XCI- XCIII; S.O.Brennan: "Substance and Definition; Reality and Logos: Metaphysics Z H", *New Scholasticism*, 59 (1985), no.1, pp.21-59.

Aristotle also accepted other meanings of this category. Namely, substance can also mean the essence of a thing, a concept (universal), or a subject[10]. Substance is that which constitutes the essence of an object (what something is). Such an entity is expressed by a general concept, e.g. of man, tree etc. Finally, substance is a subject (*hypekojmenon*) for accidentalities which cannot exist without it.

Aristotelian conception of substance was taken over by St. Thomas Aquinas. His descriptions of substance make it possible to distinguish two aspects, negative and positive. The former indicates the fact that substance does not exist in another being as its subject, since it is a subject itself[11]. Apprehended in its positive sense, substance means a being which exists independently. Such a mode of being is described in Thomistic philosophy as being in itsef (***in se***) and through itself (***per se***)[12]. Yet, it does not imply at all that substance exists exclusively due to itself (***a se***), i.e. that it has no efficient cause. The latter understanding of substance would identify it with the Absolute[13]. If in the cognitive order, the property of being a substrate for an accidentality is prior to that of independent being, the ontical order is reversed. A substantial being is "self-existent" in the sense that it is a subject for itself. This relative autonomy of beingness is the most essential property, while other properties, such as permanence, being a basis for accidental features, are already secondary. No substantial being can exist in another being as its subject of inherence, i.e. it cannot depend on another being in the very fact of existence. This does not exclude a possibility of one substance being combined with another, with which it creates a larger whole. Thomistic philosophy perceives such a combination in human nature which contains two factors, somatic and psychical.

The independence of existence and (relative) permanence are ascribed in Thomistic philosophy to individual substantial beings. This theory is called substantialism. Other philosophical currents, from Hume and Kant to Whitehead, ascribe permanence exclusively to the essence of things. In this interpretation it is possible to speak exclusively about the permanence of formal-structural features of reality, not of individual substantial beings. Thomism also accepts the category of "***subsistentia***" which is defined as substance apprehended in the aspect of the durability of existence and independence of being[14].

The conception of substance has an analogous character, because it is realized differently in the inorganic world and in the organic world, in the human world and in the extra-human world. The characterization of the human self certainly makes it possible to

---

[10]*Metaphysics* Z(VII), 3, 1028 b 34 ff.

[11]*Summa Theologiae*, I, q.29,a.2; III, q.77,a.1, ad 2.

[12]*Summa Theologiae*, I, q.3,a.5, ad 1.

[13]This is how substance was described by B.Spinoza so in consequence, as a pantheist, he accepted the singleness of the substance - deity.

[14]"Secundum enim quod per se existit et non in alio, vocatur substantia. Illa enim subsistere, quae non in alio, sed in se existunt". *Summa Theologiae*, I, q.29,a.2.

refer to it the conception of substance. Some Thomists (J.Maritain, K.Kłósak) even claim that we can directly cognize the substantiality of the human "I"[15].

The latter opinion seems acceptable, although not without some modification. The conception of substance is connected with the whole Aristotelian ontology and for that reason it would be difficult to speak about direct verification of this category. But personal experience shows us such properties of the human self which correspond to the conception of substance and only in this context do they become adequately meanignful. The human "I" is a substantial being, i.e. existentially independent, a subject, a performer of its own actions, a carrier of lasting values (among others, of rationality and freedom). It is not the category of humanity, apprehended collectively, generically or structurally, but an individual man that is a substantial being.

The category of substance has a fundamental methodological and heuristic importance in classical philosophy. It is not merely a semantic category, accepted by way of convention. The reality of substance is indicated by internal and external experience[16]. At the moment, the point concerns the substantiality of the human self. Obviously, substance alone is not directly knowable through sensory faculties. The latter only provide a rich material of observations, namely, they inform us about man's changeability, both biological-somatic and psychic-spiritual. Man's age changes, so does his appearance, state of health, external and psychic characteristics, views, knowledge, convictions etc. These constant changes imply the existence of an internal substantial self which is the basis of the changes. Without the existence of such an ontical basis it would be impossible to speak about changes (for who is to change?), attributes (who is conscious, good or evil etc.?), infra-ontical relations (who is a friend of who?). The negation of the substantiality of the human "I" reduces man to a series of successive acts, activities, impressions, experiences etc. Without it, there would be no continuity and individual identity so that in consequence cognitive, moral, social or religious categories would lose all sense. Higher values, especially moral and religious, are unexplainable and unjustifiable without a substantial basis of the self.

The reality of man's substantial self is also confirmed by inner experience. This argument has already been discussed previously, when characterizing the relation between the "I" and its accompanying acts connected with the somatic and psychic spheres of man. The fluctuations of acts constitutes a sharp contrast with the stability of the self, which makes it possible to infer about its substantial character. At any rate, even everyday speech, reflecting man's ontical situation, constantly employs expressions such as I think, my decision, will, man's character, spiritual conversion etc. This way of speaking cannot be reconciled with the negation of the substantiality of the human "I". Humanity is not collective or anonymous and that is why it cannot be interpreted a-substantially.

---

[15]J.Maritain: *Distinguer pour unir*, Paris 1948, pp.174 ff, 857 ff.

[16]R.E. McCall: *The Reality of Substance*, Washington 1959; J. de Vries: "Die Substanz im Bereich des geistigen Seins", *Scholastik*, 27 (1952) pp.34-54.

Classical philosophy is consistently bound with the theory of substance and this is also true about anthropology. Still, history of philosophy also contains records of the current of radical and moderate anti-substantialism. Extreme anti-substantialism is connected with radical empiricism whose main representatives include English sensualists, John Locke and David Hume. The latter ascribed the value of scientific cognition only to sensory cognition, or, speaking more precisely, to impressions. That thinker questioned the qualitative difference between sensory cognition and intellectual cognition, and that is why he postulated direct reducibility of concepts ("ideas") to impressions. Thus, since sensory perception does not inform us about the existence of substance, then the conception is a cluster of "simple ideas" combined due to the operation of imagination[17]. We perceive only a multiplicity of impressions following one after another. Seeking in them a single foundation, i.e., substance, is an effect of the operation of the psychological law of association which suggests combining a multiplicity into a unity. According to Hume, the existence of substance is not predicated by inner experience. We are merely conscious of a continuous flux of our impressions, but we do not discover any self, the substantial "I", as a simple and indivisible being[18]. Similar claims were made by representatives of positivism, Auguste Comte and Stuart Mill. They thought that the conception of substance comes into being in consequence of the constancy of man's perceptions; the latter produces a tendency to personify experienced impressions.

Hume's anti-substantialism is a consequence of a number of epistemological, methodological, and even ontological assumptions. The former are connected with sensualism which undermines the inventive-heuristic function of intellectual cognition. Hume's methodological assumptions imply a scientistic model of science reduced to the role of describing the material world. Finally, the ontological assumptions concern phenomenalism which, in the domain of anthropology, means putting human nature into question; the real human "I" is not directly knowable by way of impressions (internal or external) but only through intuition and intellectual reflection. Internal experience is a form of intuition, while intellectual reflection reads the presence of the substantial "I" as an ontical reason of the whole psychic life.

Anti-substantialism has a varied philosophical origin, sensualistic and idealistic. The former was represented by English empiricists and, later on, by some psychologists. Their leading representative was Wilhelm Wund († 1920), who practised psychology without the soul; he negated the substantiality of the human soul and perceived in it exclusively a set of impressions and experiences. Anthropological nonsubstantialism was also continued by the adherents of the psychological theory of associationism and the Russian physiologist, I. Pavlov. A subjectivistic - idealistic current of anti-substantialism appeared in some representatives of existentialism. Martin Heidegger questioned the sense of employing the conception of substance in the domain of anthropology, motivating it by the fact of the difference in the existence of the human and extra-human worlds. This category,

---

[17]D.Hume: *A Treatise on Human Nature*, London 1911, pp.24,222-223.

[18]Ibid., pp.238-240.

borrowed from the world of things, is thought to distort the authenticity of man's individual existence. Similar objections may be encountered in some representatives of phenomenology, although the Polish leading phenomenologist, Roman Ingarden, had a positive attitude to the conception of substance and the possibilities of its application in the description of man. On the other hand, extreme anti-substantialism is represented by Jean Paul Sartre who described man as "a series of undertakings". The French existentialist accepted an a-personal and a-substantial conception of man. It is therefore paradoxical that some psychologists attempt to develop a psychology deprived of the human self. They are accompanied in this by some existentialists who try to solve the mystery of individual existence while not noticing the need of the existence of a stable human "I". Anthropology without man is as absurd as existence without the ontical "I".

The philosophical currents mentioned above proclaim extreme and overt anti-substantialism. However, in our days one may also find evidence of another anti-substantialist current, which is moderate and, mainly, more covert. Its typical representative is Alfred North Whitehead († 1947), the creator of the so-called process theology[19]. Although when characterizing man he does use the conception of substance, he still understands it as "a stability of peception"[20]. The universe is a cosmic organism in which there co-exist "actual beings" and "eternal objects". Man is merely a fraction of the continuous process of the self-creation of being. He is a series of experiences, impressions, decisions, perceptions, actual occasions, one following the other. There does not exist a substantial-personal identity of man, and one may speak exclusively of an identity which is temporal-occasional, axiological, cognitive etc. The only real permanence of man's personal identity is achieved through values which, in turn, are included in the so-called efficient nature of God. Explaining man in the context of process theology, Whitehead defines him as a "community" of historical experiences, actual beings, and a variety of the functors of the cosmos[21]. At any rate, the English writer does not hide his affinity to Locke and Hume who reduced the human self to a stream of experiences[22]. Whitehead also understood man as a stream of experiences and acts. It was undoubtedly an actualistic and processual apprehension of man who was thus reduced to the role of a stage or rather a moment of the evolutionary transformations of the cosmos. In this way the "substantiality" of the human self was reduced to the fact of the continuity of transformations and impressions.

Whitehead's a-substantial conception of reality currently enjoys quite a widespread popularity in the United States and in Europe. Some authors propose a relational theory

---

[19]Cf. S.Kowalczyk: *Bóg w myśli współczesnej* [God in Contemporary Thought], Wrocław 1982, pp.289-344.

[20]A.N.Whitehead: *Adventures of Ideas*, Cambridge 1939, p.263; also his: *His Reflections on Man and Nature*, New York 1961, pp.28,164.

[21]A.N.Whitehead: *Process and Reality*, New York 1969, pp.125- 126,192,222; *Adventures of Ideas*, pp.240-241.

[22]*Process and Reality*, pp.163-164.

of the substance[23], that is, a renouncement of Aristotelian conception of substance as an individual being, for the sake of substance as a formal-structural unity of the world. It must be admitted that in the domain of the phenomena of the micro-world the problem of the applicability of the classical conception of substance is controversial. In this respect, there have long appeared propositions of re-interpreting Aristotle's theories, namely, the category of substance being no longer connected with the corpuscular aspect of matter but rather with its character of wave and energy. Therefore, substance may possibly be called a field energy. The relational conception of substance becomes controversial when it is universalized because it is assigned the heuristic function in explicating the human reality. The ontologicalization of the conception of substance, apprehended exclusively as an arrangement of formal-structural relations, becomes entangled in contradictions. The separation of relations from their ontical subjects is obviously a mistake. Nor is the difficulty solved by distinguishing internal and external relations, since both, at least indirectly, are meaningful only in connection with individual beings. Relations without an ontological basis cannot exist. At any rate, if conceptions are to be carriers of certain connotations, relations cannot be substantialized, nor can substances be reduced to relations alone. Whitehead's a-substantialism unavoidably leads to pantheistic monism. It does not seem that the identification of substance with an arrangement of formal relations can conjure away such a danger in this respect. The more controversial, therefore, is the exemplification of the relational theory of substance in respect to anthropology. Man interpreted exclusively or primarily as a set of relations and actions loses his ontical and axiological character.

Concluding the analysis of the substantiality of the human self one should mention the extreme substantialism of some authors. Namely, it is claimed, that the relational conception of the human person was accepted by Martin Buber, Karl Rahner and Jacques Maritain. Actually, Buber's position is not unequivocal in this matter, although he probably recognized the ontical permanence of man as a person. The two remaining Thomists were quite unequivocal in their affirmation of man's substantiality, although, at the same time, they rightly emphasized the ontical directedness of man towards other persons. In their interpretation, from the very beginning man has the status of a substantial person, but its growth and axiological actualization are achieved only in combination with God and human community. Such views, however, do not yet constitute a relational and a-substantial conception of man.

[23] J.Życiński: "Relacyjna teoria substancji" [The Relational Theory of Substance], *Studia Philosophiae Christianae*, 23 (1987) no.1, pp.53-74.

LITERATURE

ADAMCZYK, S.: *De existentia substantiali in doctrina S. Thomae Aquinatis*, Romae 1962.

BINSWANGER, L.: *Grundformen und Erkenntnis menschlichen Daseins*, München 1962.

BODAMER, J.: *Der Mensch ohne Ich*, Wien 1960.

CHUNG-HWAN-CHEN: "Aristotle's Concept of Primary Substance in Books Z and H on the Metaphysics", *Phronesia* 2 (1957), no.1, pp.46-59.

DUPREZ, L.: *La notion de la substance*, Fribourg 1932.

GOGACZ, M.: *Wokół problemu osoby* [On the Problem of Person], Warszawa 1974.

JOLIVET, R.: *La notion du substance. Essai historique et critique sur la développment des doctrines d'Aristote à nos jours*, Paris 1929.

McCALL, R.E.: *The Reality of Substance*, Washington 1959.

MARITAIN, J.: "Sur la notion de subsistence", *Revue Thomiste*, 54 (1954), pp.242-256.

NELSON, E.J.: "A Defence of Substance", *The Philosophical Review*, 56 (1947), pp.491-509.

PARKER, D.H.: *Experience and Substance*, Michigan 1948.

RANDALL, J.H.: "Substance as Process", *Review of Metaphysics*, 10 (1956-1957), pp.580-601.

RECK, A.J.: "Substance and Person", *The Personalist*, 4 (1960), pp.277-288.

ROZWADOWSKI, A.: "De perceptione substantiae et de eius habitudine ad accidentia", *Gregorianum*, 7 (1926), pp.73-96.

SCHEU, M.: *The Categories of Being in Aristotle and St.Thomas*, Washington 1944.

SIEGMUND, G.: *Der Mensch in seinem Dasein*, Freiburg im Br. 1952.

VRIES, J.de: "Die Substanz im Bereich des geistigen Seins", *Scholastik*, 27 (1952), pp.34-54.

WEISS, P.: *Modes of Being*, Carbondale 1958.

Chapter 2

Man as The Personal "I"

Man lives in the world of things or objects but he himself is a person, i.e. a subject. This fact is a source of both his greatness and his mystery. Can man cease to be a person? Can he be treated as if he was not a person? The consequences of separating the categories of man and of person are not restricted to the plane of doctrinal-philosophical deformations but they lead to existential-social dangers (from an instrumental treatment of man to his physical annihilation).

(i) The Categories of Nature, Individual,and Person

The conception of nature (***physis***) appeared in old-Greek thought where it was connected with the idea of unchangeable ontical structures[1]. In turn, such structures were explained as an effect of the endurance of generic natures, which determined a certain mode of behaviour of things and their natural dynamism. In Scholastic philosophy the term "nature" had several meanings, namely, the totality of the visible reality (***natura naturans***), the Creator of nature (***natura creatrix***), the essence of things (e.g. the nature of warmth, colour, man), natural causes operating in the world, and, finally, a source of changes[2]. The latter meaning will be in the focus of our attention at this point.

Nature, understood in its proper sense, denotes the ***first*** and internal cause of activities[3]. As the first agent of action, nature is not a direct source of movement but actually the remotest - the first "from the beginning" - source of change. Speaking more precisely, nature is an agent through which a concrete individual acts. The proper author of an action is an individual that operates according to its generic nature, by means of certain faculties. Therefore, nature is a more remote source of change (***principium quo***), while the individual is the direct cause (***principium quod***), and faculties are the instruments of change. Nature is the internal cause of changes, in contradistinction, for instance, to the artist, who is the external cause of action.

---

[1]L.Strauss: *Natural Right and History*, Chicago 1953, Chap.III.

[2]*Summa Theologiae*, I,q.29,s.1,ad 4; III,q.2,a.12.

[3]*Summa Theologiae*, III,q.2,a.1,c.

Speaking about "human nature" one may have in mind two meanings, namely, the essence of man and man's action. Human nature is qualitatively different than animal or plant nature. It is reflected in a different mode of action; man acts in a rational and free way, while an animal in its dynamism is deprived of consciousness and is totally subjected to its determinants[4].

A concrete subject of existence is the individual (***suppositum***). Thomistic philosophy describes the individual as a single substance, independent, and nontransferable to other beings[5]. This description requires some explanation. First of all, an individual can only be a substantial being, and not beings of a dependent status of existence, known as accidentals. As has already been stated above, only an individual being can be a substance, in its proper sense. An individual being is indivisible in itself and it is separate from other beings, although this does not exclude its connections with them. Secondary substances, i.e. conceptions, cannot be individuals. An individual is a substantial, complete being. Incomplete substance never creates a separate whole but is actually or potentially bound with other beings. Hence, accidentals, as incomplete substances, cannot be individuals. Accidentals co-exist in another being as their subject, whereas incomplete substances are only elements of a larger whole. For this reason, man's psychic factor (soul) cannot be an individual, since by its nature it is only a component of man and not a separate natural whole. Nothing that constitutes an element of some composite (***compositum***) and as long as it remains such an element, can be an individual. An individual is also a substantial being, i.e., it is not only subject to the action of other selves but it also acts as a causer. An important property of every individual is also the fact that it is not transferable to other beings. Even a complete and independent substantial being, if it is transferable to other substantial beings, does not constitute an individual. Theology provides examples of such complete substances which are not individuals. Christ's human nature was a substance generically complete, but it co-existed in the person of the Word and therefore was not the individual (and, in consequence, a person, either). Also the "substance" of God's nature was not a single individual because it appertains to all the persons of the Holy Trinity, endowing them with common existence. A formal feature of an individual is some positive perfection. For if a substantial being is a kind of perfection, and perfection is something positive, then an individual - the ontical "completion" of substance - undoubtedly consists in possessing in its essence some positive perfection.

Only an individual can be a person, but not every individual is one. The term "person" (Greek ***prosopon***; Latin ***persona***) appeared in ancient Greece and originally denoted the actor's mask put on during the performance on the stage. Antique theatre usually presented famous and heroic characters and, hence, the conception of person signified a distinguished man. With the passage of time, however, the term was applied to every

---

[4]Speaking about human nature, Cardinal Wojtyła (*Osoba i czyn*, op.cit., pp.79-81) has in mind passive dynamism. In common understanding human nature also covers mental faculties.

[5]St.Thomas Aquinas: *De Potentia*, q.9,a.4; In *II Sent.*, d.5,q.1,a.1; *Summa Theologiae*,III,q.2,a.3.

man as a rational and free self. The term appeared in philosophy by way of theology, namely, during the analysis of the Trinitarian and Christological dogmas[6].

Philosophical descriptions of the person are numerous and varied. One such definition of the person was provided by Boethius († 525) who described it as "an individual substance of rational nature" (rationalis naturae individua substantia). This description emphasizes the fact that only an individual rational substance can be a person; hence, only a being independent in its existence and complete can be a person. Rationality is a constitutive feature of the person, and for that reason non-rational selves are not persons. The above description concerns the person of man. Boethius's definition, although it usually constitutes the starting point for considerations on the theme of the person, is not entirely satisfactory. Existentialistic Thomists accuse it of essentialism, i.e. of disregard of the role of existence as the primary act of a substantial being. An even more significant drawback is the fact that Boethius's definition - when referred to man - obscures his personal, unique specificity. Man is apprehended as a specimen of the genus of rational beings, which means his disparagement. After all, the person is something more than an average representative of the genus ***homo sapiens***.

St. Thomas Aquinas generally accepted Boethius's definition of the person, although he also formulated his own descriptions. For him the person is what is most perfect in nature[7]. It is a rational individual. "The human person is an independent and separate being in the human nature. Man is a free being and, therefore, existing for himself"[8]. For St.Thomas the human person is a reality which is self-existent, individual and separate from other beings[9]. Although Thomists do refer to Boethius's and St.Thomas's descriptions of the person, they usually modify and supplement them. Here are a few examples. Jacques Maritain defines the person as "a complete individual substance, intellectual in nature and master of its actions"[10]. On another occasion, he states that "a person is a unity of a spiritual nature endowed with freedom of choice and so forming a whole which is independent of the world"[11]. Both descriptions stress man's two attributes, rationality and freedom. Wincenty Granat, in turn, looking for an integral definition of the human person, describes it as "a bodily-spiritual unit which can act in a rational, free and social way"[12]. This description also pays attention to the social character of humanity. Referring to Boethius's definition, Cardinal Wojtyła states briefly

---

[6]Cf. W.Kasper: *Jesus der Christus*, Mainz 1976.

[7]*Summa Theologiae*, I,q.29,a.3; II-III,q.32,a.5.

[8]"Persona humana significat subsistentem distinctum in natura humana. Homo est naturaliter liber et propter seipsum existens", *Summa Theologiae*, II-II,q.64,a.2,ad 3. Comp. I,q.29,a.3, ad 2.

[9]*Summa Theologiae*,I,q.29,a.4,c and ad 3; I,q.30,a.4.

[10]*Three Reformers*, New York 1970, pp.19-20.

[11]J.Maritain: *True Humanism*, New York 1938, p.2.

[12]*Osoba ludzka. Próba definicji* [The Human Person. An Attempt at Definition], Sandomierz 1960, p.244.

that the person is somebody - a personal ***suppositum*** (individual)[13]. Thomistic philosophy describes the person in ontological terms. First of all, it emphasizes its substantiality, ontical completeness, individual subjectiveness, independence of existence (as opposed to the co-existence of an accidental). Descriptions of the person also pay attention to man's attributes, such as, rationality, freedom, responsibility, directedness towards social life.

In contemporary philosophy there are also multiple descriptions of the human person. The phenomenological-existentialistic current perceives in man not so much a stable substantial being but mainly an existence constantly undertaking efforts of self-determination. Instead of the classical conception of man, Max Scheler spoke for an actualistic theory of the human person[14]. The change of the model of the person results in a claim that the person cannot be defined at all. Personal existence constantly undergoes self-realization, so ultimately it cannot be described and classified. Attention is also paid to the paradoxical and antinomial character of the human person, i.e. the co-existence in its nature of opposed features. That is why Wilhelm Stern († 1938) calls the human person "a manifold unity" (***unitas multiplex***)[15].

(ii) The Attributes and Structure of the Human Person

No description of the human person can completely grasp the whole of its ontical richness and that is why one cannot be satisfied with a definition alone. A fuller explication of these problems becomes possible only by indicating the fundamental properties of man as a person. St. Thomas Aquinas emphasizes three attributes, namely, autonomy of being, rationality and individuality[16]. Yet, his other statements make it possible to present a fuller list of the properties of the human person. The most important ones may include the following: spirituality, autonomy of existence, subjectiveness, individuality, nontransferability to other beings, sensitivity to values, dynamism, self-realization, directedness towards social life, religiousness.

Spirituality is the fundamental dimension of the personal being and this is also true about man[17]. Describing the person, Boethius and St.Thomas Aquinas stressed the feature of rationality. Other descriptions of the person rightly point to the attribute of freedom. Rationality and freedom occur only in the world of spirit, while they are absent in the world of matter alone. Therefore, speaking about man's spirituality we must have

---

[13]*Osoba i czyn*, op.cit., pp.75-76.

[14]It was nevertheless moderate actualism, since Scheler called man "an act- substance" (Substanz-Akt).

[15]Cf. W.Granat: *Osoba ludzka*, op.cit., pp.19-25.

[16]"De ratione personae sunt tria, scilicet subsistere, ratiocinari et individuum esse": St.Thomas Aquinas: *I Sent.*, d.25, q.1, a.3; comp. *II Sent.* d.3, q.1, a.2; H.E.Hengstenberg: *Philosophische Anthropologie*, München 1984, p.311.

[17]Cf. H.E.Hengstenberg, op.cit., pp.170-179.

in mind both these attributes. The elements of thought and consciousness in the idea of man are repeatedly stressed in modern and contemporary philosophy, especially by Descartes and Hegel. The categories of consciousness and self-consciousness, however, apprehend man on the phenomenological plane, while the category of spirit concerns already the plane of ontology. Therefore, the spirituality of the human person means something much more than thought and consciousness. Spirituality is the ***condition sine qua non*** of the existence of the person. That is why a mineral, a plant or an animal cannot be a person. As a result, all those currents which question the autonomy of man's psychic-spiritual sphere, can hardly be described as personalistic. Functionally or phenomenologically apprehended consciousness does not yet constitute the spirit. The spirit is not a sum of acts and experiences; it is a substantial self, breaking out of the limitations of time and space. The spiritual being has an existential depth which - contrary to Hegel's claims - can never be ultimately fathomed. But, on the other hand, to reduce man to subconsciousness and nonconsciousness, as Freud did, is wrong, too. The human person, containing in itself the element of the spirit, is directed by rational thought. Finally, spirituality secures for man the ontical constants of existence and activity, and then transcendence in respect to the conditions of the external world.

The next property of the human person is the autonomy of being, often called self-existence. Obviously, this cannot be absolute self-existence, since the latter is an exclusive privilege of the Absolute. Yet, man is a substantial being and a subsistence; he exists in himself and for himself (though not only for himself). Ontical independence causes that the human person cannot be treated as a component of another self, e.g. the human embryo before birth is not a fragment of its mother's organism but a separate man. Thus, since man is an ontical subject, conscious and free (at least potentially), he cannot be treated instrumentally, as a means for the realization of some "higher" aims. Ontological subjectiveness justifies juridical subjectiveness in social life.

Another significant attribute of the personal being is its individuality. It was repeatedly stressed by St.Thomas Aquinas, speaking about the person as a concrete unit of substance. The human person is an ontical individuality, i.e. a being which is complete structurally and functionally[18]. It is a whole "closed" in itself, separate in the world of nature and in human community. The individuality of the person, as the human spirit, still says something else. Man is a unity which, thanks to its ontical endowment, is unique. Every human individual is unique in its specificity, inner life, choices, values realized. Thus, the Thomistic understanding of man's individuality makes it possible to recognize his individuality and uniqueness. This aspect was discovered anew by existentialists, among others, by Sören Kierkegaard and Gabriel Marcel. Hegel glorified the universals, while depreciating individual beings and treating them as moments in the self-development of the absolute spirit. Kierkegaard rightly observed that, after all, thinking is a prerogative of an individual man[19]. The person is an individual substantial being, though, naturally,

[18]R.Guardini: *Welt und Person*, Würzburg 1939, pp.123-127.

[19]F.Copleston: *Studies of Logical Positivism and Existentialism*, London 1960, pp.105-110.

something more, too. The person is not an individualized generic nature but a separate, unique reality.

Thomistic philosophy explains the individuality of the human person in ontological terms. In our times we may find a psychological-axiological interpretation of the conception of the individual which endows this category with a pejorative sense. This is precisely done by Emmanuel Mounier who juxtaposes the individual to the person[20]. The human individual is understood by him as an embodiment of egocentrism and egoism, while the person is to be a synonym of altruism and service to the society. Thus, the process of individualization degrades man internally, while the opposite process of personalization makes man richer. Mounier's understanding of individuality is connected with the social-political domain, especially as a consequence of his critical evaluation of liberal-capitalist individualism. This departs from the ontological conception of individuality in Thomism.

The next feature of the human person is the fact that ontologically it is nontransferable[21]. After all, it is a substantial being and spirituality is one of its dimensions. Such beingness cannot be transferable; it cannot be renounced or handed over to somebody else. Man cannot renounce his subjectiveness as much as he cannot "suspend" his ontological status of being a person. Humanity cannot be transferred or imparted to somebody else. Naturally, it is possible and recommendable to hand over values, but not one's own being.

Another attribute of the human person is not always remembered, namely, sensitivity to higher values. St.Thomas Aquinas explicitly confirmed that man is the highest value in the visible world[22]. Man himself is both a value and a being realizing values which constitutes his life vocation. The strict connection between the human person and the world of values was emphasized by the Augustinian current in philosophy, paying particular attention to the role of the will and love in man's life. In contemporary times these problems are discussed, among others, by Max Scheler[23]. The metaphysics of the human person cannot therefore be narrowed down to the ontology of being and substance, but it should also cover axiology[24]. The human person is somebody who is sensitive to mental-spiritual values, such as truth, good, friendship, love, sacrifice, sacrum etc. The realization of such values also means a development of the person, while their destruction means its degradation and debasement. Perception and realization of values appertain to the ontical structure of the person and that is why the separation of humanity and values means self-debasement and self-reification. Values do not merely constitute

---

[20]"Manifeste au service du personnalisme" [in:] *Oeuvres*, vol.1, Paris 1961, p.525.

[21]*Summa Theologiae*, I,q.29,a.4,ad 3.

[22]*Summa Theologiae*, I,q.29,a.3.

[23]Comp. *Wesen und Formen der Sympathie*, passim.

[24]M.F.Sciacca: *L'Uomo. Questo "squilibrato"*, Roma 1956, pp.57 ff.

the milieu of the person, but they are actually parts of the person. There can be no full human person without values, while the latter do not exist beyond the person.

An ability of ontical self-development is another property of the human person. Many contemporary thinkers give up the description of the person as a substantial being because the category of substance is identified by them with a static character. But man is a substantial being of spiritual nature, due to which he is capable of identifying his life situation, of self-determination, choice of aims and means. Naturally, there is a certain constant in the dynamics of the personal being which enables the continuity of the history of man apprehended individually and socially. The beingness of a person is given to man and imposed on man. It is given in the ontological sense, and it is imposed on him for the realization of values corresponding to the dignity of the person. The person is a possibility which demands actualization through personal effort. It is man's calling to act, internally and externally. Thanks to this, man develops as a personal subject. Contemporary Christian thinkers (among others, Blondel, Teilhard de Chardin) describe man as a being capable of self-creation. Obviously, it is not the initial creation that they have in mind, but the finalization of the creative act of God. At any rate, the human person is capable of self-realization, of shaping its own internal and external self. Man is not so much ***homo faber*** but rather ***homo laborans***; the creation of tools is less important than self-realization through the act of labour[25].

While being a substantial self, complete and internally non-transferable to other selves, the human person is not a closed monad. Already Aristotle called man a social being. Social character is evident in man's language, facial expressions, gestures, modes of behaviour, internal need of communication and of community. Social life does not create man but it is indispensable for his somatic and psychic development. Social character also appears in the fundamental human values - truth, good, friendship, love, justice etc. They co-create the common good without which community would lose its character and turn into a mob or regimented troop. The social character of human labour causes that the individual "I" is seeking the "you" of another man. The relation between the "I" and the "you" should be a relation between subjects, for only then will it correspond to the dignity of the person.

An extension of man's social character is his religiousness. Apart from the human "you", man also seeks the absolute "You". He feels it ontical and axiological need. A believing man sees in God Him Who is the ontical reason of his existence and the ultimate sense of his life. To use Teilhard de Chardin's phrase, God is the Alpha and Omega of the human person. For that reason, man without an ontological relation to God would not be a person, while without the existential-psychological relation he would not be a discriminating person[26]. Human higher values are potentially infinite and that is why they obtain their ultimate foundation only in God. Religious life is nothing else but

[25]The subjective function of labour is also emphasized by Pope John Paul II in the encyclical *Laborem exercens* 6,9,12.

[26]Cf. R.Guardini: *Welt und Person*, pp.164-167.

participating in God, in His power, love, mercy, life. That is why religiousness belongs to the most significant attributes of the human person, while its lack undoubtedly impoverishes and often deforms man.

At the end of this analysis of the properties of the human person, one should briefly mention the problem of its ontical structure. It will be discussed in greater detail later on, so we shall restrict ourselves here only to few remarks. The human person has a spiritual dimension but it is not a pure spirit and, even less, an infinite absolute Spirit. A material body and biological life constitute its integral elements[27], although they do not decide about man's dignity (while participating in it). The person is not an effect of material-biological organization and that is why one cannot see in it only the natural element of the evolution of the biocosmos. The human person is a psycho-physical whole, a two-dimensional being. It is not a sum of corporeity and psychicism, but their ontological subject. The connection between these two factors is natural, substantial and dynamic. The human body is "stigmatized" by the soul, while the latter is an integrating and directing factor, a form, in respect to the body.

Being in its structure a psycho-somatic combination, the person acts on two levels. This raises the problem of the integration of nature and the person in man's being[28]. A concrete man is not only an exemplification of the genus of rational beings but a personal being. The function of the person does not consist in separating individuals from the indistinct "mass of humanity". The person endows man with personal existence so that thanks to this, all man's activities, both somatic-vegetative and psychic-spiritual, have one common subject. Naturally, the former form of activity is less subordinated to man's consciousness and will than the latter. But man is a single personal being in which an integration of various levels and manifestations of dynamics is possible. The integration of nature in the person does not obliterate the difference which persists between them, but only "emphasizes the unity and identity of man as a subjective being, as the ***suppositum***"[29]. Such an integration is possible thanks to the transcendence of the person in relation to its activities, both corporeal and psychic.

(iii) The Formal Element of the Human Person

The enumeration of the attributes of the human person does not yet constitute any final solution of the problem of its structure and essence. For there arises a question: What makes the human person a person? What is the formal element of the human person? Opinions in this matter are highly differentiated, both in Scholastic philosophy and in other trends. Some philosophers would like to see a significant property of the person in a specific intellectual or social quality. Hence, persons would include a scholar,

---

[27]St.Thomas Aquinas: *III Sent.* d.5,q.3,a.2; H.E.Hengstenberg, op.cit., pp.295-306.

[28]K.Wojtyła: *Osoba i czyn*, op.cit., pp.78-88.

[29]Ibid., p.88.

a ruler, a judge, a merchant, a soldier etc. Another group of thinkers perceives the most fundamental property of man in the phenomenon of thought and consciousness. Already Aristotle called man "a thinking animal". This view was then repeated by the Stoics, and, later on, by St.Augustine and St.Thomas Aquinas. Blaise Pascal called man "a thinking reed". Descartes described man as "a thinking substance"[30]. In such interpretations thinking becomes the essence of the human person. G.W.F.Hegel, J.G.Fichte and Maine de Biran are of the opinion that it is the consciousness of one's self that constitutes the essence of man. Christian Wolff regarded the remembrance of our experiences and activities as the distinctive feature of the human person. A.Rosmini perceived such an element in the freedom of the will. According to Kant, man is a personality capable of going above the mechanisms of all nature thanks to its moral value and conscience.

The above descriptions of the human person are one-sided. None of them takes fully into account all the elements of the human person. Each of them may also provoke a number of objections. To a large extent, the intellectual or social quality is realized only in some people, whereas personal dignity is an attribute of each man. This implies that a purely qualitative property cannot be a constitutive element of the human person. Nor can the possession of actual self-consciousness be an essential property of the person. It is true that this phenomenon is an exclusive ontical privilege of man. Yet, if by the person one understood first of all the owner of actual consciousness, this view would lead to disastrous consequences. Infants, mentally deficient people, drunks, and others temporarily deprived of consciousness, would thus lose the dignity of the human person. Virtual consciousness cannot be a formal element of the person; if it were so, one would have to assume that an accidental is the essence of the personal being. After all, consciousness is merely an operation of the intellect, i.e. it has the ontical status of an accidental. Consciousness, memory and possession of free will constitute merely an exteriorization of the ontical richness of the human person, but not its formal elements. Acts of memory, reflection or of will presuppose the prior existence of the subject - individual, but they do not constitute the most fundamental element of the person.

The problems of the formal element of the human person were an object of attention of medieval Christian thinkers. Their considerations took place in the context of theological issues, especially of Christological questions. Christ has a double nature, divine and human, but only one self-existence, i.e. the person. God has one eternal nature but existing in three Persons. These theological truths required distinctions to be made between the categories of substance, nature, and person.

Scholastic conceptions of the person have a common ontological - substantial character but one may still distinguish among them two currents, essentialistic and existential[31]. Duns Scotus († 1308) claimed that the essence of the person consists in a double

---

[30]*The Principles of Philosophy* [in:] *The Philosophical Works of Descartes*, Cambridge 1967, vol.1, pp.222-223.

[31]Cf. R.Garrigou-Lagrange: "De vera notione personalitatis", *Acta Pont. Academiae Romanae S.Thomae Aquinatis*, 5(1938) pp.8-92; J.B.Lotz: "Person und Ontologie", *Scholastik*, 38(1963), pp.335-360.

negation, namely, the dependence of the actual person on other beings and the dependence on the future. Christ's human nature is not a person because it is actually dependent on the person of the Word. The human soul is not a person either, because it has a natural inclination to combine with the body; it is therefore potentially dependent even when after death it is temporarily separated from the body. Every negation, even a double one, means only an absence of certain content or relation. For that reason negation alone cannot constitute an adequate explanation of the mystery of the person. No absence or negation can rationally explicate a positive perfection. At any rate, if negative apprehensions had no positive equivalents in the person, the problem of the essence of the human person would make no sense. In a similar way the person is explained by Cajetanus and Suarez. Cajetanus († 1534) asserted that the formal feature of every person is "the substantial mode" which was a positive property different from both nature and existence. However, this substantial mode is not an accidental but is accessorily reduced to the category of substance. It cannot be an accidental because the person is not merely an addition to nature but its perfection. Francisco Suarez († 1617), while questioning the real difference between existence and essence, introduced "the substantial mode" into human nature already actualized through existence. Thanks to the reception of the "substantial mode" the existing human nature becomes a person. Christ's human nature, although it had it own existence, was deprived of that "mode". Cajetanus's view was accepted by many Thomists, for instance, John of St.Thomas, while in contemporary times, among others, by Cardinal D.Mercier and R.Garrigou-Lagrange.

The above interpretation is controversial because it totally disregards the role of existence which is the highest act of every being, not excluding the person. The "substantial mode", understood as something added to the individual being before its coming into existence, cannot constitute any reality. Cajetanus forgot the proper role of existence as an act. The element of contents undoubtedly plays an important role in forming the person but it is not the only, or even the most important, element. The "substantial mode" is a kind of fiction, lacking any real foundation. It is equally difficult to accept Suarez's views. For if the substantial mode is combined with individual substance after its coming into existence, than it would be something accidental for the person. And this would imply that an accidental is a formal element of the human person which, naturally, is unacceptable.

The other existential trend referring to the problems of the human person, is represented in Scholastic philosophy by Capreolus. Referring to the teachings of St.Thomas Aquinas, he perceived the formal element of the human person in substantial existence. Naturally, not every existence realizes the person, but only the existence of a rational nature. The person is something most perfect in nature. The highest perfection of every being is substantial existence and therefore it is only the latter that determines the formation and ontical character of the person. Some texts by St.Thomas seem to confirm such an interpretation[32]. In a similar way the essence of the human person is explained by contemporary Thomists. Cardinal Karol Wojtyła, recognizing the priority of existence over any activity, accepted the act of existence as the constitutive element of every individual. That is why he asserted that man exists as an individual due to possessing a "personal existence"[33]. Existence has been accepted as the foundation of man's personal being and his proper dynamics. Another Polish author, Mieczysław A.Krąpiec, accepted the self-existing "I" as the significant element of the person. The human person is "his own existence and proportional to a given individual nature, and who can be defined in agreement with the current classical philosophy as the "I" of a rational nature"[34]. An even more emphatic statement is formulated by M.Gogacz: "The very human person appears as a being, constituted by existence, created by the first efficient cause, in existence and in essence, which this existence actualizes in itself by the power of its dynamics as its limitation"[35]. The representatives of Thomism, especially in its existential variety, perceive the formal element of the human person in existence as the superior act of every being.

The existential interpretation of the constitutive element of the human person perfectly explains the duality of natures in one person of Christ the Lord. Yet, it is incapable of a rational explanation of the triplicity of Persons in a single substantial nature of the Holy Trinity. For if it is existence that constitutes the person, then how can a single existence form the three Persons of God?[36] It also seems that the existential interpretation of the problem of the person, especially in the approaches of some authors, totally disregards the role of the elements of contents in shaping the human person. The person involves not only its very substantial existence alone, but also the generic nature. It includes both somatic-biological elements and psychic-mental elements, cognitive, aspirational, emotional, social. An integral human person is a psycho-physical whole whose realization, naturally, is existence. Therefore it seems that the existential interpretation of the human person should be combined with some elements of the essentialist interpretation[37]. The formal element of man is personal existence, i.e. that of a rational free individual.

In contemporary Thomism there has appeared still another trend whose representatives support a relational understanding of the formal element of the person. One should distinguish here two matters: (a) an interpretation of the human person; and

---

[32]"Esse pertinet ad ipsam constitutionem personae et sic quantum ad hoc se habet in ratione termini, et ideo unitas personae requirit unitatem ipsius esse complati et personalis": *Summa Theologiae*, III,q.19,a.1,ad 4. Comp. III,q.17,a.2; De Potentia, q.9,a.3,c.

[33]*Osoba i czyn*, op.cit., pp.75-87. M.Gogacz objected that Wojtyła interpreted existence conceptualistically as "existential contents"; cf. *Wokół problemu osoby*, op.cit., p.24.

[34]*I-Man*, op.cit., p.323.

[35]*Wokół problemu osoby*, op.cit., p.215.

[36]Cf. A.Rodziński: *Osoba i kultura* [The Person and Culture], Warszawa 1985, pp.23,68-69.

[37]This does not undermine in any way the coherence of the Thomistic conception of the person.

(b) the person as such (both human and divine). The relational interpretation of the human person, though understood in highly varied ways, appears in many authors, both Thomists and others[38]. They emphasize the ontical connection of the human person with God as the Necessary Being, or the indispensability of the connection of the individual man with community.

At the moment, we are interested in the relational interpretation of the formal element of every person as such. In the Polish literature the person is characterized in this way by Adam Rodziński. He distinguishes two planes in man, ontological, i.e. substantiality, and axiological, i.e. the person. Every person is in itself a leading value which, in turn, co-creates other higher values[39]. Such values exist only in the world of persons and endow their lives with sense. The person is not apprehensible exclusively through a theoretical description of its ontological structure. The comprehension of the person is possible only through the language of axiology which is a specific co-experiencing. The other element of the proposed conception of the person is the emphasis laid on the category of relation. The person is "a relation of a constitutional responding of somebody to somebody"[40]. The metaphysics of the person is not only the philosophy of being but a philosophy of community, of a communion of persons. Although interpersonal relations in themselves have a categorial - impermanent character, nevertheless they grow out of the very essence of the person and get into another person. An adequate understanding of the person is therefore impossible without the fact of relations which, hence, can be recognized as the formal medium of every person. The relational interpretation of the person makes it possible to explain the triplicity of the Persons of the Holy Trinity. Although they are connected by common existence, they relationally differ from each other[41]. The difficulty connected with the Christological dogma is explained by the hypothesis about the double existence in the person of Christ: the existence proper to human nature and the "supersubstantial" existence of God's nature[42].

The relational interpretation of the person is not quite clear enough. It recognizes the fact that the person is the subject of all relations, personal and objective[43]. Yet, at the same time, it is the relations that are to determine the differentiation of persons. Are not the two statements contradictory? At any rate, relations are derivative in respect to substantial-personal beings, so they cannot shape them. The ontical differentiation of the Persons of the Holy Trinity and of human persons seems to make it impossible to accept the identical ontical ***constitutivum***. The relational conception of the person entails still

[38]M.Gogacz: *Wokół problemu osoby*, op.cit., especially pp.195-200.

[39]*Osoba i kultura*, op.cit., pp.29,47,63.

[40]Ibid., pp.29; comp. pp.60 ff.

[41]Ibid., pp.23,44 ff.

[42]Ibid., pp.40-43.

[43]Ibid., p.61.

another difficulty. It is suggested that the substantial nature and the person are two metaphysical orders mutually complementary but, at the same time, mutually nonderivable[44]. In this interpretation man's natural unity becomes incomprehensible while it is precisely personal existence that constitutes his nature.

However, there is one valuable element in the proposed interpretation of the personal being. Namely, the person involves not only the domain of ontology, but also that of axiology. The person implies the presence of values connected with intellect, will, conscience, sense of life etc. There can be no authentic person without the logos and the ethos. The ***constitutivum*** of every person is therefore encountered in its sensitivity to values which shape and develop it. It seems that the actualization of values, besides substantial existence, is the second indispensable constitutive element of the person as such. This holds true both about the human persons and God's Persons. The latter become specific on the plane of values, of truth and love, although ontologically they are identical. Axiology is an integral element of metaphysics and for that reason the latter cannot be narrowed down to the philosophy of being. Values are rooted in being, in the act, but they also imply the plane of the personal being. Classical descriptions of the person omitted precisely its connection with the domain of values. The person is a substantial being, rational and free, sensitive to higher values and realizing them in the context of social life[45]. The person is not a monad but it is the subject of all interpersonal relations.

(iv) Person and Personality. Concluding Remarks.

The considerations carried out above seem to justify making a distinction between two categories, person and personality. Many times they are used interchangeably[46], although this is not legitimate. Person concerns the plane of metaphysical considerations which are to elucidate its structure and function. Every person is a being of spiritual nature which inheres in itself and decides about itself; it is capable of it and obliged to do it. The conception of personality concerns the psychological-moral plane and that is why it varies in each man[47]. The person is given to everybody, so in practice it is identical in all people. There are no supermen or undermen; personal humanity is a common gift of the Creator. As men - persons we are all equal. What differentiates us is personality and character. The latter are results of the personal attitude, internal work, efforts of self-perfection. This is not a gift of fate, but something worked out by each man. Person is an ontical magnitude; it neither increases nor decreases. But man's

---

[44]Ibid., pp.52-53.

[45]The proposed description of the person is a re-interpretation of the classical description.

[46]M.Krąpiec: *I-Man*, op.cit., pp.282 ff.

[47]Cf. R.Guardini: *Welt und Person*, op.cit., pp.128-138; H.E.Hengstenberg, op.cit., pp.315-321.

personality changes; it develops, is stunted, and may even be destroyed. Personality deformations do not mean the death of the person. Human organism decays, but the person, in its spiritual dimension, does not. Positive personality is characterized by active involvement in the realization of higher values, by internal simplicity, righteousness, directness and similar virtues.

A different understanding of the category of personality is proposed by Wincenty Granat. He distinguished a triple personality of man, psychic, ethical and social. Psychic personality concerns mainly the subjective "I" apprehensible in human consciousness, its features, ontical structure etc.[48]. Man is a morally appraising being and this aspect of human nature constitutes precisely ethical personality[49]. It is connected with the phenomena of freedom and conscience. Finally, social personality concerns man perceived in a variety of social relations, in the family, nation, state[50]. It is the author's conviction that an analysis of the three enumerated types of personality allows a reconstruction of the conception of an integral person, taking into account all its fundamental dimensions and attributes. Yet such considerations merely seem to obscure the categories of person and personality which, naturally, is controversial. Psychic, ethical and social personalities are simply different aspects of the human person. They are more or less emphasized in particular philosophical currents. Thus, for instance, phenomenology stresses the psychic aspect of the person ("I"), Kantianism - the ethical aspect, while Marxism - the social aspect. Obviously, the one-sided emphasis laid on particular planes cannot result in an integral description of man. It should also be added that particular philosophical trends employ various methods and begin with various assumptions. Hence, one can speak not so much about ethical or social personality but rather about ethical or social aspects of the human person. These are man's real aspects or frames of reference and that is why their analysis is justified[51]. By analogy, it is also justified to apply various philosophical methods in the analysis of the human person, although undoubtedly a leading method should be specified.

The above considerations seem to indicate some final reflections. First of all, one should accept the qualitative difference between the world of person and that of things - individuals[52]. Only man is a person and every man is a person. The person is an ontological datum which cannot be taken away from man. Man cannot cease to be a person, out of his own or somebody else's will. As long as man lives, personal humanity is his inalienable property. The person is an individual being. Nature creates genera but is incapable of creating a person. The human person is not only a specimen of the genus of thinking beings but a separate subject capable of spiritual self-realization. The person

---

[48]W.Granat: *Osoba ludzka*, op.cit., pp.153-184.

[49]Ibid., pp.185-203.

[50]Ibid., pp.204-206.

[51]It would be a mistake to claim that there is no real existence of the ethical, psychic or social dimensions of the human person.

[52]H.E.Hengstenberg, op.cit., pp.323-329.

does not occur in man at a definite temporal moment or as a result of a favourable existential or social situation. From the very beginning man is a person and remains a person till the end of his life. The human person has a complex psycho-physical structure but it is not a sum or aggregate of various ontical levels and properties. Finally, the person is a substantial being, subject of a multitude of personal relations, but it is not their result. Man is not exclusively a relation to society or even God, although he is actualized thanks to them. God is the Creator of the human person and that is why its ontical and existential sense disappears when it is separated from Him. Man's actions, if they are fully conscious and free, involve the totality of his person. This holds true about both mental life and the life directly connected with the somatic-biological plane.

The spiritual dimension of the human person enables and obliges man to a creative development of his personality. The person is a substantial being, though not a static one. The development of one's own personality is achieved in the domain of higher values. Their realization expands man's personality, while a departure from them means its moral degradation. A threat to man occurs primarily as contempt of values, their betrayal or destruction. Personality disorders do not yet mean the death of a person. That is why there always exists a possibility of an inner conversion as a consequence of which the person's beingness will find its correlate in moral personality.

LITERATURE

ARRESE,D.de: *La persona humana*, Madrid 1962.

BALLARD,E.G.: "Individual and Person", *Philosophy and Phenomenological Research*, 18 (1957-1958), pp.59-67.

BINDER,H.: *Die menschliche Person*, Stuttgart 1964.

COMFORT,A.: *Nature and Human Nature*, London 1966.

DEGL',Innocenti U.: *Il problema della persona nel pensiero di S. Tommaso*, Roma 1967.

DERISI,O.N.: *La persona. Su essencia, se vida, su mundo*, La Plata 1950.

FEBRER,M.: *Il concepto de persona y la union hipostatica*, Valencia 1951.

FELDSTEIN,L.C.: "Reflections on the Ontology of the Person", *International Philosophical Quarterly*, 9 (1969) pp.313-341.

FRINGS,M.S.: *Person und Dasein*, Den Haag 1969.

GARRIGOU-LAGRANGE,R.: "De vera notione personalitatis", *Acta Pont. Academiae Romanae S.Thomae Aquinatis*, 5 (1938) pp.8-92.

GAZZANA,H.: "De constitutione personae", *Gregorianum*, 26 (1946) pp.310-326.

GOGACZ,M.: *Wokół problemu osoby* [Concerning the Problem of the Person], Warszawa 1974.

GRANAT,W.: *Osoba ludzka. Próba definicji* [The Human Person. An Attempt at Definition], Sandomierz 1961.

GUARDINI,R.: *Welt und Person*, Mainz 1988.

GUILFORD,J.P.: *Personality*, New York 1959.

HÄRING,B.: *Personalismus in Philosophie und Teologie*, München 1968.

JERPHAGNON,L.: *Qu'est-ce que la personne humaine?*, Toulouse 1962.

LOTZ,J.B.: *Der Mensch in Sein*, Wien 1967.
MARCEL,G.: *La dignite humaine*, Paris 1964.
MINKUS,P.A.: *Philosophy of the Person*, Oxford 1960.
MONTAGU,A.: *Anthropology and Human Nature*, New York 1963.
MUNIZ,F.P.: *El constitutivo formal de la persona creada en la tradicion tomista*, Salamanca 1947.
NÉDONCELLE.M: *Personne humaine et nature*, Paris 1963.
PAREYSON,L.: *Esistenza e persona*, Torino 1950.
PAUL,L.: *The Meaning of Human Existence*, Philadelphia 1950.
PITTERI,L.: *Lapersona umana. Sua struttura ontologica nella filosofia di Tommaso d'Aquin*, Pescara 1969.
RODZIŃSKI,A.: *Osoba i kultura* [The Person and Culture], Warszawa 1985.
SCHWARTLÄNDER,J.: *Der Mensch ist Person*, Stuttgart 1968.
STEFANINI,L.: *Metafisica della persona*, Padova 1950.
STRAWSON,P.E.: *Individuals. An Essay in Descriptive Metaphysics*, London 1959.
THOMAE,H.: *Das Individuum und seine Welt. Eine Persönlichkeitstheorie*, Göttingen 1968.
VENABLE,V.: *Human Nature*, Cleveland 1966.
VETTER,A.: *Personale Anthropologie*, Freiburg 1966.
WINCKELMANS de Cléty Ch.: *L'univers des personnes*, Paris 1969.

Chapter 3

Man as a Psycho-Somatic Reality

The considerations presented so far indicate that the human self is a substantial and personal being. These are evidently metaphysical propositions explaining the nature of the human being. The next stage of the analysis will constitute an attempt to characterize man as a psycho-somatic reality, i.e. as a composite of the body and the soul. If the material body is an object of direct experience[1], the category of soul is deduced from the systemic metaphysical analysis. It finds its confirmation in personal-axiological experience, but it is not directly read from it. The concepts of soul, spirit, and body are differently understood in particular philosophical trends, religions, cultures, historical traditions etc. Therefore, their explication makes it necessary to take into account the cultural-temporal context within which they function.

(i) Human Soul: Its Existence and Nature

The concept of soul played a crucial role in old-Greek thought, including philosophy. The Greek term "psyche" most often finds its equivalent in Latin "anima" or "spiritus"[2]. Almost every philosophical current offers at least partly different interpretations of the nature of soul, although most frequently it is understood as the sphere of man's psychic-mental life. Classical philosophy, initiated by Aristotle, defines soul as the act of the material body or as a substantial form of the human body.

Speaking about soul in its Christian interpretation we cannot be restricted to the semantic-phraseological plane. And this is precisely what is done in many philosophical currents, among others, in various kinds of materialism, biologism, sociologism and behaviourism. A follower of mechanistic materialism, T.Kotarbiński describes soul as an element of the material body (e.g. the brain). Dialectical materialism interprets soul as an epiphenomenon of biological-neurological processes, as their function, product, accompanying phenomenon etc.; it questions soul's ontical autonomy and reduces it to

---

[1]Comp. Part II, Chap.1 of this study.

[2]Aristotle also used the term "nous" to denote soul and in Latin many terms were used, too. Cf. G.Verbeke: *L'évolution de la doctrine du pneume du stoicisme à saint Augustin*, Louvain 1945; V.White: *Seele und Psyche*, Salzburg 1964.

the role of a secondary and temporal phenomenon. Also behaviourism questions the reality of soul and perceives in it an expression of vegetative life. In this respect a somewhat unclear position was taken by P.Teilhard de Chardin who frequently described soul as an effect of the organization of the material body[3]. The Christian scholar did not exclude the creative function of God and yet he interpreted the origin of the human soul on the phenomenological plane in a reductionistic manner. In the exposition of classical Christian philosophy the soul is by no means a product of matter, a final stage in the evolution of the cosmos, a result of the specific organization of the human body and so on. Explications of this kind in fact undermine the soul's real existence as an objective-autonomous reality.

Christian philosophy recognizes not only the existence of the soul but also its substantiality and spirituality. St.Thomas Aquinas proves this on the basis of the fact that the human soul is not a material reality[4]. Such an argumentation refers to Augustinian thought[5], because it emphasizes the opposition between the properties of material beings and man's spiritual "I". The greatness of the human spirit cannot be described in material-spatial terms but only in cognitive, moral, aesthetic and religious terms. Man's biological maturity cannot be identified with his internal-moral maturity and that is why the "courses" of the developments of "external man" and of "internal man" differ. Therefore, since soul has no material properties, it must constitute an immaterial reality. The subject of human consciousness has different properties than the material body; hence, there is a difference between, for instance, colour or height and friendship. The immateriality of man's internal "I" has not only a functional character but also a substantial one. For that reason St.Thomas speaks about the self-existence of the human soul[6]. This is confirmed, among others, by the fact that man's conscious activity has an intentional character. Although located in a determined space-time continuum, man transcends the categories connected with the world of matter. That is why he may apprehend every being, love all the good etc. Biological-vegetative life is completely "closed" within the borders of matter, while man's mental life is intentionally directed towards absolute higher values.

The spiritual substantiality of man's internal "I" is also supported by the argument which refers to the specificity of the acts of mental life[7]. This concerns two domains, cognition and the will. In their essence and functioning, intellectual-cognitive acts are immaterial, although in a specific way they are dependent on the nervous system. The human mind is not a mirror which passively records the picture of the world; nor is it a

---

[3]R.Lischer: *Marx and Teilhard. Two Ways to the New Humanity*, New York 1979.

[4]*Summa Theologiae*, I,q.75,a.1,c.

[5]St.Augustine: *De quantitate animae* 3,4 PL 32,1037; 14,24 PL 32,1049.

[6]*Summa Theologiae*, I,q.75,a.2,c.

[7]*Summa Theologiae*, I,q.61,a.2,ad 3; J.Seifert: *Das Leib-Seele- Problem in der gegenwärtigen philosophischen Diskussion*, Darmstadt 1979, pp.86-93.

kind of a computer, since the latter is lacking the substantial personal-spiritual "foundation". The acts of intellectual cognition are characterized by immateriality,universalization, intentionality, prospectiveness, and self-reflectiveness. These properties are not included in the potential of matter, for, can it ever be self-conscious, for instance? The aspirational-volitional domain also implies the substantial spirituality of the human "I". The acts of decisions, choices, moral self-realization, classification of higher values, love, friendship etc., all require a personal-spiritual centre. The immateriality of the acts of mental life, both cognitive and aspirational, is impossible without a stable substantial basis. Such a basis clearly cannot be provided by matter since then the effect would qualitatively surpass the cause. Man's mental activity finds a rational explanation only in the reality of a substantial spiritual person as the ontical foundation. Without a substantial soul, intellectual cognition or man's free choices would be impossible.

The substantiality of human immaterial soul also finds confirmation in internal experience[8]. It is true that under the conditions of earthly life we have no direct experience of the soul as such. The category of soul has a philosophical-systemic character and therefore it is not a direct result of intuitive-spontaneous cognition. Nevertheless, the importance of the concept of soul is confirmed by the data of human consciousness. Man's conscious experiences have an immaterial character, analogous to that of the internal "I". This is the primordial datum of human consciousness. We are conscious of its stability and ontical self-existence in respect to the material-biological determinants of humanity.

The substantiality of human soul justifies some conclusions concerning its nature. First of all, it is evident that it is precisely immaterial soul that constitutes the foundation of the personal identity of the human being. The personal "I" includes soul as its integral element, for due to it man preserves the continuity of his existential consciousness. The spiritual being is indivisible and simple, although this does not exclude a possibility of possessing a multiplicity of faculties, powers, potentials etc. Although enclosed in the sphere of corporeity in a natural manner, the spiritual "I" is self-existent and internally autonomous. It is a reality, not merely an expression or function of the material body. Being immaterial, man's soul is not a supernatural reality or, even less, a divine reality. Thanks to it man is open to supernatural values and to God, yet the spiritual "I" is a natural element of the human person. The nature of the soul also entails its connection with the material body.

---

[8]J.Seifert, op.cit., pp.94-98. This problem is a subject of a controversy: some Thomists recognize the fact of the direct experience of human soul, although a majority questions it. It seems that two matters have been confused here; the conception of soul is connected with the philosophical system, although this does not exclude an experiential apprehension of its connotative contents.

(ii) Human Soul as a Form Organizing the Body

Man's substantial and personal "I" is adequately explained only through an affirmation of the existence of immaterial soul. Nevertheless, soul is not man's property. Christian philosophy, including St.Thomas Aquinas[9], quite unambiguously describes man as a compound of two substantial factors, the body and the soul. Their mutual relation is explained in Aristotelian-Thomistic philosophy on the basis of the theory of hylomorphism. The latter is derived from the domain of ancient learning about nature and today it is sometimes questioned by advances made by modern natural sciences[10]. Yet, in fact, this theory has a metaphysical character, being combined with the categories of act and potency[11]. The theory of hylomorphism is a model commonly accepted in classical philosophy to help in explaining the ontical structure of the material world, especially the organic world[12]. According to this theory, all the material and material-spiritual beings constitute a combination of two substantial elements, matter (***hyle***) and form (***morfe***). Aristotle understood matter as an unformed and featureless medium, i.e., as a pure potential. Strictly speaking, such a potential occurs exclusively as primordial matter which has not yet come into contact with any form. A component of being is found only in secondary matter which constitutes a passive-receptive factor. If matter constitutes a potential, then form is an act and perfection of being[13]. A substantial form is precisely what makes being determined qualitatively and generically. Form is an act integrating the whole of being and its activating agent. Form combines particular individuals into a determined genus[14]. Form is a primary substantial act (***entelechia***), while action (***energeia***) is a secondary act.

The theory of hylomorphism is employed in Thomistic philosophy to explicate the structure of the human being. This theory suggests a natural and necessary mutual subordination of both components of being, matter and form, i.e. the body and the soul. The ontical specificity of human soul does not undermine its natural directedness towards its connection with the material body. St.Thomas Aquinas states this quite clearly: "Although the body does not belong to the essence of soul, the essence of soul still has a tendency to become unified with the body. [...] And since soul, to some extent, needs the body to perform its tasks, this proves that in the hierarchy of beings endowed with

---

[9]"Post considerationem creaturae spiritualis et corporalis, considerandum est de homine, qui ex spirituali et corporali substantia componitur"; *Summa Theologiae*, I,q.75, prologue.

[10]Such a view is accepted by A.Mitterer: *Wandel des Weltbildes von Thomas von Aquin auf heute*, Innsbruck 1935.

[11]*Summa Theologiae*, I,q.76,a.1.

[12]Cf. T.Wojciechowski: *Teoria hylomorfizmu w ujęciu autorów neoscholastycznych* [The Hylomorphic Theory as Approached by Neo- Scholastic Authors], Warszawa 1967.

[13]St.Thomas: *In Phys.*, I,1.

[14]The problem of individuation will be mentioned later on.

reason soul has a lower rank than an angel which does not combine with the body"[15]. The body and the soul are substantial parts of the human being, yet none of them, in isolation from the other, can constitute the genus ***homo sapiens***. Hence, this is also true about the substance of the self-existing soul; it is complete in existence, but incomplete as a genus. Man constitutes a compound of the material body and immaterial soul, i.e. of matter and of form. Only together do they co-create a complete human nature. Such an anthropological perspective departs from the Platonic-Cartesian approaches, which narrow down the essence of man to the factor of soul and reduce the role of the body to a temporarily employed tool. In the Thomistic interpretation, the body and soul together create the person of man, mutually conditioning and complementing each other. None of them can exist before the becoming of the compound such as the psycho-physical human being. Their relation is natural and direct.

As a metaphysical theory, hylomorphism concerns the whole reality which is exclusively or partially material. This is implied by the analogous character of the concept of substantial form. Form is the soul. Plato distinguished three souls in man, vegetative, sensible and mental. Aristotle inclined to accept a thesis about man's single soul, though endowed with various powers and fulfilling three functions, biological, sensible and mental[16]. Even more emphatically was the unity of the substantial form of the human being emphasized by St.Thomas Aquinas. In his times the matter provoked a widespread controversy. Avicenna recognized the existence of at least two forms, the form of corporeity and the concretizing form, in an individual being. A similar view was held by the representatives of Scotism, ascribing to man the possession of two substantial forms: one of them was the form of corporeity, while the other endowed man with individual properties. St.Thomas decisively spoke for the unity of the substantial form while recognizing, after Aristotle, a plurality of the powers it possesses. Thus, man has one and only one substantial form, i.e. soul, which fulfils the basic vital functions, biological-vegetative, sensible and mental. This same soul causes that man is an animate, feeling and rational substance. Soul ultimately constitutes the foundation and explanation of both biological-sensual life (drives) and mental-spiritual life (intellect, will)[17].

Ontical gradualism demands a recognition of the plurality of qualitatively differentiated substantial forms and that is why it is possible to speak about vegetative, animal and human souls. The inanimate world possesses exclusively the form of corporeity due to which a concrete being has a determined shape, structural organization, properties etc. Plant organisms are endowed with the vegetative soul, whose effects include an ability of nutrition, growth, continuation of the species. Animal organisms possess a higher kind of substantial form since it results in the sphere of drives and instincts and in sensible

---

[15]*Summa Theologiae*, I,q.75,a.7,ad 3; J.Seifert, op.cit., pp.154-163.

[16]Aristotle: *On Soul*, II,2,411 a-b.

[17]*Summa Theologiae*, I,q.76,a.4,ad 3; A.Forest: *La structure métaphysique du concret selon saint Thomas d'Aquin*, Paris 1956, pp.199 ff.

cognition. Between the animal and the human souls there are qualitative differences[18]. Of the latter, the most significant ones include: sensible cognition - intellectual cognition, determinism of the drives - freedom of choice, biological emotionality - emotionality of the higher affections (e.g. moral), immanence - self-transcendence, unconsciousness - self-consciousness, psychically static character - spiritual-mental development, cognitive passivity - cognitive inventiveness and intentionality, objectiveness - subjectiveness (personality). The differences enumerated above confirm the ontical uniqueness of the human soul. It is a substantial form of the material body, but in its nature and functions it significantly departs from the restricted potentials of the vegetative and animal souls. The latter are not self-existent, i.e. in their origin and activity they are entirely dependent on the material bases.

According to hylomorphism, man is a combination of matter and form. The latter appears to be a rational soul, fulfilling its functions of the formal cause of the human ontical composite. Although matter and form create a uniform whole, in their natures and operations they are mutually opposed. The formal cause is an act which gives a thing its existence, substantial or accidental. The function of actualizing is not something accidental for form but it results from the beingness of this form. With its beingness, form perfects and actualizes matter which is a potential. And since form is an act which organizes and integrates matter, it also endows being with existence and perfection; it achieves this directly, omitting intermediate elements[19]. The causality of matter consists in the reception of determined properties, whereas the causality of form is connected with the fact of actualizing the potentials contained in the material medium. This role appertains to form due to its internal nature, not because of some external additions. One can only speak about the necessity of certain conditions so that a substantial form can in fact realize its proper causality. First of all, such a condition appears to be the very existence of form. Such an existence is merely the existence of an element (***ut quo***), i.e. co-existence. Form does not exist before the appearance of the composite; the "priority" appertains to it only in respect to its nature[20]. The next condition of the causality of form is the "proximity" between matter and form as the two components of one being. The existence of a causal agent, which leads to the combining of matter and form into one whole, is also necessary here. Between matter and form there should also occur an adequacy or proportionality. The effect of the causality of form is perceived as the actualization of primary matter and the appearance of a new composite. In itself matter has no existence and it is only substantial forms that endow it with existence, forms whose task is the actualization of the potential of this matter. Another, secondary effect of the

[18]J.Seifert: *Leib und Seele. Ein Beitrag zur Philosophischen Anthropologie*, Salzburg-München 1973, pp.84-115.

[19]*Summa Theologiae*, I,q.76,aa.6 and 7; In Metaph., V,2.

[20]Cf. J.A.Peters: "Matter and Form in Metaphysics", *The New Scholasticism* 31 (1957), pp.447-483; S.Adamczyk: *De existentia substantiali in doctrine Sancti Thomae Aquinatis*, Roma 1962, pp. 153-186.

causality of form is the removal of the previous form from an object. But this question is marginal in respect to the problem of human soul.

The causality of form outlined above is specifically realized in the case of man's substantial form, i.e. his soul. St. Thomas draws attention to this issue when he writes: "And the human soul is the most perfect form and that is why it so greatly surpasses in its power corporeal matter that it has activity and power without any participation of matter at all; this power is called intellect by us"[21]. The human soul is a self-existent form because the mental activity (intellect and will) it inspires becomes to a large extent independent of the material body. The higher mental activities of the soul, as immaterial, cannot be a result of the material being, that is, the body. Obviously, the ontical and functional self-existence of the soul is not identical with man's ontical self-existence understood as autonomy of existence. No creation, even a rational one, ever loses its ontically derivative status in respect to God.

St.Thomas's thesis about the self-existence of man's soul, though explicitly formulated only by him[22], goes back in its origin to Aristotle's metaphysics. The latter's work *On Soul* repeatedly formulates the thesis that soul is the substantial form of the body. This also holds true about the human soul, thanks to which "we live, perceive and think"[23]. The old-Greek thinker clearly ascribes to the human soul, as a substantial form, differentiated activities, vegetative and mental. Moreover, he emphasizes the specificity of the human soul as a possessor of intellect (***nous***). He writes: "For this is, it seems, quite a different type of soul which alone is capable of existing as an eternal entity after separation from the destructible thing [from the body]"[24]. This statement is not unequivocal, especially in respect to the problem of the relation between the categories of spirit and intellect. Nevertheless, it certainly raises some doubts about the validity of the claim that Aristotle did not know the idea of the immortality of the human soul[25].

Coming back to the chain of St.Thomas's reasoning, one should more strongly emphasize the specificity of the formal causation of the human soul. The completely immaterial human soul is a form of the material body. Vegetative and animal souls, being totally dependent on the matter they have actualized, share its fate. They come into being and disintegrate together with it. The human soul is a self-existent form and that is why, although it organizes and actualizes the material body, it does not crumble together with it; also thanks to its activity, it dominates over the body. For that reason St.Thomas notices that "the more perfect the form, the more entirely it masters the bodily matter,

---

[21]*Summa Theologiae*, I,q.76,a.1,c.

[22]*Summa Theologiae*, I,q.75,a.2,c.

[23]Aristotle: *On Soul*, II,2,414 a, p.41.

[24]Ibid., II,2,413 b, p.40.

[25]E.Gilson: *Elements of Christian Philosophy*, New York 1960, Chap.9; M.Krąpiec: *I-Man*, op.cit., pp.101-102.

the less it sinks into it and the more it surpasses it in its power"[26]. The human soul is not an emanation of matter (as is the case of vegetative and animal souls) but it imparts its own existence to the body. Naturally, the point does not concern a temporary priority of the soul over the totality of the human person, but ontical priority. According to St. Thomas, the human soul has its own act of existence which it imparts to the body it actualizes[27]. Therefore, man's existence is, first of all, the existence of his soul as a self-existent substantial form, and only then is it the existence of the composite of matter and form. Man's psycho-somatic complexity is his natural structure and that is why in the beingness of the human person the soul does not retain an existence separate from the body[28]. It imparts its existence to the material body which it organizes and activates, co-existing together with it. In every being, also including man, there exists only one substantial form. That is why the immaterial soul fulfils all the functions connected with man's person. It is the soul that causes that "man is an actual being, a body, a living self, an animal and a man"[29]. The predominant role of the soul does not push to the margin the role of the material body because it still remains a natural component of the human person. The body participates in man's beingness, in his dignity, his calling and his tasks.

Characterizing the relation between the soul and the body, Thomism discusses the so-called principle of individuation[30]. Namely, it claims that the reason for the individualization of the human soul is matter connected with quantity (***materia quantitate signata***). Without discussing this matter in any greater detail (this is clearly a very complex issue), one should nevertheless note that the question derives from Platonism. According to the latter, ideas were interpreted as universals. A continuation of the Platonic idea in Aristotle appears in the category of form. That is why it seems necessary to seek such an agent which could individualize the carrier's generic features, i.e. the form. But must form be apprehended as a genus? After all, it is not only the body but also the soul of an individual man that constitutes a source of his idiosyncratic properties[31]. On the other hand, matter always differentiates and individualizes, whereas the generic form is a source of a somatic and psychic unity.

---

[26]*Summa Theologiae*, I,q.76,a.1,c.

[27]"Anima illud esse in quo ipsa subsistit, communicat materiae corporali, ex qua et anima intellectiva fit unum, ita quod illud esse quod est totius compositi, est etiam ipsius animae. Quod non accidit in aliis formis, quae non sunt subsistentes. Et propter hoc anima humana remanet in suo esse, destructo corpore; non autem aliae formae"; *Summa Theologiae*, I,q.76,a.1,ad 5.

[28]*Summa Theologiae*, I,q.76,a.7, ad 3.

[29]*Summa Theologiae*, I,q.76,a.6, ad 1.

[30]Cf. St.Thomas: *De ente et essentia*, c.2-3.

[31]J.Seifert: *Leib und Seele*, op.cit., pp.343 ff.

(iii) Man as a Heterogeneous Totality

The separation of the two elements in the human being, i.e., the body (matter) and the soul (form), implies a problem of their mutual relations. Is man, therefore, a unity at all? Does the duality of human nature make it possible to speak of his ontical unity? Finding an appropriate solution between dualism and monism is a true dilemma of any anthropology.

We should begin with some semantic explanations. The categories of dualism and monism are ambiguous[32]. Dualism can be phenomenal and substantialist. The former perceives an opposition between bodily and psychic processes which take place in man's being. This is acknowledged even by Marxist epiphenomenalism and process theology, although they question the substantial differentiation of the body and the soul. Classical Christian philosophy recognizes the substantialist dualism of human nature. Such dualism, in turn, may be extreme or moderate. The adherents of the former included Plato and, to some extent, also Descartes. Moderate dualism was accepted by St. Augustine and St.Thomas Aquinas, who recognized the natural character of the relations between the material body and the immaterial soul. Varieties of radical dualism can be found in the theories of occasionalism and parallelism, which treat corporeity and spirituality as two spheres functioning side by side and mutually independent. In another respect, one may distinguish ontological and axiological dualism. The latter proclaims an opposition between body and soul in moral categories. Manichaeism interpreted the material body as the seat of evil while the sphere of the spirit - as the incarnation of good. Ontological dualism implies a possibility of separating the soul from the body at the moment of man's death which, of course, is unacceptable for phenomenological dualism.

The category of monism is also ambiguous. At the moment we are not concerned with the general-ontological monism, but exclusively anthropological monism. The most significant semantic distinction concerns homogeneous and heterogeneous varieties of monism. The former explains the unity of the human being as ontical homogeneity and uni-dimensionality; the body and the soul are here interpreted as substantially identical. This is an extreme, monistic conception of man. Homogeneous monism may also occur in several varieties such as materialistic, idealistic or pantheistic. Heterogeneous monism recognizes exclusively the functional unity of the human being which does not contradict the acceptance of substantialist dualism. Classical Christian philosophy is in favour of the latter interpretation of human nature.

Man is a unity of body and soul but he is not their identity. They are two elements of the ontical-substantial character and not only a double operation of the same substance[33]. Both elements constitute integral parts of human nature, mutually constituting it. This substantialist dualism has recently been questioned. The point does not concern the challenge posed by reductionistic materialism or extreme Platonic

[32] J.Seifert: *Das Leib-Seele-Problem...*, op.cit., pp.126-129.

[33] *Summa Theologiae*, I,qq.75 and 76.

spiritualism which perceive the essence of man in a single factor, matter or spirit. The influence of Protestant theology caused that also some Catholic authors undermine anthropological dualism. Josef Pieper follows precisely this line of reasoning when he refers to the statement by St.Thomas: "Soul, as a part of human nature, does not possess its proper perfection otherwise than in the unity with the body"[34]. In this utterance by St.Thomas Pieper chose to omit the phrase that soul is "a part of human nature" and, therefore, it is not surprising that he could then claim: "On the basis of this fundamental conception it is not only man but also soul itself that must be described as something, in a sense, corporeal"[35]. The proposed explication of man departs from Thomistic anthropology (and others, as well), because it implies the "corporeity" of soul. Departure from traditional anthropological dualism is also typical of some followers of Teilhard de Chardin, who are in favour of the evolutionary origin of the human soul. "And if the human soul - it is suggested - came into being in the evolutionary way, then it cannot constitute a separate, self-existent substance. Together with the soul, there came into being not so much a new substance but rather a new actual ontical level in man's nature"[36]. The difference between the soul and the body is therefore reduced to the phenomenological sphere and for that reason one finds here such terms as "levels", "aspects", "manifestations", "actions" etc.

The renouncement of substantialist dualism, signalled above, is hard to reconcile with classical Christian philosophy[37]. For if the soul is merely an aspect or an ontical level, it is difficult to speak about its immortality. Only a substantial element of human nature, to some extent ontically independent of the body, can be permanent and immortal. At any rate, the unity of the somatic-biological and psychic-spiritual factors need not be interpreted as their ontical identity. The mutual dependence of the soul and the body, an evident fact for Christian philosophy, does not justify substantialist monism. Hence, the soul is not only a specific aspect of the body or its ontical layer, but a substantial element co-constituting human nature.

The problem of the relations between the body and the soul was solved in a variety of ways. Recognizing the natural character of these relations, Christian philosophy separates itself from the theories of occasionalism and parallelism which question the mutual influence of both factors. Anthropology, combined with the theory of hylomorphism, accepts the mutual inter-dependence and inter-action of the body and the soul[38]. The somatic-biological factor plays a significant role in many experiences of man,

---

[34]*De spiritualibus creaturis*, q. unica, a.2,ad 5.

[35]*Tod und Unsterblichkeit*, München 1968, p.56.

[36]T.Wojciechowski: *Teoria hylemorfizmu* ..., op.cit., pp.264-269. The author seems inclined to the meromorphic model of being which acknowledges the unity of the generic form but also recognizes a plurality of substantial forms in individual being. Such a model corresponds with the evolutionary picture of the world but, similarly to Scotism, undermines the unity of a concrete being.

[37]Cf.J.Seifert: *Leib und Seele*, op.cit., pp.329-338.

[38]J.Seifert: *Das Leib-Seele-Problem* ..., op.cit., pp.139-148.

among others, in the phenomena of suffering and sexuality. Yet, in both cases man's sensations differ principally from analogical sensations in an animal, for they are incorporated into the domain of the operation of mental faculties and higher emotions. Psychic suffering is absent in the animal world, as well as the higher forms of love (friendship, love of one's neighbour, religious love). There also occurs a reversed influence, that of the soul on the body, which is confirmed by the phenomena of conscience, self-determination, self-sacrifice etc. The interdependence of the soul and the body is evident in man's activities, such as manual labour, mental reflection, social life, the domain of culture etc. The soul is the form organizing the body, and, therefore, there is in man nothing that would be purely material and corporeal. Biological and vegetative life is interpenetrated by the influence of the internal "I", connected with the soul and its powers. At the same time, man is not a pure spirit (***anima separata***) and that is why his mental-spiritual sphere is connected with the somatic-biological sphere. The influence of the body, in its ontological aspect, is positive for the functioning of the soul[39]. Without its co-participation the substantial form cannot realize some of its tasks, e.g. sensible cognition.

The connection of the body and the soul, even though it is so close, is not realized in a local-spatial manner. For that reason it is impossible to localize the soul in a determined element or organ of the body. In keeping with the tradition of Christian thought, St. Thomas states that the whole soul exists in the whole animate body and in each of its parts[40]. The influence of the soul is realized in the manner of the vital force, whose domain of operation involves the totality of the human organism.

Summing up the solutions offered so far, one may formulate some conclusions. Man is a psycho-somatic composite and, hence, a single totality of various elements[41]. It is a heterogeneous rather than homogeneous whole. In man there exist various elements, material, biological, vegetative, psychic-mental. They are not separate but they create a structural-ontical and functional unity. Thanks to that, although man has ontical levels in common with inorganic, vegetative and animal worlds, he is not a mineral, a plant or an animal. Human nature has an ontical centre, namely, the personal "I". It is individual, self-existent, nontransferable, permanent, and immaterial. It constitutes the ontical foundation of the totality of human nature. The person is, first of all, a spiritual self, most often called the soul. It is an organizing and active factor of the human being, but it does not exhaust its totality. The material body also constitutes man's integral part, included in his natural and eschatological tasks. The body and the soul together constitute the human person in equal measure, though in different ways. Man's ontical dualism does not undermine in any way his dynamic-functional monism.

---

[39]St.Thomas: *De Potentia*, q.5,a.10, ad 5.

[40]*Summa Theologiae*, I,q.76,a.8,c.

[41]Cf. E.Coreth: *Was ist der Mensch?*, Innsbruck 1977, pp.152-158.

The controversy between the monistic and dualistic understandings of man also occurred in the interpretations of the Bible[42]. The first Books of the Old Testament favour the interpretation of human nature which is somewhat monistic[43], but later on, beginning with the Book of Wisdom, they already contain elements of dualism. Similar intimations can be found in the New Testament, among others, in the teachings of St. Paul[44]. However, it should be remembered that the Holy Gospel in fact passes over a philosophical interpretation of the human being, focussing attention on his relation to God. That is why, for instance, the conception of the body often denotes the state of sinfulness rather than an element of man. At any rate, there is no justification for the claim that the Bible contains anthropological monism and undermines the truth about the immortality of man's soul. The later Books of the Old Testament and the New Testament distinguish the elements of the body and the soul, differentiating their nature and destiny.

Frequently one may also find a triadic interpretation of man. Trichotomy is found by some authors in the Bible, among others, in the Book of Wisdom (2,3; 9,15), which speaks about the spirit (***pneuma, nous***) as an element different from the soul (***psyche***) and the body (***soma***). Most likely, such an interpretation is an effect of the lack of unambiguous terminology of the Holy Scriptures. In the domain of philosophy, the trichotomic interpretation of man is accepted by Viktor Frankl[45]. In the structure of the human person he distinguished the body, the soul and the spirit. He understood the soul as psychic life in its somatic determinants, whereas the term "spirit" was used by him to denote what is traditionally explicated as the soul. The Austrian psychiatrist stressed the autonomy of the spirit in respect to the organic-vegetative plane, and, to some extent, he also separated both these spheres.

---

[42]Cf. A.Gelin: *L'homme selon Bible*, Paris 1968.

[43]But already the Book of Ecclesiastes contains the text: "before the dust returns to the earth as it began and the spirit returns to God who gave it" (12,7).

[44]J.Coppens: "L'anthropologie biblique" [in:] *De homine. Studia hodiernae anthropologiae*, Romae 1970, vol.1, pp.7-21.

[45]V.Frankl: Homo patiens, Wien 1950.

LITERATURE

BERNATH,K.: *Anima forma corporis. Eine Untersuchung über die ontologischen Grundlegen des Anthropologie des Thomas von Aquin*, Bonn 1969.

BICKEL,L.: *Aussen und Innen. Beitrag zur Lösung des Leib-Seele-Problems*, Konstanz 1960.

BIER,A.: *Die Seele*, München 1965.

CONRAD-MARTIUS,H.: *Die Geistseele des Menschen*, München 1960.

COPPENS,J.: "L'anthropologie biblique" [in:] *De homine. Studia hodiernae anthropologiae. Acta VII Congressus Thomistici Internationalis*, Romae 1970, vol.2, pp.7-21.

GEYER,H.: *Von der Natur des Geistes*, Freiburg 1969.

HIRSCHBERGER,J.: *Seele und Leib in der Spätantike*, Frankfurt am M. 1969.

HÖRZ,H.: *Materie und Bewusstsein*, Berlin 1965.

LAVELLE,L.: *De l'Ame humaine*, Paris 1951.

LOTZ,J.B.: *Die Identität von Geist und Sein*, Rom 1972.

LOTZE,R.H.: *Das Dasein der Seele*, Leipzig 1923.

MULLIN, Mc E, [ed.]: *The Concept of Matter*, Notre Dame 1963.

PEGIS,A.C.: *At the Origins of the Thomistic Notion of Man*, New York 1963.

PEURSEN,C.A.Van: *Le corps - l'âme - l'esprit. Introduction à une anthropologie phénoménologique*, The Hague 1979.

ROSSI,G.L.: *L'uomo, animalità e spiritualit à*, Torino 1967.

ROYCE,J.E.: *Man and his Nature*, New York 1961.

SCHULTZ,H.J.: "Was weiss Man von der Seele?", *Erforschung und Erfahrung in Psychologie, Philosophie und Theologie*, Bonn 1967.

SEIFERT,J.: *Leib und Seele. Ein Beitrag zur philosophischen Anthropologie*, Salzburg 1973.

SEIFERT,J.: *Das Leib-Seele-Problem in der gegenwärtigen philosophischen Diskussion*, Darmstadt 1979.

STYBE,S.F.: *"Antinomias" in the Conception of Man. An Inquiry into History of Human Spirit*, Copenhagen 1962.

ULRICH,F.: "Zur Ontologie des Menschen", *Salzburger Jahrbuch für Philosophie* 7 (1963) pp.25-128.

VANNI-ROVIGHI,S.: *L'anthropologie filosofica de San Tommaso d'Aquino*, Milano 1968.

VRIES, de J.: *Materie und Geist*, München 1970.

WHITE,V.: *Seele und Psyche*, Salzburg 1964.

Chapter 4

Faculties of the Human Being

The ontical structure of the human person, besides the subject ("I") and his actions, also covers a qualitatively differentiated multiplicity of faculties. St.Thomas motivates their existence by the fact that only in infinite and absolutely simple God there occurs a complete identity of existence, nature and action[1]. On the other hand, in every created being, including man, there occurs a real difference between the being, on the one side, and, on the other - the faculties and actions. The former and the latter are not identified with the nature of an accidental being and that is why they do not constitute its substantial endowment. The potentiality of the nature of a created being suggests the existence of faculties which, in turn, are actualized in a concrete action.

(i) The Notion and Typology of Faculties

The existence of faculties was proved by St.Thomas Aquinas in two ways, by referring to the material of empirical experience and to the systemic assumptions of metaphysics. Empirical material shows an abundance of human vital actions which demand an adequate ontical foundation. Reductionistic reasoning[2], often employed in Thomistic philosophy, is connected with the metaphysical principle of causality. Actions - effects require the existence of man's appropriate abilities as their cause. The ultimate subject of action is man himself but his faculties constitute the direct principle of these actions. St.Thomas demonstrates this by referring to the fundamental metaphysical thesis about the existence of a potential and an act, and then by their correlation[3]. Only God is a pure act and for that reason His actions and beingness are identical. Man is a being that is both real and also potential. His actions are not identified with his substantial beingness and that is why one should see them as accidentals. At the same time, not all kinds of actions appertain to all the creatures, and therefore one may speak of their ontical, stable

---

[1]*Summa Theologiae*, I,q.54,a.1,c; I,q.77,a.1,c.

[2]Reductionistic reasoning, also known as "aprioristic" in Scholastic philosophy, is fundamental in the domain of the philosophy of God.

[3]*Summa Theologiae*, I,q.77,a.1,c.

abilities to perform specific actions. Such abilities are precisely faculties. The substantial subject is endowed with certain faculties and the existence of substance is finalized in the operation of precisely these faculties. The faculties of the human person ensure the possibility of action. The possibility is of two kinds, passive and active. The former concerns the possibility of reception, e.g. of impressions from the external world. The faculties of the human being constitute an active possibility, since it concerns the abilities to perform certain functions.

What are faculties? They are not substantial and self-existent beings, i.e., they do not exist in separation from the personal foundation of the human being. To use the terminology of Aristotelian ontology, one may say that faculties are accidentals. However, they are accidentals of a special kind because they constitute a natural and indispensable endowment of the human being. For that reason St.Thomas calls them properties, for although they do not belong to the essence of being, still they directly result from generic features. "In this way, one may say that the faculties of soul (***potentiae animae***) are something intermediate between substance and accidentals, in a sense constituting the natural properties of soul"[4]. Although man's faculties have the status of accidental beings, they constitute his universal and indispensable endowment. St.Thomas recognizes a multiplicity of faculties in man's being, really different both from the substantial foundation and from each other[5]. Nevertheless, this does not undermine the psycho-physical unity of the human person, because particular faculties are ontically and functionally interconnected. They determine the richness and transcendence of the person in respect to the external world whose actions and faculties are not so greatly differentiated as those of man.

Man is the subject of faculties. St.Thomas distinguished a double subjectiveness of faculties. The human soul is a direct subject of mental, i.e. immaterial faculties, the mind and the will. The subject of the remaining faculties was perceived in the totality (***compositum***) of the human nature[6]. That is why, for instance, man's sensible cognition is realized as a result of the co-operation of the body and the soul. Although the soul is a direct substantial subject of psychic-mental actions, it nevertheless constitutes the ultimate ***principium*** of all man's actions, also of lower actions[7]. This distinction does not negate either the organic ties between man's somatic and spiritual elements or their mutual influence. The point is simply the fact that the higher psychic functions have no material organ that would be analogical to sensible powers.

The human person is a seat of many faculties. Their division assumes as a criterion the abundance of their acts which, in turn, are differentiated according to their appropriate

---

[4]*Summa Theologiae*, I,q.77,a.1,ad 5.

[5]*Summa Theologiae*, I,q.77,a.2,c.

[6]Comp. *Summa Theologiae*, I,q.77,a.5,c.

[7]*Summa Theologiae*, I,q.77,a.6,c.

objects[8]. Speaking about the object of faculties, St.Thomas obviously had in mind their formal object. The material object of man's faculties is the whole existing world, although its various aspects or sectors constitute formal objects of particular faculties. Philosophical tradition, referring to Plato's theory of three souls, distinguishes three levels of life, vegetative, sensual and mental. St.Thomas also distinguished three kinds of soul, the vegetative soul of the plant world, the sensory soul of the animal world, and the mental soul of the human world[9]. Yet, at the same time he also separated four levels of life, because, apart from the three forms of life mentioned above, he also distinguished the ability of local movement. Finally, his classification also included the following faculties: vegetative, sensory, appetitive, locomotory, and mental[10].

In another respect, he distinguished cognitive and appetitive faculties, but the latter he applied primarily to man. In this case the criterion of the division is no longer the object of the faculty but their manner of operation and ontological finalism[11]. Cognitive faculties have a different character and aims than appetitive faculties.

Constituting a natural endowment of the human being, faculties do not function in isolation from each other. First of all, they are connected with man's substantial form, i.e. soul. In its existence and dynamics the multiplicity of faculties is an ordered unity[12]. Sensory faculties initiate man's action but ontologically they are subordinated to mental faculties. The latter constitute a new quality so that in consequence man transcends the world of plants and of animals.

(ii) Vegetative and Sensory Faculties

Apart from its specific mental faculties, the human person also possesses vegetative and sensory faculties. The former connect man with the world of plants, while the latter with the animal world. Naturally, in man both of them are realized in a specific way since they remain there in the sphere of the influence of intellect and will. Vegetative faculties are lacking the distinction between the cognitive and appetitive spheres, characteristic of both sensory and mental faculties of man.

St.Thomas Aquinas distinguished three vegetative faculties, namely, nutrition, growth and procreation[13]. The faculty of nutrition is permanently connected with every living organism, vegetative, animal or human. The process of nutrition begins at the moment of birth and lasts till death. The faculty of growth has an active character only in a certain

[8] *Summa Theologiae*, I,q.73,a.3,c.

[9] *Summa Theologiae*, I,q.78,a.1,c.

[10] *Summa Theologiae*, I,q.78,a.1, sed contra.

[11] *Summa Theologiae*, I,q.77,a.5,c.

[12] *Summa Theologiae*, I,q.77,a.4,c.

[13] *Summa Theologiae*, I,q.78,a.2.

period of life, causing the quantitative development of the organism. Finally, the faculty of procreation is more perfect than the other two because its ontological aim is the creation of a new organism. All the three faculties function in a specific manner in human psycho-physical being since man's biological immanence does not exclude his psychic-spiritual transcendence in respect to his surrounding world. While the phenomenon of growth is entirely independent of man's consciousness and will, the functioning of the faculties of nutrition and procreation are subject to axiological categories. For that reason the separation of these two domains from ethical norms is an error of biological reductionism. In the human person the faculty of procreation is connected with the rich sphere of emotional-sensory sensations, whose crowning is the phenomenon of love. St.Thomas recognized love as the foundation of human life, especially of the emotional-appetitive sphere. Love is the primary act of the whole sphere of affections; it is at the beginning of the whole life of emotions; it is also an end because everything we want, everything we impose on ourselves, everything we bear, has no other aim but that of maintaining or gratifying love[14]. Thus, in human nature the vegetative faculty of procreation is connected with the sensory and mental domains, co-creating a rich world of human love.

Another integral element of the human being is found in his sensory faculties which connect man with the world of animals. In keeping with tradition, St.Thomas accepted the dichotomic division of sensory faculties into external and internal. The object of the former is the material world with its properties. External senses are directed at concrete material things, and their object is what is sensible (***sensibile***). They include colours, shapes, sounds, kinaesthetic sensations etc. Each external sense has its proper object, e.g. the eye and colour. Traditionally they are described as the so-called secondary properties[15]. Some attributes of material things can constitute objects of perception of two sensory faculties, e.g. shapes; these are the so-called primary properties. Primary properties have an objective character, whereas secondary properties have a more subjective-individual character.

Following tradition, St.Thomas distinguished five external senses, namely, those of touch, taste, smell, hearing and sight[16]. Touch is the lowest of external senses since in fact it is merely a set of receptors sensitive to movement and rest, temperature, pain, resistance etc. The seat of this sense is the whole surface of the skin in which there are the nerve endings of the organism. Although the sense of touch is the lowest in the hierarchy, it still constitutes a foundation for the remaining external senses. The senses of taste and smell constitute a kind of particularization of touch, for they are directed at specific stimuli acting on separated centres of the human organism. On the other hand, according to St.Thomas the highest rank should be given to the sense of sight and then

[14]*Summa Theologiae*, I,q.20,a.1,c; II-II,q.27,a.2,c.

[15]Comp. *Summa Theologiae*, I,q.78,a.3,ad 1-4.

[16]*Summa Theologiae*, I,q.78,a.3.

to hearing. Both constitute sources of the richest cognitive sensations, and, at the same time, they are closest to intellect.

In the system of the faculties of the sensory sphere a particularly privileged position is assumed by internal senses which are characterized by the highest degree of immateriality[17]. Such senses have no material organs. Their objects are not material things but impressions connected with the functioning of external senses. St.Thomas accepted the existence of four internal senses in man, namely, the correlative sense, imagination, sensory memory and the faculty of estimation. The enumerated senses play an important role in man's life since they constitute a transitional stage between the purely sensory stage and the mental sphere.

The "correlative sense" constitutes a specific centre of all the sensible impressions, and first of all, of their synchronization and integration. Due to it, the so far "scattered" sensations of particular external senses are transformed into a coherent whole. The "correlative" sense co-operates with imagination and together they create images. If sensations are fragmentary and unstable, images constitute a total - though still only sensible - apprehension of material objects. Kinaesthetic sensations, sensations of sight, hearing etc. are transformed into an image, for instance, of a man or an animal. Imagination not only creates images but it also serves as their "storage room". As modern philosophy notices (among others, J.P.Sartre), images can be of two kinds, reproductive and creative. This distinction makes it possible to question the claims of extreme idealism which reduces the external world to subjective sensations. The third faculty of internal senses is sensory memory, common to man and to animals. The latter do not have yet the active ability of recollection (***reminiscentia***), but they are only capable of retaining experienced sensations and created images. Memory makes it possible for man to have a feeling of a continuity of experienced sensory sensations which then provide valuable material for intellectual reflection.

The most perfect sense of man is the faculty of estimation (***vis aestimativa***), also called the faculty of thought appraisal (***vis cogitativa***) or a particular reason (***ratio particularis***). In its character and function this faculty approaches the cognitive-intellectual sphere[18]. In animals it is simply an instinct which indicates the right way of behaviour in a given existential situation. In man the faculty of estimation, as a result of its functional connection with the mental sphere, enables a recognition of the existence of a concrete material being. It is still an identification of an individual being but regarded as an embodiment of some generality. Since the fact of existence is already universal and holistic, its cognition - within the realm of the particular reason - begins the domain of mental cognition[19].

---

[17]*Summa Theologiae*, I,q.78,a.4.

[18]*Summa Theologiae*, I,q.78,a.4,ad 4-6.

[19]M.A.Krąpiec: *Realizm ludzkiego poznania* [The Realism of Human Cognition], Poznań 1959, pp.500-511.

Man's sensory sphere, apart from the domain of cognition, also covers the appetitive sphere. This is a sphere of emotions, in which the feelings of anger and appetites are distinguished[20].

(iii) Mental Faculties

As a psycho-physical being, man is capable of actions connected with both vegetative-sensitive life and mental-spiritual life. The latter is realized by means of the cognitive mental faculty, i.e. intellect, and of the mental appetitive faculty, i.e. the will. Man's intellect is proportional to his accidental being connected with the world of matter. In God intellect belongs to His essence, while in created beings intellect is a faculty[21]. Only in the broad sense can one say that intellect is the essence of man. The intellect of pure spirits (angels) functions regardless of sensory cognition, whereas man's intellect - in the stage of his earthly life - utilizes the empirical material provided by sensory faculties.

St.Thomas states quite clearly that intellect is one cognitive faculty, although it performs various functions[22]. In view of the multiple operations of intellect one can give it different names, such as mind, reason, intellect, mental memory, speculative or practical intellect, higher and lower reason. In Thomistic terminology mind (***mens***) denotes the whole of man's mental sphere, i.e. both intellect and will. The term "intellect" (Latin ***intellectus*** from ***intus*** - ***legere***) denotes the mental-cognitive faculty which plays three basic roles: creation of concepts, formulation of judgements, and inference. The creation of concepts, intentionally recreating the essence of the examined objects, is the domain of the intellect capable of reading the internal nature of reality. Reason (***ratio***) is the faculty of mental cognition in so far as it is capable of passing from some judgements to others; such an activity is called reasoning. Mental memory is not a faculty different from intellect and the difference between them is only functional. Mental memory stores the concepts created out of images in order to recreate them at any time. Finally, speculative and practical intellects are different in respect to their aims and tasks; the former aims at discovering some truth, while the latter takes care of practical activities.

In Thomistic philosophy, the existence of intellect as a separate faculty of mental cognition is motivated by numerous arguments[23]. One of them points to the fact of the creation of concepts which significantly differ from sensations and images of sensory cognition[24]. The latter refer to concrete material things, whereas concepts are

---

[20]Comp. Part II, Chap.4 of this study.

[21]*Summa Theologiae*, I,q.79,a.1,c and ad 1,2.

[22]Cf. *Summa Theologiae*, I,q.79,aa.6-11.

[23]Cf. *Summa Theologiae*, I,q.79,aa.1-11.

[24]*Summa Theologiae*, I,q.79,a.4,c; *Contra Gentes* II,76; *De Veritate*, q.1.a.9.

universals; their object is what is common and necessary. Concepts abstract from individual properties of the examined things and concentrate on substantial properties; they denote a class of beings, not individuals. Thanks to this there appears an unpassable border between images and concepts. This makes it possible to infer that they are products of man's different psychic faculties. Thus, a universal idea cannot be interpreted as a cumulation of images; their intentional structure and object are completely different. A noncontradictory explanation of the ontical sources of concepts requires the acceptance of a separate, immaterial cognitive faculty, namely, intellect. An argument derivative in respect to the one presented above concerns the fact of creating concepts of immaterial beings, such as moral values, conscience, soul, God. Such ideas, denoting structurally immaterial beings, could not arise in consequence of the infiltration of the material world. Only an immaterial faculty has been able to create concepts which cognitively apprehend immaterial values.

The next argument speaking for the existence of the immaterial faculty of intellect concerns the ability of reflection and self-reflection. An animal does not separate its own self from its surrounding world, analogically to man (an infant) before he can use his reason. A mentally mature man separates the subject from the object, his own "I" from the world of things and of other persons. The presence of the faculty of intellect is also indicated by the phenomenon of mental reflection, the ability of a critical evaluation of one's own cognition, the skill of apprehending universal rules of being and of thought, the possibility of cognitive corrections etc. Only an immaterial faculty ontologically enables activities of this kind; it also explains man's constant mental progress which makes possible the development of material and spiritual culture. Intellect also conditions the formulation of various judgements, assertions, negations, questions, exclamations, comparisons, conditional clauses etc. The faculties of sensory cognition in animals provide no basis for an active-creative attitude towards the world. Intellect is not only a passive copy of the perceived reality, but also a conscious and critical attitude towards it. This is achieved precisely through judgements and reasoning whose ontical foundation can be provided exclusively by immaterial intellect.

In Thomistic epistemology and anthropology a crucial role is played by the theory of intellect or, more precisely, the theory of two intellects, agent and possible[25]. Their distinction was proposed already by Aristotle when he stated laconically that agent reason, as capable of being "separated", is immortal, whereas passive reason (as if passive) undergoes demolition[26]. Aristotle's commentators did not interpret his words in an unequivocal way. Alexander of Aphrodisias was of the opinion that the possible intellect constituted part of man and was mortal, while the agent intellect was identified by him with the deity. Themistius interpreted the agent intellect as a single spiritual light, common for all men. The nature of both intellects became a subject of much attention of medieval Arab thinkers, Avicenna and Averroes. They both recognized the agent

---

[25]E.Gilson: *Le Thomisme*, Paris 1947, Part II, Chap.4.

[26]Aristotle: *On Soul*, III, 5,430 a 17-19.

intellect as extra-individual intelligence which enables mental cognition. Yet, if Avicenna († 1037) accepted the individual character of the possible intellect, Averroes († 1198) thought that also this intellect is common for all men. Hence, the latter philosopher also spoke for monopsychism, undermining man's spiritual individuality.

St.Thomas also took his stand in this discussion and wrote a treatise ***De unitate intellectus contra averroistas parisienses***. The Christian thinker opposed the theory of monopsychism and accepted the existence of two intellects, agent and possible, as the faculties of the human soul. The alternative of the common intellect leads to evidently false propositions, for instance, that Plato and Aristotle had an identical common mind and, therefore, that they were one man[27]. Analogically, one could claim that all humankind possesses a common mental cognition, common intellect and common humanity.

Recognizing the individual character of mind, St. Thomas, following Aristotle, distinguished two intellects, agent and possible. Both are faculties which inhere in the ontical structure of the human soul[28]. Why did St.Thomas Aquinas accept the necessity of both intellects? First of all, he pointed to a significant difference between human intellect and God's intellect. The latter is a pure act and that is why the act of cognition has an entirely intuitive character. God's cognition is direct and perfect in respect to everything, doing without concepts and inference. Human intellect, because of its finiteness and man's psycho-physical nature, is possible - in spite of all its perfection - in relation to the apprehended objects[29]. For that reason we may speak of the possibility of cognition rather than about actual cognition. The human intellect is passive also because the first object of its cognition is the material world. However, the proper objects of intellect are universals and that is why concrete-material beings cannot be direct objects of the mind's perception. Therefore there must exist a faculty which will perform a specific "dematerialization" of impressions and images. The process of cognition demands the existence of "some power which would actualize the objects of mental cognition through abstracting the cognitive forms from [their] accompanying material properties"[30]. The function of the agent intellect consists in discovering in material beings immaterial elements, connected with the existence of the substantial form. Thus, it is necessary to separate intentionally universal features from individual properties, immaterial from material structures. And this is precisely the task of the agent intellect. Often it was called the light. St.Thomas accepts the term, although he understands it as man's natural skill of "exposing" generic features in the material of sensory impressions[31]. The agent intellect constitutes cognitive-intellectual forms (***species***

---

[27]*Summa Theologiae*, I, q.76, a.2, c; I, q.79, a.5, c.

[28]*Summa Theologiae*, I, q.79, a.4, c.

[29]*Summa Theologiae*, I, q.79, a.2, c.

[30]*Summa Theologiae*, I, q.79, a.3, c; comp. I, q.79, a.4, ad 4.

[31]*Summa Theologiae*, I, q.79, a.3, ad3; I, q.79, a.4.c.

impressa) which are then passed on to the possible intellect in order to create appropriate concepts. Its role therefore amounts to the ability of discovering significant and universal features in the muddle of information provided by sensory perception. "Besides this faculty, there may also occur in the soul another faculty, receiving cognitive forms of this kind; we call it possible intellect since it appertains to the soul for that reason that the soul is in the state of possibility in respect to those cognitive forms"[32].

As a representative of genetic empiricism, St. Thomas confirmed the indispensability of sensory cognition as a starting point of the cognitive process. Impressions and images constitute the necessary foundation of human knowledge and intellect makes use of the information contained in images[33]. Man's cognitive process is achieved through gradual dematerialization[34]. Its first stage is the creation of cognitive sensory forms, i.e. impressions. They come into being as a result of the operation of the stimuli of the external world on man's receptors. The next stage consists in transforming those fragmentary impressions into images which, although they apprehend cognitively an ontical concrete thing, already constitute an intentional synthesis of knowledge about the examined object. In turn, the sensitive form (***species sensibilis***) is then subjected to the operation of the agent intellect which "dematerializes" the material presented to it. This consists in an intentional separation of significant general features from individual, accidental and purely material properties. Before the operation of the agent intellect, images cannot be grasped by the possible intellect, because of the opposition between materiality and mind[35]. Only an image dematerialized by the agent intellect can be transformed into an impressed mental-cognitive form (***species impressa***) which, in turn, becomes an object of proper intellectual cognition. The possible intellect creates its own proper concepts, i.e. an expressed mental cognitive form (***species expressa***). It is already a product of the human spirit whose faculty is intellect. Hence, the concept is described in Thomistic philosophy as "a mental word" (***verbum mentis***). The final stage of the process of human cognition is therefore something like a spiritualization of its object, whose expression is its intentional character.

The Thomistic theory of the agent and possible intellects is connected with the totality of his ontology and, in consequence, it can be accepted only in its context. Other currents of Christian philosophy, including Augustinianism and Scotism, explain the process and structure of man's intellectual cognition in a different way. When accepting the Thomistic conception of mental cognition one should not separate it from his whole epistemology. The theory of the two intellects cannot therefore mean a renouncement of other forms of man's cognition, such as, internal experience, intuition, axiological experience etc. The agent and possible intellects should not be interpreted in isolation from the totality of the

---

[32]*Summa Theologiae*, I, q.79, a.4, ad 4; cf. *Contra Gentes*, II, 77.

[33]*Summa Theologiae*, I, q.84, a.7, c.

[34]*Contra Gentes* II, 77; *De Veritate*, q.10, a.6, ad 1; ***Summa Theologiae***, I, q.85, a.1, ad 3; *III Sent.*, d.14, q.1, a.1.

[35]*Summa Theologiae*, I, q.85, a.1, ad 3; *De Veritate*, q.10, a.6, ad 1; *I Sent.*, d.17, q.2, a.1.

human person whose tools they constitute. It is man who apprehends by means of intellect and not intellect as an autonomous being.

There still remains the problem of the object of man's intellectual cognition to be discussed. Thomistic philosophy distinguishes material and formal objects. A material object is anything that somehow is subordinated to some faculty. A formal object is what particularly interests a given faculty. Each faculty has only one formal object because otherwise it would be dissociated in its nature[36]. Among Thomists there were heated discussions concerning the formal object of human intellect. Some of the thinkers thought that such an object is being as a whole[37]. Yet, most Thomists distinguish a double formal object, adequate and proportional. A proportional object is only that which does not exceed the average possibilities of the faculty of intellect and which can be achieved in a natural way (in the stage of man's earthly life). An adequate (complete) object is all that which actually or in the future is apprehensible to intellect in whatever way, direct or indirect[38]. Thus, a proportional formal object is the nature of material beings. It is in this spirit that St.Thomas Aquinas speaks when he draws attention to the connection between the human intellect and the faculties of sensory cognition on the stage of earthly life[39]. Human cognition is undoubtedly initiated in the material world and only then does it turn toward the whole reality, also including the world of spirit (soul, God). The genetic connection of intellectual cognition and sensory cognition does not yet nullify the specificity of the former. Intellect as such implies possible infinity which, to some extent, also concerns human intellect. For that reason it is possible to conclude that an adequate formal object is being as a whole, i.e. everything that exists. That is why St.Thomas claimed that human "intellect apprehends its object in the aspect of the general reason of being; for possible intellect is that, due to which it can become everything"[40]. Man's intellect, although based on the material of sensory perception, is capable of apprehending the general nature of being and its ultimate genesis. As a result, intellectual cognition is ultimately directed towards the infinite being, i.e., towards God.

The other mental faculty of man is that of the will. It belongs to the aspirational-appetitive sphere. St. Thomas distinguished appetite in a broad and strict sense[41]. The former denotes the so-called natural appetite (***appetitus naturalis***), deprived even of the least degree of consciousness and connected with the structure of being. Appetite understood in its proper sense refers to the faculty of elicited appetite (***appetitus elicitus***), i.e. an appetite realized in acts. It can be further divided into a sensible appetite,

---

36 *Summa Theologiae*, I-II, q.1, a.5, c; *Contra Gentes*, II, 83.

37 S.Adamczyk: *De obiecto formali intellectus nostri*, Romae 1933, pp.45-50, 64-80, 110-118.

38 Cf. M.A.Krąpiec: *Realizm ...*, op.cit., pp.621-625.

39 "Intellectus autem humani, qui est coniunctus corpori, propium obiectum est quidditas sive natura in materia corporali existens": *Summa Theologiae*, I, q.84, a.7, c; cf. I, q.84, a.8,c.

40 *Summa Theologiae*, I,q.79,a.7,c.

41 *Summa Theologiae*, I,q.80,a.1,c.

connected with the domain of affections, and a mental appetite. In man there occur both forms, i.e. sensible and mental appetites[42]. The latter is precisely the faculty of the will (***liberum arbitrium***), which St. Thomas also calls man's free decision[43]. "Free decision is that due to which we can make a choice. Free decision is an appetitive faculty"[44].

What is the mechanism of the functioning of the will? It belongs to man's aspirational sphere and that is why it is connected with the domain of affections. Among others, they are related by being directed towards values. Yet, if man's sensory appetites have concrete values, connected with the material world, as their object, then the will is directed towards good as such[45]. Man's psycho-physical nature causes that he usually desires certain concrete values but, with his will, he discovers in them an aspect of universal and permanent good. That is the reason why he seeks the infinite and absolute good, that is, God[46]. He constitutes the adequate object of man's will. The immateriality of the faculty of the will causes that man discovers the presence of the highest good and desires it. Although there are many ties which connect the will with the domain of affections, yet in its nature it does not include the dichotomy of irascible and concupiscent spheres[47]. The will means man's conscious aspiring to good, and, as St.Thomas stated, that is why intellect is the foundation of the will. "Man must have free decision for the very reason that he is a rational being"[48]. The connection between the will and intellect is close and permanent, that is why some Thomists ascribe to the will the ability of reflection. It is understood in such a way that every act of the will (e.g. of love) may become an object of our reflection. Strictly speaking, reflection is the domain of intellect but a holistic explication of the human being makes it possible to combine it also with the functioning of the will. The decision of the will is always preceded by a deliberation of intellectual cognition, although it cannot be reduced to it[49]. The basic feature of the faculty of the will is freedom of choice. Although by its very nature, the will desires good, the multiplicity and qualitative differentiation of values do not impose on man in the necessary manner any specific good[50]. We can make free choice from among many goods, preferring some values to others.

One should finally touch the question of the mutual relation between intellect and the will. St.Thomas was a proponent of the priority of intellect over the will. This priority

---

[42]*Summa Theologiae*, I, q.80, a.2, c.

[43]*Summa Theologiae*, I, q.83, a.2, c and ad 1. Comp. Part II, Chap.5 of this study.

[44]*Summa Theologiae*, I, q.83, a.2, sed contra.

[45]*Summa Theologiae*, I-II, q.10, a.1, c; I, q.80, a.2, ad 2.

[46]*Summa Theologiae*, I, q.93, a.2, ad 3.

[47]*Summa Theologiae*, I, q.82, a.5, c.

[48]*Summa Theologiae*, I, q.83, a.1, c; comp. *De Veritate*, q.24, a.2, c.

[49]*Summa Theologiae*, I, q.83, a.4, c.

[50]*Summa Theologiae*, I, q.82, a.2, c and ad 1-3.

takes into account the nature of both faculties rather than the temporal aspect[51]. The problem concerns the fact that the object of intellect is more universal than that of the will. Mental cognition is directed towards the totality of being, whereas the will usually defines itself in relation to a determined good. Nevertheless, St.Thomas admitted that sometimes the will is more perfect than intellect, namely, when its object is qualitatively higher than the object of cognition. "Therefore, love of God is better than knowing Him"[52]. Intellect and the will, as man's mental faculties, are mutually subordinated to each other. "Both these faculties embrace each other in their acts since intellect apprehends what the will wants, while the will wants intellect to know"[53]. The real difference between intellect and the will does not undermine the fact of their mutual co-operation in the activities of the human person. Thomistic intellectualism is not identical with the omnipotence of intellect or its exclusiveness. On the other hand, the priority of intellect over the will, characteristic of Thomism, is undermined by Augustinian voluntarism[54]. The multiplicity of mental faculties, analysed above, should not be regarded as their separation. The final principle of every activity is man, while faculties constitute the direct subjects of his activity.

LITERATURE

ADAMCZYK,S.: *De obiecto formali intellectus nostri secundum doctrinam S. Thome Aquinatis*, Romae 1933.

GOGACZ,M.: *Obrona intelektu* [The Defence of Intellect], Warszawa 1969.

HART,C.A.: *Thomistic Concept of Mental Faculty*, Washington 1930.

KLUBERTANZ,G.P.: "The Root of Freedom in St.Thomas's Later Works", *Gregorianum*, 42 (1961), pp.701-724.

KRĄPIEC,M.A.: *Realizm ludzkiego poznania* [The Realism of Human Cognition], Poznań 1955.

MAZZANTINI,C.: *Il problema filosofico del "libro arbitrio" in S. Tommaso e Duns Scoto*, Torino 1966.

Phenomenology of Will and Action. The Second Lexington Conference on Pure and Applied Phenomenology, Louvain 1967.

RABEAU,G.: *Species. Verbum. L'activité intéllectuelle élémentaire selon S. Thomas d'Aquin*, Paris 1938.

RAHNER,K.: *Geist in der Welt. Zur Metaphysik der endlichen Erkenntnis bei Thomas von Aquin*, München 1964.

ROUSSELOT,P.: *L'intéllectualisme de saint Thomas*, Paris 1936.

SIWEK,P.: *La psychophysique humaine d'après Aristote*, Paris 1930.

WERKMEISTER,W.H.: *The Basis and Structure of Knowledge*, New York 1968.

WERNER,C.: *L'âme et la liberté*, Paris 1960.

---

[51] *Summa Theologiae*, I, q.82, a.3, c.

[52] Ibid.

[53] *Summa Theologiae*, I, q.82, a.4, ad 1.

[54] S.Kowalczyk: *Człowiek i Bóg ...*, op.cit., pp.43 ff, 82.

Chapter 5

The Origin of Man

The question of the origin of man is a fundamental problem of philosophical anthropology. It has an interdisciplinary character because it involves not only philosophy and theology, but also natural sciences. Christian thought accepts the theory of creationism, connecting the fact of the appearance of man with the creative intervention of God. The category of creation occurs today also in empirical sciences, among others, in cosmology[1]. It is understood there as a natural process of matter coming into being from nothing, a process which probably should be seen as a transformation of the structures of the material world. The philosophical conception of creation has been closely connected with Christianity, while today some followers of dialectical materialism speak about immanent creationism[2].

(i) The Theory of Classical Creationism

The concept of creation, in its proper sense, has a philosophical-theological character. Speaking about the genesis of man, the problem should be perceived in a wider context. For there arises a question: Why does there exist a universe in which man - the person, appeared? Explaining the origin of the world and man, theistic-personalistic philosophy refers to the creative act of God. The term "creation", denoting here the action of creation, is sometimes used synonymously with the term "creature", i.e. the effect of such an act. analogically to Latin words, ***creation*** as the action of creating, and ***creatura***, as the effect of the creative action. It should therefore be at once noted that at this point we are concerned with God's creative action. St.Thomas Aquinas relates the conception of creation with that of causality; namely, creation is the endowing of a being with existence[3]. In its scope, the concept of the creative act is narrower than the category of causality. Namely, the creative act means the endowment of a thing with being out of previous subjective nothingness (the created thing did not exist) and objective nothingness

---

[1]H.Bondi: *Cosmology*, Cambridge 1961, Chap.8.

[2]J.Kuczyński: *Homo creator*, Warszawa 1979, pp.7,17 ff.

[3]"Creare est causare sive producere esse rerum": *Summa Theologiae*, I,q.45,a.6,c; comp. I,q.45,a.2,c.

(there was no material of any kind)[4]. Nothingness is not some kind of a lower status of being but its total negation. In turn, creation is not a change of some existing thing, its generic shaping or perfecting the already existing material[5]. It is not an actualization of a real potential constituting a germinal being. Therefore, the act of creation should not be interpreted as a fact of a normal change. The starting point of creation is the objective nothingness and the nothingness of the created being. Giving the world existence, the Creator did not use any material[6]. Therefore, creation cannot be understood analogously to the activity of man who designs a plan, looks for appropriate material, chooses appropriate means of production, and, finally, successively realizes his aims. The creative act of God cannot be explained anthropomorphically, taking advantage of imagination.

The category of creation can be apprehended in two ways, actively, i.e. from the point of view of God, and passively, i.e. from the point of view of the created beings. Understood in the former sense, creation means the operation of God endowing a thing with existence in spite of previous nothingness[7]. Naturally, this is an entirely immanent action, i.e. really identical with God's nature, not an external activity. Creation apprehended from the perspective of the created beings denotes their relation of dependence on the Creator. In consequence of the act of creation there occurs a specific relation between the Creator and the creatures; from the perspective of God it is only a "mental" relation (the created world does not add anything to Him), whereas from the perspective of the accidental beings it a relation of real dependence connected with being endowed with existence[8]. Creation is not an accidental relation, added to the already existing world. The whole universe, apprehended in its beingness, is dependent on God's creative power. That is why St.Thomas recognized the act of creation as the exclusive prerogative of Almighty God[9]. All creatures, though capable of efficient action, must always make use of the already existing material.

The theory of creation, also concerning man, is strictly connected with the ontological analysis of reality. This analysis makes it possible to state that the accidental being - and only such being occurs in the sphere of human cognition - is "neutral" in respect to existence. It exists really but in its nature it does not contain an autonomous necessary

---

[4]"Creatio est productio rei ex nihilo sui et subiecti". Ch.Boyer: *Cursus Philosophiae*, Paris 1938, vol.2, p.396.

[5]*Contra Gentes*, II,18; *De Potentia*, q.3,a.2; A.D.Sertillanges: *L'idée de création et ses retentissements en philosophie*, Paris 1945, pp.43 ff.

[6]*De Potentia*, q.3, a.1, c and ad 7; q.3, a.3.

[7]"Creare est ex nihilo aliquid facere": *Summa Theologiae*, I,q.45,a.2,ad 2. Cf. I,q.45,a.3,ad 1. Sertillanges rightly connects the conception of creation with the relation of dependence of the creation on the Creator, but he excessively stresses the opposition between creation and action. Cf. *L'idée de création* ..., op.cit., p.7; L.Wciórka: *Ewolucja a stworzenie* [Evolution and Creation], Poznań 1976, pp.42 ff.

[8]*Contra Gentes*, II,19; *De Potentia*, q.3, a.3, ad 6.

[9]*Contra Gentes*, II,21; *Summa Theologiae*, I, q.65, a.3, ad 3.

existence[10]. A being of this kind, regardless of the length of its duration, never explains the genesis of its existence. Each accidental being is an owner of existence but in itself it is not existence. The existence of a contingent being does not explain itself in an immanent way, and that is why it requires an external-transcendental cause. The appearance of the contingent world is an effect of God's creative power[11]. Action is always correlated with the efficient power of every being. Hence, since only God exists thanks to His own nature, only He could create the contingent being, by endowing it with existence[12].

The explication of the concept of creation demands its further specification in respect to the category of time. Christian philosophy does not assume any unified view in this matter. St.Bonaventura describes creation as a temporal initiation of the existence of being, and that is why he formulates a number of arguments against the hypothesis of the eternity of the world[13]. St.Thomas Aquinas tends to combine the concepts of creation and time in some of his statements. Thus, for example, he says that "creation is nothing else but a relation towards God consisting in the novelty of being"[14]. The expression "the novelty of being" was understood by the medieval thinker in the ontological sense rather than categorial-chronological. He wanted to stress the ontic heteronomy of created beings receiving their existence from God. Yet, the creative act is not a historical event, taking place in some space and time, but the metaphysical action of God. The world has been created out of nothing (***ex nihilo***) which does not automatically mean that it must have been created after nothingness (***post nihilum***)[15]. St.Thomas thought that the temporal order of the world becomes evident only in the light of the Revelation (*Genesis* 1,1) and that is why philosophical motivation is incapable of excluding the hypothesis about the eternal existence of the accidental being[16]. Still, the thinker evidently experienced some doubts in this respect[17]. Summing up, one may state that the necessity of the act of creation of the world is first of all a consequence of the lack of its ontic autonomy, whereas the question of its temporal duration is a secondary matter. Even the eventual eternal existence of the contingent being does not find explanation in its nature since it will always be a participatory existence, received from somebody. The visible world is connected with the categories of time and space, but its creation

---

[10]S.Kowalczyk: *Filozofia Boga* [The Philosophy of God], Lublin 1980, pp.101-121.

[11]*Summa Theologiae* I, q.45, a.5,c.

[12]*Contra Gentes*, II,65; *Summa Theologiae*, I, q.8, a.1.

[13]P.Böhner, E.Gilson: *Christliche Philosophie*, Paderborn 1954, pp.487-488.

[14]"Creatio nihil est aliud realiter quam relatio quaedam ad Deum cum novitate essendi": *De Potentia*, q.3, a.3.

[15]*Summa Theologiae*, I, q.46, a.2, ad 2.

[16]*Summa Theologiae*, I, q.46, a.2; *Quodlib.*, XII, q.6, a.7; Sertillanges, op.cit., pp.25-42.

[17]Cf. *Summa Theologiae*, I,q.7,a.4, where St.Thomas proves the impossibility of the actual infinite quantity, and, hence, indirectly, also of the eternity of the material cosmos.

happened independently of both these categories. Otherwise, the creative action would constitute an attribute of such a cause which would be an immanent factor of the world. And such an explication of creation would lead to pantheism.

The accidental being, called into existence by God's creative power, never loses its status of contingency. That is why the conception of creation is organically connected with the conception of "preserving in existence" (***conservatio in esse***)[18]. In God's action both elements, the initiation of existence and its preservation, constitute a real unity.

In St.Thomas's interpretation, the problem of the genesis of man concerns primarily the question of the appearance of the immaterial human soul. The human body, similarly to the bodies of animals, is formed out of a material medium. It is not so in the case of the soul whose appearance can be explained only through the direct act of creation by God[19]. Thanks to its immateriality, the human soul cannot be derived from the potential of matter. St.Thomas also rejects two other hypotheses, those of pre-existence and of generationism. The former is characteristic of Oriental thought, among others, of Hinduism. The theory of generationism, also known as traducianism, suggests the propagation of the soul through the biological act of giving birth[20]. These alternatives were questioned by St. Thomas. The material body cannot be regarded as the primaeval source of the immaterial soul and that is why the propagation of the body (along with its properties, features etc.) is not identical with the propagation of the soul. The parents of a child, as contingent beings, cannot constitute a creative cause of its soul. Only God can create the substantial-spiritual soul.

Justifying the indispensability of the creation of the human soul by God, St. Thomas refers to its immaterial manner of existence and functioning[21]. Man's spiritual "I" cannot be a product of matter or its expression, function, transformation etc. Between the mode of existence (***esse***) and the mode of the initiation of existence (***fieri***) there must pertain an ontological correlation. What functions in an immaterial (non-corporeal) way cannot come into existence from an exclusively material being. Therefore, matter cannot provide the reason for the existence of mental-psychic life. If one accepted such a possibility, then, trying to be logically consistent, one would have to reject the principle of noncontradiction. A noncontradictory explication of the human being makes it necessary to question the claim that a material cause can produce a qualitatively higher effect, i.e. the human soul. Yet, if matter contains no features proper to man's spiritual "I", either actually, or even potentially, then the fact of its existence demands the reference to God. The primaeval source of the human soul, therefore, is not the material world and the processes occurring in it, but only God. He is the creative cause of man, although not a

[18]*Contra Gentes*, II,65 and 67; *De Potentia*, q.3,a.7; Sertillanges, op.cit., p.43.

[19]*Summa Theologiae*, I,q.75,a.6,ad 1; I,q.90,a.3,c; *Contra Gentes*, II,87.

[20]St.Augustine hesitated between creationism and generationism; cf. *De libero arbitrio*, 3,21,59 PL 32,1299.

[21]*Summa Theologiae*, I,q.90,a.2.

material cause[22]. The human soul comes from God but it is not an element or emanation of God's nature.

(ii) Anthropogenesis in the Empirical-Naturalistic View

While explaining the genesis of humankind it is impossible to ignore the achievements of natural sciences, especially of biology. A crucial role in these disciplines is played by the idea of evolution and therefore a philosophy of man should also take some attitude towards it. A relatively small group of Christian authors totally question the theory of evolutionism[23]. The apodictically negative attitude towards the idea of evolution is today hard to maintain, although, on the other hand, one should not confuse the naturalistic theory of evolution with the philosophy of evolution[24].

The concept of evolution is interdisciplinary, as it occurs in both natural and humanistic sciences. The problem of the origin of man is connected with the naturalistic understanding of the term. The question therefore concerns biological evolution which is "a process developing in time and, practically, irreversible, thanks to which there occurs some novelty, variety, and higher levels of organization"[25]. This description refers to the fact of progressive transformations of the organic world which result in a successive becoming of ever higher morphologically and functionally species of animals. The conception of evolution (resp. evolutionism) may also denote naturalistic theories which attempt to explain the mechanism of biological evolution. It is in the latter sense that we speak about Darwinism, Lamarckism, transformism etc.[26]. The philosophical explication of the evolution of the biocosmos, where theistic-personalistic philosophy finds its counterpart in materialistic-atheistic evolutionism, is still something else. Finally, one may speak about a theology of evolution[27] which analyses the phenomenon of evolutionary changes in the light of the Revelation. The meanings of the category of evolution (evolutionism) cannot be identified with one another and for that reason the semantic confusion in this respect leads to demagogic claims of the type, for instance, that natural sciences undermine creationism.

The problems of the phylogenesis of man are considered within the frameworks of several natural sciences, especially such as comparative anatomy, morphology, embryology,

---

[22]*Summa Theologiae*, I,q.90,a.1.

[23]Cf. P.Siwek: *Ewolucjonizm w świetle nauki* [Evolutionism in the light of Science], London 1973.

[24]R.I.Nogar: "From the Fact of Evolution to the Philosophy of Evolutionism", *The Thomist*, 24 (1961), pp.463-501.

[25]S.Skowron: *Ewolucjonizm* [Evolutionism], Warszawa 1966, p.7.

[26]Ibid., pp.20-115.

[27]H.Folk: *Schöpfungsglaube und Entwicklung*, Münster 1958.

biogeography, palaeontology and palaeoanthropology[28]. At the moment we shall restrict ourselves to the latter disciplines whose hypothesis are based on discovered bone relics of primordial peoples and their supposed ancestors. Palaeoanthropology is looking for intermediate links between the world of animals and the human world. However, there arises a question: How can one draw a precise line between them? The Rubicon separating man from animals appears to be the ability of abstract-discursive thinking and the use of symbolic language[29]. A direct grasping of this border, on the basis of bone fossils, is practically impossible. For that reasons scholars make use of biological-morphological criteria, such as, an advanced stage of cerebralization, upright posture, development of the palm, use of tools etc.[30]. Still, the data so far accumulated by palaeoanthropology do not yet allow any conclusive decisions. Hence, it is not surprising that the origin of man is presented in a variety of ways in specialist studies.

Generally it is assumed that about thirty million years ago (i.e. in Oligocene or only in Pliocene) the family of hominids (***Hominidae***) and the family of anthropoids (***Pongidae***) were distinguished[31]. The anthropoids are the ancestors of today's apes. Among the excavated forms, they included among others the African ***Proconsul*** and ***Oreopithecus***[32].

The family of the hominids that interest us here includes first of all the Australopithecus (***Australopithecinae***), living in Africa (from Latin: australis - southern, and pithecus - ape). They are traditionally included in the phylogenesis of man. Some authors perceive in the Australopithecus a pre-human form[33], while others classify it among the proto-hominids[34]. Although their brain was relatively small (500 - 700 cm2), the rich excavated materials imply the presence of features characteristic of man, both somatic and psychic[35]. The somatic features include first of all the erect posture, moving on two limbs, and human dentition. The Australopithecus produced cultures connected with the so-called bones-teeth and horn industry. It was a fairly rich set of tools proving an ability of passing over acquired skills. Numerous bone fossils of the Australopithecus, among others, those discovered in the valley of Olduvai (today in Tanganyika), make it possible to conclude that the process of hominisation was initiated in Africa. That was the

---

[28]S.Skowron, op.cit., pp.116,194.

[29]E.Thenius: *Stammesgeschichte des Säugetiere (einschlislich der Hominiden)*, Berlin 1969, pp.219 ff.

[30]F.M.Wuketis: *Grundriss der Evolutionstheorie*, Darmstadt 1982, p.157.

[31]S.Skowron, op.cit., pp.286-290; P.Overhage: "Das Problem der Hominisation" [in:] P.Overhage and K.Rahner: *Das Problem der Hominisation*, Freiburg 1962, pp.98-112.

[32]Formerly Oreopithecus was included in the geneaology of man although today this is no longer accepted as valid.

[33]T.Wojciechowski: *Wybrane zagadnienia z filozoficznej antropologii* [Selected Problems in Philosophical Anthropology], Kraków 1985, pp.57-58.

[34]S.Skowron, op.cit., p.292.

[35]P.Overhage: "Das Problem der Hominisation", op.cit., pp.118-129.

view of Charles Darwin and, today, also of Teilhard de Chardin[36]. Initially, the Australopithecus was quite commonly included in the genealogy of man. Yet, later on the fact of the co-existence of those beings with Homo habilis was discovered; it was about three million years ago in Africa. This discovery does not definitively exclude the Australopithecines as an intermediate link because they lived already five and a half million years ago. Hence, one cannot exclude a possibility that some early population of the Australopithecines led to the evolutionary appearance of man. As a result, today there are two models of anthropogenesis: one of them removes the Australopithecus from the evolutionary line of man, while the other includes them in it[37]. It seems likely that there existed several species of the Australopithecus; one of them was the Zinjanthropus which displays a particularly great similarity to the anatomical structure of modern man.

Further links in man's genealogy include the Pithecanthropus and the Neanderthal man. The Pithecanthropus, living from two million to about 100,000 years ago, among others in modern Indonesia and China, were formerly called ape-men (***Pithecanthropus***). Today they are seen mainly as extinct human species and that is why they are described as ***Homo erectus***[38]. Those men already lived in caves, knew the use of fire, produced tools, and used speech. The more famous discoveries of the Pithecanthropus specimens include the so-called Peking man, whose remains were examined by Teilhard de Chardin in the cave Chow-Kow-Tien.

A close link in the lineage of modern man is the so-called Neanderthal man who appeared about seventy - forty thousand years ago[39]. He lived in Western Europe, although most probably also in Africa and Palestine. His characteristic feature is the size of his brain which was already 1300 - 1600 cm2. The Neanderthal men already displayed developed culture; they buried their dead, most probably had some religious beliefs and ethical ideas. The final stage in the development of man is ***Homo sapiens*** who appeared about fifty thousand years ago; one of his characteristic features was an advanced aesthetic faculty whose results can now be seen in the cave paintings in France and Africa[40].

The phylogenesis of man outlined by palaeoanthropology is neither complete nor definitively established. Some doubts have already been mentioned above. The empirical material, limited quantitatively and qualitatively, makes it impossible to determine unequivocally the developmental lines of man and his ancestors from the world of animals. The reconstruction of the process of hominisation, in both biological-somatic and

---

[36]Teilhard de Chardin: "L'afrique et les origines humaines" [in:] *L'apparition de l'homme*, Paris 1956, pp.283 ff.

[37]Cf. F.G.Fothergill: *Evolution und christlicher Glaube*, Würzburg 1969, pp.282-324.

[38]S.Skowron, op.cit., pp.296-299; W.Henke and H.Rothe: *Der Ursprung des Menschen*, Stuttgart 1980, pp.156-160.

[39]W.Henke and H.Rothe, op.cit., pp.161 ff.

[40]Ibid., pp.166 ff; W.F.Le Gros Clark: "The Antiquity of Homo sapiens in Particular and the Hominidae in General", *Scientific Progress*, 42 (1954), pp.377-389.

especially psychic respects, has not been finished yet[41]. Nevertheless, most naturalists speak for monophyleticism, whereas monogenism is usually questioned. As is rightly obeserved[42], the evolution of man is not limited to external-biological transformations. It is also a process of psychic-mental development, self-realization, personalization, entry into the world of higher values (ethical, religious). Hence, man is not only the end of evolution but also its subject, namely, the person taking free decisions and responsible for his subsequent fate.

In spite of common somatic origin with the organic world, man is a unique being in nature. This is indicated both by his structure (the higher degree of cerebralization, erect posture, structure of the palm etc.) and by his activities. The dynamics of man differs qualitatively from the behaviour and activities of animals. Man possesses an entirely new dimension, namely, mental-spiritual culture. Its fundamental element, as well as a source, is the ability to think. Although it is possible to speak about the intelligence of higher animals, still this is merely a sensible-pragmatic intelligence. Some authors go even so far as to ascribe to animals specific "thinking", for instance, connected with their ability to recognize geometric figures, to formulate "nonverbal judgements" etc.[43]. Nevertheless, it is never universal-abstract, discursive, reflective-conceptual thinking. The "visual thinking" of animals constitutes a sharp contrast with man's conceptual thinking. Only man is capable of grasping a causal relation, thanks to which he apprehends the nature of things, genetic connections of phenomena in the visible world, ability of using fire etc. Man's mental intelligence conditions his heuristic-inventive thinking, thanks to which, in turn, progress in civilization and culture is possible. Man's spiritual culture is also characterized by a cognitive passion for discovering truth, as well as by ethical consciousness of good and evil, artistic sensibility, religious life, awareness of family and national ties. All this is absent in the world of animals while their maternal instinct is often purely biological and periodical. The intelligence of animals does contains some rudiments of thinking but in fact it never crosses the border of universal-inventive thinking. The sensory view of higher animals is qualitatively different from the apprehension and intellectual appraisal of man.

There are also other fundamental differences between the world of animals and that of man[44]. One of them is the ability of speaking. Animals also have their specific "language" by means of which they communicate to each other messages necessary for survival in various circumstances. Some experiments with the chimpanzees showed that, for instance, they were capable of partly learning the language of signs designed for

---

[41]Sharp criticism of the empirical material of palaeontology has been carried out by P.Siwek, although it would be difficult to accept his conclusion questioning the genetic tie between man and the animal world, even in respect to the body. Cf. P.Siwek, op.cit., pp.128-164.

[42]M.J.Hildebrand: "Die seelisch-geistige Entwicklung in anthropologischer Betrachtung", *Studia Generalia*, 7 (1954) pp.491-500.

[43]P.Overhage: *Die biologische Zukunft der Menschheit*, Frankfurt am M. 1977, pp.115-117.

[44]T.Wojciechowski, op.cit., pp.67-88.

deaf-and-dumb people[45]. However, the similarities between the language of animals and of people do not nullify the sharp border that separates them: only the latter are capable of mastering a significative, universal and symbolical language. Only man has created a conceptual language which constitutes a basis of science, literature, philosophy etc. The educational experiments with animals, undoubtedly interesting in some respects, have never crossed the barrier of conceptual language and for that reason it seems that their expansion stopped at a certain point. Tool-making is also a specifically human property. Animals certainly possess some motory-manipulative skills that are usually connected with the use made of, for instance, a stick or other natural elements of the surrounding world. Yet, only man is capable of fully conscious and intentional production of tools, having in mind their future use, grasping relational connections between things and situations. Already the primordial man produced tools in a systematic, "industrial" way, which makes it possible to evaluate the stage of his civilizational developments. Human tools have a character which is not merely pragmatic but also aesthetic as well as socially integrative. None of these features has been observed in animals.

(iii) The Theory of Evolutionary Creationism

Constituting a practically unquestionable datum of modern science, the theory of evolutionism must have exerted some influence on Christian creationism. More and more often traditional creationism is interpreted in agreement with the dynamic-evolutionary picture of the cosmos. A particularly emphatic example of that influence may be found in the evolutionary creationism of the Reverend Pierre Teilhard de Chardin[46]. He accepted a double understanding of evolution, cosmic and biological. The explication of "the phenomenon of man" was organically connected by him with the idea of evolution, while acknowledging a unity of the process of development - from inanimate matter to man. In the cosmic process of transformation, a particularly significant role was seen in the stage of the "noo-genesis", i.e. hominisation. The French Jesuit questioned the traditional distinction between matter and spirit which he regarded as "pernicious dualism". Man's body and soul are not two distinct elements but rather two different phases of the same process or two aspects[47]. The stage of hominisation is included in the totality of the evolution of the organic world. It is characterized by the phenomenon of consciousness and self-consciousness thanks to which there occur both man's interiorization and integration[48]. Man is a unity of two forms of energy: physical-biological, i.e. tangential, and psychic-spiritual, i.e. radial. The former is

[45]P.Overhage, op.cit., pp.109 ff; R.Leaky and R.Lewin: *Die Menschen vom See*, Berlin 1982, pp.169 ff.

[46]Cf. R.Lischer: *Marx und Teilhard*, New York 1979, pp.123-142.

[47]P.Teilhard de Chardin: "Du cosmos à cosmogénèse" [in:] *Oeuvres*, vol.7, Paris 1964, pp.266-267.

[48]"La place de l'homme dans la nature" [in:] *Oeuvres*, vol.8, Paris 1965, pp.17-20.

connected with the domain of the body, while the latter - with that of spirit. The spirit is an effect of the organization of the material body[49]. The latter proposition does not mean an acceptance of the naturalistic interpretation of the genesis of both the cosmos and man. Teilhard clearly recognized the efficient-creative function of God in relation to the universe, although he interpreted the creative act mainly as a process of the unification of being[50]. He recognized the need of God's creative act also in respect to man. He motivated it by the fact that "the threshold of reflective consciousness" necessarily requires the "psychic agent of intervention"[51]. Thus, the transformation of the animal organism into a human organism was not spontaneous but it required God's creative power.

Although Christian creationism was not questioned by Teilhard, still he re-interpreted its classical explication. To a large extent, his anthropology is an anthropogenesis based on the cosmic-biological perception of reality. In his interpretation, the stage of hominisation had antecedents functioning for a long time, primarily, the intensifying process of cerebralization of the higher forms of the animal world. And then there successively appeared on the earth first pre-hominids and proto-hominids, and, finally, at the end of the Tertiary there appeared ***Homo sapiens***. At that time the animal psychism was transformed into a reflective thought, while the tangential energy - into the radial energy. There "gushed consciousness" of the primordial man[52], thus initiating the stage of the noosphere. At the same time it was also the beginning of a new era in the history of the earth because reflective thought is a consciousness of the second degree (self-consciousness) enabling invention, universalization and anticipation[53]. Animal psychism is restricted to the domain of instinct (often very complex and amazing), while human thinking initiates the world of the person. A further consequence of the hominisation will be a planetarization[54]. The latter will consists in a conscious directing of one's own psychic-social evolution which will result in the unification of humanity and its encounter with the transcendental Omega, i.e. with God.

Teilhard de Chardin wanted to integrate creationism with the modern state of natural science. Classical Christian creationism implied a direct act of creation of the human soul out of prior nothingness. Explaining the genesis of the psychic factor (soul) of man, the French scholar referred to the theory of the evolution of the biocosmos. Namely, he

---

[49]P.Teilhard de Chardin: "Le phénomène humain" [in:] *Oeuvres*, vol.1, Paris 1955, pp.193-195.

[50]P.Teilhard de Chardin: *Ecrits du temps de la guerre*, Paris 1965, pp.114,178.

[51]"La place de l'homme dans la nature", op.cit., p.49.

[52]"Le phénomène humain", op.cit., pp.185 ff.

[53]"Le phénomène spirituel" [in:] *Oeuvres*, vol.6, Paris 1962, pp.129- 130; K.H.Schmitt: "Der 'kritische Punkt der Hominisation' innerhalb der Kosmischen Evolution in der Aussage Teilhard de Chardin", *Acta Teilhardiana*, 4 (1967), pp.60-74.

[54]"Les singularités de l'Espèce humaine" [in:] *Oeuvres*, vol.2, Paris 1957, p.315.

suggested that "God does not act otherwise but evolutionally"[55] The are no clear explanations of details, but most likely the point is that, creating man's psychic-spiritual sphere, God utilized the natural material in the form of animal psychism. And this is the theory of evolutionary creationism.

The above interpretation of creation was, generally, accepted by Karl Rahner. He started with a distinction between the transcendence and immanence of God whom he interpreted in a somewhat different way. God's efficient-creative action cannot be realized in a way analogous to the natural causes in nature, although it is still their foundation[56]. God does not act in the existing cosmos by disregarding the natural laws and forces of nature; He acts through them and that is why the results of the operation of natural causes exceed the possibilities contained in their nature. It is as if matter accomplished self-transcendence, directing itself towards spirit. The destiny and sense of matter is making the realization of spirit possible. The real growth of being, evident in the course of the process of evolution, implies the co-participation of the efficient-creative First Cause[57]. God is neither a material nor an element of finite being, but He constitutes its causal activity - enabling it to operate[58]. Therefore, the evolutionary development of the world is realized through a harmonious co-operation of God and of natural causes. This hypothesis refers to the traditional theory of "God's co-operation" (***concursus divinus***) but apprehended together with the evolutionary vision of the cosmos. The German theologian quite openly acknowledges God's creative function, while simultaneously presenting the natural antecedents of the evolutionary transformations of the cosmos.

His conception of the creative act Rahner applied to an explication of the genesis of the human soul. Namely, he stated that ontogenesis corresponds to phylogenesis[59]. God directly created the soul of the first men, similarly as He creates the soul of every man. Yet, it is possible to say that the parents give birth to the whole man, since God always co-operates with natural causes and maintains them in existence. The body and the soul are different spheres of the human person but, in opposition to Platonism, they are not heterogeneous spheres. The integral unity of the body and the soul makes it possible to speak about the evolutionary development of matter towards spirit[60]. The internal subordination of the body and the soul causes that the pre-history of the human body, explained in the context of the theory of evolution, is, at the same time, the pre-history

---

[55]"L'hominisation" [in:] *Oeuvres*, vol.3, p.104, footnote 1; "Les fondements et le fond de l'idée d'évolution" [in:] ibid., p.190.

[56]K.Rahner: "Die Hominisation als theologische Frage" [in:] P.Overhage and K.Rahner: *Das Problem der Hominisation*, op.cit., pp.13- 90.

[57]K.Rahner: "Die Hominisation ...", op.cit., pp.61 ff.

[58]Ibid., pp.68-69.

[59]Ibid., pp.79 ff.

[60]Ibid., pp.82-83; K.Rahner: "Die Einheit von Geist und Materie im christlichen Glaubensverständnis" [in:] *Schriften zur Theologie*, Einsiedeln - Zurich 1965, vol.6, pp.201-204.

of the whole man. Hence, the human soul is not a natural transformation of the animal psychism, although one can speak about man's biological pre-history.

The evolutionary conception of creationism seems to win over more and more followers although their detailed explanations often differ quite radically. Referring to Bergson, Paul Chauchard identifies connotatively two expressions, creative evolution and evolutionary creation[61]. God is the creator of the human soul but its organic unity with the material body makes it possible to speak about the evolutionary origin of the whole man. During evolution there occurs a spiritualization of matter. God is the creator of the world and an initiator of evolution and for that reason biological evolutionism is not identical with the theory of philosophical-materialistic evolutionism. The noncontradiction of the naturalistic theory of evolution and of the philosophical-theological theory of creation is also accepted and discussed by A.D.Sertillanges. He concentrates his attention mainly on the co-operation of natural causes and of God as the First Cause of any being[62]. Other Christian authors, when explaining the theory of creationism, re-interpret the conception of the creation out of "nothingness". The first act of creating the world was of course its calling into being from the absolute non-being. However, later on God creates new beings out of nothingness in the sense that they have not existed in themselves, while their genesis is conditioned by the transformation of the already existing entities[63].

(iv) Evolution and Creation

Evolutionary creationism (also known as intermediate creationism) occurs in several varieties, radical and moderate. The latter version acknowledges the genetic ties of man with the organic world in respect to the domain of the material body. After the encyclical Humani generis (36) of Pope Pius XII, the matter provokes no more doubts. Teilhard de Chardin and Rahner also speak about the evolutionary origin of the human soul, having mainly in mind the ontical and functional unity of man's psycho-physical being. Their views have not been conclusively and clearly presented, while the meaning of many formulations still remains obscure and ambivalent. Perhaps it is possible to accept that, while creating the human soul, God could utilize the "material" of the psychic life of higher animals. However, God's direct intervention is necessary for the appearance of the human person and its psychic-mental life. This is not questioned by the followers of evolutionary creationism, but some of them, when explaining the idea of the creative act, employ formulations which seem doubtful.

The category of creation implies, ***ex definitione***, the existence of the ontical ***novum*** of the human soul. Such a ***novum*** is not yet created by a "transformation" of the animal into

[61]*La création évolutive*, Paris 1957, p.125; comp. pp.121-134.

[62]*Sertillanges*, op.cit., pp.139,153.

[63]R.T.Francoeur: *Perspectives in Evolution*, London 1965, Part II, Chap.4.

the human psychism or by "raising" sensible psychism to the level of spiritual psychism. Expressions of this kind do not take into account the qualitative difference which obviously separates man from animals. It would also be difficult to accept the thesis that the human soul is lacking substantial reality. But if it was merely a transformation of substantial corporeity and sensuality, then its reality would only have an accidental and functional character. In such an interpretation there arises a threat of anthropological reductionism connected with the ontology of materialism[64]. Hence, it is not surprising that the radical variety of evolutionary creationism is frequently criticised[65]. It is not strange because it seems doubtful that the human soul could come into being "out of" man if it is precisely the ***conditio sine qua non*** of humanity. Soul could not come into being before its own existence. At the basis of evolutionary creationism (in its extreme variety) there occurs an obliteration of the methodological differences of natural sciences and philosophy. The latter depends on empirical sciences, at least in the epistemological-methodological aspect. The idea of evolution does not explain all the ontic levels of human nature, including the human soul. The unity of the body and soul is not identical with the genetic reduction of one of these elements to the other. The classical variety of Christian dualistic anthropology does not mean parallelism, either.

Juxtaposing creationism and evolutionism one should bear in mind their epistemological-methodological differences[66]. Creationism is a philosophical-theological theory, pointing to God as the First Cause of all being. The theory of evolution, belonging to the domain of empirical-natural sciences, explains the mechanism of ever higher species coming into being in the biocosmos. The former case concerns the existence of the world; the latter - the phenomenology of transformations. The thesis about the creation of the world goes beyond the scope of empiricism and that is why it can neither be verified nor negated by the data of natural sciences. In spite of the numerous still unanswered questions, evolutionism constitutes a scientifically justified explanation of many transformational stages of the animate world. Still, this fact by no means abolishes theistic creationism because the natural theory of evolution does not at all take up the question why the world exists. The fact that it existed yesterday and still earlier does not explain its ontical reason of being. Empirical sciences speak about the world that exists but they say nothing about its eternity or beginning in time. Constituting an integral part of modern natural knowledge, the theory of evolution refers to the immanent forces and factors of the cosmos. Because of the method he applies, the naturalist is "closed" in the domain of the material world, so out of necessity his explanations must be only partial. Therefore, the theory of evolution does not solve the metaphysical problems of the genesis of the world and man. Both these problems enter the domains of philosophical and theological reflection.

---

[64]Marxism interprets the human "soul" as a function of biological organism, and the radical variety of evolutionary creationism closely approaches this interpretation.

[65]Cf. F.G.Fothergill, op.cit., pp.337 ff.

[66]Ibid., pp.325-377.

Obviously, the natural theory of evolution throws much light on the problems of the origin of man, especially in its phenomenological aspect. Still, evolutionism neglects many aspects of the human person, such as its ontological connotation, subjectiveness, personal character, values connected with mental life etc. An adequate explanation of these problems and facts makes it necessary to refer to philosophy in whose domain the thesis about the creation of the world and of man has been formulated in a valid manner. Creationism does not exclude evolutionism[67]. God is the Creator of everything, yet He did not have to create directly all the levels of being. For that reason the act of creation does not undermine the fact of the evolutionary transformations of the organic world which, in turn, led to the appearance of man. Only God is absolutely unchangeable, while the world of nature necessarily undergoes these or those transformations. Hence, philosophical creationism is not a challenge to the theory of evolution, including the evolutionary explanation of the natural antecedents in the origin of man. It is the directedness and progressiveness of evolution, explained on the basis of logical-ontological principles, that require the presence of the efficient-creative Cause. The creation out of objective and subjective nothingness refers to the primary act of creation but then God could have taken advantage of the material of the functioning cosmos. This mode of creation may also be referred, obviously, as a hypothesis, to the problem of the genesis of man. Evolutionary creationism can be reconciled with classical Christian thought, provided, however, that the objects and methods of philosophy and of natural sciences are kept distinct. The latter cannot question the substantiality of the immaterial "I" of the human person and thus to reduce it to the sphere of corporeity.

God is the First Cause of everything but not the only cause. The theory of creationism explicitly confirms the co-participation of natural causes, i.e. the secondary causes, dependent on the Creator, in the process of the transformations of the world. The activities of the creatures constitute a finalization of the creative act, since the world has been endowed with its dynamics by God[68]. The act of the creation of the world was combined with endowing it with activity, i.e. a possibility of real causality. This makes it possible to explain the evolutionary development of the organic world, together with the stage of the hominisation, as an organic co-operation of the First Cause and secondary (natural) causes[69]. In spite of His transcendence, God is immanent in existence, in functioning, and in the efficient power of natural-earthly causes. The results of their operation are therefore conditioned by the continuous influence of the Creator in a way analogous to the operation of tools understandable as an expression of the action of the main cause. Hence, there exists a strict connection between the operation of the First Cause and that of secondary causes[70]. The latter participate in the efficient power of

---

[67]H.Volk, op.cit., pp.9-12.

[68]*Summa Theologiae*, I,q.105,a.5; P.Overhage: "Das Problem der Hominisation", op.cit., pp.197-203.

[69]*Contra Gentes*, III,70; W.H.Kane: "Existence and Causality", *The Thomist*, 28 (1964), pp.76-92.

[70]L.Wciórka, op.cit., pp.114-142.

God, thanks to which the effects of their activities are simultaneously fruits of the efficient influence of the Creator. The Thomistic theory of the efficient co-operation of God and of creatures does not clash in any way with the natural theory of the evolutionary development of the biocosmos but it requires a complementation. That is why it is controversial to attempt and undermine the need of special creative intervention when, in consequence of evolution, there appear ever higher forms of being. The Thomistic theory of the co-operation of various kinds of causes does not negate the need of specific God's intervention in the origin of man. This is suggested not only by the Revelation but also by the personalistic interpretation of philosophical anthropology. The naturalistic understanding of anthropogenesis, connected with the theory of evolution, does not contradict creationism. The activity of the natural factors of nature, although so significant, does not yet explain the facts of hominisation and personalisation. That is why it is possible to speak about the creative act of God included in the process of evolutionary transformations which have ultimately led to the appearance of humanity. Evolutionism does not contradict creation nor does it cancel out its necessity in respect to the human person.

LITERATURE

ASHLEY,M.B.: "Causality and Evolution", *The Thomist*, 36 (1972), pp.199-230.

BUYTENDIJK,F.J.: *Mensch und Tier*, Hamburg 1958.

CHAUCHARD,P.: *La création évolutive*, Paris 1957.

COLLIN,F.: *L'evolution. Hypoth èses et probl èmes*, Paris 1961.

CORTE,N.: *The Origins of Man*, New York 1958.

FOTHERGILL,F.G.: *Evolution und christlicher Glaube*, Würzburg 1969.

FRANCOEUR,R.T.: *Perspectives in Evolution*, London 1965.

MESSENGER,E.C.: *Evolution and Theology. The Problem of Man's Origin*, London 1931.

OVERHAGE,P.: *Die Evolution des Lebendigen. Die Kausalität*, Freiburg 1965.

OVERHAGE,P.: "Das Problem der Hominisation" [in:] P.Overhage and K.Rahner: *Das Problem der Hominisation*, Freiburg - Basel - Wien 1961, pp.91-374.

RAHNER,K.: "Die Hominisation als theologische Frage" [in:] ibid., pp.13-90.

SERTILLANGES,A.D.: *L'idée de création et ses retentissement en philosophie*, Paris 1945.

SIMPSON,G.: *The Meaning of Evolution*, New Haven 1949.

SŁOMKOWSKI,A.: *Problem pochodzenia człowieka* [The Problem of the Origin of Man], Poznań 1957.

TEILHARD DE CHARDIN,P.: *Oeuvres*, vols.1-13, Paris 1955-1976.

VOLK,H.: *Schöpfungsglaube und Entwicklung*, Münster 1958.

WCIÓRKA,L.: *Ewolucja i stworzenie* [Evolution and Creation], Poznań 1976.

WUKETIS,F.M.: *Grundriss der Evolutiontheorie*, Darmstadt 1982.

Chapter 6

The Problem of Death and Immortality

The paradox of the human being consists in the clash of two phenomena, his somatic-biological transience and his psychic-internal longing after immortality. Are the two phenomena mutually exclusive? Answers to this question differentiate philosophical trends, religions, ideologies, existential attitudes of men. Differences are noted not only in individual attitudes towards the perspective of death, but also in various ideological-religious and philosophical views on the problems of death. In consequence, one can distinguish passive-negative and active-positive doctrinal attitudes[1]. The former do not propose any doctrinal solution of the phenomenon of death and, in fact, restrict themselves to the acknowledgement of its senselessness (J.P.Sartre) or, at best, attempt to overcome verbally the paralysing fear of death. Active-positive attitudes combine the phenomenon of man's death with variously understood conceptions of immortality. Christianity recognizes man's individual immortality; pantheism acknowledges a kind of collective immortality in the Absolute; finally, some ideologies of naturalism (Marxism) speak about man's participation in immortal history, progress, victorious class etc. In this way the perspective of death is being connected with a hope for this or that kind of immortality.

(i) The Notion and Sense of Death

The fact of death has always assumed a central position in man's thought. In consequence, since ancient Greece and Rome, many thinkers have called for reflection on death and a determination of an appropriate attitude towards it. Even philosophy was often understood as considerations about death[2]. In the Middle Ages fascination with death was often combined with an almost panicky fear of it which in some cases found expression in morbid forms. In modern times attempts at first were made to avoid or

---

[1]S.Kowalczyk: "Les attitudes de l'homme à l'egard de la mort", *Divus Thomas*, 79 (1976) Nr 1/2, pp.3-27.

[2]J.Pieper: *Tod und Unsterblichkeit*, op.cit., pp.14 ff.

make light of the problem of death, yet, ultimately, the rich thanatological literature constitutes evidence of the unavoidability of taking up this theme[3].

Every analysis of the event of death has to face the question whether this is a natural phenomenon for man. An unequivocal answer is impossible because the psycho-physical person of man is ontologically differentiated. This was already accepted by St. Thomas Aquinas when he distinguished in man two ontical levels, material and psychic[4]. Apprehending man in the aspect of his material body and biological life, one can speak about the natural character of death. After all, man is part of the biocosmos and biological life has a restricted time of duration; it has its beginning and its end. Man, being included in the material world, is born and he dies. He is a being of fragile existence, transient, accidental, mortal. But at the same time the human person, apprehended in the aspect of internal-spiritual life, is directed towards immortality. He desires it and perceives in it the sense of his life. That is why the perspective of death often evokes a reaction of rebellion or protest even against God. The complexity of the human being is a cause of a dialectical attitude towards death: we perceive its unavoidability, yet at the same time we speak about its absurdity.

Hence, the problem of death has again an interdisciplinary character; it is an object of study in biology, medicine, psychology, philosophy, theology, literature and the arts. In the considerations that follow we shall distinguish three planes, biological-medical, psychological-phenomenological, and philosophical-theological. The first aspect will be outlined only briefly, while more attention will be paid to the other two.

Biological sciences, especially medicine, speak about death in the strict sense, as about the final stage of human life. They distinguish pathological and physiological death; the former is a result of a disease, while the latter is a consequence of natural quantitative and qualitative transformations of the human organism. A more significant problem is the distinction between clinical and biological death. The former initiates the latter but a precise determination of the moment of death is still very difficult in contemporary medicine[5]. Clinical death, also described as somatic or relative, denotes lack of functioning of man's vital organs, such as blood circulation, the operation of the heart and of the lungs; other organs still continue to operate for some time, and for that reason reanimation is still possible in spite of clinical death. Today, the extinction of the brain functions confirmed by a flat plot on the electroencephalograph which registers bioelectric

---

[3]J.Choron: *Death and Modern Man*, New York 1964, pp.245-269; W.Shibles: Death: *An Interdisciplinary Analysis*, Whitewater 1974.

[4]"Sic ergo corruptio naturalis est homini secundum necessitatem materiae; sed secundum rationem formae esset ei conveniens immortalitas; [...] Et inquantum immortalitas est nobis naturalis, mors et corruptio est nobis contra naturam": St.Thomas Aquinas: *De Malo*, q.5, a.5.

[5]H.Bon: *La mort et ses problémes*, Paris 1941, pp.1-24; Ch.Käufer: "A Medical View of the Process of Death", *Concilium* (1974) Nr. 10, pp.33- 42; E.Becker: *The Denial of Death*, New York 1973; E.Kübler-Rose: *On Death and Dying*, New York 1974.

currents of the brain cortex has been accepted as the proper criterion of death[6]. The atrophying of the brain, which controls the whole of the organism, initiates biological death, also called molecular or absolute. Particular tissues and organs do not die out at the same time since, as a rule, the more perfect the organ, the quicker is its biological disintegration. Biological death is the final moment of man's dying; the disruption of the processes of respiration and circulation causes the poisoning of the brain cortex and, in consequence, irreversible processes of disintegration in the organism. Actually, the reanimation of man is possible only within a few minutes after the halting of the operation of the heart and lungs. Still, there have been cases of clinical death persisting for several days and there still occurred a restoration of the normal vital functions of the human organism[7]. Therefore, a precise determination of the border between man's life and death remains impossible in its biological-medical aspect so far.

The second level on which the phenomenon of death can be characterized is the psychological-phenomenological plane. In this context attention is paid to the psychological-existential and personal experiencing of the perspective of death. After all, it is not only the last moment of life but a process, a totality of one's life directed towards this ending. St. Augustine stressed precisely that aspect when he wrote that "The course of life is nothing else but a run towards death"[8]. Hence, man's whole life can be seen as a constant drawing towards death, in a way, a "ripening" to death. Death was similarly understood by Martin Heidegger who described man's existence as "being-towards-death" (Sein-zum-Tode)[9]. Man is not only a mortal self but a being stigmatized with the perspective of annihilation. Death is hidden at the very foundations of life. That is why already at the moment of birth man is sufficiently old to die[10]. Death is not man's accidental fate but it is contained in his ontical structure. The thought of death should therefore accompany man, because life and death are inseparable. Having in mind the existential-psychological plane, one may speak about death as an end and as a fulfilment. Death means the end of biological life and the end of man's status of a "pilgrim" (***homo viator***). Yet, at the same time, death is a "fulfilment" since it is a termination of the aims and tasks undertaken in life. Although death is unavoidable, it may nevertheless be either internally accepted or rejected in rebellion. That is why one may speak of death as of man's internal act[11]. The phenomenological description of death additionally makes it possible to distinguish two aspects, internal and external. The former concerns our death (its perspective), while the latter - the death of somebody else. The internal experience

---

[6]Ch.Käufer (op.cit., pp.40-41) is of the opinion that even the EEG record cannot constitute an absolute proof of death because the weakened activity of the brain may be beyond the sensitivity threshold of the apparatus.

[7]This is discussed in medical and thanatological literature.

[8]St.Augustine: *De civitate Dei*, 13,10 PL 41,373.

[9]M.Heidegger: *Sein und Zeit*, Halle 1941, pp.245-247.

[10]Ibid., p.245.

[11]J.Pieper, op.cit., pp.125-127.

of suffering and death differs significantly from an external observation of both phenomena. A broad understanding of death, i.e. death as a process, makes it possible to speak about experiencing it by every one of us.

The phenomenon of death is also described on the philosophical-theological plane. The classics of Christian thought, St. Augustine and St. Thomas Aquinas, defined death as a separation of the soul from the body[12]. Yet, when this relatively simple definition is subjected to closer scrutiny, it appears to cause serious difficulties. The notion of "separation" is derivative in respect to that of the "unification" of the soul and the body. Thus, the understanding of death becomes dependent on philosophical-systemic premises, namely, on the conception of man. Plato described man as a soul using the body and, in consequence, he understood death as a liberation of the soul from the constraining body[13]. The metaphors employed by the Greek thinker are particularly telling in this context: he compared death to an escape from prison or to stepping out of a boat after crossing the river. Plato's influence was long-lasting and widespread in the domain of the interpretation of death. Even St.Augustine frequently described death as "an escape and liberation from the body"[14], although he had in mind the moral-religious plane rather than the ontological one. According to Plato's conception of man, death does not violate the essence of man, reduced to the spiritual sphere. This is a diminishment of the role of death which is regarded almost as something merely apparent[15].

The truly Christian interpretation of death is different because it acknowledges the participation of man's whole person in the process and fact of death. This is emphasized especially in Thomistic philosophy. It is not only the body that dies but the whole man - a psycho-physical person. Death destroys the most fundamental components of the human person, although man's immaterial "I" survives. This "I", which in the language of peripatetic philosophy is described as the soul, is indestructible, but its natural relations to matter are violated. As a separation of the soul and the body, death means a disruption of essential-natural ties of the two components of human nature. Therefore, death is not a departure of a sailor from his boat or a dismissal of the instrument of the body, but a tragic destruction of the ontical bonds of human existence. It does not even omit man's spiritual element, although it does not completely destroy its being. Thomistic anthropology is opposed to extreme dualism in apprehending human nature; the body and the soul are not mutually opposed or accidentally bound together, but they interpenetrate and mutually shape each other[16]. Thus, although Christian philosophy rejects

---

[12]"Mors nempe [...] separatio est animae a corpore". St.Augustine: *Enarr.* in ps., 48, sermo 2,2 PL 36,556. Comp. St. Thomas Aquinas: *Compendium theologiae* I,230.

[13]Plato: *Alcibiades* I,130 E-F; *Phaedrus* 247 F.

[14]*De quantitate animae*, 33,76 PL 32,1077.

[15]J.Pieper, op.cit., pp.45-50; K.Rahner: *Zur Theologie des Todes*, Freiburg im Br. 1959, pp.17-26.

[16]J.Möller: *Zum Thema Menschsein. Aspekte einer philosophischen Anthropologie*, Mainz 1967, pp.47-48.

materialistic anthropology, it does not follow Platonism which diminishes the importance of death, either.

While stressing the organic unity of "psychicism" and "corporeity" of human nature, Thomistic philosophy simultaneously recognizes their heterogeneity. The psychic-spiritual element is not identical with the sphere of corporeity, and, hence, the question about the subsequent fate of immaterial soul is meaningful. Death is a crucial stage in human existence but it is not man's absolute end. This understanding of the human being is in strong contrast with the extreme monistic comprehension of man, typical of materialistic anthropologies. In recent years, many Protestant theologians have also accepted the monistic conception of the human being. They are of the opinion that it is not only the body, but also the soul that dies. The thesis about the immortality of human soul, they claim, has been taken over by Christianity from the Hellenic philosophy and is not contained in the Bible; the latter speaks only about resurrection. Questioning "the old-fashioned idea of soul", Wolfhart Pannenberg writes:

"*The inner life of our consciousness is so strictly connected with bodily actions that it would be unable to survive on its own. It is necessary to acknowledge the gravity of death whenever we somehow visualize life after death if it is to be meaningful at all for modern man. Yet, on the other hand, such life can be imagined exclusively as corporeal, since we have no other.*"[17]

This statement quite unequivocally indicates a departure from personalistic anthropology towards materialistic monism. "Making death real" has in fact become a negation of the spirituality and immortality of human soul. It is not only a departure from Christian philosophy but also a false cognizance or misconstruction of statements contained in the sources of the Revelation.

The presence of the idea of man's immortality in the Holy Scriptures is quite generally acknowledged. St. Thomas Aquinas wrote about a large number of Biblical texts which confirm the immortality of human soul[18]. Catholic authors most often also accept a similar opinion although some of them evidently diminish the significance of scripturalist texts[19]. For example, they maintain that the Bible speaks about the resurrection rather than of immortality. The Biblical conception of man and soul in fact did undergo some evolution, though already the Book of Wisdom and the Books of the Maccabees of the Old Testament speak quite clearly about the immortality of the spiritual factor. At the same time, the New Testament (Luke 16,19-31; 23,43; Matthew 16,26; Mark 8,36; James

[17] *Was ist der Mensch?*, Göttingen 1962, p.37. Cf. also ibid., pp.31- 40. A similar view is held by O.Cullman: *Immortality of the Soul or Resurrection of the Dead?*, London 1958, pp.27 ff. Cf. F.Crosson: "Psyche and Persona" [in:] *New Themes in Christian Philosophy*, Notre Dame - London 1968, pp.279-298.

[18] *Contra Gentes* II, 79.

[19] Comp. W. de Pater: *Immortality. Its History in the West*, Leuven 1984, pp.71-99. For instance, the author claims that the idea of resurrection in the Book of Ezekiel has an exclusively nationalistic character, while the Books of the Maccabees consider resurrection to be an exclusive privilege of the martyrs.

5,[20]; 1 Peter 4,19) repeatedly suggests the immortality of the human soul20. The idea of immortality pervades the whole Bible and it is particularly evident at the basis of Christ's evangelical teachings. The life of the body is not the only sector of man's existence and death does not mean an annihilation of his whole being.

The phenomenon of death raises the question about its existential sense apprehendible for man. The idea of man's immortality, of which we shall say more later on, makes it possible to overcome the horror of death. At the moment, however, the point concerns an attempt of explaining the sense of death as a phenomenon in itself. Death means a destruction of the form of the human being existing so far, and in this sense it is a physical evil. But can it become a moral good? Philosophical and theological Christian anthropology allows an affirmative answer. Every man, regardless of the stage of his life, may undertake an inner-moral act due to which an ontical evil is transformed into a moral good. Still, it is neither easy, nor frequent. Endowing death with sense, similarly to the whole life, is an effect of man's internal maturity.

A fascinating interpretation of the sense and role of death has been proposed by the authors following the so-called theory of ultimate choice. Its leading adherents include: Laszlo Boros, Robert W.Gleason, Pierre Glorieux, Josef Pieper, Roger Troisfontaines, and, to some extent, also Karl Rahner. Particular renown has been won by the study of the Hungarian Jesuit, L.Boros, entitled ***Mysterium mortis***. According to the author, it is only at the moment of death that man is capable of taking a completely conscious and free decision. He refers to St. Augustine and distinguishes between "the internal man" and "the external man"[21]. Their lines of development are not identical, for when the corporeal element of the human person weakens, the spiritual element is intensified and becomes autonomous.

> "*In death, in the total loss of externality, there comes into being a total internality. In this way, only in death does man become himself, the ultimate person, a completely independent centre of decision. [...] Thus, death would be a fully personal and total assumption of a stand in respect to personal God*".[22]

The author refers not only to St. Augustine but also to contemporary thinkers, such as M.Blondel, J.Maréchal, H.Bergson and G.Marcel[23]. Maurice Blondel stressed the role of the will in man's life, for thanks to it we seek absolute-infinite values. Boros suggests that in life the human will is unsteady and for that reason the permanent, ultimate act of will is possible only at the moment of death. Taking advantage of J.Maréchal's epistemology, the author tries to demonstrate that only the liberation of the soul from the body enables the first, perfect act of the cognition of God[24]. In his book he also

---

[20]N.Luyten: *Unsterblichkeit*, Basel 1957, pp.11 ff. C.Tresmontant: *Le probl éme de l'âme*, Paris 1971.

[21]L.Boros: *Mysterium mortis. Der Mensch in der letzten Entscheidung*, Freiburg im B. 1962, pp.8 ff.

[22]"Hat das Leben einen Sinn?" *Concilium* 6 (1970) Nr. 12, p.676.

[23]L.Boros: *Mysterium mortis*, op.cit., pp.37-58.

[24]L.Boros maintains that his theory is opposed to the Platonic theory of anamnesis. The moment of death is regarded not as a recollection but as an anticipation of a full cognition of God in the future life.

employs H.Bergson's theory of intuition and suggests that death is the stage of the most perfect intuitive cognition of God. Boros also refers to G.Marcel's existentialism and claims that at the moment of death the most perfect act of the love of God is realized. Hence, death is to constitute the culminating moment of man's spiritual development for then there occurs an utmost intensification of the acts of cognition and love, due to which man takes the ultimate decision of choosing God.

The theory of the ultimate choice has found many followers. Some of them even proclaim an opinion that it is supported by biblical and theological arguments[25]. Karl Rahner, who also sympathizes with this conception of death, makes a distinction between two of its senses, passive and active[26]. Apprehended passively, death refers to the biological aspect where the dilapidation of personality is absolutely independent of man's will. The active meaning of death is connected with the spiritual plane where inner development and self-perfection become possible. Actively apprehended death is therefore man's spiritual-personal act and a culminating moment in the development of his spirit. On the plane of biological life death undoubtedly means destruction, while on the plane of spiritual life death is a complementation of the human person in dialectical development.

Analysing the phenomenon of death, the followers of the theory of ultimate choice also touch on theological aspects. Namely, they maintain that death is the beginning of resurrection. As Boros writes: "The resurrection occurs directly in death, although it is not yet finished. The resurrection of the body still requires a transformed and transmuted world for its existential space. Immortality and resurrection would therefore constitute one and the same reality"[27]. K.Rahner pronounces similar opinions. He observes that the human soul, as a form of a material body, is permanently bound to it, actually or potentially. Death is not a complete separation of the soul from the body and that is why, as its consequence, the soul does not become "non-cosmic", i.e. having no relation to matter, but "pan-cosmic"[28]. Death is a liberation of the soul from the limitations of a single body but at the same time it makes possible an opening to the totality of the universe; then the soul's ontical tie with it is created. The adherents of this theory compare the moment of death with that of birth[29]. After birth the child loses its mother's nourishment but becomes capable of assimilating all the foods of the earth. Similarly, the man who dies loses his body but enters into contact with the totality of the universe. In this way death is to constitute a beginning of resurrection.

In the theory of ultimate choice the moment of death is described as the achievement of the highest spiritual maturity which only then enables man to take the fully conscious

---

[25]R.Troisfontaines: *Je ne meurs pas*, Namur 1960, pp.128-151.

[26]*Zur Theologie des Todes*, op.cit., pp.29-30, 38-39. The theory of "ultimate choice", especially in the interpretations of L.Boros and K.Rahner, is accepted by M.Krąpiec: *I - Man*, op.cit., pp.335-362.

[27]L.Boros, article quoted above, p.677.

[28]K.Rahner: *Zur Theologie des Todes*, op.cit., pp.19-22.

[29]L.Boros: *Erlöstes Dasein*, Mainz 1965, pp.104-108.

and free choice of God. The human spirit separates itself from the limitations of the concrete-material body, and faces God, who appears to man in all His splendour. God calls man to Himself and then there occurs the moment of the ultimate decision, of the acceptance or rejection of God. However, since at the moment of death man achieves, or rather freedom of the will, he chooses God with the whole power of recovers, the fullness of mental recognition and total his spirit. That is why man's ultimate decision is the decision of choosing God[30].

The theory of ultimate choice contains many elements that are interesting and, to some extent, valid. But it also includes controversial elements and its problems concern several planes, such as medical-psychological, philosophical and theological. The theory as a whole is beyond any empirical or psychological verification[31]. The phenomenon of human death is still veiled in mystery (e.g., it is not known when and how man definitively dies), so all suggestions on this subject must have a hypothetical character. Boros suggests that at the moment of death every man performs a recapitulation of his whole life and makes the ultimate choice. The confessions of people who have experienced direct threat of death (e.g. by drowning) confirm the psychic phenomenon of the "summing up" of life. In spite of that, it is difficult to accept the claim that the final moment of death is a stage of full consciousness and freedom, because biological disintegration of the human person causes a loss of consciousness. The beginning of life (birth) and its end (death) are beyond man's consciousness and freedom. It is not death but pangs of death that can be conscious, half conscious or unconscious. The final stage of man's dying unavoidably leads to the disappearance of consciousness and that is why it seems doubtful that it can just be death that would make us capable of taking "the ultimate decision", totally conscious and free. At any rate, is every death conscious, as J.Pieper suggests?[32] One may agree with him that man's "inner sight" may balance one's whole life in a short time. Still, it is doubtful that this moment can be the moment of death which, by its nature, eludes consciousness. Besides, there are frequent cases of sudden death, when there is no dying. Then the inner process of ripening to the fullness of personality and, thus, taking a conscious decision are impossible. The Gospels confirm that Christ was warning against a possibility of being surprised by death. This seems to undermine the generally formulated theory that death is precisely the most appropriate moment of choosing God by man.

The theory of ultimate choice is difficult to reconcile with the views of classical Christian thinkers, St.Augustine and St.Thomas Aquinas. St.Augustine stressed the variety of deaths of good and evil people which can hardly conform to the aprioristic optimism

---

[30]L.Boros: *Mysterium mortis*, op.cit., pp.90-110.

[31]Cf. J.M.Pohier: "Death, Nature and Contingency" *Concilium* (1974) Nr. 10, pp.64-79; G.Greshake: "Towards a Theology of Dying", ibid., pp.80-98; P.Evst: "La théologie et la mort de l'homme", *Nouvelle Revue Théologique* (1974), pp.471 ff.; H.Bon: *La mort et ses probl émes*, Paris 1941, pp.25-52.

[32]J.Pieper, op.cit., pp.133-149.

of the theory in question[33]. St.Thomas was opposed to Platonic conceptions of the human person and that is why he did not treat the material body as a barrier to the achievement of internal maturity. Because of its evident Platonism, the theory of ultimate choice is far from Thomistic realism.

This theory is also controversial in its fundamental philosophical aspects[34]. The suggestion that death is the culminating stage in man's development implies a Platonic understanding of human nature. Man is a psycho-physical whole and for that reason he is active and authentically human in both dimensions of his person, material and spiritual. Therefore, if the stage of the cessation of biological processes in death is treated as a fullness of man's development, this constitutes an angelical-Platonic interpretation of humankind. The theory of ultimate choice reveals a depreciation of the body which is in opposition to classical Christian thought. Anyway, can death be interpreted in positive categories? If every suffering (physical and psychic) is evil, it is difficult to apprehend death as perfection and a good. It seems unquestionable that the phenomenon of death means a "devastation" of the human person which is connected with intense pain and fear.

The discussed theory also means a devaluation of the totality of human life, its decisions, intentions, achievements, activities, and moral wants. Boros's analyses hide a dilemma: if only "the ultimate decision" constitutes a fullness of consciousness and freedom, then all the acts and activities of human life are not authentically free; on the other hand, if man's decisions taken during his life are free, then the ultimate decision differs from others only in its intensity, not quality, and then it does not constitute the necessary ending of human life[35]. If man became free only after "parting" with his body, then the material dimension of personality would be a transient state and a sad necessity. Obviously, man can "re-orient" himself in relation to God, as it often happens precisely in the last stage of human life. In this sense the validity of the theory of ultimate choice can be acknowledged but it can hardly be accepted as a general interpretation of the role and sense of death. Undoubtedly, the moment of death is important but it cannot constitute the leading criterion in evaluating the human attitude towards death. The whole life is a God's gift that can either be put to good use or wasted. In some way Boros's theory "equalizes" the lives of good and bad people, because it shifts the decisive criterion to the moment of death when - and only then - they choose the ultimate option.

The adherents of the theory of ultimate choice suggest that the moment of death is also a beginning of resurrection in whose consequence the human soul enters into contact with the totality of the material world. Naturally, leaving aside objections of theological

---

[33]S.Kowalczyk: "La problème de la mort dans la doctrine de saint Augustin" *Estudio Augustiniano* 10 (1975) Nr.3, pp.357-372.

[34]E.H.Schillebeeckx: *Vatican II. A Struggle of Mind and Other Essays*, Dublin 1963, pp.61-91.

[35]M.J.O'Connel: "The Mystery of Death: A Recent Contribution", *Theological Studies* (1966) pp.433-442.

character[36], one should observe a possibility that the conception of the pan-cosmic soul betrays a tendency towards pantheism. For how can soul become combined with the totality of the cosmos? De-individualization is unavoidably connected with the process of depersonalization. And, therefore, it is difficult to explicate death as the moment of the fullest development of the human person. The theory of ultimate choice is doctrinally controversial, while existentially it departs from the realities of the biological-medical processes of man's dying. Even in the evangelical description of Christ's Passion, death is a tragic and painful experience. An overcoming of this tragic character is possible only in the context of faith in eternal life. And a philosophical preamble of this faith is the conviction about the immortality of human soul.

(ii) The Immortality of Human Soul

The problems of justifying man's immortality have given rise to abundant literature, especially their historical aspect[37]. There are various types of motivation connected with particular currents of philosophy, such as Platonism, Augustinianism, Thomism, Christian existentialism, intuitionism (Bergson) etc. We shall concentrate in greater detail on the views of Thomism, but at the beginning some reflections of Plato and St. Augustine should be outlined.

In the writings of the old-Greek thinker there appear several kinds of arguments for the immortality of human soul. Some of them will be mentioned later on, since they constitute the starting point of the analyses by St. Thomas Aquinas. At this point three conceptions should be stressed. Firstly, Plato demonstrates the immortality of soul as a being capable of self-motion[38]. Soul is a being capable of movement out of its nature. A material body is described as animate when it does not receive movement from the outside. The more so, the soul, as an independent agent of action, cannot be activated by something else. The soul does not come into being, nor does it die, and therefore it is immortal.

Similar in nature is another motivation which starts with the assumption that soul is a source of life[39]. It belongs to the essence of soul and hence the alternative of a dying soul is absurd, for soul, as a synonym of life, can never cease to exist. An opposition to it is evil and therefore only absolute evil can be equivalent to its death[40]. Naturally, since evil is usually connected with the body, it can do harm to the good of the soul; still,

---

[36]J.Kremer: "Paulus: Die Auferstehung Jesu, Grund und Vorbild unserer Auferstehung", *Concilium* 6 (1970) Nr.12, pp.707-712.

[37]Cf. Q.Huonder: *Das Unsterblichkeitsproblem in der abendländischen Philosophie*, Stuttgart 1970; W.A. de Pater: *Immortality. Its History in the West*, Leuven 1984.

[38]Plato: *Phaedrus* 245 C - 246 A.

[39]*Phaedo* 103 C - 107 A.

[40]*Republic X*, 608 A - 611 A.

it can never lead to its total death, so in consequence it is possible to speak about the immortality of the soul.

The problem of the immortality of soul is still controversial in the writings of Aristotle. Some authors are of the opinion that he did not accept the immortality of the human soul[41]. In reality, he claimed that immortality appertains to active intellect, as opposed to the possible intellect[42]. Hence, in soul there is something that is immortal.

The idea of the immortality of man was consolidated in the thought of early Christianity which is evident in the works of St. Augustine. His conception of the immortality of the human soul was based on its immateriality. He presented a double motivation of the thesis about soul's immortality, a negative one, derived from the properties of soul and its functions, and a positive one, inferred from the direct obviousness of soul's self-cognition[43]. His reflections were continued and deepened by St.Thomas Aquinas, among others, in respect to the problems of intellectual cognition. St.Augustine also formulated arguments overtly confirming the immortality of the human soul. Two of them seem particularly significant, one derived from the cognition of truth and the other from the conception of life. Both arguments reveal Platonic inspiration.

St.Thomas Aquinas was quite unequivocal in affirming the theory of the immateriality and immortality of the human soul, although it was not a view commonly acknowledged by medieval scholastic philosophy. Duns Scotus accepted soul's immortality on the theological plane, while philosophical considerations about this issue were regarded by him as hypothetical[44]. As the best argument he acknowledged the one which starts with the analysis of man's intellectual activity. However, in his opinion, the autonomy of such activities does not prove in an absolute way the autonomy of the existence of incorporeal human spirit. Scotus's reasoning was followed by Cardinal Cajetan who also regarded the philosophical arguments for man's immortality as merely probable.

In our times the idea of the immortality of the human soul is undermined by Protestant theologians, among others, by Karl Barth and W.Pannenberg[45]. They consider this idea to be a relic of the Hellenic thought and instead refer to the biblical idea of the resurrection of the totality of the human being. The influence of Protestantism is marked in some Catholic authors. Thus, for instance, Edward Schillebeeckx clearly sympathizes with the Protestant thought, although at the same time he acknowledges the permanence of some element of the human being after death[46].

---

[41]W.de Pater, op.cit., pp.41-45.

[42]Aristotle: *De Anima II*, 2,413 b, 430 a.

[43]J.Pastuszka: *Niematerialność duszy ludzkiej u św. Augustyna* [The Immateriality of the Human Soul according to St. Augustine], Lublin 1930; S.Kowalczyk: *Człowiek i Bóg w nauce św. Augustyna*, op.cit., pp.97-105.

[44]W.de Pater, op.cit., pp.72-73.

[45]K.Barth: *Unsterblichkeit*, Basel 1966, pp.43-51; W.Pannenberg, op.cit., pp.364 ff.

[46]W.de Pater, op.cit., p.132.

Classical philosophy formulated several arguments for the immortality of the human soul. The most significant of them include: the teleological argument derived from the desire of happiness; the ethical argument inferred from the sense of justice; and metaphysical proofs. The latter refer to three phenomena: the immateriality of the inner "I", man's cognitive-intellectual activity, and the activity of his will[47]. Occasionally there appear attempts of justifying the existence and immortality of soul on the basis of the domain of para-psychological phenomena[48] but they are completely ignored by Christian thought. The arguments for man's immortality have also been subject of many critiques[49]. The latter result most often from aprioristic epistemological (sensualism, scientism) or ontological (materialism) assumptions.

The teleological argument is derived from a relatively common conviction about the finalistic structure of the world. Natural beings are ontologically directed towards their appropriate aims, thus realizing their tasks. Man is incorporated in the teleology of the cosmos although he realizes it in a manner proper to himself. In Contra Gentes St. Thomas wrote:

> "*Man should satisfy his inborn desires if he reaches his ultimate goal. But this does not take place in life.Hence, if man does not achieve the happiness which is his proper goal in this life, he must achieve it in his future life. It is impossible for a natural desire to be vain.For nature does not do anything in vain. And the natural desire would be vain if it could not be fulfilled. Thus, it is possible for man to fulfil his natural desire. It is not realized in this life, and that is why it must be realized after this life. Therefore, man's ultimate happiness exists in the future life.*"[50]

At the basis of this argumentation there is the metaphysical principle of purposefulness expressed by the sentence: natural desires cannot be objectless. If man could not absolutely realize his desire of happiness, which is a universal and fundamental phenomenon, it would be a striking breach in the finalism of nature. Thus, the very ontical structure of the human person indicates the necessity of its immortality. St. Thomas's ***Summa Theologiae*** constitutes an attempt of specifying the character and object of man's desire of happiness. We read there:

> "*Every being, by its nature, wants to exist in a manner appropriate to it. And in beings capable of cognition desire applies to cognition. A sense is capable of cognition restricted in time and place, whereas intellect apprehends existence in an abstracted way and as existence realized in every time. Therefore, by its very nature, every being endowed with*

---

[47]Cf. *L'anima*, ed.by M.P.Sciacca, Brescia 1954; A.Wenzl: *Unsterblichkeit. Ihre metaphysische und anthropologische Bedeutung*, Bern 1951; J. de Vries: *Materie und Geist*, München 1970.

[48]H.Price: "The Problem of Life after Death", *Religious Studies* (1968), pp.447-459.

[49]D.Hume: *A Treatise of Human Nature*, op.cit., pp.221-237; C.J.Ducasse: *A Critical Examination of the Belief in a Life after Death*, Springfield 1961.

[50]*Contra Gentes* III, 48.

a mind wants to exist permanently. And a natural desire cannot be vain. Thus, every substance endowed with a mind is indestructible."[51]

This passage combines two threads of thought: it indicates the immaterial character of the activities of intellect and it describes the phenomenon of human happiness as transcending the borders of time and space. As a rational and conscious being, man seeks absolute and infinite values. They demand the permanence of his existence, i.e. immortality. The desire of lasting happiness, therefore, derives from the ontical structure of the human person and that is why such an argument has a teleological-philosophical character. The desire of complete happiness is a desire of immortality.

Another argument for the immortality of the human soul is called ethical because it refers to the indispensability of respecting the moral order. Such a thread of thought occurred already in St. Bonaventura who combined the need of man's immortality with the idea of God's justice[52]. The negation of the permanent existence of the spiritual "I" of the human person would be wrong for just people, since their faithfulness to good would not be granted due reward; at the same time, the evil of the unjust would not receive adequate punishment. Somewhat differently is the ethical argument apprehended by Immanuel Kant who starts his analysis with the fact of the imperative of moral law. Man feels in himself an inner command: Do good. An explanation of this phenomenon demands the acceptance, as a postulate, of man's immortality. Kant was a follower of ethical rigorism which requires a total submission to moral commands. Self-identification with the laws of ethics is extremely difficult and that is why it is impossible within the narrow temporal scope of earthly life. The process of inner perfection has an infinite character. That is why the highest good, i.e. God, is possible only under the assumption of the existence of an immortal soul[53]. Only man's immortality ensures man's inner unification with the commands of the moral law, indispensable for the shaping of his personality. Kant regarded the ethical argument merely as a postulate, while questioning its metaphysical value. One may agree with him in the sense that it really has a psychological-hypothetical character.

For Christian thought the most important arguments for man's immortality have a metaphysical character, being based on the analyses of the nature of soul, cognitive-mental activity, and the operation of appetitive-volitional faculties.

The first argument, referring to the nature of the internal "I", can be found already in the writings of St.Augustine. He accepted direct self-obviousness of the cognition of soul, of its existence, ontical independence in beingness of the material body, capability of immaterial actions[54]. As a subject of memory, intellect and will, soul cannot be a

[51]*Summa Theologiae* I,q.75,a.6,c; *Contra Gentes* II,79; W. de Pater, op.cit., pp.165 ff.

[52]St.Bonaventura: *II Sent.* 19,1,1.

[53]I.Kant: *Kritik der praktischen Vernuft*, Leipzig 1929, pp.142-151.

[54]St. Augustine: *De Trinitate* 9,3,3 PL 42,963; 10,10,14 PL 42-981; cf. S.Kowalczyk: *Człowiek i Bóg ...*, op.cit., pp.101-104.

material being, although it is connected with material body. Its immateriality constitutes a foundation of its immortality.

St.Thomas Aquinas repeatedly emphasized the immateriality of the human soul. The above thesis was explained and justified by him on the basis of the theory of hylomorphism. The human soul is a substantial form in the psycho-physical totality of the human person. The permanence of being is derivative in respect to the permanence of its form[55]. That is why the indestructibility of the human soul justifies its immortality. St.Thomas described the soul as "an intellectual substance", that is, incorporeal and immaterial[56]. It is neither the body nor an effect of its organization, while in its mode of existence and operation it differs significantly from the body[57]. St. Thomas's idea can be broadened by explicating it on the basis of various conceptions of materiality and immateriality. The Aristotelian-Thomistic philosophy understands matter as a potential, a lack of ontical structure and action. The human soul is immaterial because it is a source of the organization of the human ***compositum*** and its activity. In our times matter is apprehended as a space-time continuum. Man's spiritual "I" is therefore immaterial because it is weightless, indivisible, immeasurable, impenetrable; on the other hand, it is simple, incorporeal, self-conscious, active, transcending time and space. These kinds of attributes of the personal "I", being a soul (though not only a soul), prove the immateriality of the self. Man's soul has its own beingness, which is self-existent, immaterial, and, hence, indestructible and immortal. Only God could annihilate the human soul but such an alternative would clash with God's wisdom and goodness. The nature of man's personal-spiritual self, explained on the basis of the principle of noncontradiction, proves its immortality. What is immaterial in its nature cannot undergo destruction through the biological decomposition of the body. The co-operation of the soul with the material body does not constitute their ontical identity and therefore the death of the body does not mean an end of the existence of the soul.

The next two metaphysical arguments for the immortality of the human soul refer to the specificity of man's mental activity, intellectual cognition and the will. St.Thomas refers to the classical principle that the mode of operation indicates the mode of existence - ***operatio sequitur esse***[58]. Man's permanent property is self-consciousness and the ability of intellectual cognition. The activities of intellect include, among others, the ability of abstraction and universalization, the skill of invention and prospective thinking, the ability of correcting cognitive results, the transcending of material-biological conditions of the acts of cognition. Man's mental life cannot be contained in the material categories of place, time, number etc. Immaterial acts - actions of intellect demand the existence of an

---

[55]*Contra Gentes*, II,55.

[56]*Contra Gentes*, II,79.

[57]*Summa Theologiae*, I,q.75,aa.2 and 6; M.Krąpiec: *I - Man*, op.cit., pp.108-116.

[58]"Operatio enim rei demonstrat substantiam et esse ipsius": *Contra Gentes*, II,79.

immaterial subject, i.e. soul[59]. It is impossible for a material being to have immaterial properties and actions. The hypothesis about matter being a supposed subject of thinking is absurd because the nature of thought and the nature of matter are irreducible to each other. Just as a mineral cannot have biological life, thinking matter is an even more ontically contradictory conception. The phenomena of human self-consciousness and discursive thought, though functionally dependent on material body, are totally different from matter in their nature. Matter is incapable of thinking, inference, evaluation; it has no consciousness of its own being and is totally lacking cognitive sensitivity.

The immateriality and indestructibility of the human soul are also implied by the object of intellectual cognition. This argument was already formulated by Plato, according to whom he who discovers eternal truth participates in its immortality[60]. This conception was often quoted by St.Augustine when emphasizing the difference between man's sensory and intellectual cognition. The object of sensory cognition, localized in space and time, is concrete and material. The object of intellectual cognition concerns universal truths, indestructible and absolute[61]. Through mental cognition man discovers the truths of being and thought, and he comes to know the rich world of spiritual values (moral, artistic, religious). Such a train of thought may also be found in St.Thomas Aquinas. He states that man, being capable of apprehending an indestructible truth, is an owner of an immaterial and immortal soul[62]. The argument is succinctly expressed by J.Pieper who writes:

> "*Since the human soul is capable of grasping truth as such; since it is able to do something that is principally beyond any possible material process and remains independent of it; since, thus understood, it is capable of absolute operation - for these reasons it must also possess esse absolutum; it must also have a being independent of the body; it must be something that remains in existence beyond the decomposition of the body and beyond death.*"[63]

Therefore, both the structure of man's intellectual cognition and its object are meaningful only when we acknowledge the existence of the immaterial - and hence also immortal - spiritual subject.

Justifying the immortality of the human soul, personalistic philosophy also refers to the ontical structure of the operation of the will and its object. St. Thomas extensively analysed the mechanism and character of the functioning of the will, stressing its

---

[59]*Summa Theologiae* I,q.75,aa.1 and 6; J.Y.Jolif: "Affirmation rationelle de l'immortalité de l'âme chez saint Thomas", *Lumière et Vie*, (1955) Nr.24, pp.59-77; R.Troisfontaines: *Je ne meurs pas*, Namur 1960, pp.81-85.

[60]Plato: *Phaedo* 79 D, 102 A - 107 D.

[61]A sensory view of a concrete triangle differs significantly from the concept of triangle. The former phenomenon is strictly connected with the functioning of the neurological system, while the latter transcends man's somatic activity.

[62]*Summa Theologiae*, I,q.61,a.2,ad 3; *II Sent.*, d.19,q.1.a.1.

[63]*Tod und Unsterblichkeit*, pp.184-185; cf. M.Krąpiec: *I - Man*, op.cit., pp.110-115.

connections with the domain of higher values[64]. By its nature, the will is directed towards good. Yet, whereas man's emotional sphere is connected with finite and destructible values, the will has its adequate object in absolute and infinite good. Particularized goods are incapable of satisfying the deepest desires of the human person which seeks the highest values, such as truth, good, love, beauty, sacrum. Not only the object, but also the mode of operation of the human will are characteristic. The will recognizes and then joins the world of moral norms while the life of the will becomes interlocked with the domain of conscience. The material world does not absolutely explain the freedom of the will, the abilities of self-control and self-obligation, the criteria of good and evil, acts of love or hatred. Only an immaterial and indestructible being can be a subject of the activities of the will and of conscience.

The domain of the will and its object has been analysed extensively, though in a specific way, by contemporary Christian thinkers, Maurice Blondel[65] and Gabriel Marcel. Let us concentrate on the considerations of the latter. He constantly emphasizes that man is not any abstract idea or a set of acts and experiences, but a concrete and personal "I". The human person expresses itself in acts of faith, hope, love and loyalty. Man is a constant pilgrim, ***homo viator***, opening himself internally to other people and their needs. In interhuman relations there appear love and faithfulness. Authentic love is capable of sacrifice, hence it transcends the borders of time and space[66]. Even the death of a loved person does not completely destroy the "I - you" relation because faithfulness does not know material barriers. Love does not die, only the material body incorporated in the earthly "horizon". Hence, authentic and faithful love implies man's immortality. Human love, as much as the whole person, must undergo the experience of death. And yet, in spite of death, there exists something eternal in man directed towards good and expressing himself in acts of love[67]. Death is man's second birth to another life. It is a transition to another plane of being, virtually contained in the human being sensitive to indestructible values.

There still remains one problem to be mentioned, namely, the question of the ontological status of the human soul after death. Speaking more generally, the issue concerns the nature of man's immortality. Classical Christian philosophy quite explicitly acknowledges individual immortality of every man, thus standing in opposition both to materialism and to pantheism. St. Thomas describes the ontological status of man after death as "the soul separated from the body" (***anima separata***) and then undertakes an attempt to characterize the scope and mode of intellectual cognition. He accepts not only the continuity of the mental faculties of individual man but also a continuation of skills

[64]*Summa Theologiae*, I-II,q.2,a.7; q.10,a.1; I,q.87,ad 1.

[65]Cf. S.Kowalczyk: *Bóg w myśli współczesnej*, op.cit., pp.216-228.

[66]G.Marcel: *Présence et immortalit é*, Paris 1959, p.186; J.Choron: *Death and Western Thought*, New York 1963, pp.254-261.

[67]*Présence et immortalit é*, op.cit., pp.73-183.

developed during his earthly life[68]. As St.Thomas states, the souls of the saved get to know the transformations of the world through God which, however, does not mean an ontological-substantial identity with Him[69]. The individual character of the soul is not lost at the moment of death because the soul retains its potential directedness towards its ties with the material body. The philosophical truth about the immortality of the human soul finds a complementation in the theological truth about the resurrection of the bodies. Although the soul separated from the body does not undergo biological death, it no longer constitutes an integral person of man; the latter can only be the psycho-physical totality of human nature.

In our times man's individual immortality is often questioned, among others in trends referring to pantheism. A typical example may be found in the so-called "process theology" whose initiator was Alfred North Whitehead. He detached himself from the conception of individual immortality which he called subjective. He himself was for the "objective", i.e. collective, immortality. He did not restrict it exclusively to people but referred it to the whole world. He thought that "God's efficient nature is a changeable world receiving 'eternity' through its objective immortality in God"[70]. The realization of this collective immortality is achieved mainly through man's connection with the world of values. Participating in the realization of values, such as truth, good, or beauty, man transcends the borders of destruction and death. The immortality of values is a way towards the immortality of man. Yet, it does not mean individual duration after death but only "a unification of a multiplicity of persons" in God where they constitute component elements[71]. Other representatives of process theology most often also question man's immortality and try to show that it does not clash with Christian philosophy and theology[72]. The idea of collective-social immortality, proposed by the followers of process theology, obliterates man's single identity. Hence, it also questions his personality, responsibility for good or evil, consciousness of further survival. "Objective" immortality is a negation of individual-personal immortality.

A new interpretation of death and immortality, of an evidently naturalistic-biological character, has been proposed by Pierre Teilhard de Chardin. The French scholar most probably accepted man's individual immortality although he understood it as a unification of human persons in a supra-personal divine Omega[73].

The idea of immortality is also connected with the Oriental theory of reincarnation (metempsychosis) which assumes a possibility of a specific "transmigration of souls",

---

[68]*Summa Theologiae*, I, q.89, aa.1 and 5; cf. *De Veritate*, q.19, aa.1-2.

[69]*Summa Theologiae*, I, q.89, a.8.

[70]A.N.Whitehead: *Process and Reality*, New York 1969, p.409; comp. ibid., pp.286,410-411.

[71]A.N.Whitehead: "Immortality" [in:] *His Reflections on Man and Nature*, New York 1961, p.170.

[72]A.Koothottil: "Life 'after' Death: Individual Survival or Universal Communion?" [in:] *God, Man, the Universe*, Leuven 1981, pp.85-90.

[73]P.Teilhard de Chardin: "Les directions et les conditions de l'Avenir" [in:] *Oeuvres*, Paris 1961, vol.5, pp.304-305.

combined with a succession of bodies[74]. The conception, however, is alien to Christian thought because it undermines the individual self-identity of man as a unique combination of the soul with a determined body.

LITERATURE

BECKER,E.: *The Denial of Death*, New York 1973.

BON,H.: *La mort et ses probl èmes*, Paris 1946.

BOROS,L.: *Erlöstes Dasein*, Mainz 1965.

BOROS,L.: *Der Mensch in der letzten Etnscheidung*, Freiburg im B. 1962.

CHORON,J.: *Death and Modern Man*, New York 1964.

CULLMAN, O.: *Immortality of the Souls or Resurrection of the Dead?*, London 1958.

DEMSKE,J.M.: *Sein, Mensch und Tod. Das Todesprobleme bei Martin Heidegger*, München 1963.

Di NAPOLI, G.: *L'immoralit à dell'anima nel Rinascimento*, Torino 1963.

HOUNDER,Q.: *Das Unsterblichkeitsproblem in der abendländischen Philosophie*, Stuttgart - Mainz 1970.

JOLIF,J.Y.: "Afirmation rationelle de l'immortalité de l'âme chez saint Thomas", *Lumière et Vie* (1955), nr 24, pp.59-77.

KOWALCZYK,S.: "Les attitudes de l'homme à l'egard de la mort", *Divus Thomas* 79 (1976) Nr.1/2, pp.3-27.

KOWALCZYK,S.: "Le problème de la mort dans la doctrine de saint Augustin", *Estudio Augustiniano*, 10 (1975) Nr.3, pp.357-372.

LEVELLE,L.: *Le Moi et son destin*, Paris 1936.

MARCEL,G.: *Présence et immortalit é*, Paris 1959.

MARTELET,G.: *Victoire sur la mort. Eléments d'anthropologie chrétienne*, Lyon 1962.

MORIN,E.: *L'homme et la mort*, Paris 1970.

PATER,W.A.de: *Immortality. Its History in the West*, Leuven 1984.

PIEPER,J.: *Tod und Unsterblichkeit*, München 1968.

RAHNER,K.: *Zur Theologie des Todes*, Freiburg im B. 1959.

SCIACCA,M.F.: *Morte e immortalit à*, Milano 1968.

SHIBLES,W.: *Death: An Interdisciplinary Analysis*, Whitewater 1974.

THIELICKE,H.: *Tod und Leben. Studien zur christlichen Anthropologie*, Tübingen 1946.

TRESMONTANT,C.: *Le probl ème de l'âme*, Paris 1971.

VIVES,G.L.: *De anima et vita*, Padova 1974.

VOEGELIN,E.: "Immortality. Experience and Symbol", *The Harvard Theological Review*, 60 (1967), pp.235-279.

WENZL,A.: *Unsterblichkeit. Ihre metaphysische und anthropologische Bedeutung*, Bern 1951.

WHITEHEAD,A.N.: "Immortality" [in:] *His Reflections on Man and Nature*, New York 1961, pp.157-177.

[74]P.Siwek: *The Enigma of the Hereafter: The Reincarnation of Souls*, New York 1952.

Chapter 7

The Individual in Social Community

Philosophical anthropology, usually concentrating on the ontic structure of man and the axiological dynamics connected with it, cannot omit the problems of social life. Although an individual person is not something analogous to a cell of the social organism, yet, neither is it a monad closed to the external world. Man is a substantial-autonomous being, psychically interiorized, but he is not an embodiment of egocentrism. Relations between the individual and society abound in tensions and conflicts, still, this opposition does not mean an antinomy of interests. Although mutually opposed, the individual and society also complement and enrich each other. The latter is possible, however, when both partners of the relation between man and society are properly apprehended. A harmonious solution of the dilemmas of their co-existence is conditioned by the perception of a person in the human individual, and of a community in society.

(i) Extreme Views

There is a variety of models of the relations between the individual and society. In contemporary culture three such models seem most representative, namely, collectivism, extreme individualism, and personalism[1]. The first two constitute a certain deformation since they solve the problem in extreme ways. The theory of anthropological sociocentrism makes an absolute of the role of the collective (race, class), thus degrading individual man to the rank of an epiphenomenon of social life. Extreme individualism, on the other hand, connected with liberalism, makes an absolute of the human individual, reducing social life to the "play of interests". Both socio-ideological trends neglect the personal dimension of man. These are not always consciously accepted doctrinal systems; often they are merely existential attitudes, patterns of behaviour or mentality etc.

The organistic theory which stresses the priority of the collective over the individual had many representatives in the history of human thought. They also included Plato who, in his vision of the "ideal state", proposed state intervention in the private lives of

---

[1]K.Wojtyła: *Osoba i czyn*, op.cit., pp.297-301.

citizens[2]. Hence, he allowed an infringement of their rights, sanctioned by law. The instrumental treatment of the individual man, contained in the Platonic conception of state, has been realized in the dictatorship systems in modern times[3]. They ignored the fundamental rights of the human person and demanded blind obedience to the authorities which tolerated no objection to them (e.g. in the form of parliamentary opposition).

The organistic theory was also accepted by Hegel who ascribed to the collective a substantial-absolute being. His theory of pan-logicism speaks about three stages in the development of the deity: individual, collective, and absolute. In this interpretation the collective (state, humankind) constitutes a higher form of the self-realization of the Absolute. Individual men are merely moments in the dialectic development of the universe of being. Also Herbert Spencer († 1903), a follower of evolutionary utilitarianism, sympathised with socio-centrism. He spoke about analogies between society and a biological organism and, thus, interpreted all the behaviours of individuals as effects of their long-lasting bonds with society.

Yet, a classical example of anthropological collectivism is found in Marxism. In his *Theses on Feuerbach* Karl Marx wrote: "The human self is not an abstraction inherent in a single individual. In its reality it is a totality of social relations"[4]. This formulation, presented as a definition of man, is directed against L.Feuerbach whom Marx accused of ignoring the role of social-economic structures in explaining the origin of man. An individual is "an abstraction", because the real man is a result and expression of social relations; it is in and through the latter that man comes into being. For Marx society is not an assembly of human individuals as their ***juxtapositio***. There are no people before and beyond society, therefore society does not come into being out of human individuals. Such an understanding of community is typical of individualism from which Marx detached himself. In *Economic-Philosophical Manuscripts* he wrote: "As society itself produces man as man, so man produces society [...]. The human natural self exists only for social man; for only then does nature become a tie binding man with man [...]. Only then his natural being becomes for him a human being"[5]. This utterance quite explicitly posits a thesis: society "produces" man as a human being. The pre-social and extra-social mode of existence means a degradation of man to the domain of biological vegetation.

Marx's collectivism is continued in contemporary Marxism. The latter still retains the classical thesis that man is always and everywhere a "product" of society and, in some sense, a reflection of social relations[6]. Such an interpretation of man favours the

---

[2]Plato: *Laws* 631-632,942.

[3]J.Messner: *Das Naturrecht*, Wien 1960, pp.729 ff.

[4]K.Marx: *Thesen über Feuerbach* [in:] *K.Marx, F.Engels: Werke*, Berlin 1962, vol.3, p.6.

[5]K.Marx: *Ökonomisch-philosophische Manuskripte*, Leipzig 1974, p.190.

[6]Cf. A.Schaff: *Marxismus und das menschliche Individuum*, Wien 1965, pp.82-95; also his: *Marx oder Sartre. Versuch einer Philosophie des Menschen*, Wien 1966, pp.98-100.

instrumental treatment of the human person. For if man is "a real use of social being"[7], then he loses his ontic and axiological autonomy for the sake of the collective. Society in a way absorbs the individual man since it constitutes and wholly contains him. Although Marxism does not reify the state, still it restricts man's real personality to social dimensions of life. "Man is a man only in unity with other people and only thanks to this unity"[8]. Thus, there are no men beyond society, as much as there can be no society beyond people.

The Marxist interpretation of the relation between individual man and society is contradictory to personalism. Sociopriorism and sociocentrism, contained in Marxist anthropology, turn society into an absolute and depreciate the human individual. For if "at the basis of the Marxist thesis about the genetic conditioning of the individual by society there is a conception of society as a real being, constituting the existence of the individual, providing the source and productive force of all the elements of the psychic and external life of the individual", then this individual "is necessarily degraded to the rank of an epiphenomenon of society, of a secondary and derivative element"[9]. In this interpretation man ceases to be a person by his very nature, but becomes a "collective" man. Contemporary re-interpretations of collectivism, proposed by Polish Marxists, do not change this theory in any significant way. They still accept the chronological and ontological priority of society over the chronological and ontological priority of society over the individual, the personal autonomy of the latter is still questioned and its rights are interpreted as a concession of the class collective. "Socialist collectivism" still remains collectivism[10]. If hominization is still explained by the phenomenon of socialization, then the priority and permanence of the human being are undermined. Man is no longer an individual person who in its nature contains factors creating the person. Man is a man exclusively as a social being, i.e. a member of a class, state etc. His psychic-spiritual life, personality and rights exist exclusively within the framework of social life and thanks to it[11]. Such an interpretation does not ensure ontical autonomy to the individual person in its relation to the social collective. That is why Christian personalism cannot accept such a solution, either in its philosophical aspect or in its axiological aspect. By his nature man is a social being but his personal "I" transcends the actual social-economic relations.

On the opposite pole to Marxist collectivism there is extreme individualism. It derives from the philosophical theories of atomism and nominalism, while today it is connected with the model of social-economic liberalism. Greek atomists claimed that only individual

---

[7]K.Marx: *Ökonomisch-philosophische Manuskripte*, op.cit., p.191.

[8]M.Fritzhand: *Człowiek, humanizm, moralność* [Man, Humanism, Morality], Warszawa 1966, p.91.

[9]T.Ślipko: "Pojęcie człowieka w świetle współczesnej filozoficznej antropologii marksistowskiej w Polsce" [The Conception of Man in the Light of Modern Marxist Philosophical Anthropology in Poland], *Zeszyty Naukowe KUL* 10 (1967) Nr.2, p.14 (3-16).

[10]M.Fritzhand: "Indywidualizm czy kolektywizm?" [Individualism or Collectivism?], *Człowiek i światopogląd*, (1972) Nr.2, pp.7-28.

[11]Cf. J.Y.Calvez: *Le pensée de Karol Marx*, Paris 1956, pp.401 ff.

beings have real existence, whereas wholes are merely products of the human mind. The adherents of nominalism also ascribed reality only to individuals, reducing composites and universals to the rank of abstractions. The proper creators of individualism and liberalism include: Thomas Hobbes († 1679), John Locke († 1794), and Jean Jacques Rousseau († 1778). It was their shared conviction that, in his nature, man is egoistic and asocial. Although social life is a threat to man, it is nevertheless indispensable for him. Its complete rejection leads to excesses of individual egoisms and anarchy in everyday life, and that is why "fear and reason" incline people to accept a vital compact in society. Hobbes suggested that in his nature man is hostile towards other people (***homo homini lupus***). The alternative of total egoism and general strife constitutes a premise for the acceptance of "the social contract"[12]. Social life is interpreted as "a play of egoisms" of human individuals, regulated by the accepted contracts. Society should be subordinated to the individual; its task consists in ensuring unhindered freedom of activity, especially in the domain of economic life. Every man is a sovereign for himself[13]. Thus, liberal individualism loses the idea of common good, since it explicates social good as a sum of the goods of particular people. On the other hand, the merit of liberalism is its defence of human rights, although, on the other, it is accompanied by a depreciation of the ideals of equality and social justice for the sake of freedom. The right of private property becomes an absolute, although contemporary liberalism allows state intervention in this respect.

Classical individualism is also followed by the French philosopher, Jean-Paul Sartre. According to him, our "brother", another man, is not only different from our "I" but is also its negation[14]. Other people restrict us, which unavoidably leads to conflicts. For instance, Sartre extensively analyses the phenomenology of human look[15]. When looking at us, another man deprives us of our subjectiveness; for we become for him merely objects of observation when we are more or less unobtrusively watched. This creates in us a sense of embarrassment, often of shame, which, in turn, deprives us of subjectiveness and privacy. That is why another man becomes an enemy that robs us of our existence[16]. Another man becomes a kind of a harbinger of nothingness, and, therefore, frequent contacts with other people lead to a diminishment or even annihilation of our "I". Antipathy and distrust towards people constitute man's natural attitude. Even the necessity of making use of the assistance of other people produces in us a sense of dependence. Man should therefore consciously accept the fate of a recluse. Another man is not our "brother" but a stranger and, frequently, an enemy. People are objects for each

---

[12]T.Hobbes: *Leviathan*, London - New York 1953; J.J.Rousseau: *Du contrat social*, Paris 1971; J.Majka: *Filozofia społeczna* [Social Philosophy], Warszawa 1982, pp.33-50.

[13]Only Hobbes, although he started with the assumptions of individualism, sympathized with the conception of a centralistic- totalitarian state.

[14]J.P.Sartre: *L'être et le néant*, Paris 1943, p.26.

[15]Ibid., pp.310-364.

[16]Ibid., pp.328,338-340,350 ff.

other but, out of necessity, they must live side by side, be in contact, while often hating and diminishing each other. Even the phenomenon of love is interpreted by Sartre in keeping with the assumptions of egocentric individualism. Love is to be an expansion of one's interests and plans. Because of love, man becomes a slave of another man, since one wants to be "the whole world" for the other. Human speech has also been interpreted as an attempt on the freedom of another man. Finally, Sartre reaches the shocking conclusion that other people are our hell[17]. Authentic community is therefore impossible. Self-realization is exclusively a work of an individual man, while social life is most often a threat to him.

The followers of liberalism are aware of their critical evaluation by their opponents, mainly because of their individualistic option. Still, they think that the neo-liberalism currently accepted no longer continues radical individualism. Michael Novak, author of *The Spirit of Democratic Capitalism*, admits that the individualistic model of social life departed from the traditional conception of society. Still, the tradition was connected with the no longer existing social-economic system, e.g., the rural system. The apologist of democratized capitalism proclaims an opinion that today even this system accepts multiple forms of collective life, especially productive-industrial assemblies (called "corporations")[18]. Liberalism acknowledges a mutual dependence of social groups and of countries; it also revalues the ethos of co-operation. Particularly highly esteemed are the family, trade unions, circles of friends etc. It is therefore possible to speak about a positive conception of the society of liberalism, and even about propagating various types of communities.

The liberal-individualistic conception of society is very sharply criticised by Marxism[19]. The social teaching of the Church also points to some drawbacks in the proposed social-economic model. In *Octogesima adveniens* Paul VI warns against the idealization of liberalism and states that "philosophical liberalism includes an erroneous claim about the autonomy of the individual in his activities, motivations and uses of freedom" (OA 35). The same Pope also notes the one-sidedness of the conception of freedom in individualism; namely, it was a freedom from something, rather than freedom to something. The sense of freedom is not a negation but co-participation - usually communal - in the realization of higher values. John Paul II points to another drawback of liberalism, namely, the depreciation of the dignity of abour for the sake of the priority of the capital (*Laborem exercens* 11-12). The same Pope also draws attention to the lack of sufficient concern of the rich North about the poor South; the former covers precisely countries of the liberal-capitalist model, while the latter is known as "the Third World" (*Sollicitudo rei socialis* 14-19).

In spite of its defence of the rights of the human individual, individualism provokes objections for many reasons. The picture of man it offers is one-sided and deformed. In

[17]J.P.Sartre: *Huis-Clos*, Paris 1947.

[18]M.Novak: *The Spirit of Democratic Capitalism*, New York 1982, Chap.6.

[19]Ibid., Chaps.15-19.

spite of egocentric tendencies, the human "I" is nevertheless capable of altruistic sacrifice for the sake of other persons. Society is not an aggregate of individuals of the same kind, but a co-operation and community of persons. The interpretation of social life proposed by liberalism has lost the idea of common good. And the latter is necessary for the functioning of society in a way appropriate for the requirements of humanism and ethics. The social unions discussed by M.Novak are based exclusively on tradition, emotional bonds, or economic interests. Still, there is no appreciation of the conception of common good which often requires a self-limitation of freedom. Individualistic liberalism quite rightly defends freedom but it does not seem to perceive that its conception of social life tolerates licence and ruthlessness of stronger individuals who take over power in society and then tyrannize others. Social-economic disproportions, which result from violation of the principles of equality and justice, provoke an intensification of sympathies to revolutionary solutions. Contemporary fascination with historical materialism of Marxism, evident in the countries of Latin America, provides appropriate confirmation. In spite of so many differences between them, liberal individualism and Marxist collectivism have one feature in common. Namely, they see in man primarily a material-biological individual, while underestimating the personal-spiritual dimension - its specificity, its correspondent values and goals[20]. Even the absolutization of the individual, typical of liberalism, distorts the sense of the human person and reduces man's activity to the material plane. A distorting mirror of individualism appears in Sartre's anthropology, pervaded by the apology of egoism and pessimism[21]. The trend has lost here the ability of recognizing one's "brother" in another man, perceiving in him only a threat or an enemy. And then, in fact, social life would turn into an imaginary hell.

(ii) Foundations of Social Life

The anthropology of Christian personalism is in opposition to both collectivism and individualism. Society is perceived as neither a result of a convention nor a creature equivalent to biological organism. The theory of collectivism deprives human individuals of their subjectiveness and autonomy, while the theory of individualism degrades social life to the level of egoistic patterns of behaviour. In neither case can one speak about the social life worthy of man as a person. Christian personalism accepts a double source of social life, namely, the person and values. Naturally, these are not separated realms of reality because they are organically connected. There are no persons without values and there are no values without persons[22]. The proper conception of social life is

[20]Cf. F.Copleston: *Studies of Logical Positivism and Existentialism*, London 1960, pp.111-112.

[21]Cf. S.Kowalczyk: "Jednostka a społeczeństwo w interpretacji egzystencjalizmu" [The Individual and Society in the Interpretation of Existentialism], *Studia Płockie* 10 (1982), pp.151-157.

[22]S.Kowalczyk: "Philosophical Concepts of Values", *Collectanea Theologica* 57 (1987), fasc.specialis, pp.115-129.

conditioned by a correct conception of man. Man is a substantial and personal being, a psycho-physical unity. He is rooted in the world of matter and biological life and, yet, he transcends them through the mental life of intellect and will. The person is a subject, a psychically interiorized being, shaping the rich world of lower and higher values. A natural horizon of each man is social life; it is there that his creative potentials and aspirations are actualized and the continuity of human history is ensured. Hence, society is not an effect of any convention, but it is man's natural calling.

Personalism constitutes a common platform of Christian thought which, however, does not exclude some differentiation in explicating the relations binding the individual with society[23]. Some authors (e.g. Eberhard Welty, A. Van Leeuven) stress the role of society as a whole. They believe that the social "whole" is more perfect than a "part" (human individual). Man exists in society and through society, and that is why the human person is subordinated to the common good of the whole. This interpretation, to some extent based on the writings of St.Thomas Aquinas[24], correctly emphasizes the idea of common good, yet, without a simultaneous overestimation of "the rights of the whole" to the disadvantage of individual persons.

Some other authors (e.g. E.Link) lay particular stress on the principle of complementarity[25]. They claim that the human person is a foundation of common good and that is why the aim of society is only a complementation of the actions of individuals. The complementarity principle constitutes the most important rule of social life. This opinion, in turn, perfectly illustrates the importance of the human person but it is inadequate in its appreciation of the role and requirements of common good in social life.

In his analysis of the relation between the individual and society, the French Thomist, Jacques Maritain, distinguished two levels in man, the individual and the person. Man as a material individual is subordinated to society, whereas as a personal spirit he is above society[26]. This conception has been questioned many times, also from the Christian point of view[27]. Maritain's opponents point out that the division of man into a person and an individual is unsatisfactory because all elements of human nature - both material and psychic - have a personal character. Obviously, the French Thomist did not question the fact that man, precisely as a person, is directed towards social life[28].

There have also been attempts at finding a middle way between the above conceptions of the relation "individual - society". For instance, T.Geppert accepts "the law of the

---

[23]Cf. E.Kurz: *Individuum und Gemeinschaft beim heiligen Thomas von Aquin*, München 1932, pp.9-18.

[24]*Summa Theologiae*, I-II,q.96,a.4,c.

[25]E.Link: *Das Subsidiaritätsprinzip. Sein und Bedeutung für die Sozialethik*, Freiburg im Br. 1955.

[26]J.Maritain: *Three Reformers*, New York 1970, pp.19-23; also his: *La personne et le bien commune*, Paris 1947, pp.27-34.

[27]J.Croteau: *Les fondements thomistes du personalisme de Maritain*, Ottawa 1955, pp.21,80-81.

[28]J.Majka: *Filozofia społeczna*, op.cit., pp.262-269.

interpolar centre"[29]. He observes that there are always certain tensions between individual men and society. Still, society exists thanks to interpersonal relations which create the unity of order. Social life is directed by two laws, the law of the whole (solidarity) and the law of complementarity. The former protects the interests of the whole community, while the latter - the interests of individual men.

Man, as a psycho-physical person, is a social being by nature. Directedness towards social life is encoded in man's ontic structure and it is actualized in action. Although man is a person, he is still a being that is accidental, finite and potential. He has no complete self-sufficiency, either biological or psychic. For this reason, he is directed towards the external world. Impersonal cosmos, although it is man's natural environment, cannot constitute a partner for man. A person is seeking contact with another person and that is why man is a social being. He is an authentically rational and free self from the first moment of his existence, but it is only social life that actualizes and develops his humanity. The human person is a co-existing (***mit-sein***) with others and that is why he forms various communities, such as family, the circles of professions and schools, social, national, ideological communities. Man has a social instinct and predispositions necessary for social life.

Social life is, first of all, man's need and necessity because in many respects he is not self-sufficient[30]. This is also evident on the biological-material plane. A human infant, deprived of social care (especially of family), is doomed to die. Even a grown-up man is capable of physical survival only with the help of society which provides him with food, tools, general and vocational education, protection from dangers. Contemporary man has grown used to high technological civilization, whose lack might expose him to quick ruin. Animals are stable and restricted in their needs, whereas man broadens the scope of his material and psychic needs. This, in turn, increases his economic and biological dependence on society. Today one can observe an extension of the period of education and vocational studies which also delays the achievement of independence of individual man.

Man's ontical predilections incline him to assume social life. The material-biological insufficiency of human individuals in their everyday lives forces them to form various social groups. However, it would be a mistake to think that it is precisely this fact that constitutes the essence of social life. An analogical ontical limitation also characterizes animals which, after all, do not create society in the strict sense of the word. Animals live in herds, not in communities. Thus, social life in its proper sense, although it is conditioned by material and biological needs, is initiated only on the psychic-personal plane[31]. Biological specimens constitute a species called ***homo sapiens***, but social

[29]Th.Geppert: *Teleologie der menschlichen Gemeinschaft*, Münster 1965.

[30]St.Thomas Aquinas: *Summa Theologiae*, II-II,q.188,a.8; *Contra Gentes* III, 85; In *Ethicam Nicom.* I,1,1.

[31]Cf. Cz.Strzeszewski (pseudonym: S.Jarocki): *Katolicka nauka społeczna* [Catholic Social Teaching], Paris 1954, pp.16-19.

community is co-created only by rational and free persons. Hence, in social life one may distinguish two levels: the lower level comprising man's somatic-biological aspect, and the higher level connected with the functioning of mental life.

As the analysis of the structure of human being indicates, social life is realized primarily on the level of psychic-spiritual life. Man's specific feature is his ability of self-transcendence. Man's authentic life is not an egocentric concentration on himself but a pursuit of community. It is not the very fact of becoming involved in social life that is important but rather its "quality". Only internal establishment in community ensures positive effects. Man's emotional-spiritual life develops within community and that is why, for instance, the upbringing of a child apart from its family is so difficult and even risky. A mature man also needs the psychic support of others, of his family, friends, neighbours. Only a benevolent atmosphere of community quarantees man's normal psychic life. The man who separates himself from others or is removed from social life suffers an impoverishment of his psychic life and often develops psychic distortions.

Man's psychic life has a dialogic-social character because it is a continuous communication of a variety of values, cognitive, moral, artistic, ideological etc. The human person, through its many-sided dynamics, is a social being. Life in society means an active exchange of values which requires, first of all, a mental-cognitive dynamics. Only a rational being identifies its current and future needs, perceives the scope and hierarchy of values, determines ends and means. Another element of social life is the human language (spoken or written) which enables a transmission of experiences, communication of messages and education of the young. Thanks to speech, the individual man need not discover everything by himself but he can learn from others. This takes place precisely on the level of social life. Man not only discovers the structure of the world but, thanks to his intellect, he can also transform and perfect it. The human person is called to co-create the cosmos[32]. Yet, it is possible only through social action. ***Homo rationalis*** is at the same time ***homo socialis***. Animals do not create society because they are incapable of intellectual cognition; they do not consciously set goals for themselves; they are incapable of creative inventiveness.

The essence of social life is the communication of values and for that reason man's will is a constant element in constructing authentic human assemblies[33]. Human intellect conditions a conscious and free choice of values, of ends and means, of a given life style. Social life is something necessary but its forms and range result from man's personal choice. At the same time, the foundation of the permanence of social relations is freedom. Freedom makes it possible to choose and create good which, by its nature, goes beyond the sphere of individual interests. A free and rational person creates a pro-social good which in the Catholic social teaching is described as "common good" (***bonum commune***). The communication of truth is complemented by the communication

---

[32]*Summa Theologiae*, I-II,q.91,a.2.

[33]O.Spann: *Gesellschaftslehre*, Leipzig 1930, pp.130 ff.; D.von Hildebrand: *Metaphysik der Gemeinschaft*, Regensburg 1975, pp.99 ff.

of good in a variety of its forms. Moral life, connected with the realization and exchange of values, always has a social character. The family, the school, labour teams, groups of friends and acquaintances, various kinds of organizations - they all significantly influence the formation of moral paradigms and attitudes. Man's individual conscience is also affected by the social moral atmosphere. Man makes his own ethical choices but the approval or disapproval of his social environment exerts a strong influence on his behaviour, scale of perceived values and accepted moral criteria. Thus, although social life implies co-operation on the material-somatic plane, it is also expressed in the proper way in mental-spiritual life, i.e., cognitive, appetitive, and axiological. Intellectual cognition is a basis of evaluation, although both are interpenetrating. A more perfect cognition reveals a richer scale of human possibilities and choices, but it does not automatically guarantee better choices. The latter demand an appropriate formation of conscience and exercise of the will, which, again, is impossible without participation in social life. Values are the elements which unite society most deeply because they shape it from within, through man's mind and will. Human society is primarily a community of values - their realization, propagation, and protection.

(iii) Society as Community

Man is ontically directed towards community and he desires to live in it. But what is community? The classics of Christian thought were undertaking attempts to define it. St.Augustine described the community of the state as an organized assembly of rational beings united by love of common good[34]. In this description love was accepted as the material of social life; naturally, it was love inspired by intellectual cognition. St. Thomas Aquinas called community a conjunction of people acting in harmony to achieve a common goal[35]. This description essentially repeats the formulation of St.Augustine, although it speaks about the common goal instead of common good.

Each community contains a material element and a formal element. The former concerns the multiplicity of human individuals as members of a certain community. The formal element denotes the bond which unites rational and free persons organized in a certain way. Community is not a substantial being but only an accidental-relational one. Nor is it a mental being because the unity of people has a real, though only relational, character[36]. Community is a result of the co-operation of those people who perceive some common goal and, hence, who coordinate their actions for its realization. Community (from Greek ***koinonia***; Latin ***communio***) denotes mutual understanding and co-operation.

---

[34]"Populus est coetus multitudinis rationalis rerum quam diligit concordi communione sociatus": *De civitate Dei* 19,24 PL 41, 655.

[35]"Cum societas nihil aliud esse videatur, quam adunatio hominum ad unum aliquid communiter agendum": *Contra impugnantes Dei cultum et religionem*, c.3.

[36]*Summa Theologiae*, I,q.28,a.1; q.77,a.1,ad 5.

Authentic community is possible only in the world of rational beings since only such beings are capable of recognizing supra-individual aims. It is indispensable to go beyond the realm of one's individuality and the current moment. The recognition of social aims is fulfilled in the appetitive sphere and through the decision of the will concerning joint realization which, naturally, is impossible without at least a certain minimum of sympathy to shared values. Hence, the material of community means intentional directedness to a certain good. Although concrete social relations usually have a categorial character and that is why they are unstable, yet, thanks to an organic connection with the sphere of absolute values it is possible to speak about the transcendental dimension of these relations[37].

An ideal society is the one which constitutes a community. It can be formed only by rational, free persons, and that is why animals are incapable of accomplishing this aim. A community is not an organism[38]. A biological organism is a substantial being, while community is not. People exist before the whole - the society, while cells are ontically derivative in respect to the organism. A social bond does not come into being mechanically, as in the case of a living organism, but is a result of a conscious and free choice of persons. Community is not an ontological hyper-person; only in the juridical-moral sense can one speak about society as a person. Social life has its source in persons, in their consciousness, intellect, will, conscience. When the cognitive and appetitive-emotional spheres are integrated in pursuit of certain values, a community comes into being. An average society has utilitarian aims, while community is founded on higher values[39]. Community has no existence beyond or above persons because it exists in them. Persons cannot be turned into instruments in social life since it is their good that constitutes the sense of social life. On the other hand, social community has nothing to do with individual or group egoism, since it is founded on the idea of common good.

Community is a polymorphic reality, for it exists in a variety of forms. There are also various classifications of social life. Some authors write about duo-personal and pluri-personal communities[40]. A duo-personal community occurs, for instance, in friendship or marriage. A pluri-personal community has more variants and may appear as a family, clan, tribe, nation, state. One may also speak about material and formal communities; the former may be exemplified by the nation, and the latter by the state. Sociology, in turn, distinguishes micro- and macro-communities.

The human person is open in both cognitive and appetitive-emotional spheres to other people. Our individual "I" wants to initiate dialogue with the "you" of another person, whose final result is "we", the germ of community[41]. The life of the human person goes

---

[37]J.Majka: *Filozofia społeczna*, op.cit., pp.290-294.

[38]D.von Hildebrand: *Metaphysik der Gemeinschaft*, op.cit., pp.127 ff.

[39]H.E.Hengstenberg: *Philosophische Anthropologie*, Münster 1984, pp.106 ff.

[40]D.von Hildebrand: *Metaphysik der Gemeinschaft*, op.cit., pp.114, 136 ff, 171 ff.

[41]M.Buber: "Ich und Du" [in:] *Das dialogische Prinzip*, Heidelberg 1965, pp.10-20, 66-68, 100 ff.

beyond the scope of individual experiences and aims. Nobody is a closed monad or a lonely island, and that is why man desires to meet and be united with other people. We feel the need of social life, i.e., contact, conversation, dialogue, understanding, friendship, love, help. Cognitive communication is complemented by the communication of good which initiates social life. Friendship and love mean a unification of two persons, "I" and "you", yet without destroying their autonomy. An opposition to the interpersonal relation "I - you" is found in the relation "I - it" which leads to a reification of another man. The personalistically experienced relation "I - you" requires the fulfilment of several conditions. Only a person can be a subject and an object of such a relation because only a person can say "I am". Next, it is important that the object of such a relation, i.e. "you", be always apprehended as an ontological subject. This, in turn, implies the recognition of the otherness of another person, acceptance of this person's subjectiveness and appropriate rights. A further condition of the proper experiencing of the "I - you" relation is the sense of mutual responsibility for each other. The persons who are friends or who are in love are to be not only close to each other but also for each other. The "I - you" relation, experienced in a personal way, forms a micro-community, i.e. "we". It is a community of mutual cognition, understanding, benevolence, devotion. One's own interests and aims are then subordinated to common good.

An authentic community is never egoistic and for that reason the "we" cannot be closed within the narrow circle of the affairs of two people. A duo-personal community is usually transformed into a pluri-personal community. Friendship does not consist in an egocentric infatuation with one another. A marriage begins a family, the family co-creates a nation. In turn, the love of one's nation should not turn into chauvinism but should be connected with goodwill to other nations. And thus there exists a logical and axiological transition from the community of "we" to a general community of all humankind. And only then can one speak about the love of every man as one's brother. Brother is not merely a moral category but also an ontological one. True love means the involvement of the individual "I" in a community, in a family, nation, humankind. The consciousness of shared aims and communion of values constitute the sources of social community. It is precisely there that human potentials are realized and humanity is developed.

It is also worthwhile noting one more semantic distinction, namely, that between community and association[42]. Community (German ***Gemeinschaft***) denotes every assembly founded on biological ties (family, nation) and constituting a basis of common history, tradition, language, often religion, ethos etc. A community of this kind usually shares some common good whose realization, protection and development constitute an integrating factor. In social awareness there persists a strong consciousness of the "we" which is a foundation of spiritual self-identity. On the other hand, the community of the association type (German ***Gesellschaft***) is an artificial creation, a result of reflection and free decision. Incorporation in such a community occurs through accession, which may

---

[42]F.Tönies: *Gemeinschaft und Gesellschaft*, Stuttgart 1887; J.Majka: *Filozofia społeczna*, op.cit., pp.306-314.

later on be withdrawn. Family and national membership has occurred without our will, while state membership is no longer so stable. Community involves us internally, while association usually means only a partial participation in jointly undertaken tasks (it does not "reach" all the sectors of our personality). Such associations are encountered, for instance, in trade unions or various clubs.

(iv) The Axiology of Social Life

Our characterization of the axiology of social life will emphasize mainly two elements, namely, the principle of solidarity and the social consequences of the command of the love of one's brother. The principle of solidarity is strictly connected with the idea of common good[43]. This principle has an ontological, legal and ethical character. It has an ontical character because its observation conditions the existence of community. It also constitutes a legal and ethical norm because it binds all the members of a concrete community. Naturally, it differs from detailed juridical norms whose infringement entails determined penitentiary consequences. The principle of solidarity is a general postulate which describes an ideal of social life. The role of this principle is strongly emphasized by the trend of the so-called social solidarity (H.Pesch, O. von Nell-Breuning). Solidarity differs from universalism or internationalism, in that it implies a variety of persons and their subjectiveness in social life.

Practically all man's actions are realized in social life but only some of them have a social character in the proper sense of the term. Social actions are those which are directed towards common good. The latter is accepted internally, i.e. consciously and voluntarily, rather than being enforced by some social power. People are united in society precisely by common good, by common needs, aims, activities. The idea of common good derives from man's ontic structure but at the same time it should also be referred to the axiological plane. Common good is perceived only by rational beings and realized only by free persons[44]. Common good is "a social-moral value whose contents is the fullness of the personal development of all the members of societies, realized by them together on the basis of natural human properties and institutional social conditions"[45]. Community is an assembly of persons whose integration results from their being directed towards common good. Community is what it is thanks to common good. The latter constitutes the formal principle of every social being, of the family, nation, state, association etc. Even accidental communities have a common goal, if only a temporary one. Natural communities and communities organized for the realization of long-lasting aims accept common good as superior in respect to individual aims. Common good has

[43]Cz.Strzeszewski: *Katolicka nauka społeczna*, op.cit., pp.395-399.

[44]Cf. J.Krucina: *Dobro wspólne. Teoria i zastosowanie* [The Common Good. Theory and Application], Wrocław 1972.

[45]J.Kondziela: *Filozofia społeczna* [Social Philosophy], Lublin 1972, p.31; cf. also ibid., Chaps.1-2.

a double character, personal and institutional. The former concerns a group of people of a certain community, while the latter is a set of institutions and structures necessary for its functioning. In the interpretation of Christian personalism the essence of common good is the good of the people living in a community. Institutions and structures of power, though necessary, constitute a secondary element of common good. For that reason common good cannot be identified with the profits or interests of the currently ruling elites, because the sense of the latter consists in common good of the whole society.

The relation between the common good of a society and the good of an individual is a complex problem. Individualism claims that social integration mainly amounts to the skill of defending the interests of particular citizens. Totalitarianism, in turn, proposes a complete subordination of the good of individuals to the interests of the society. Without questioning the difficulties and possible tensions, Christian personalism acknowledges the convergence of the good of the human person and the common good of society. St.Thomas Aquinas actually claims that it is something more than convergence, namely, the good of persons and social common good in fact mutually imply each other. A complete good of a human person is impossible without referring to it the good of the society[46], since many individual aims can be realized only in the social dimension. Man has certain duties towards society and therefore the range of common good does not depend on his arbitrary decision. Yet, at the same time, common (universal) good and the good of individuals differ not only quantitatively but also qualitatively; they differ in their formal reasons[47]. For that reason personalism questions the validity of individualism, especially its egocentrism and interpretation of human nature. After all, the individual "I" is not threatened or impoverished by the social "we" because society enriches the human person in multiple ways. By giving something of himself to others, man develops spiritually. That is why the priority of common good over individual interests should be accepted. This principle is applicable to qualitatively homogeneous values, especially economic and those connected with biological life. Therefore, society has a right to demand sacrifice from individuals, especially at moments crucial for its further existence.

Speaking about common good, Christian personalism is by no means in agreement with the views of collectivism. Therefore, the priority of common good over individuals has certain restrictions. The spiritual good of the human person is higher than the economic values of societies and, as a result, the state cannot demand from its citizens a renouncement of their worldviews, moral or political convictions etc.[48] Social and state authorities cannot issue unethical orders and enforce their execution. There is no authentic common good when an internal good of the human person is destroyed, for instance, freedom, conscience, subjectiveness. Man is not a passive cell of society, and that

---

[46]"Bonum proprium non potest esse sine bono communi": *Summa Theologiae*, II-II,q.47,a.10,ad 2. Cf. I-II,q.92,a.1,ad 3.

[47]*Summa Theologiae*, II-II,q.58,a.7,ad 2.

[48]*Contra Gentes*, III,113; *De virtutibus in communi*, q.unica, a.9.

is why social norms and structures cannot infringe on the inalienable rights of the human person. Man has not received these rights from the society because they result from his ontical structure and personal dignity. Authentic common good is achieved only through the realization of the good of the persons constituting the community, and not against their good. This is formulated in the principle of complementarity which protects the good of the human person[49]. Therefore, there is no contradiction of interests between the individual and the community. On the other hand, there persists a chronic opposition between the "I" of the human person and the totalitarian model of society which consciously renounces the separateness and richness of human persons for the sake of a specifically understood social interest (in practice it is usually the interest of the ruling elites of power). In his encyclical Pacem in terris John XXIII set up a catalogue of man's fundamental rights. The questioning and violation of these rights amounts to the destruction of common good of society whose aim and sense is the development of the human person.

In the interpretation of Christian personalism another element of the axiology of social life is the principle of the love of one's brother. This is a basic norm of human life, in both individual and social dimensions. The words of Christ are quite explicit: "This is my commandment: love one another" (*John* 15, 12). The love of another man constitutes a criterion of belonging to Christianity (1 *John* 4, 20-21). St. James very sharply condemned the rich whose faith was not accompanied by deeds since they did not share their goods with the needy (*James* 2, 14-19; 5, 1-6). Christ Himself threatened with damnation precisely for that lack of love and charity (*Matthew* 25, 31-46). The Holy Scripture demands from Christians the realization of social virtues such as justice, solidarity, responsibility, mutual assistance.

The role of love in social life is so important because it alone guarantees fully man's subjectiveness. The depreciation of love in contemporary social thought derives from Hegel who, as a basis for his explication of social mechanisms, accepted the dialectics of the relation "master - slave"[50]. In this interpretation the predominant social attitude is to be opposition and strife rather than love and solidarity. The idea of social justice, when separated from the idea of love, is insufficient for personalistic social axiology. This is discussed by Pope John Paul II in his encyclical *Dives in misericordia* which points to the consequences of separating justice from love. "On behalf of supposed justice (e.g. historical and class justice), men are often broken, killed, deprived of freedom, robbed of their fundamental rights" (DM 12). Naturally, justice is a necessary factor of social order, but only love initiates interhuman personal relations. Love is certainly a foundation of social life, not only in a family but also in a macro-community[51]. On the other hand,

---

[49]Cz.Strzeszewski: *Katolicka nauka społeczna*, op.cit., pp.390-394.

[50]J.Y.Calvez, op.cit., pp.402 ff.

[51]D.von Hildebrand: *Metaphysik der Gemeinschaft*, op.cit., pp.32 ff., 315 ff, 324 ff. Although the author rightly recognizes love as the main medium of social life, he pays too little attention to the postulates of justice.

the love abstracted from the demands of justice is transformed into hypocritical cant. Justice is binding not only for individuals or classes but also for nations. That is why "the states cannot - without committing a crime - pursuit the expansion of their possessions by way of injuring or feloniously oppressing other nations" (John XXIII, *Pacem in terris* 92). Analysing the problem of international justice in his encyclical *Popularum progressio* (48-76), Pope Paul VI stressed the necessity of a more universal treatment of the command of the love of one's brother. The axiology of personalism is founded in equal measure on the commands of both justice and love. On behalf of justice collectivism departs from love, while individualism depreciates the role of justice, being satisfied with the ideal of love, if it mentions it at all. Christian personalism proclaims the inseparability of justice and love. Only their joint acceptance ensures the solution of the dilemmas of the relation "individual - community".

LITERATURE

ALBERT,K.: *Das gemeinsame Sein*, Sankt Augustin 1981.

BRUNNER,P.: *Der Mensch im Widerspruch*, Berlin 1937.

BUBER,M.: "Ich und Du" [in:] *Das dialogische Prinzip*, Heidelberg 1965.

CAMPBELL,T.: *Seven Theories of Human Society*, Oxford 1981.

DIEHL,K.: *Der Einzelne und die Gemeinschaft*, Jena 1940.

FRODL,F.: *Gesellschaftslehre*, Wien 1936.

GEPPERT,T.: *Teleologie der menschlichen Gemeinschaft*, Münster 1965.

GILSON,E.: *Le société de masse et sa culture*, Paris 1967.

JANSSENS,L.: *Personne et société*, Louvain 1939.

HILDEBRAND D.von: *Metaphysik der Gemeinschaft*, Regensburg 1975.

KONDZIELA,J.: *Osoba we wspólnocie* [The Person in Community], Katowice 1987.

KOWALCZYK,S.: "Jednostka a społeczeństwo w interpretacji marksistowskiej" [The Individual and Society in Marxist Interpretation], *Studia Płockie* 10 (1982), pp.159-168.

KRUCINA,J.: *Dobro wspólne. Teoria i zastosowanie* [The Common Good. Theory and Application], Wrocław 1972.

KURZ,E.: *Individuum und Gemeinschaft bei heiligen Thomas von Aquin*, München 1932.

LANGEMAYER,B.: *Der dialogische Personalismus*, Paderborn 1962.

LINK,E.: *Das subsidiaritätsprinzip. Sein und Bedeutung für die Sozialethik*, Freiburg im Br. 1955.

LOTZ,J.B.: *Ich - Du - Wir. Fragen um den Menschen*, Frankfurt am M. 1968.

LÖWITH,K.: *Das Individuum in der Rolle des Mitmenschen*, Bonn 1969.

MAJKA,J.: *Filozofia społeczna* [Social Philosophy], Warszawa 1982.

Man and Society, New York 1966.

MARITAIN,J.: *La personne et le bien commune*, Paris 1947.

MARITAIN,J.: *Man and the State*, Chicago 1951.

MARITAIN,J.: *Principes d'une politique humaniste*, Paris 1945.

NOVAK,M.: *The Spirit of Democratic Capitalism*, New York 1982.

ORAISON,M.: *Etre avec la relation à autrui*, Paris 1968.

PANNENBERG,W.: *Anthropologie in theologischer Perspektive*, Göttingen 1983.
PLAMENATZ,J.: *Man and Society*, London 1965.
PLESSNER.H.: "Diesseits der Utopie" [in:] *Immer noch philosophische Anthropologie? Soziale Rolle und menschliche Natur*, Köln 1966.
POCOCK,D.F.: *Social Anthropology*, New York 1961.
POPPER,K.R.: *The Open Society and Its Enemies*, London 1948.
RIEZLER,K.: *Man. Mutable and Immutable. The Fundamental Structure of Social Life*, Chicago 1950.
SPANN,O.: *Gesellschaftslehre*, Leipzig 1930.
THEUNISSEN,M.: *Der Andere. Studien zur Sozialontologie der Gegenwart*, Berlin 1965.
TOULEMOND,R.: *L'essence de la société selon Husserl*, Paris 1962.
WALGRAVE,J.H.: *Cosmos, personne et société*, Paris 1968.
WELTY,B.: *Gemeinschaft und Einzelmensch*, Leipzig 1935.
WILDMAN,G.: *Personalismus. Solidarismus und Gesellschaft*, Wien 1961.
WOJTYŁA,K.: "Osoba: podmiot i wspólnota" [The Person: The Subject and Community], *Roczniki filozoficzne* 24 (1976), Nr.2, pp.5-39.

Chapter 8

Humanism and Personalism

(i) Humanism

The presentation of the philosophy of man outlined above cannot neglect a problem so frequently discussed today, namely, the questions of humanism and personalism. The mutual relation of the two categories is not always correctly explained and, hence, it often becomes a cause of many misunderstandings. The conception of humanism is broader in its scope than that of personalism and therefore we shall start with its analysis first.

Today the category of humanism seems to be enjoying its peak popularity. First of all, the lively interest in the philosophy of man results in a special sensitivity to the problems of humanism. For if we speak about man's nature and calling, we are also seeking the ways of the development of humankind. The variety of the kinds of anthropology (philosophical, cultural, sociological, natural, theological etc.) makes it necessary to distinguish various aspects of humanism, among others, to introduce a distinction between theoretical and pragmatic humanism. The conception of humanism covers a rich set of generally acknowledged values, cognitive, artistic, moral etc. Their mutual relations and their hierarchy are understood in various ways, often antithetically, yet, in spite of that, humanism constitutes the most neutral plane of ideological encounters. Finally, humanism provides a bridge between various trends of broadly understood culture, as well as between religious, ideological, social, philosophical and other currents.

Still, the vitality of the idea of humanism does not necessarily contribute to its semantic clarity and unambiguousness. The term itself (from Latin ***humanus*** - human) has been introduced into European culture only at the beginning of the nineteenth century. It was used for the first time in 1808 by F.I.Niethammer, a German pedagogue, who postulated a model of education and upbringing founded on ancient culture[1]. In 1848, in his *Economic-Philosophical Manuscripts* Karl Marx made a distinction between theoretical humanism, i.e. atheism, and practical humanism, i.e. communism, as a socio-economical model. In 1859 G.Voigt used the term humanism to describe the European culture of the Renaissance (the 14th - 16th centuries). In turn, F.C.S.Schiller

[1]*Die Streit des Philanthropismus und Humanismus in der Theorie der Erziehungs-Unterrichts unserer Zeit*, Jena 1808.

(† 1937) understood humanism as an opposition to rationalism and, hence, he postulated that philosophy should take into account all man's impressions and experiences[2].

Here we are interested mainly in philosophical humanism which is also highly differentiated. Its elements can be found already in Pythagoras, namely, in his anthropocentric view of reality. The maxim that "Man is the measure of all things" is particularly emphasized in lay humanism. However, it has been rightly noted that the leading founders of the Hellenic culture, namely, Plato, the author of the *Dialogues*, and Aristotle, the writer of the *Metaphysics and Nicomachean Ethics*, were men far from relativism[3]. Greek and Roman culture, in turn, constituted the frame of reference for many Fathers of the Church, which is particularly evident in the case of St.Augustine. The Christian Middle Ages also took advantage of the achievements of ancient thought; among others, St.Thomas Aquinas was a creative continuator of Aristotle. Yet, it is a common conviction that a particularly important role was played by the humanism of the Renaissance. It found its expression mainly in the domain of literature, art and music, but could also be observed in philosophy, primarily as a return to Platonism and Aristotelianism, interest in man and his place in the cosmos. A classical example of a Renaissance humanist can be found in the Italian poet, Francesco Petrarch († 1374)[4]. The nineteenth century witnessed great popularity of lay humanism, often of an anti-religious and anti-Christian character. Finally, today there occur many variants of humanism, Christian, existential, phenomenological, Marxist, scientistic-evolutionary.

This plurality of humanisms makes a description of the conception particularly difficult. An attempt at defining humanism can make use of several methods, historical, comparative, linguistic, and ontological[5]. The first two methods are connected with the historical development of the conception of humanism, which has already been remarked above. The linguistic and ontological methods can, in turn, be combined, thus indicating the close tie between the conception of humanism and the interpretation of the human being. We shall return to this point when discussing the dominant forms of contemporary humanism. Most often the term humanism is applied to denote such a doctrinal or existential attitude which perceives the highest value of visible reality in man[6]. Wincenty Granat defines humanism as "a set of theories and practical attitudes affirming and accepting the postulate of the dignity and value of every human person as well as its freedom, inviolability of rights, and especially the possibilities of individual and social

[2]Schiller's pragmatism is not identical with the acceptance of Pythagoras's relativism.

[3]W.Jaeger: *Humanism and Theology*, Milwaukee 1943, pp.40-56.

[4]W.Pater: *Renaissance. Studies in Art and Poetry*, New York 1959.

[5]The first three methods have been examined by M.Fritzhand: "O pojęciu humanizmu metodologicznie" [Speaking Methodologically about the Conception of Humanism], [in:] *Humanizm socjalistyczny*, Warszawa 1969, pp.85-103.

[6]This description refers to a remark by St.Thomas Aquinas that the human person is something most perfect in nature. Cf. *Summa Theologiae*, I, q.29, a.3.

development"[7]. Each description is to some extent controversial, because it is a result of some accepted doctrinal or methodological assumptions (not always with full awareness). The term humanism may cover all those philosophical trends which accept man's ontical specificity (phenomenological or ontological), psycho-physical integrity of his nature, his subjectiveness, activeness, relations with society, ability of creating a culture, and which are opposed to an instrumental treatment of the human person. In man humanism always sees an end, never a means of realizing others aims.

The ideas of humanism are connected with the philosophy of being, anthropology, an accepted worldview, axiology etc., and that is why they change together with the latter. There are several criteria used to distinguish varieties of humanism. In the subjective respect one may distinguish the following forms of humanism: pragmatic, ontological, and ethical. A pragmatic-epistemological variant of humanism appeared in Schiller who interpreted the world through man's experiences and his mental activities. Ontological humanism recognizes man as the highest being, either in the absolute sense (and then it is atheistical humanism) or in a relative sense (which is the case of theistic humanism). In turn, ethical-social humanism regards man as the central value of the universe, which should be ascribed priority over the world of things.

Having in mind the relation between individual people and society, one may distinguish three forms of humanism: collectivist, individualistic and communal. Collectivist humanism, particularly typical of Marxism, regards individual people as functions and products of social life. Individualistic humanism, connected with the doctrine of liberalism, treats the state as a guardian of private-individual interests. Finally, social-communal humanism, accepted by Christian philosophy and theology, emphasizes the ontological foundations of social life, simultaneously perceiving its formal basis in the category of common good.

J.Maritain, having in mind the problem of the Absolute, distinguished two types of humanism, theocentric and anthropocentric[8]. Theocentric humanism accepts God as the First Cause of the world and man's ultimate aim. On the other hand, anthropocentric humanism, especially in its extreme variety, endows man with the self-creating function on both ontological and axiological planes (cognitive, moral, social). Theocentric humanism has a religious-eschatological character, being opened to the reality of God and the realm of absolute values, both natural and sacral. Anthropocentric human often has a naturalistic-secular character, negating the transcendence of man and God, acknowledging the priority of economic values over the spiritual ones, and accepting the relativity of truth and moral good. The latter form of humanism refers to Greek - Roman antiquity and the epoch of the Renaissance, whereas theocentric humanism is usually connected with the acceptance of religion. Moderate anthropocentrism does not exclude

---

[7]W.Granat: *U podstaw humanizmu chrześcijańskiego* [At the Foundations of Christian Humanism], Poznań 1976, p.46.

[8]*True Humanism*, New York 1938, pp. 19 ff.

theocentrism by any means, as exemplified by Christianity[9]. God's ontical priority over the world of creatures does not undermine man's exceptional status in the world, man being regarded as its centre and culmination (*Gaudium et spes* 12).

History of philosophical anthropology makes it possible to distinguish between personalistic and non-personalistic variants of humanism. The former emphasizes man's qualitative differentiation as a person from the extra-human world. Such humanism is accepted by I.Kant (man is always an aim in itself, never a means), M.Scheler (man is a person inspired by love and discovering personal God through values), M.Heidegger (man is a being that discovers truth and is called to be faithful to that truth). Personalistic humanism is especially stressed by Christian philosophy which interprets the human being as a person - subject, whose permanent attributes include spiritual life irreducible to biological life. Non-personalistic humanism also occurs in many variants, among others, as pantheistic and materialistic. Oriental pantheism questions man's individual personality, reducing it - in this or in future life - to the a-personal Original Unity. L.Feuerbach combined lay humanism with a conviction that man as a species is an absolute and an object of natural-immanent religion. Nonpersonal humanism is also characteristic of Marxism, according to which hominisation is a result of man taking up labour and social life, whereas mental-spiritual life is a product of the economic base.

Naturally, the classifications of humanism presented above are not the only ones. Bearing in mind an ontological interpretation of man's nature, one may distinguish three forms of humanism: extremely static, typical of Platonic anthropology and the pantheism of the old-Hindu thought; evolutionary-processual, characteristic of Marxism, A.N.Whitehead and P.Teilhard de Chardin; and active-personalistic, encountered in St. Augustine, St.Thomas Aquinas, H. Bergson, and M. Blondel. André Niel, in turn, perceived in the culture of contemporary world the following types of humanism: Christian (G.Marcel), spiritualistic (K.Jaspers), Marxist, existentialist (J.P.Sartre), heroic (F.Nietzsche), evolutionist, and scientistic[10]. The author is trying to order somehow this plurality of humanisms and distinguishes two predominant trends among them, namely, anthropomorphic and cosmic[11]. Among the former he included existentialism, Marxism and Christianity, while among the latter - the humanisms based on the idea of cosmic evolution.

In the survey of contemporary lay varieties of humanism an important position is taken by humanism inspired by Marxism. In his writings Marx uses the term humanism to denote the following elements: postulative-Promethean atheism, interpreted as the liberation of man from the Absolute; acknowledgement of labour and society as ontical-creative factors of human nature; socio-economic emancipation; rejection of religion regarded as spiritual alienation; and the postulate of man's axiological-moral

---

[9]W.Granat: *U podstaw humanizmu chrześcijańskiego*, op.cit., passim.

[10]*Les grandes appels de l'humanisme contemporain*, Paris 1966, p.9.

[11]Ibid., pp.11-17.

autonomy[12]. Marxists describe humanism as an affirmation of man's ontical and moral autonomy, i.e. recognizing man as his own creator, a self-existent centre of life, the highest value, and an exclusive creator of moral norms in both individual and social life[13]. Man, or, speaking more precisely, collective man, has thus been turned into his own demiurge and saviour. That is why "man himself should grant himself his own rights"[14]. The foundations of the Marxist theory of humanism are various, e.g. historical (the Renaissance, ancient and 18th-century materialism, Hegelian pantheism), philosophical (dialectical and historical materialism), and socio-economic (communism understood as the abolishment of private ownership of means of production). The adherents of Marxism particularly emphasize the following features of their variety of humanism: radicalism - destruction by force of the social and economic structures of capitalism; autonomy - the negation of God and the whole supernatural domain, the postulate of class struggle and revolution as necessary means for the realization of the principles of social justice and equality, combining the love of people towards their own class with hatred of other classes; optimism - a vision of a classless society; eudemonism - realization of complete happiness on earth; collectivism - priority of society over the interests of human individuals[15].

The theory of Marxist humanism is a conglomerate of valid and controversial elements, and of realistic and utopian conceptions. The former include the ideas of social justice and equality, the condemnation of exploitation and injustice, a revaluation of labour, the postulate of the subjectiveness of the worker[16]. In turn, utopian is the ideal of a classless society, based on the common or social ownership of means of production, in which, ***ex definitione***, all social evil is to disappear[17]. Marxist historical materialism is an apotheosis of struggle and violence, uncritical glorification of the proletariat as a collective saviour from socio-economic serfdom, utopian belief in the disappearance of social stratification and in ideal justice, depreciation of man's existential problems

---

[12]S.Kowalczyk: *Z problematyki dialogu chrześcijańsko- marksistowskiego* [On the Problems of the Christian-Marxist Dialogue], Warszawa 1977, pp.147-180.

[13]A.Schaff: *Marxismus und das menschliche Individuum*, op.cit., pp.220-226.

[14]M.Fritzhand: "Humanizm w filozofii i etyce Marksa" [Humanism in Marx's Philosophy and Ethics] [in:] *Humanizm i kultura świecka* [Humanism and Lay Culture], Warszawa 1958, p.209. Cf. A. and J.Kuczyńscy: *Humanizm socjalistyczny* [Socialist Humanism], Warszawa 1966; T.Płużański: *Człowiek między niebem a ziemią* [Man between the Heaven and Earth], Warszawa 1977.

[15]A.Schaff: *Marxismus ...*, op.cit., pp.219-238; *Humanizm socjalistyczny*, ed.by T.M.Jaroszewski, Warszawa 1980; *Humanizm socjalistyczny a osobowość człowieka pracy* [Socialist Humanism and the Personality of the Worker], ed.by J.Jędrzycki, Warszawa 1980.

[16]S.Kowalczyk: "Christian and Marxist Theory of Liberation", *Occasional Papers on Religion in Eastern Europe*, 7 (1987), Nr.1.

[17]This is admitted by A.Schaff: *Marxismus ...*, op.cit., pp.233-238.

(happiness, sense of life and death, individual immortality), aprioristic hostility towards religion as a fundamental dimension of man's life, extreme apriorism[18].

There are still other forms of lay humanism whose common element is postulative-voluntaristic atheism as an arbitrary option. J.S.Huxley was a propagator of scientistic-evolutionary humanism and he maintained that in the future science would take the place of religion in its formative-moral and social functions. J.P.Sartre, in turn, propagated extremely individualistic humanism, claiming that freedom constitutes man's essence and that is why it cannot be surrendered to God or society. Existential-pessimistic humanism was proclaimed by Albert Camus; in his interpretation, man's calling consists in bringing help to the needy, although evil is predominant and permanent. Ontical humanism is represented by Nicolai Hartmann who suggested that authentic morality demands man's autonomy, i.e., a rejection of God as the giver of ethics.

In the trend of personalistic humanism a leading role is played by Christian humanism[19]. However, the latter is by no means monolithic and static because it also appears in a variety of forms. The Augustinian trend of Christian humanism emphasizes the activity of the will and the emotional domain (especially of love) and it reveals the dynamic role of values in man's life[20]. Thomistic humanism explains the structure of man as a personal being, his faculties, attributes and activities, thanks to which the person is the most perfect being in nature and therefore owns special dignity. Thomistic-phenomenological humanismis characteristic of Cardinal Karol Wojtyła, the author of *Osoba i czyn* [The Person and the Act]. He represents an apprehension of man in his concrete activity, in his internal act and in personal experiencing of values. There is also a Christian-existential variety of humanism initiated by G.Marcel who has most clearly demonstrated the priority of personal values ("being") over economic values ("having"). In the category of Christian humanism one should also include dialectical humanism of Jean Lacroix, social humanism of Emmanuel Mounier, integral humanism of Jacques Maritain, and the humanism of Vaticanum II. The plane common to Christian humanism is the affirmation of the ontical specificity of man in his surrounding world, connected with the psycho-physical richness of his nature, subjectiveness, activeness of intellect and will, ability to create spiritual culture, and inclination to form a social-personal community. Christian humanism is inseparably connected with personalism.

The multiplicity of ideas and trends of humanism is an evident fact. Still, this plurality does not discredit the very conception of humanism, nor does it justify a shift towards the position of ideological-moral relativism. The clamorous boasting of the idea of humanism

---

[18]The evaluation of Marxism can be carried out in various aspects, such as historical, systemic-immanent logic, metaphysical, ethical, pragmatic etc.

[19]R.Rombers and R.Rieks: "Humanismus" [in:] *Historisches Wörterbuch der Philosophie*, Basel 1974, vol.3, cc.1217-1232.

[20]S.Kowalczyk: *Człowiek i Bóg w nauce św, Augustyna* [Man and God in the Teachings of St.Augustine], Warszawa 1987, part II: "Człowiek i świat wartości" [Man and the World of Values].

need not be connected with authentic and full humanism. What is "integral humanism", to use J.Maritain's term? And what disqualifies apparent humanism? Nineteenth-and twentieth-century representatives of postulative atheism indicate that full humanism demands a recognition of man's ontical and moral autonomy, i.e. a negation and rejection of God. That is why F.Nietzsche proclaimed the death of God, K.Marx understood philosophy as "a challenge of faith issued to all gods of the heaven and earth"[21], while J.P.Sartre saw in God a rival jealous of man's freedom. Atheistic humanism is a consequence of one-sided and distorted conceptions of both God and man. The conviction shared by the adherents of postulative atheism is the assumption that man is ... a superman. This was openly stated by F.Nietzsche; L.Feuerbach perceived the fullness of humanity only in a "generic man"; Marx turned into absolute the collective (especially the class of the proletariat); while Sartre regarded freedom as an absolute. However, man is not an absolute being, either on the plane of the material body or of psychic life. Man is not omnipotent, omniscient or infinitely good, hence all attempts of turning him into an absolute or a deity (resp. of the species, class, race, nation) lead to illusions. Quite often the claim that man is a superman or a creator of himself is simply false. Yet, neither is true the thesis that man is subhuman (***subhumanum***), e.g. a tamed, civilized animal (as Nietzsche claimed), a bundle of blind instincts (S.Freud), or a machine running towards self-destruction (structuralism). Authentic humanism demands an acceptance of the integrality of the human being in which both corporeity and spirituality, in spite of their natural connection, are irreducible to each other. Recognizing the existence of the human person as an immaterial subject, personalism is an indispensable condition of integral humanism.

Another criterion of authentic humanism is found in the integral character of the apprehension of man, of his nature, needs, and calling. For this reason a one-sided or reductionistic understanding of the human person abolishes humanism, e.g. by reducing man to the role of a link in biological evolution, a creature of blind chance, an effect of the play of economic forces etc. The French Thomist, Jacques Maritain, reserves the term integral humanism only for such humanism which

> "*essentially tends to render man more truly human and to make his original greatness manifest by causing him to participate in all that can enrich him in nature and in history (by 'concentrating the world in man', as Scheler has almost said, and by 'dilating man to the world'). It at once demands that man make use of all the potentialities he holds within him, his creative powers and the life of the reasons, and labour to make the powers of the physical world the instruments of his freedom*".[22]

---

[21]K.Marx: *Doktordissertation. Differenz der demokritischen und epikureischen Naturphilosophie*, Jena 1964, p.24.

[22]J.Maritain: *True Humanism*, op.cit., p.XII.

Karl Rahner briefly remarks that humanism means an attitude and a conviction that the shaping of the spirit makes man fully man[23]. That is the reason why materialistic reductionism undermines the very foundations and sense of humanism. Christian integral humanism perceives and revalues all the significant elements (or aspects) of the human person, i.e. the body and the spirit, biological and spiritual life, scientific search for truth and the social-moral praxis, man's autonomy but also his connection with God. Integral humanism acknowledges the need of man to become involved in society but it opposes any imperialism of class, nation or race.

The next criterion of full humanism is the respect of the principle: man - the person can only be an end, never a means. "The human person is and should be a principle, subject, and end of all social institutions" (*The Council Constitution about the Church in the Modern World* 25). Because of its inalienable dignity, rationality and moral sensitivity, the human person should never be apprehended instrumentally. It cannot be treated instrumentally even by society and therefore any form of dictatorship, infringing on man's subjectiveness and freedom, breaks the requirements of humanism. The beautiful phrase, "Man is the highest value", turns into an empty slogan when, on behalf of anonymous society, present or future, the health and life of concrete people are exposed to danger and, even more so, when their fundamental personal rights are ignored. Obviously, the rights are organically interconnected with duties towards society but society is not an arbitrary decision-maker in respect to human rights. The foundation of the latter is perceived by Christian humanism in the dignity of the human person and in natural law. Humanism must protect everything that is contained in the deepest layers of the human person: sensitivity to truth and good, freedom of conscience, possibility of an unhindered choice of a worldview and of a way of life. Authentic humanism also means the moral-social praxis, i.e. respect of a concrete man as a person. And this fact cannot be substituted by any declarations or postulates.

The theory of Christian humanism has various philosophical-ontological, axiological and theological foundations. The philosophical premises include: the superiority of the human person over material nature, man's inalienable dignity, rationality, freedom and moral sensitivity as man's universal attributes, the presence of the internal-spiritual "I", natural character of ties with society. The axiological bases of humanism concern mainly the acknowledgement of man's inner life, his mental culture (cognitive, moral, artistic, religious), natural law as a foundation of moral norms, individual and social sense of labour. The theological premises of Christian humanism refer to the fundamental truths of the Revelation, especially of Christology[24].

The critical evaluation of various forms of lay humanism, sketched out above, does not exclude a possibility of understanding and cooperation between adherents of various

---

[23]K.Rahner: "Christliche Humanismus" [in:] *Lexikon für Theologie und Kirche*, Freiburg 1961, vol.5, pp.528-530.

[24]W.Granat: *U podstaw humanizmu chrześcijańskiego*, op.cit.; also his: *Personalizm chrześcijański. Teologia osoby ludzkiej* [Christian Personalism. The Theology of the Human Person], Poznań 1985.

worldview and social options. After all, the preservation of one's own philosophical and ideological identity does not cancel out a chance of a friendly dialogue and cooperation for the good of man. A defence of humankind can and should constitute a common platform for all varieties of humanism[25].

(ii) Personalism

Similarly to humanism, in recent decades the idea of personalism has gained great popularity and renown. Representatives of most contemporary philosophical and social trends declare themselves to be personalists. This is even done by the adherents of dialectical and historical materialism[26]. Therefore, what is personalism? The origin of the term "personalism" goes back to the nineteenth century when it was used for the first time by Friedrich Schleiermacher († 1834). He combined personalism with the idea of personal God[27]. Personalism was understood similarly by Ludwig Feuerbach although he added that person is an abstract category. Charles Renouvier († 1903) divided philosophers into two groups, personalists and nonpersonalists[28]. He included himself in the group of personalists because he recognized human nature as a real and fundamental dimension of being. The conception of personalism was popularized by Wilhelm Stern († 1938), the author of *Person und Sache*[29]. He described himself as a follower of "critical personalism" because he renounced the metaphysical analysis of person for the sake of psychological and epistemological approaches. The term and the ideas of personalism were then quickly diffused and became part of the commonly used language of philosophy[30].

Personalism was quickly assimilated by theistic thinkers, also the Christian ones. Today there are many trends and schools of personalism. And, thus, there are: Augustinian personalism (J.Hessen, F.M.Sciacca, F.Sawicki), Thomistic personalism (J.Maritain, C.Fabro, K.Wojtyła[31]), phenomenological-axiological personalism (M.Scheler, L.Lavelle, R.Guardini), existentialistic personalism (G.Marcel, K.Jaspers, M.Buber, N.Berdiayev), sociological personalism (E.Mounier, J.Lacroix), theological personalism

---

[25]S.Olejnik: "Etyka chrześcijańska a humanizm ateistyczny" [Christian Ethics and Atheistic Humanism], *Ateneum Kapłańskie* 65 (1973), vol.80, pp.221-238; S.Kowalczyk: "Chrześcijaństwo a dialog światopoglądowy" [Christianity and the Dialogue about Worldviews] [in:] *Z zagadnień światopoglądu chrześcijańskiego* [On the Problems of the Christian Worldview], Lublin 1989, pp.189-210.

[26]They speak about "socialist humanism".

[27]*Über die Religion*, Leipzig 1868.

[28]Ch.Renouvier: *Le personalisme suivi d'une étude sur la perception externe et sur la force*, Paris 1903.

[29]It was first published in 1906.

[30]In the United States, in California, R.T.Flewelling began to publish the journal *The Personalist*.

[31]K.Wojtyła: "Personalizm tomistyczny" [Thomistic Personalism], *Znak* 13 (1961), pp.664-674.

(K.Rahner, E.Schillebeeckx, W.Granat)[32]. Naturally, the classifications of forms of personalism may vary, depending on the accepted criteria. Thus, one may speak about personalism of particular philosophical trends (past and present), aboutmetaphysical, theological, humanistic, pedagogical, social, political personalism and so on. Personalism is derived from the domains of philosophy and theology but it affects all the domains of man's individual and social activity. Personalism predominates in Polish Christian philosophy, making its presence evident on both cognitive-intellectual and social-pragmatic planes. Particularly strong has been the influence of J.Maritain and E.Mounier[33].

The plurality of the variants of personalism does not facilitate its clear and unambiguous characterization. It is perhaps worth quoting some of the more interesting descriptions of personalism, especially those connected with the Christian point of view. Maritain does not give a definition of personalism in the proper sense of the term, yet, he states that it constitutes the natural foundation of integral humanism. Christian personalism has a theocentric, pluralistic and communal character[34]; one of the consequences of this is the conception of personalistic democracy. Emmanuel Mounier made a distinction between two main forms of personalism, theoretical and pragmatic. The former denotes a certain kind of philosophy accepting man's ontical specificity and his personal dignity. Personalism apprehended pragmatically constitutes an existential-social attitude of concern about man[35]. The French author stresses the close connection between both apprehensions of personalism and observes that "the theory of activity is not an addition to personalism"[36]. He is also right in emphasizing the necessity of social activity for the good of people.

There are many descriptions of personalism[37]. Most often the term is used to denote any philosophical, religious or social trend which accepts: (a) man's personal being; (b) material and spiritual dimensions of his nature; (c) rationality, freedom and sensitivity to higher values; (d) the superior value of the human person over the world of things as well as socio-economic and political structures. Personalism is in opposition both to extreme individualism and to collectivism; it acknowledges the necessity of social life for the actualization of full humanity, but it is simultaneously opposed to the instrumental treatment of the human person.

Characterizing the philosophical personalism of Christianity one should recall its fundamental ontological and axiological determinants. The former concern the

[32]W.Granat: *Personalizm chrześcijański*, op.cit.

[33]Cf.S.Kowalczyk: "Personnalisme polonais contemporain", *Divus Thomas* 88 (1985) Nr.1-3, pp.58-76.

[34]*True Humanism*, op.cit., pp.105 ff., 157 ff.

[35]Initially Mounier claimed that personalism is not an "intellectual scheme" or "system"; cf. *Qu'est-ce que le personnalisme?*, Paris 1946, p.10. Later on he admitted that "personalism is a philosophy, not merely an attitude": *Introduction aux existentialismes*, Paris 1946, pp.36 ff.

[36]*Introduction aux existentialismes*, pp.93-108.

[37]They are quoted and discussed by W.Granat: *Personalizm chrześcijański*, op.cit., pp.76-77.

philosophical foundations of the theory of personalism, while the latter constitute its moral-social consequences[38]. The ontological foundations of personalism should include, first of all, three elements: the conception of personal being, recognition of its dynamics occurring on many levels and in many directions, and the conception of social community.

First of all, personalistic anthropology acknowledges man's ontical self-identity. Although man is fragile in his existence, he is nevertheless permanently identical in his humanity. Man is not only a stream of experiences, acts, impressions, decisions etc. They are all rooted in the inner "I" as their ontical centre and causer. The human self is not only a succession of temporal moments or their synthesis, but a personal subject. The continuity of the human "I" cannot be reduced exclusively to the unity of the biological organism, because it also, and primarily, concerns the psychic-mental plane, namely, memory, consciousness, conscience, character. The relative permanence and identity of man's self is described by Thomistic philosophy as the substantiality of the "I". Therefore, man is not only a system or result of relations, qualities, cognitive and emotional etc., but also a substantial being and his own subject[39]. Hence, he is a being independent both structurally and functionally, though, obviously, immersed in the cosmos that surrounds us. Material and biological immanence in relation to the world does not, however, exclude man's internal-spiritual transcendence in relation to the world and to society.

An integral element of personalistic anthropology is the acknowledgement of the fact that man, from the very beginning of his existence - and not only from the moment of his birth - is a person. An individual man is not merely another specimen of the species called ***homo sapiens*** but also a person. The personal being constitutes a completely new and higher dimension of reality. "The person is a universe of spiritual nature, endowed with freedom and therefore constituting a totality independent of the world"[40]. Man as a person is somebody, a subject, a mysterious world of interiority and spirit. He is a self-conscious being, free, sensitive to higher values, capable of self-control and self-direction. Hence, it would be difficult to speak about the person (resp. personalism) when man is interpreted as: thinking matter, exclusively a final stage in the evolution of the organic world, a higher form of animal life, or an act of accident. A mineral, a plant or an animal cannot be a person; only a man can. Animals have a biological personality but they are not persons. The world of animate and inanimate matter is exclusively a world of things - objects, not of persons - subjects. Materialism explains man's psychic life as a function of material structures and as an epiphenomenon of biological life. In this perspective there is no place for the person - the ontical subject, internally autonomous in respect to the external world. As a psychic-physical whole and the internal "I", the

---

[38]Cf. A.C.Knudson: *The Philosophy of Personalism*, New York 1927; L.Stefanini: *Personalismo filosofico*, Rome 1954; M.Nedocelle: *Vers une philosophie de l'amour et de la personne*, Paris 1957; Rotenstreich: *Man and His Dignity*, Jerusalem 1983; *Problem wyzwolenia człowieka* [The Problem of the Liberation of Man], Roma 1987.

[39]R.Guardini: *Das Ende der Neuzeit*, Würzburg 1951, pp.51-60.

[40]J.Maritain: *True Humanism*, op.cit., p.2.

person is an inalienable endowment of every man. All people are everywhere equal as persons. There are no supermen or undermen, for in its essence humanity is identical in everybody. Individual people differ in their biological and psychic personality which is a gift of nature and an effect of man's activities.

The ontological determinant of the human person is its multifarious activity. This aspect was already noted by St.Augustine who apprehended man in his dynamics and concrete experiences. Although Thomism described activity as the highest ontical act, it nevertheless paid too little attention to the problems of man's activity. Traditional anthropology treated marginally the function of the actions of man as the person and rested satisfied with a schematic-static conception of the human being. The role of human activity was recalled by Maurice Blondel, the phenomenologist Max Scheler, and, recently, Cardinal Karol Wojtyła[41]. In their interpretation, an act is not only an expression of the human person but also its actualization and finalization. It is a dynamic conception of man, revealing the specificity of internal and external activities. The human person is a continuous ***fieri***. It is within man's possibilities to achieve both internal and external self-realization or self-destruction. Man lives within the framework of the world of values and has to take a definitive attitude towards them; he must choose and create some values, while neglecting or destroying others. It is an opportunity for the human person to become involved in the world of persons, of people and of God. This involvement can be achieved only through personal values, such as truth, good, freedom, friendship, love, justice, sacrifice, trust. The values of the "having" type are naturally necessary for man's existence but they cannot substitute the values which serve the "being" of the person. Man's dynamics occurs on many levels, manual and mental, biological and internal-spiritual, cognitive, moral and artistic, contemplative and creative, individual and social. Ontical integrality appertains to man from the beginning of his existence and its element is the self-teleology appropriate to him as a person. One may therefore say that "man fulfils himself" as a person[42]. The person is not a static, ontically petrified reality, but an active subject. It constantly undergoes the processes of self-realization or self-degradation. Dynamics is incorporated in the ontical structure of the person and corresponds with its attributes, rationality and freedom.

The ontological premises of personalism also include the conviction that man, in his nature, is a social being. He is a "being-towards-another-man". He not only lives in society but also needs society biologically and psychically for his own survival and development. Explaining the relations binding the individual man with society, personalism is opposed both to individualism and collectivism. Individualism diminishes the role of social life, perceiving in the latter merely a result of a collective convention. In turn, collectivism interprets man as a set of social relations and as their "product", which undoubtedly constitutes an undermining of his subjectiveness and internal autonomy. The latter

[41]*Osoba i czyn* [The Person and the Act], Kraków 1969; also his: "Osobowa struktura samostanowienia" [The Personal Structure of Self- Determination], *Roczniki Filozoficzne*, 29 (1981), Nr.2, pp.6-11.

[42]*Osoba i czyn*, op.cit., pp.126-127.

interpretation also facilitates an instrumental treatment of the human person which is practically realized in the totalitarian model of social and state life. As E.Mounier rightly noticed, authentic personalism rejects both "the imperialism of private interests" and "the tyranny of collective forces"[43].

The theory of personalism suggests that the individual man be internally and externally involved in social life. At the same time, however, he is to remain a subject of social life. "The human person is and should be the principle, subject, and aim of all social institutions, because, by its nature, it necessarily needs social life" (*Gaudium et spes* 25). Man constitutes an integral part of society and has certain obligations towards it. However, at the same time, in the domain of higher values, man as a person is autonomous in respect to society and always remains in it as a free subject of his decisions and actions. The relation between man and society cannot be explained in terms of the "individual - species" because it would then be merely an external-biological relation. The essence of social life is the creation and transmission of values, economic and spiritual, cognitive and moral, artistic and ideological (also including the religious ones). If this communication of values is to respect man's personal dignity, it should be realized in the atmosphere of complete freedom. Only a free man discovers truth and seeks good, the values which in their essence have a social dimension. In turn, society is not a mechanical gathering of people living side by side, deprived of a sense of a community of values and aims. Explaining the mechanism of the coming into being of an authentic social community, Christian personalism introduces the conception of participation. The essence of social life is co-existence and co-operation, that is, participation in the community, in its history, decisions, experiences, obligations, aims, values[44]. Participation is an antithesis of alienation. A badly functioning community, especially one based on various forms of coercion and enslavement, alienates and destroys man as a person. An individual man involves himself actively in the community when he perceives in it an opportunity of the development of his own personality, precisely through unification with other people. The material of social life is common good which covers a rich set of values, from economic to moral-ideological. Common good often demands sacrifice from human individuals, e.g. in cases of a threat to the nation. Yet, social community, if it is a real one, never destroys the human person, its autonomy, conscience, personal convictions, rights. Authentic common good can be achieved only through the realization of the good of man as a person.

The ontological criteria of personalism are organically connected with moral-social criteria. The former constitute the foundations of personalism, while the latter follow as its natural consequences. The axiological criteria of authentic personalism include respect of man's personal dignity and his necessary rights. In the universe known to us only man is the person and subject, a thinking being, conscious of its existence, free and having the right to freedom, distinguishing truth from falsehood, good from evil etc. The human

---

[43]E.Mounier: *Qu est'ce que le personnalisme?*, op.cit., pp.58-59, 105-105.

[44]K.Wojtyła: *Osoba i czyn*, op.cit., pp.294-295, 304-305.

person has its face, external and internal, which should never be destroyed or obliterated. Man's natural dignity requires respect for his necessary rights, personal, economic, social, cultural, political. It is not enough to care for some of these rights, while ignoring or suspending others. The values of the "having" type are, obviously, necessary for man's existence, but they do not substitute the personal "being". The priority of the person in respect to the world of things is a paragon of personalism.

The dignity of the human person is something natural, and, therefore, universal and ineffaceable. Only man is a person and every man is one. The person is not a product of the material world or socio-economic structures. Man is a person from the beginning of his existence till the end of his life and his human dignity cannot be taken away from him or simply suspended. That is why personalism cannot be reconciled with the undermining of such a fundamental human right as the right to live. The human foetus, though still unborn, is already a man and a person. Personalistic ethics, pedagogy or economy cannot therefore justify or even allow the destruction of children's lives before birth. Man is a person by his very nature and that is why personal humanity is his inalienable property. One can never cease to be a person, out of one's own or somebody else's will. Nature creates species but the person is a fruit of love - for the faithful, also of God's love.

The axiological-social consequences of the idea of personalism also include the postulate of pluralism in socio-political life. Pluralism is indispensable for the existence of social freedom and personal responsibility of citizens. This has been discussed by Pope John Paul II: "The 'health' of the political community - reflected in voluntary and responsible participation of all citizens in public affairs, safeguarding of laws, respect and support of human rights - constitutes a necessary condition and a sure quarantee of the development of 'the whole man and of all people'" (*Sollicitudo rei socialis* 44). Personalism postulates equality of all citizens before law and founding social life on the principle of pluralism in the domains of culture, worldview, profession, society, politics. Such pluralism is impossible when there are corrupted or totalitarian governments in power. A correct state and social life demands co-responsibility and co-participation in the undertaken social tasks. This is realized through real participation and influence in taking decisions concerning the good of the country, determining aims and selecting means, controlling the state-social mechanisms etc. The sense of responsibility comes into being only in pluralistic state structures. The theory of collectivism, connected with the historical materialism of Marxism, departs from the requirements of personalism at many points. Although the ideas of social equality, justice, liberation from poverty etc. do correspond with personalism, in the interpretation of classical Marxism "the kingdom of freedom" becomes an almost eschatological future. It is a distant ideal whose realization is to be accomplished by the "temporary" dictatorship of the proletariat and monoparty structures of the state organism. The idea of the dictatorship was later on somewhat suppressed for the sake of the so-called "leading role of the party". Some countries resigned from the constitutional provision about such a role of the party, yet in other regions of the world the idea of the dictatorship of the proletariat is still maintained and enforced. Obviously, this cannot be reconciled with personalism because it infringes the subjectiveness of individual persons and of nations. An unavoidable consequence of personalism is pluralism whose optimal model is personalistic democracy[45]. Personalism cannot be reconciled, either, with any discrimination against classes, nations, races, religions etc., or economic exploitation (the latter also infringes the dignity of the human person).

Another consequence of personalism is the stress laid on the principle of solidarity in social life. However, it cannot be exclusively a class or professional solidarity, because it would then be limited to the defence of the interests of particular groups. Class solidarity most often provokes hatred for people belonging to other classes[46]; as a result, the rich would treat the poor with contempt or vice versa. The solidarity embracing the whole society is based on other assumptions than individual or class interests. At its basis there is benevolence, love, all-human brotherhood. Christian personalism emphasizes the leading role of love in man's individual and social life. Only love introduces harmony into man's life, integrates man's personality, opens man to the needs of others, integrates in the common good of society. The idea of the love of one's brother, derived from the Revelation, is the main foundation of the principle of social solidarity. Social justice is a command of love, while simultaneously constituting its exemplification and realization. There can be no authentic love without justice, but there can be no full justice without love, either. Justice means an "equalization" of people in respect to objective goods, whereas love is something more: "People meet each other in the same good, that is, man with his proper dignity" (John Paul II: Dives in misericordia 14). The postulates of social equality and justice must therefore be complemented by "the civilization of love"[47].

The theories of humanism and personalism are organically interconnected, that is, the axiology of humanism demands the ontology of personalism. Humanism is a guardian of the ***humanum***, i.e., humanity. The latter is impossible without the recognition of the personal dimension in man's being. In spite of its existential and spiritual imperfections, the human person is the highest and inviolable good of the visible world.

---

[45]J.Maritain: *True Humanism*, op.cit., pp.156-161; also his: *Christianisme et democratie*, Paris 1943, pp.65-67.

[46]*True Humanism*, op.cit., pp.38-40, 164-165.

[47]John Paul II: *Dives in misericordia* 14; K.Ryczan: "Miłość- miłosierdzie w życiu społecznym" [Love-Charity in Social Life] [in:] *Jan Paweł II, Dives in misericordia. Tekst i komentarze.* [John Paul II. Dives in misericordia, Text and Commentaries], Lublin 1983, pp.223-233.

LITERATURE

ADLER,M.: *L'humanisme travailliste*, Paris 1927.

BIGO,P.: *Marxisme et humanisme*, Paris 1953.

BLACKHAM,H.J.: *Humanism*, Baltimore 1968.

ETCHEVERRY,A.: *Le conflit actuel des humanismes*, Paris 1955.

GRANAT,W.: *U podstaw humanizmu chrześcijańskiego* [At the Foundations of Christian Humanism], Poznań 1976.

GRANAT,W.: *Personalizm chrześcijański. Teologia osoby ludzkiej* [Christian Personalism. The Theology of the Human Person], Poznań 1985.

GRASSI,E.: *Humanismus und Marxismus*, Berlin 1973.

HÄRING,B.: *Personalismus in Philosophie und Theologie*, München 1968.

HEIDEGGER,M.: *Lettre sur "l'humanisme"*, Paris 1964.

JAEGER,W.: *Humanism and Theology*, Milwaukee 1943.

KNUDSON,A.C.: *Philosophy of Personalism*, New York 1927.

KESSLER,E.: *Das Problem des frühen Humanismus*, München 1968.

KOWALCZYK,S.: "Personalisme polonais contemporain", *Divus Thomas* 88 (1985), Nr.1-3, pp.58-76.

KWEE SWAN LIET: *Bibliography of Humanism*, Utrecht 1957.

LACHANCE,L.: *L'humanisme politique*, Paris 1964.

LUBAC,H. de: *Le drame de l'humanisme athée*, Paris 1945.

MARITAIN,J.: *True Humanism*, New York 1938.

MARITAIN,J.: *La personne et le bien commune*, Paris 1947.

MODZELEWSKI,E.: *Humanizm marksistowski* [Marxist Humanism], Warszawa 1981.

MOUNIER,E.: *Qu'est-ce que le personalisme?*, Paris 1946.

NEDONCELLE,M.: *Vers une philosophie de l'amour et de la personne*, Paris 1957.

NIEL,A.: *Les grands appels de l'humanisme contemporain*, Paris 1966.

SCHAFF,A.: *Marxismus und das menschliche Individuum*, Wien 1965.

SARTRE,J.P.: *L'existentialisme est un humanisme*, Paris 1946.

SINKO,T.: *Od filantropii do humanitaryzmu i humanizmu* [From Philanthropy to Humanitarianism and Humanism], Warszawa 1960.

WOJTYŁA,K.: "Personalizm tomistyczny" [Thomistic Personalism], *Znak* 13 (1961), pp.664-674.